CHECKLIST OF PARISH REGISTERS 1986

RÉPERTOIRE DE REGISTRES PAROISSIAUX 1986

Fourth Edition, revised by Patricia Birkett

Quatrième édition, révisée par Patricia Birkett

Manuscript Division
Ottawa
1987

Division des manuscrits
Ottawa
1987

National Archives of Canada

Archives nationales du Canada

Publishing History

First edition 1969, compiled by Marielle Campeau

Second edition 1975, revised by Patricia Kennedy

Third edition 1981, revised by Patricia Birkett with the assistance of Janine Roy and Lorraine St-Louis

Fourth edition 1987, revised by Patricia Birkett

Canadian Cataloguing in Publication Data
National Archives of Canada. Manuscript Division.
   Checklist of parish registers, 1986 = Répertoire de registres paroissiaux, 1986
    Text in English and French.
    First ed. 1969, compiled by Marielle Campeau.
    DSS cat. no. SA2-47/1986
    ISBN 0-660-53863-6
   1. Registers of births, etc.–Canada–Bibliography–Catalogs. 2. Church records and registers – Canada – Bibliography – Catalogs. 3. Canada – Genealogy – Bibliography – Catalogs. 4. National Archives of Canada. Manuscript Division. I. Campeau, Marielle. II. Birkett, Patricia. III. Title. IV. Title: Répertoire de registres paroissiaux, 1986.

CD3648.A1N37 1987   016.929'371   C87-099009-8E

© Minister of Supply and Services Canada 1987

Available in Canada through
Associated Bookstores
and other booksellers

or by mail from

Canadian Government Publishing Centre
Supply and Services Canada
Ottawa, Canada K1A 0S9

Cat. No.: SA2-47/1986
ISBN: 0-660-53863-6

Canada: $12.00
Other countries: $14.40

All rights reserved. No part of this publication may be reproduced, stored in a retrieval system, or transmitted by any means, electronic, mechanical, photocopying, recording or otherwise, without the prior written permission of the Publishing Services, Canadian Government Publishing Centre, Ottawa, Canada, K1A 0S9.

Cover: Notre-Dame de Bon-Secours, first stone church in Montreal, erected through the efforts of Marguerite Bourgeoys. Print. (C-4623)

Éditions successives

1re édition 1969, préparée par Marielle Campeau

2e édition 1975, révisée par Patricia Kennedy

3e édition 1981, révisée par Patricia Birkett avec l'aide de Janine Roy et Lorraine St-Louis

4e édition 1987, révisée par Patricia Birkett

Données de catalogage avant publication (Canada)
Archives nationales du Canada. Division des manuscrits.
   Checklist of parish registers, 1986 = Répertoire de registres paroissiaux, 1986
    Texte en anglais et en français.
    Première éd. 1969 préparée par Marielle Campeau.
    Cat. MAS nº SA2-47/1986
    ISBN 0-660-53863-6
   1. Registres de l'état civil–Canada – Bibliographie – Catalogues. 2. Registres ecclésiastiques – Canada – Bibliographie – Catalogues. 3. Canada – Généalogie – Bibliographie – Catalogues. 4. Archives nationales du Canada. Division des manuscrits. I. Campeau, Marielle. II. Birkett, Patricia. III. Titre. IV. Titre: Répertoire de registres paroissiaux, 1986.

CD3648.A1N37 1987   016.929'371   C87-099009-8F

© Ministre des Approvisionnements et Services Canada 1987

En vente au Canada par l'entremise des
librairies associées
et autres librairies

ou par la poste auprès du

Centre d'édition du gouvernement du Canada
Approvisionnements et Services Canada
Ottawa (Canada) K1A 0S9

Nº de cat. : SA2-47/1986
ISBN : 0-660-53863-6

Canada : 12 $
à l'étranger : 14,40 $

Tous droits réservés. On ne peut reproduire aucune partie du présent ouvrage, sous quelque forme ou par quelque procédé que ce soit (électronique, mécanique, photographique), ni en faire un enregistrement sur support magnétique ou autre pour fins de dépistage ou de diffusion, sans autorisation écrite préalable des Services d'édition, Centre d'édition du gouvernement du Canada, Ottawa, Canada, K1A 0S9.

Couverture : Notre-Dame-de-Bon-Secours a été la première église de pierre bâtie dans l'île de Montréal grâce à Marguerite Bourgeoys. Gravure. (C-4623)

TABLE OF CONTENTS	Page
Introduction	
Abbreviations	vii
Civil Registration of BMD	vii
Church Records of BMD	viii
Parish Registers at the National Archives	ix
Microfilm Loans	ix
Restrictions on HBC Reels	ix
Advice to Genealogical Researchers	ix
List of Registers	x
Cross-References	x
Additional Material	xi
Archives of the Hudson's Bay Company	
Rupert's Land	3
Canada	
British Columbia	7
Manitoba	9
New Brunswick	15
Newfoundland and Labrador	25
Northwest Territories	27
Nova Scotia	29
Ontario	39
Prince Edward Island	131
Quebec	133
Saskatchewan	163
Yukon Territory	165
Outside Canada	
Czechoslovakia	169
French Guiana	173
Great Britain	171
Hungary	175
India	177
Poland	179
Saint-Pierre-et-Miquelon	181
Union of Soviet Socialist Republics	183
United States of America	185
Geographic Index	
Archives of the Hudson's Bay Company	
Rupert's Land	195
Canada	
British Columbia	195
Manitoba	195
New Brunswick	196
Newfoundland and Labrador	197
Northwest Territories	197
Nova Scotia	197
Ontario	197
Prince Edward Island	201
Quebec	202
Saskatchewan	204
Yukon Territory	204
Outside Canada	
Czechoslovakia	204
French Guiana	204
Great Britain	204
Hungary	204
India	204
Poland	204
Saint-Pierre-et-Miquelon	204
Union of Soviet Socialist Republics	204
United States of America	204

TABLE DES MATIÈRES	Page
Introduction	
Abréviations et sigles	vii
Registres d'état civil (BMD)	vii
Archives des Églises (BMD)	viii
Registres paroissiaux aux Archives nationales	ix
Prêts de microfilms	ix
Consultation des bobines de la CBH	ix
Conseils aux généalogistes	x
Répertoire de registres	x
Renvois	x
Ressources supplémentaires	xi
Archives de la Compagnie de la Baie d'Hudson	
Terre de Rupert	3
Canada	
Colombie-Britannique	7
Île-du-Prince-Édouard	131
Manitoba	9
Nouveau-Brunswick	15
Nouvelle-Écosse	29
Ontario	39
Québec	133
Saskatchewan	163
Terre-Neuve et Labrador	25
Territoire du Yukon	165
Territoires du Nord-Ouest	27
Hors du Canada	
États-Unis	185
Grande-Bretagne	171
Guyane française	173
Hongrie	175
Inde	177
Pologne	179
Saint-Pierre-et-Miquelon	181
Tchécoslovaquie	169
Union des républiques socialistes soviétiques	183
Index géographique	
Archives de la Compagnie de la Baie d'Hudson	
Terre de Rupert	195
Canada	
Colombie-Britannique	195
Île-du-Prince-Édouard	201
Manitoba	195
Nouveau-Brunswick	196
Nouvelle-Écosse	197
Ontario	197
Québec	202
Saskatchewan	204
Terre-Neuve et Labrador	197
Territoire du Yukon	204
Territoires du Nord-Ouest	197
Hors du Canada	
États-Unis	204
Grande-Bretagne	204
Guyane française	204
Hongrie	204
Inde	204
Pologne	204
Saint-Pierre-et-Miquelon	204
Tchécoslovaquie	204
Union des républiques socialistes soviétiques	204

Introduction

Abbreviations

B   Baptism or birth
M   Marriage
D   Death or burial

CMS   Church Missionary Society
HBC   Hudson's Bay Company
SPG   Society for the Propagation of the Gospel

Civil Registration of BMD

The following provincial and territorial offices are in charge of civil registration and have records covering the periods indicated. Inquiries should be addressed directly to the respective offices:

Alberta: Complete records from 1898, with some birth records from 1853 onward and death records from 1893, are now in the custody of the Division of Vital Statistics, Department of Social Services and Community Health, 10405-100th Avenue, 4th Floor, Edmonton, Alta., T5J 0A6.

British Columbia: Although civil registration officially began in 1872, early records are incomplete. Some baptismal records date back to 1849. The originals or copies are held by the Division of Vital Statistics, Ministry of Health, Victoria, B.C., V8V 1X4.

Manitoba: The Office of Vital Statistics, Department of Community Services and Corrections, Room 104, Norquay Building, 401 York Avenue, Winnipeg, Man., R3C 0V8, has complete records from 1882, together with some incomplete church records prior to that date (searched when the denomination is known).

New Brunswick: The Registrar General, Vital Statistics Division, P.O. Box 6000, Fredericton, N.B., E3B 5H1, has complete records from 1920 and incomplete records for 1888-1920. A few county records prior to that date have been retained.

Newfoundland: Civil registration began in 1892. The records are in the custody of the Registrar General, Vital Statistics, Department of Health, Confederation Building, St. John's, Nfld., A1C 5T7. For earlier years the only source is church records, which are numerous for the period 1860-1891, though some date from the 1820s. For information, apply to the Provincial Archives of Newfoundland and Labrador, Colonial Building, Military Road, St. John's, Nfld., A1C 2C9.

Northwest Territories: Complete records date from 1925. Address inquiries to the Registrar of Vital Statistics, P.O. Box 1320, Yellowknife, N.W.T., X1A 2L9.

Nova Scotia: Records of births and deaths from 1 October 1908, and of marriages since 1907-1918 (depending on the county), are with the Deputy Registrar General, Department of Health, P.O. Box 157, Halifax, N.S., B3J 2M9. Civil records of births and deaths were kept 1865-1876, and of marriages from the late 1700s. Inquiries concerning these earlier records should be addressed to the Public Archives of Nova Scotia, 6016 University Avenue, Halifax, N.S., B3H 1W4.

Ontario: Civil registration began 1 July 1869. Address inquiries to the Deputy Registrar General, MacDonald Block, Queen's Park, Toronto, Ont., M7A 1Y5.

Abréviations et sigles

B   baptême ou naissance
M   mariage
D   décès ou sépulture

CBH   Compagnie de la Baie d'Hudson
CMS   Church Missionary Society
SPG   Society for the Propagation of the Gospel

Registres d'état civil (BMD)

On trouvera ci-dessous la liste des divers bureaux provinciaux chargés de l'enregistrement des actes de l'état civil. Pour obtenir des renseignements, s'adresser à ces organismes :

Alberta : La Division of Vital Statistics, Department of Social Services and Community Health, 10405-100th Avenue, 4th Floor, Edmonton, Alta., T5J 0A6, conserve des registres complets depuis 1898, ainsi que quelques registres de naissances qui remontent à 1853 et des registres de décès de 1893 à nos jours.

Colombie-Britannique : Bien que l'enregistrement des actes de l'état civil soit obligatoire depuis 1872, les registres des premières années sont incomplets. Certains registres de baptêmes remontent à 1849. La Division of Vital Statistics, Ministry of Health, Victoria, B.C., V8V 1X4, conserve les originaux ou les copies de ces documents.

Île-du-Prince-Édouard : L'enregistrement des actes de l'état civil date de 1906, mais il existe des registres de mariages remontant à 1787, quelques registres de baptêmes de la plupart des églises de l'Île à partir de 1800, ainsi que quelques registres de sépultures. Pour en obtenir des copies, prière de s'adresser au Director, Division of Vital Statistics, Department of Health and Social Services, P.O. Box 3000, Charlottetown, P.E.I., C1A 7P1.

Manitoba : L'Office of Vital Statistics, Department of Community Services and Corrections, Norquay Building, Room 104, 401 York Avenue, Winnipeg, Man., R3C 0V8, possède des archives complètes remontant à 1882, ainsi qu'un certain nombre de registres paroissiaux incomplets antérieurs à 1882 (on doit connaître la confession religieuse pour qu'une recherche soit entreprise).

Nouveau-Brunswick : Les bureaux du Registrar General, Vital Statistics Division, P.O. Box 6000, Fredericton, N.B., E3B 5H1, possèdent des archives complètes depuis 1920. Les archives des années 1888 à 1920 sont cependant fragmentaires. Quelques documents antérieurs à cette date ont été conservés.

Nouvelle-Écosse : Des registres de naissances et de décès, 1865 à 1876, et de mariages, commençant à la fin du XVIIIe siècle, se trouvent aux Public Archives of Nova Scotia, 6016 University Avenue, Halifax, N.S., B3H 1W4. C'est dans les bureaux du Deputy Registrar General, Department of Health, P.O. Box 157, Halifax, N.S., B3J 2M9, que se trouvent les registres de naissances et de décès à compter du 1er octobre 1908, et de mariages à compter de 1907 à 1918 selon le comté.

Ontario : C'est le 1er juillet 1869 qu'eurent lieu les premiers enregistrements d'actes de l'état civil. Les demandes doivent être adressées à l'attention du Deputy Registrar General, MacDonald Block, Queen's Park, Toronto, Ont., M7A 1Y5.

Prince Edward Island: Civil registration began in 1906, but there are some marriage records dating back to 1787. There are also baptismal records from most of the Island churches from 1800, as well as a few burial records. Records are in the custody of the Director, Division of Vital Statistics, Department of Health and Social Services, P.O. Box 3000, Charlottetown, P.E.I., C1A 7P1.

Quebec: Since the early seventeenth century, clergymen have been required to keep duplicate registers, one of which is retained in the parish where the event occurred, while the other is deposited in the office of one of the 39 district protonotaries. The protonotaries' copies of registers more than 100 years old are deposited in the appropriate one of the nine regional offices of the Archives nationales du Québec. Extracts from the registers may be obtained directly from the parish or, depending on the age of the registers, by writing to the district protonotary or the regional office of the provincial archives. In the case of Quebec, the National Archives of Canada is unable to supply researchers with the address of a central office.

Saskatchewan: Vital Statistics, Department of Health, 3475 Albert Street, Regina, Sask., S4S 6X6, holds complete records from 1920, with incomplete records for 1878-1920.

Yukon Territory: Vital Statistics, Government of the Yukon Territory, P.O. Box 2703, Whitehorse, Y.T., Y1A 2C6, holds some birth records for 1898, an index of births c. 1900-1924, and complete records from 1924.

Note

The authorities vary considerably in the services provided for genealogists and in the fees charged. Copies of records can be obtained by the persons immediately concerned, or by their next-of-kin. Researchers should remember that compliance with the laws requiring civil registration was irregular as late as the 1920s in rural districts, owing to unfamiliarity with the law. Minor errors in dates and divergent spelling of names may also cause difficulties.

Church Records of BMD

Since the civil registration of vital statistics did not become general practice in Canada until it was undertaken as a provincial responsibility late in the nineteenth century, the chief sources of such information for earlier periods are the records of local churches.

The preservation of parish registers is the responsibility of the parishes themselves, or of the denominational or provincial archives, rather than of the National Archives of Canada. A number of such microfilmed registers in the custody of the Provincial Archives of New Brunswick (Box 6000, Fredericton, New Brunswick, Canada, E3B 5H1) and of the Saskatchewan Archives Board, Regina Office (5th Floor, Library Building, University of Regina, Regina, Saskatchewan, Canada, S4S 0A2) can be borrowed from those institutions through the interlibrary loan service. In the majority of cases, inquirers must know the names of the parishes or mission districts and of the denominations relevant for their search, and should write directly to the clergyman or priest of the particular parish in which they are interested.

The National Archives of Canada is unable to direct researchers either to the local churches or to the archival repositories in which their records are deposited.

Québec : Des registres d'état civil existent au Québec depuis les débuts du XVIIe siècle. Ils sont tenus en double copie dont l'une est conservée à la paroisse où a eu lieu l'événement, et l'autre est déposée auprès du protonotaire concerné. Les protonotaires des 39 districts judiciaires versent les copies de registres âgés de plus de cent ans aux Archives nationales du Québec qui comptent neuf bureaux régionaux. Les extraits des registres d'état civil sont obtenus de la paroisse ou, selon qu'il s'agit de registres ayant plus ou moins de cent ans, en s'adressant au protonotaire du district ou au bureau régional des archives provinciales. Pour le Québec, les Archives nationales du Canada ne peuvent fournir au chercheur une adresse de bureau central.

Saskatchewan : Les bureaux des Vital Statistics, Department of Health, 3475, Albert Street, Regina, Sask., S4S 6X6, possèdent des registres complets depuis 1920, ainsi que des registres incomplets pour les années 1878 à 1920.

Terre-Neuve et Labrador : L'enregistrement des actes de l'état civil remonte à 1892. Ces renseignements sont conservés par le Registrar General, Vital Statistics, Department of Health, Confederation Building, Saint John's, Nfld., A1C 5T7. Pour les années antérieures à 1892, il faut consulter les archives religieuses, assez complètes pour la période allant de 1860 à 1891. Certaines de ces archives remontent à 1820. Pour d'autres informations, s'adresser aux Provincial Archives of Newfoundland & Labrador, Colonial Building, Military Road, Saint John's, Nfld., A1C 2C9.

Territoire du Yukon : Les bureaux des Vital Statistics, Government of the Yukon Territory, P.O. Box 2703, Whitehorse, Yukon, Y1A 2C6, détiennent des registres de naissances de 1898, un répertoire des naissances de 1900 à 1924 environ et des registres complets depuis 1924.

Territoires du Nord-Ouest : Il existe des registres complets depuis 1925. Adresser les demandes au Registrar of Vital Statistics, P.O. Box 1320, Yellowknife, N.W.T., X1A 2L9.

Note

Les services offerts aux généalogistes et les frais exigés varient énormément d'un bureau à l'autre. Les personnes concernées ou leurs proches parents peuvent obtenir un extrait des registres. Il est à noter que jusqu'aux années 20, l'obligation d'enregistrer les actes de l'état civil n'était pas toujours respectée dans les districts ruraux, parce que la loi était mal connue. En outre, la tâche est parfois rendue difficile par les erreurs mineures dans les dates et les variantes orthographiques des noms de famille.

Archives des Églises (BMD)

Comme l'enregistrement de l'état civil n'est devenu une pratique courante au Canada qu'à partir du moment où les provinces s'en sont chargées, vers la fin du XIXe siècle, les registres paroissiaux restent la principale source pour obtenir ce genre de renseignements pour la période précédant les recensements officiels.

La conservation des registres paroissiaux incombe aux paroisses mêmes, ou aux archives provinciales ou confessionnelles, plutôt qu'aux Archives nationales du Canada. Un certain nombre de registres microfilmés se trouvent aux Archives provinciales du Nouveau-Brunswick, Case postale 6000, Fredericton, N.-B., Canada, E3B 5H1 et au Saskatchewan Archives Board, Regina Office, 5th Floor, Library Building, University of Regina, Regina, Sask., Canada, S4S 0A2, et peuvent être

Parish Registers at the National Archives

Although preservation of parish registers is not the responsibility of the National Archives of Canada, its holdings do include a small number of these records, which are fully described mainly in the inventories of manuscript groups 8 and 9. This collection comprises only a small fraction of the parish registers of the country, and is in no way comprehensive even for the National Capital Region, which is the area of greatest coverage. It should also be noted that in most cases the Archives has only copies — either transcripts, photocopies, microfilms or microfiches — of the original registers, and that it does not reproduce them for sale.

Microform Loans

Researchers wishing to borrow the microfilms and microfiches listed in this checklist may do so through the intermediary of any institution that possesses the necessary microform readers for their use and participates in the interlibrary loan arrangement. Requests should be submitted on authorized forms by the borrowing institution, and should indicate clearly both the place and church name and the microform call number(s) of the material desired. Microfilms may be borrowed, three reels at a time (and microfiche, four fiche at a time), for a period of one month. The microforms must be used on the premises of the borrowing institution, and no copies may be made from any borrowed material while on loan. Copies of individual entries in the registers may be obtained from the National Archives of Canada (395 Wellington Street, Ottawa, Ontario, Canada K1A 0N3), at the standard charge for photoduplication, provided that there is no restriction prohibiting such copying. **No requests for copies of complete registers will be entertained.**

Restrictions on HBC Reels

Access to the registers of returns of BMD made to the Hudson's Bay Company by its chaplains and other Church Missionary Society missionaries (on reels HBC-4M4 and HBC-4M5) is controlled by the Archives of the Hudson's Bay Company. All **interlibrary loan requests** and **research inquiries** should be addressed to:

> The Keeper, Hudson's Bay Company Archives,
> Provincial Archives of Manitoba,
> Manitoba Archives Building,
> 200 Vaughan Street, Winnipeg, Manitoba,
> Canada R3C 1T5.

Researchers in Ottawa who wish to consult the reels at the National Archives of Canada should apply for permission to the British Archives Section of the Manuscript Division.

The returns on these two reels are listed separately on page 3. The listing is not reproduced either as a whole or in part anywhere else in this checklist, but cross-references to the place names found in it appear in the appropriate places in the listings for British Columbia, Manitoba, the Northwest Territories, Ontario, and Saskatchewan.

Advice to Genealogical Researchers

1) Learn as much as possible about your family before beginning archival research.
2) Study the historical background of the area you are researching.

empruntés de ces établissements par l'entremise du prêt entre bibliothèques. Dans la plupart des cas, cependant, les chercheurs doivent connaître le nom des paroisses ou des missions, et des confessions pertinentes et doivent s'adresser au ministre ou au prêtre de la paroisse dont les archives les intéressent.

Les Archives nationales du Canada ne sont pas en mesure de renseigner les chercheurs sur l'emplacement des églises ou des dépôts d'archives.

Registres paroissiaux aux Archives nationales

Bien que la conservation des registres paroissiaux n'incombe pas aux Archives nationales du Canada, on y trouve, néanmoins, quelques registres dont la plupart sont décrits entièrement dans les inventaires des groupes de manuscrits 8 et 9. Cette collection ne comprend qu'une petite fraction des registres paroissiaux du pays et elle est incomplète même pour les registres de la région de la capitale nationale, dont les documents sont les plus nombreux. En outre, dans la plupart des cas, les Archives ne possèdent que des reproductions d'originaux, sous forme de transcriptions, de photocopies, de microfilms ou de microfiches, et elles ne les reproduisent pas pour les vendre.

Prêts de microfilms

Tout établissement qui possède les lecteurs pour microforme et qui participe au système de prêt entre bibliothèques peut emprunter des microfilms et des microfiches inscrits dans le présent *Répertoire*. Les demandes doivent être faites par l'entremise de l'établissement au moyen des formules réglementaires. Le nom de l'église et de son emplacement et les numéros de microformes doivent être clairement indiqués. On peut emprunter jusqu'à trois bobines ou quatre microfiches à la fois, pour une durée d'un mois. Les microformes doivent être consultées dans l'établissement qui les a empruntées et il est strictement interdit d'en faire des reproductions durant toute la durée du prêt. Les chercheurs peuvent obtenir des copies de données de registres, à la condition qu'il n'existe aucune restriction en interdisant la reproduction. Les demandes de photocopies devront être adressées aux Archives nationales du Canada, 395, rue Wellington, Ottawa, Ont., Canada, K1A 0N3, qui vous fourniront des copies au tarif régulier. **Les Archives ne reproduisent pas de registres complets.**

Consultation des bobines de la Compagnie de la Baie d'Hudson

Les Archives de la Compagnie de la Baie d'Hudson contrôlent l'accès aux registres des rapports sur l'état civil qui lui ont été transmis par des aumôniers de la Compagnie et d'autres missionnaires de la Church Missionary Society (bobines HBC-4M4 et HBC-4M5). Toutes les **demandes de prêt entre bibliothèques** et **de recherche** doivent être envoyées à l'adresse suivante :

> The Keeper, Hudson's Bay Company Archives,
> Provincial Archives of Manitoba,
> Manitoba Archives Building,
> 200 Vaughan Street, Winnipeg, Manitoba,
> Canada R3C 1T5.

Les chercheurs, qui désirent consulter ces bobines à Ottawa, aux Archives nationales du Canada, doivent en demander l'autorisation à la Section des archives britanniques de la Division des manuscrits.

3) Consult good maps and gazetteers constantly.
4) Remember that you cannot expect consistency of any sort when using parish registers:
    a) Entries in the registers are often found in an unexpected part or parts of one book or of several books.
    b) Birth dates and ages are sometimes found in registers of marriages and burials, while marriages and deaths are occasionally noted in baptismal registers. The dates of such additional information are sometimes, but not always, taken into consideration in this checklist.
    c) Denominations change. Lutheran records, for example, may sometimes be found in Anglican registers, while Presbyterian and Methodist records are now frequently found with those of successor congregations belonging to the United Church of Canada.
    d) Parish boundaries change, and settlements may be served by different parish churches at different dates.
    e) Political boundaries are often misleading. For example, persons living in Ottawa, Ontario, may be baptized, married, or buried in Hull, Quebec.
    f) The dates provided in this checklist sometimes, but not always, take into consideration information of considerably earlier or later date than that of the actual entries in the registers.

List of Registers

This checklist provides a listing (valid to 31 December 1986) of all the registers on microfilm or microfiche at the Archives that may be borrowed through the interlibrary loan service. It presents the registers in alphabetic order by place name within each province or region. The descriptions are in English or French, according to the language used in the registers. The call number of the microfilm reel or microfiche on which an item appears is shown in bold type on the right of each description, for example:

Shelburne, Shelburne Co., [N.S.]

Christ Church Anglican Church
BMD   1783-1869   **C-3026**

Cross-References

If the listing for a register mentions the presence of material relating to another place or places, the entry is repeated under all the place names mentioned.

Where the listing is broken down into parts, only the main summary listing and the relevant part(s) are repeated in the cross-reference entry, and researchers wishing to see the complete listing should turn to the main entry. For example, the main listing for Dundas, Ontario:

Dundas, Wentworth Co.

Dundas and Ancaster Presbyterian Church
M   1848-1852   **C-3028**
comprises:

   Dundas
   M   1848-1852   **C-3028**

   Ancaster, and West Flamboro
   M   1848-1852   **C-3028**

Les rapports figurant sur ces deux bobines de microfilm sont énumérés séparément à la page 3. Cette liste n'est reproduite ni en totalité ni en partie ailleurs dans le *Répertoire*, mais des renvois aux noms de lieux qui y sont mentionnés paraissent sous ces noms dans les sections consacrées à la Colombie-Britannique, au Manitoba, à l'Ontario, à la Saskatchewan et aux Territoires du Nord-Ouest.

Conseils aux généalogistes

1) Renseignez-vous le plus possible sur votre famille avant de commencer vos recherches.
2) Étudiez l'histoire de la région qui vous intéresse.
3) Consultez très souvent de bonnes cartes et de bons répertoires toponymiques.
4) Rappelez-vous que les registres paroissiaux manquent souvent d'uniformité :
    a) Certaines données ont souvent été inscrites dans une ou plusieurs parties d'un ou de plusieurs livres;
    b) Les âges et les dates de naissance ont parfois été inscrits dans les registres de mariages et de sépultures, et les dates de ces derniers événements sont parfois mentionnées dans les registres de baptêmes;
    c) Les confessions religieuses sont appelées à changer : les dossiers de l'Église luthérienne, par exemple, se trouvent parfois dans les registres de l'Église anglicane, tandis que ceux des Églises presbytérienne et méthodiste sont fréquemment intégrés aux registres des paroisses qui appartiennent à l'Église unie du Canada;
    d) Les limites des paroisses changent aussi et il se peut que certaines collectivités aient été rattachées à différentes paroisses, à différentes époques;
    e) Les limites administratives sont souvent trompeuses. Des personnes qui ont vécu à Ottawa (Ontario), par exemple, peuvent avoir été baptisées, mariées ou enterrées à Hull (Québec);
    f) Les dates qui figurent dans ce répertoire ne tiennent pas toujours compte des renseignements qui ont été ajoutés après l'inscription initiale.

Répertoire de registres

Ce répertoire dresse la liste de tous les registres paroissiaux disponibles sur microfilm ou microfiche aux Archives nationales du Canada, au 31 décembre 1986, qu'on peut obtenir par le système de prêt entre bibliothèques. Les registres sont disposés alphabétiquement par nom de lieu, pour chaque province ou région. Les descriptions sont dans l'une ou l'autre des deux langues officielles selon la langue utilisée dans les registres. Le numéro de la bobine de microfilm ou de la microfiche est dactylographié en caractères gras, à droite de chaque description, par exemple :

Sainte-Marie, Baie (Church Point), comté de Digby, [N.-É.]

Ste-Marie (Église catholique)
BMD   1799-1801   **C-3026**

Renvois

Lorsque l'entrée de registre mentionne l'existence de documents sur d'autres endroits, la notice est répétée sous chacun des noms de lieux énumérés.

would have as one of its cross-references:

West Flamborough Township, Wentworth Co.

Dundas and Ancaster Presbyterian Church, Dundas
M   1848-1852   **C-3028**
includes:

    Ancaster, and West Flamboro
    M   1848-1852   **C-3028**

Researchers should note that while this method of cross-referencing is convenient to use, it makes the collection appear far larger than it really is.

Researchers should also note that although the names listed follow the usages of modern gazetteers as much as is possible, the names in the bodies of the entries sometimes follow the historical usages and spellings found in the material listed.

Additional Material

The checklist has not been compiled in a purist spirit. In addition to parish registers proper, a small amount of other material that provides information on BMD has also been included. This diverse material includes such items as civil registers; military registers; personal registers, indexes and diaries of clergymen and others; and a collection of funeral invitations. The Ontario Cemetery Recordings (MG 9, D 7-40) and the Quebec Cemetery Recordings (MG 8, G 54) have not been included, but a few miscellaneous cemetery recordings found in other units, such as those for Horton Township, Nova Scotia, and Breadalbane, Ontario, have been included. Again, there are a few registers of marriage licences, such as those for Thorold, Ontario, found in units of private material, but the checklist does not include the Bonds, Licences and Certificates, Lower Canada (RG 4, B 28), and Upper Canada (RG 5, B 9). Researchers interested in using these latter should use the microfilmed indexes to the two series:

Lower Canada Marriage Bonds, Index

Benjamin Abbott	— William Woodhead	H-1125
Matthew Wood	— Philip Zell	H-1126

Upper Canada Marriage Bonds, Index

Hester Abbah	— Richard Grant	H-1126
Robert Grant	— Thomas Pattenson	H-1127
Ann Patterson	— Charles Zeins	H-1128

Lorsqu'une entrée comprend plusieurs sections, seules la notice principale et la (les) section(s) pertinente(s) sont répétées dans la notice du renvoi. C'est pourquoi les chercheurs qui désirent l'entrée au complet doivent consulter la notice principale. Par exemple, la notice principale pour Montebello au Québec serait la suivante :

Montebello, comté de Papineau

Notre-Dame-de-Bon-Secours-de-la-Petite-Nation
(Église catholique)
BMD   1830-1849   **C-3023**
             avec :
Missions des cantons de Grenville, comté d'Argenteuil, et Buckingham, comté de Papineau (Église catholique)
BMD   1836-1838, 1840-1850   **C-3023**
             et :
Mission de Buckingham (Église catholique)
BMD   1839-1845   **C-3023**
         1845-1850   **C-3024**

cette entrée pourrait avoir comme notice de renvoi :

Grenville, canton de, comté d'Argenteuil

Notre-Dame-de-Bon-Secours-de-la-Petite-Nation
(Église catholique), Montebello, comté de Papineau
BMD   1830-1849   **C-3023**
comprend :

Missions des cantons de Grenville, comté d'Argenteuil, et Buckingham, comté de Papineau (Église catholique)
BMD   1836-1838, 1840-1850   **C-3023**

Ces renvois sont commodes mais ils font paraître la collection plus volumineuse qu'elle ne l'est réellement.

Les usages des répertoires toponymiques modernes ont été respectés dans la mesure du possible, mais il arrive parfois que les noms figurant dans le corps des notices suivent l'usage historique et l'orthographe utilisé dans les documents cités.

Ressources supplémentaires

Le répertoire n'a pas été établi de façon puriste. En plus des registres paroissiaux, il comprend quelques documents dans lesquels figurent des renseignements sur les naissances, les mariages et les décès. On y trouve notamment des registres d'état civil; des registres militaires; des registres, index et journaux établis entre autres par des ecclésiastiques; ainsi qu'une série d'invitations à des obsèques. Les registres des cimetières de l'Ontario (MG 9, D-7-40) et ceux du Québec (MG 8, G 54) ne sont pas mentionnés, mais le répertoire comprend quelques registres de cimetières, notamment les sections sur le canton de Horton en Nouvelle-Écosse et sur Breadalbane en Ontario. Il y a également des registres d'actes de mariage, notamment pour Thorold en Ontario, qui se trouvent dans les séries de papiers personnels, mais le répertoire ne comprend pas les titres, permis et certificats du Bas-Canada (RG 4, B 28) et du Haut-Canada (RG 5, B 9). Les chercheurs désirant consulter ces documents doivent se servir des index microfilmés pour ces deux séries :

Lower Canada Marriage Bonds, Index

Benjamin Abbott	— William Woodhead	**H-1125**
Matthew Wood	— Philip Zell	**H-1126**

Upper Canada Marriage Bonds, Index

Hester Abbah	— Richard Grant	**H-1126**
Robert Grant	— Thomas Pattenson	**H-1127**
Ann Patterson	— Charles Zeins	**H-1128**

Archives of the Hudson's Bay Company

Archives de la Compagnie de la Baie d'Hudson

Territories of the Hudson's Bay Company

Returns made to the HBC by its (Anglican) Chaplains and other Missionaries of the Church Missionary Society

B	1820-1831	**HBC-4M4*** (index)
	1831-1841	**HBC-4M5*** (index on reel **HBC-4M4***)
MD	1820-1841	**HBC-4M5*** (index)
B/MD	1841-1851	**HBC-4M5*** (index)

comprises:

Territories of the HBC

Returns of the HBC Chaplains and CMS Missionaries

B	1820-1831	**HBC-4M4*** (index)
	1831-1841	**HBC-4M5*** (index on reel **HBC-4M4***)
MD	1820-1841	**HBC-4M5*** (index)

includes: **Ontario:** [Fort] Rainy Lake
Manitoba: Beaver Creek, Berens River House, Brandon House, Fort Alexander, Fort Douglas, Fort Garry, Fort Gibraltar, Nelson River District, Norway House, Oxford House, Pembina, Pi[d]geon River, Red River Settlement (including the Church Mission House and School, the Upper Church, the Middle Church, the Lower Church at the Grand Rapids, and the Indian Church), Rock River Depot, Swan River, White Horse Plains, and York Factory
Saskatchewan: Cumberland House, Fort Île-à-la-Crosse, and Fort Pelly
Northwest Territories: Fort Simpson
British Columbia: [Fort] New Caledonia

Winnipeg, Manitoba

The Upper Church, Red River Settlement [at Upper Fort Garry (later, St. John's Anglican Cathedral, Winnipeg)]
B/MD   1841-1851   **HBC-4M5*** (index)
includes: **Manitoba:** Albany [House]
Saskatchewan: Fort Île-à-la-Crosse
Northwest Territories: Peel's River [Fort McPherson]
British Columbia: Thompson's River [Post (Fort Kamloops)]

Lockport, Manitoba

The Lower Church, Red River Settlement [at the Grand Rapids, Lower Fort Garry (later, St. Andrew's-on-the-Red Anglican Church)]
B/MD   1841-1851   **HBC-4M5*** (index)

St. Peter's Indian Reserve, Manitoba

The Indian Church, Red River Settlement [at Dynevor (later, St. Peter's Anglican Church)]
B/MD   1841-1850   **HBC-4M5*** (index)
confirmations, 1844   **HBC-4M5***

Rivière-du-Pat [The Pas, Manitoba]

Anglican Church Mission Station
BM   1842   **HBC-4M5*** (index)

---

* Access to reels **HBC-4M4** and **HBC-4M5** is controlled by the Archives of the Hudson's Bay Company. All **interlibrary loan requests** and **research inquiries** should be addressed to: The Keeper, Hudson's Bay Company Archives, Provincial Archives of Manitoba, Manitoba Archives Building, 200 Vaughan Street, Winnipeg, Manitoba, Canada R3C 1T5. Researchers in Ottawa who wish to consult the reels at the National Archives of Canada should apply for permission to the British Archives Section of the Manuscript Division.

Canada

Fort Kamloops (Thompson's River Post), Yale District
See: Hudson's Bay Company returns (page 3)

Fort New Caledonia (Fort St. James), Cariboo District
See: Hudson's Bay Company returns (page 3)

Fort St. James (Fort New Caledonia), Cariboo District
See: Hudson's Bay Company returns (page 3)

Fort Simpson (later, Port Simpson), West Coast area

William Duncan's Metlakahtla Christian Mission, Annette Island, Alaska, U.S.A.
B	1861-1918	**M-2331**
M	1881-1899	**M-2331**
D	1881-1918	**M-2331**

includes:

C.M.S. Anglican Mission of Fort Simpson and Metlakatla, B.C.
B	1861-1863, 1874-1884	**M-2331**
D	1862	**M-2331**

William Duncan's Metlakahtla Christian Mission, Metlakatla, B.C.
B	1882-1887	**M-2331**
M	1881-1886	**M-2331**
D	1881-1887	**M-2331**

Kamloops, Fort (Thompson's River Post), Yale District
See: Hudson's Bay Company returns (page 3)

Metlakatla, West Coast area

William Duncan's Metlakahtla Christian Mission, Annette Island, Alaska, U.S.A.
B	1861-1918	**M-2331**
M	1881-1899	**M-2331**
D	1881-1918	**M-2331**

includes:

C.M.S. Anglican Mission of Fort Simpson and Metlakatla, B.C.
B	1861-1863, 1874-1884	**M-2331**
D	1862	**M-2331**

William Duncan's Metlakahtla Christian Mission, Metlakatla, B.C.
B	1882-1887	**M-2331**
M	1881-1886	**M-2331**
D	1881-1887	**M-2331**

New Caledonia, Fort (Fort St. James), Cariboo District
See: Hudson's Bay Company returns (page 3)

Port Simpson (formerly, Fort Simpson), West Coast area

William Duncan's Metlakahtla Christian Mission, Annette Island, Alaska, U.S.A.
B	1861-1918	**M-2331**
M	1881-1899	**M-2331**
D	1881-1918	**M-2331**

includes:

C.M.S. Anglican Mission of Fort Simpson and Metlakatla, B.C.
B	1861-1863, 1874-1884	**M-2331**
D	1862	**M-2331**

William Duncan's Metlakahtla Christian Mission, Metlakatla, B.C.
B	1882-1887	**M-2331**
M	1881-1886	**M-2331**
D	1881-1887	**M-2331**

St. James, Fort (Fort New Caledonia), Cariboo District
See: Hudson's Bay Company returns (page 3)

Thompson's River Post (Fort Kamloops), Yale District
See: Hudson's Bay Company returns (page 3)

MANITOBA

Albany House, North District
See: Hudson's Bay Company returns (page 3)

Arden (formerly, Beautiful Plains), North Central District

Union Church, White Mud River [Palestine (later, Gladstone) Presbyterian Mission]
B	1877-1883	**H-1813**
M	1876-1884	**H-1813**
D	1879-1880	**H-1813**

includes: among other settlements west of Lake Manitoba, Beautiful Plains (later, Arden), Hamilton (later, Hamiota), Little Saskatchewan (later, Minnedosa), and Westbourne

Beautiful Plains (later, Arden), North Central District

Union Church, White Mud River [Palestine (later, Gladstone) Presbyterian Mission]
B	1877-1883	**H-1813**
M	1876-1884	**H-1813**
D	1879-1880	**H-1813**

includes: among other settlements west of Lake Manitoba, Beautiful Plains (later, Arden), Hamilton (later, Hamiota), Little Saskatchewan (later, Minnedosa), and Westbourne

Beaver Creek, Ellice District
See: Hudson's Bay Company returns (page 3)

Berens River House, North District
See: Hudson's Bay Company returns (page 3)

Brandon House, Cornwallis Municipality
See: Hudson's Bay Company returns (page 3)

Dynevor (Sugar Point), Portage La Prairie Municipality

Rupert's Land Anglican Missions, Red River Settlement
B	1838 extracts	**H-1812**
M	1821, 1823 extracts	**H-1812**
D	1821-1822, 1864 extracts	**H-1812**

comprises:

St. John's Anglican Cathedral, Winnipeg
B	1838 extracts	**H-1812**
M	1821, 1823 extracts	**H-1812**
D	1821-1822 extracts	**H-1812**

includes: Norway House, Pembina, Red River Settlement, Indian Settlement, and York Factory, Man.; as well as Cumberland House, Sask.

St. Peter's Anglican Church, Dynevor, and St. Clement's Anglican Church, Mapleton
D	1864 extracts	**H-1812**

includes: Lower Mapleton

(cont.)

See also:
    Hudson's Bay Company returns (page 3)

Fort Alexander, North District
See: Hudson's Bay Company returns (page 3)

Fort Douglas, Winnipeg Municipality
See: Hudson's Bay Company returns (page 3)
    Red River Settlement (page 11)
    Winnipeg (page 12)

Fort Garry, Winnipeg Municipality
See: Hudson's Bay Company returns (page 3)
    Red River Settlement (page 11)
    Winnipeg (page 12)

Fort Gibraltar, Winnipeg Municipality
See: Hudson's Bay Company returns (page 3)
    Red River Settlement (page 11)
    Winnipeg (page 12)

Gladstone, (formerly, Palestine), North Central District

Union Church, White Mud River [Palestine (later, Gladstone) Presbyterian Mission]
B	1877-1883	**H-1813**
M	1876-1884	**H-1813**
D	1879-1880	**H-1813**

includes: among other settlements west of Lake Manitoba, Beautiful Plains (later, Arden), Hamilton (later, Hamiota), Little Saskatchewan (later, Minnedosa), and Westbourne

Hamilton (later, Hamiota), Southwest District

Union Church, White Mud River [Palestine (later, Gladstone) Presbyterian Mission]
B	1877-1883	**H-1813**
M	1876-1884	**H-1813**
D	1879-1880	**H-1813**

includes: among other settlements west of Lake Manitoba, Beautiful Plains (later, Arden), Hamilton (later, Hamiota), Little Saskatchewan (later, Minnedosa), and Westbourne

Hamiota (formerly, Hamilton), Southwest District

Union Church, White Mud River [Palestine (later, Gladstone) Presbyterian Mission]
B	1877-1883	**H-1813**
M	1876-1884	**H-1813**
D	1879-1880	**H-1813**

includes: among other settlements west of Lake Manitoba, Beautiful Plains (later, Arden), Hamilton (later,

(cont.)

Hamiota), Little Saskatchewan (later, Minnedosa), and Westbourne

Little Saskatchewan (later, Minnedosa), Southwest District

Union Church, White Mud River [Palestine (later, Gladstone) Presbyterian Mission]
B	1877-1883	**H-1813**
M	1876-1884	**H-1813**
D	1879-1880	**H-1813**

includes: among other settlements west of Lake Manitoba, Beautiful Plains (later, Arden), Hamilton (later, Hamiota), Little Saskatchewan (later, Minnedosa), and Westbourne

Lockport, Interlake District

Kipling transcripts, on alphabetically arranged cards, of parish registers of the Red River Settlement

BMD   1820-1884 Index   **H-1344**
includes:

St. Andrew's-on-the-Red Anglican Church, Lockport
M	1835-1876, 1878-1883 Index	**H-1344**
D	1835-1876, 1878-1884 Index	**H-1344**

Registers of the Rev. William Cockran, Assistant Chaplain (Anglican) to the Hudson's Bay Company and Missionary of the Church Missionary Society

BMD   1828-1829   **A-86**
includes: Oxford House, the Red River Settlement (later, St. John's Cathedral, Winnipeg), the Rapids of the Red River (later, St. Andrew's-on-the-Red, Lockport), and York Factory, Man.; as well as Carlton House (Fort Pelly), and Cumberland House, Sask.

See also: Red River Settlement (page 11)
          Hudson's Bay Company Returns (page 3)

Lower Mapleton, Interlake District

Rupert's Land Anglican Missions, Red River Settlement
B	1838 extracts	**H-1812**
M	1821, 1823 extracts	**H-1812**
D	1821-1822, 1864 extracts	**H-1812**

includes:

St. Peter's Anglican Church, Dynevor, and St. Clement's Anglican Church, Mapleton
D	1864 extracts	**H-1812**

includes: Lower Mapleton

Mapleton, Interlake District

Rupert's Land Anglican Missions, Red River Settlement
B	1838 extracts	**H-1812**
M	1821, 1823 extracts	**H-1812**
D	1821-1822, 1864 extracts	**H-1812**

includes:

St. Peter's Anglican Church, Dynevor, and St. Clement's Anglican Church, Mapleton
D	1864 extracts	**H-1812**

includes: Lower Mapleton

Minnedosa (formerly, Little Saskatchewan), Southwest District

Union Church, White Mud River [Palestine (later, Gladstone) Presbyterian Mission]
B	1877-1883	**H-1813**
M	1876-1884	**H-1813**
D	1879-1880	**H-1813**

includes: among other settlements west of Lake Manitoba, Beautiful Plains (later, Arden), Hamilton (later, Hamiota), Little Saskatchewan (later, Minnedosa), and Westbourne

Nelson River District, North District
See: Hudson's Bay Company returns (page 3)

Norway House, North District

Rupert's Land Anglican Missions, Red River Settlement
B	1838 extracts	**H-1812**
M	1821, 1823 extracts	**H-1812**
D	1821-1822, 1864 extracts	**H-1812**

includes:

St. John's Anglican Cathedral, Winnipeg
B	1838 extracts	**H-1812**
M	1821, 1823 extracts	**H-1812**
D	1821-1822 extracts	**H-1812**

includes: Norway House, Pembina, Red River Settlement, Indian Settlement, and York Factory, Man.; as well as Cumberland House, Sask.

See also:
Hudson's Bay Company returns (page 3)

Oxford House, North District

Registers of the Rev. William Cockran, Assistant Chaplain (Anglican) to the Hudson's Bay Company and Missionary of the Church Missionary Society

BMD   1828-1829   **A-86**
includes: Oxford House, the Red River Settlement (later, St. John's Cathedral, Winnipeg), the Rapids of the Red River (later, St. Andrew's-on-the-Red,

(cont.)

Lockport), and York Factory, Man.; as well as Carlton House (Fort Pelly), and Cumberland House, Sask.

See also: Hudson's Bay Company returns (page 3)

Palestine (later, Gladstone), North Central District

Union Church, White Mud River [Palestine (later, Gladstone) Presbyterian Mission]
B	1877-1883	**H-1813**
M	1876-1884	**H-1813**
D	1879-1880	**H-1813**

includes: among other settlements west of Lake Manitoba, Beautiful Plains (later, Arden), Hamilton (later, Hamiota), Little Saskatchewan (later, Minnedosa), and Westbourne

Pembina, South Central District

Rupert's Land Anglican Missions, Red River Settlement
B	1838 extracts	**H-1812**
M	1821, 1823 extracts	**H-1812**
D	1821-1822, 1864 extracts	**H-1812**

includes:

St. John's Anglican Cathedral, Winnipeg
B	1838 extracts	**H-1812**
M	1821, 1823 extracts	**H-1812**
D	1821-1822 extracts	**H-1812**

includes: Norway House, Pembina, Red River Settlement, Indian Settlement, and York Factory, Man.; as well as Cumberland House, Sask.

See also:
Hudson's Bay Company returns (page 3)

Pigeon River, North District
See: Hudson's Bay Company returns (page 3)

Red River Settlement, Winnipeg District

Kipling transcripts, on alphabetically arranged cards, of parish registers of the Red River Settlement
BMD	1820-1884 Index	**H-1344**

comprises:

St. John's Anglican Cathedral, Winnipeg
M	1820-1878, 1881-1882 Index	**H-1344**
D	1821-1823, 1825-1838, 1841-1875 Index	**H-1344**

St. Andrew's-on-the-Red Anglican Church, Lockport
M	1835-1876, 1878-1883 Index	**H-1344**
D	1835-1876, 1878-1884 Index	**H-1344**

St. Boniface's Roman Catholic Basilica, St. Boniface
B	1824-1825, 1829-1830, 1832-1834 Index	**H-1344**
MD	1825, 1828-1830, 1832-1834 Index	**H-1344**

Registers of the Rev. William Cockran, Assistant Chaplain (Anglican) to the Hudson's Bay Company and Missionary of the Church Missionary Society
BMD	1828-1829	**A-86**

includes: Oxford House, the Red River Settlement (later, St. John's Cathedral, Winnipeg), the Rapids of the Red River (later, St. Andrew's-on-the-Red, Lockport), and York Factory, Man.; as well as Carlton House (Fort Pelly), and Cumberland House, Sask.

Rupert's Land Anglican Missions
B	1838 extracts	**H-1812**
M	1821, 1823 extracts	**H-1812**
D	1821-1822, 1864 extracts	**H-1812**

comprises:

St. John's Anglican Cathedral, Winnipeg
B	1838 extracts	**H-1812**
M	1821, 1823 extracts	**H-1812**
D	1821-1822 extracts	**H-1812**

includes: Norway House, Pembina, Red River Settlement, Indian Settlement, and York Factory, Man.; as well as Cumberland House, Sask.

St. Peter's Anglican Church, Dynevor, and St. Clement's Anglican Church, Mapleton
D	1864 extracts	**H-1812**

includes: Lower Mapleton

See also: Hudson's Bay Company returns (page 3)

Rivière du Pat [The Pas, Consol District]
See: Hudson's Bay Company returns (page 3)

Rock River Depot, North District
See: Hudson's Bay Company returns (page 3)

St. Boniface, Winnipeg Municipality

Kipling transcripts, on alphabetically arranged cards, of parish registers of the Red River Settlement
BMD	1820-1884 Index	**H-1344**

includes:

St. Boniface's Roman Catholic Basilica, St. Boniface
B	1824-1825, 1829-1830, 1832-1834 Index	**H-1344**
MD	1825, 1828-1830, 1832-1834 Index	**H-1344**

(cont.)

St. Peter's Indian Reserve (Sugar Point), Portage La Prairie Municipality

Rupert's Land Anglican Missions, Red River Settlement
B	1838 extracts	**H-1812**
M	1821, 1823 extracts	**H-1812**
D	1821-1822, 1864 extracts	**H-1812**

comprises:

    St. John's Anglican Cathedral, Winnipeg
B	1838 extracts	**H-1812**
M	1821, 1823 extracts	**H-1812**
D	1821-1822 extracts	**H-1812**

    includes: Norway House, Pembina, Red River Settlement, Indian Settlement, and York Factory, Man.; as well as Cumberland House, Sask.

    St. Peter's Anglican Church, Dynevor, and St. Clement's Anglican Church, Mapleton
D	1864 extracts	**H-1812**

    includes: Lower Mapleton

See also: Hudson's Bay Company returns (page 3)

Sugar Point (Dynevor), Portage La Prairie Municipality

Rupert's Land Anglican Missions, Red River Settlement
B	1838 extracts	**H-1812**
M	1821, 1823 extracts	**H-1812**
D	1821-1822, 1864 extracts	**H-1812**

comprises:

    St. John's Anglican Cathedral, Winnipeg
B	1838 extracts	**H-1812**
M	1821, 1823 extracts	**H-1812**
D	1821-1822 extracts	**H-1812**

    includes: Norway House, Pembina, Red River Settlement, Indian Settlement, and York Factory, Man.; as well as Cumberland House, Sask.

    St. Peter's Anglican Church, Dynevor, and St. Clement's Anglican Church, Mapleton
D	1864 extracts	**H-1812**

    includes: Lower Mapleton

See also: Hudson's Bay Company returns (page 3)

Swan River House, Parklands District
See: Hudson's Bay Company returns (page 3)

[**The Pas** (Rivière du Pat), Consol District]
See: Hudson's Bay Company returns (page 3)

Westbourne, North Central District

Union Church, White Mud River [Palestine (later, Gladstone) Presbyterian Mission]
B	1877-1883	**H-1813**
M	1876-1884	**H-1813**
D	1879-1880	**H-1813**

includes: among other settlements west of Lake Manitoba, Beautiful Plains (later, Arden), Hamilton (later, Hamiota), Little Saskatchewan (later, Minnedosa), and Westbourne

White Horse Plains House, Winnipeg District
See: Hudson's Bay Company returns (page 3)

White Mud River, [North Central District]

Union Church, White Mud River [Palestine (later, Gladstone) Presbyterian Mission]
B	1877-1883	**H-1813**
M	1876-1884	**H-1813**
D	1879-1880	**H-1813**

includes: among other settlements west of Lake Manitoba, Beautiful Plains (later, Arden), Hamilton (later, Hamiota), Little Saskatchewan (later, Minnedosa), and Westbourne

Winnipeg, Winnipeg District

Kipling transcripts, on alphabetically arranged cards, of parish registers of the Red River Settlement
BMD	1820-1884 Index	**H-1344**

includes:

    St. John's Anglican Cathedral, Winnipeg
M	1820-1878, 1881-1882 Index	**H-1344**
D	1821-1823, 1825-1838, 1841-1875 Index	**H-1344**

Registers of the Rev. William Cockran, Assistant Chaplain (Anglican) to the Hudson's Bay Company and Missionary of the Church Missionary Society
BMD	1828-1829	**A-86**

includes: Oxford House, the Red River Settlement (later, St. John's Cathedral, Winnipeg), the Rapids of the Red River (later, St. Andrew's-on-the-Red, Lockport), and York Factory, Man.; as well as Carlton House (Fort Pelly), and Cumberland House, Sask.

(cont.)

Rupert's Land Anglican Missions, Red River Settlement
B	1838 extracts	**H-1812**
M	1821, 1823 extracts	**H-1812**
D	1821-1822, 1864 extracts	**H-1812**

includes:

   St. John's Anglican Cathedral, Winnipeg
B	1838 extracts	**H-1812**
M	1821, 1823 extracts	**H-1812**
D	1821-1822 extracts	**H-1812**

   includes: Norway House, Pembina, Red River Settlement, Indian Settlement, and York Factory, Man.; as well as Cumberland House, Sask.

See also: Red River Settlement (page 11)
         Hudson's Bay Company returns (page 3)

Holy Ghost Roman Catholic Church
B	1850-1920	**H-1812**
M	c. 1901	**H-1812**

comprises:

   Poland
B	1850-1920	**H-1812**

   (In Latin and Polish)

   Galicia (Austrian Empire, later the U.S.S.R.)
B	1861-1898	**H-1812**
M	c. 1901	**H-1812**

   (In Latin, Polish, Russian, Ukrainian, and German)

   Russia
B	1869, 1884	**H-1812**

   (In Russian)

   Czechoslovakia
B	1873-1918	**H-1812**

   (In Latin, Czech, and German)

   Hungary
B	1877	**H-1812**

   (In Hungarian)

   Winnipeg, Manitoba
B	1910	**H-1812**

   (In Latin)

Registers of Rabbi Israel Isaac Kahanovitch, of Beth Jacob Orthodox Jewish Synagogue
M	1931-1943	**M-6509**

York Factory, North District

Registers of the Rev. William Cockran, Assistant Chaplain (Anglican) to the Hudson's Bay Company and Missionary of the Church Missionary Society
BMD	1828-1829	**A-86**

includes: Oxford House, the Red River Settlement (later, St. John's Cathedral, Winnipeg), the Rapids of the Red River (later, St. Andrew's-on-the-Red, Lockport), and York Factory, Man.; as well as Carlton House (Fort Pelly), and Cumberland House, Sask.

Rupert's Land Anglican Missions, Red River Settlement
B	1838 extracts	**H-1812**
M	1821, 1823 extracts	**H-1812**
D	1821-1822, 1864 extracts	**H-1812**

includes:

   St. John's Anglican Cathedral, Winnipeg
B	1838 extracts	**H-1812**
M	1821, 1823 extracts	**H-1812**
D	1821-1822 extracts	**H-1812**

   includes: Norway House, Pembina, Red River Settlement, Indian Settlement, and York Factory, Man.; as well as Cumberland House, Sask.

See also: Hudson's Bay Company returns (page 3)

Apohaqui, Kings Co.

L. Allison's Cemetery Recordings, Kings Co.
B	1725-1890	**H-1806**
D	1793-1895	**H-1806**

includes:

    Kings County Cemetery Recordings
B	1730-1890	**H-1806**
D	1793-1893	**H-1806**

    includes: Apohaqui, Hampton, Lester [Brook], Milliken [Milligan Brook], Penobsquis, Smiths Creek, Sussex, and Wards Creek, Kings Co.

Baie-des-Vents (aujourd'hui, Baie-Sainte-Anne), comté de Northumberland

St-Laurent-de-la-Baie-des-Vents (Église catholique)
B	1801-1828, 1851-1870	**C-3016**
M	1801-1831, 1851-1868	**C-3016**
D	1801-1830, 1854	**C-3016**

Baie-Sainte-Anne (antérieurement, Baie-des-Vents), comté de Northumberland

St-Laurent-de-la-Baie-des-Vents (Église catholique)
B	1801-1828, 1851-1870	**C-3016**
M	1801-1831, 1851-1868	**C-3016**
D	1801-1830, 1854	**C-3016**

Barachois, comté de Westmorland

St-Henri-de-Barachois (Église catholique)
BD	1812-1870	**C-3016**
M	1820-1870	**C-3016** (index)

comprend : Didiche, Naboiyagan (Naboujagan), et Haute-Aboujagane

Botsford, comté de Westmorland

St-Barthélemy-du-Cap-Tourmentin (Église catholique)
B	1839-1842, 1844-1853	**C-3016**
M	1846-1847	**C-3016**
D	1839-1848	**C-3016**

Bouctouche/Buctouche, comté de Kent/Kent Co.

St-Jean-Baptiste-de-Bouctouche (Église catholique)
BMD	1800-1870	**C-3016**

(cont.)

St. Martin's in-the-Woods Anglican Church, Shediac Cape, Westmorland Co.
B	1825-1835	**C-3020**
M	1829-1834	**C-3020**
	1868-1874	**H-1806**
D	1830-1833	**C-3020**

comprises:

    Register for the Parish of Shediac, Westmorland Co.
B	1825-1835	**C-3020**
M	1829-1834	**C-3020**
D	1830-1833	**C-3020**

    includes: Shediac, Shediac River, [Shemogue], and Petitcodiac, Westmorland Co.; and Buctouche, and Cocagne, Kent Co.

    Register for the Parish of Richibucto, Kent Co.
B	1833-1835	**C-3020**

    includes: Richibucto Harbour, Richibucto River, and Buctouche, Kent Co.; and Petitcodiac River, Westmorland Co.

    Register for the Parishes of Dundas and Wellington, Kent Co.
M	1868, 1870-1872, 1874	**H-1806**

    includes: Buctouche, and the Parishes of Wellington, and Dundas

Burton Parish, Sunbury Co.

S.P.G. Anglican Mission of Maugerville, Burton, etc.
BM	1787-1803	**H-1806**
D	1788-1801	**H-1806**

Cap-Tourmentin, comté de Westmorland

St-Barthélemy-du-Cap-Tourmentin (Église catholique)
B	1839-1842, 1844-1853	**C-3016**
M	1846-1847	**C-3016**
D	1839-1848	**C-3016**

Caraquet, comté de Gloucester

St-Pierre-aux-Liens-de-Caraquet (Église catholique)
BMD	1768-1799	**C-1449**

Carleton Parish, Kent Co.

S.P.G. Anglican Mission of Gagetown, Queens Co.
BM	1786-1792	**H-1806**

includes: Carleton Parish, Kent Co.; Kingston, and Sussex, Kings Co.; Hampstead, Long Island, Waterborough, and Wickham, Queens Co.; Lancaster, and St. John, St. John Co.; Maugerville, Sunbury Co.; Fredericton, York Co.; and Woodbury, Connecticut, U.S.A.

Chimogoui (Chimougoui, Shemogue), comté de Westmorland / Westmorland Co.

St-Timothée-de-Shemogue (Église catholique)
BD	1813-1899	**C-3020**
M	1818-1899	**C-3020**

St. Martin's-in-the-Woods Anglican Church, Shediac Cape
B	1825-1835	**C-3020**
M	1829-1834	**C-3020**
	1868-1874	**H-1806**
D	1830-1833	**C-3020**

includes:

    Register for the Parish of Shediac
B	1825-1835	**C-3020**
M	1829-1834	**C-3020**
D	1830-1833	**C-3020**

    includes: Shediac, Shediac River, [Shemogue], and Petitcodiac, Westmorland Co.; and Buctouche, and Cocagne, Kent Co.

Chipoudy (Chipoudie, Shepody), comté d'Albert

Registres d'état civil d'Acadie et Gaspésie, N.-É.
BM	1679-1686	**C-3021**
BMD	1751-1757	**C-3021**

comprend :

    Chipoudy (Hopewell), N.-B.
B	1755-1756	**C-3021**
M	1756	**C-3021**

    comprend : Petitcoudiac (Hillsborough), N.-B.

    Petitcoudiac (Hopewell), N.-B.
BMD	1753-1755	**C-3021**

Coates Mills, Kent Co.

L. Allison's Cemetery Recordings, Kings Co.
B	1725-1890	**H-1806**
D	1793-1895	**H-1806**

includes:

    Coates [Mills] Old Triangular Burying Ground
B	1763-1856	**H-1806**
D	1829-1882	**H-1806**

Cocagne, comté de Kent / Kent Co.

St-Pierre-de-Cocagne (Église catholique)
BMD	1800-1870	**C-3016**
	1801-1824	**C-3016**

St. Martin's-in-the-Woods Anglican Church, Shediac Cape, Westmorland Co.
B	1825-1835	**C-3020**
M	1829-1834	**C-3020**
	1868-1874	**H-1806**
D	1830-1833	**C-3020**

includes:

    Register for the Parish of Shediac, Westmorland Co.
B	1825-1835	**C-3020**
M	1829-1834	**C-3020**
D	1830-1833	**C-3020**

    includes: Shediac, Shediac River, [Shemogue], and Petitcodiac, Westmorland Co.; and Buctouche, and Cocagne, Kent Co.

Didiche, comté de Westmorland

St-Henri-de-Barachois (Église catholique)
BD	1812-1870	**C-3016**
M	1820-1870	**C-3016** (index)

comprend : Barachois, Didiche, Naboiyagan (Naboujagan), et Haute-Aboujagane

Dumfries Parish, York Co.

S.P.G. Anglican Mission of Woodstock, etc., Carleton Co.
BMD	1791-1816	**H-1806**
communicants,	1803-1820	**H-1806**

includes:

    Prince William Parish, York Co.
BMD	1792-1815	**H-1806**
communicants,	1803-1820	**H-1806**

    includes: the Parishes of Dumfries, Kingsclear, and Queensbury, York Co.

Dundas Parish, Kent Co.

St-Martin's-in-the-Woods Anglican Church, Shediac Cape, Westmorland Co.
B	1825-1835	**C-3020**
M	1829-1834	**C-3020**
	1868-1874	**H-1806**
D	1830-1833	**C-3020**

includes:

    Register for the Parishes of Dundas and Wellington, Kent Co.
M	1868, 1870-1872, 1874	**H-1806**

    includes: Buctouche, and the Parishes of Wellington, and Dundas

(cont.)

Ekoupag (Ekoupahag, Ekouipahag), comté d'York

Ste-Anne-d'Ekoupahag, en la Rivière St-Jean
(Mission catholique)
BMD	1767-1768	**M-4604** (originaux)
	1767-1768	**H-1806** (copies)
	1767-1768 extraits	**C-3109**

Ste-Anne-de-Fredericton, ou des Pays-Bas
(Mission catholique)
BMD	1806-1824	**M-4604** (originaux)
	1806-1824	**C-3019** (copies)
	1806-1824 extraits	**C-3109**

Ste-Anne-de-Fredericton, ou Kingsclear (Église catholique)
BMD	1824-1859	**M-4604** (originaux, index)
	1824-1859	**C-3019** (copies, index)

Fredericton, comté d'York/York Co.

Ste-Anne-d'Ekoupahag, en la Rivière St-Jean
(Mission catholique)
BMD	1767-1768	**M-4604** (originaux)
	1767-1768	**H-1806** (copies)
	1767-1768 extraits	**C-3109**

Ste-Anne-de-Fredericton, ou des Pays-Bas
(Mission catholique)
BMD	1806-1824	**M-4604** (originaux)
	1806-1824	**C-3019** (copies)
	1806-1824 extraits	**C-3109**

Ste-Anne-de-Fredericton, ou Kingsclear (Église catholique)
BMD	1824-1859	**M-4604** (originaux, index)
	1824-1859	**C-3019** (copies, index)

L. Allison's Cemetery Recordings, Kings Co.
B	1725-1890	**H-1806**
D	1793-1895	**H-1806**

includes:

Fredericton Cemetery, York Co.
B	1754-1853	**H-1806**
D	1821-1879	**H-1806**

S.P.G. Anglican Mission of Gagetown, Queens Co.
BM	1786-1792	**H-1806**

includes: Carleton Parish, Kent Co.; Kingston, and Sussex, Kings Co.; Hampstead, Long Island, Waterborough, and Wickham, Queens Co.; Lancaster, and St. John, St. John Co.; Maugerville, Sunbury Co.; Fredericton, York Co.; and Woodbury, Connecticut, U.S.A.

Gagetown Parish, Queens Co.

S.P.G. Anglican Mission of Gagetown, Queens Co.
BM	1786-1792	**H-1806**

includes: Carleton Parish, Kent Co.; Kingston, and Sussex, Kings Co.; Hampstead, Long Island, Waterborough, and Wickham, Queens Co.; Lancaster, and St. John, St. John Co.; Maugerville, Sunbury Co.; Fredericton, York Co.; and Woodbury, Connecticut, U.S.A.

Grande-Digue, comté de Kent

Notre-Dame-de-la-Visitation (Église catholique)
B	1800-1859	**C-3016**
	1859-1875	**C-3017**
M	1800-1875	**C-3017**
D	1802-1875	**C-3017**

Hampstead, Queens Co.

S.P.G. Anglican Mission of Gagetown, Queens Co.
BM	1786-1792	**H-1806**

includes: Carleton Parish, Kent Co.; Kingston, and Sussex, Kings Co.; Hampstead, Long Island, Waterborough, and Wickham, Queens Co.; Lancaster, and St. John, St. John Co.; Maugerville, Sunbury Co.; Fredericton, York Co.; and Woodbury, Connecticut, U.S.A.

Hampton, Kings Co.

L. Allison's Cemetery Recordings, Kings Co.
B	1725-1890	**H-1806**
D	1793-1895	**H-1806**

includes:

Kings County Cemetery Recordings
B	1730-1890	**H-1806**
D	1793-1893	**H-1806**

includes: Apohaqui, Hampton, Lester [Brook], Milliken [Milligan Brook], Penobsquis, Smiths Creek, Sussex, and Wards Creek, Kings Co.

Haute-Aboujagane, comté de Westmorland

St-Henri-de-Barachois (Église catholique)
BD	1812-1870	**C-3016**
M	1820-1870	**C-3016** (index)

comprend : Barachois, Didiche, Naboiyagan (Naboujagan), et Sacré-Cœur-de-Haute-Aboujagane

Hillsborough (Petitcoudiac), comté d'Albert

Registres d'état civil d'Acadie et Gaspésie, N.-É.
BM	1679-1686	**C-3021**
BMD	1751-1757	**C-3021**

comprend :

    Petitcoudiac (Hillsborough), N.-B.
B	1755-1756	**C-3021**
M	1756	**C-3021**

    comprend : Chipoudy (Hopewell), N.-B.

Hopewell, comté d'Albert

Registres d'état civil d'Acadie et Gaspésie, N.-É.
BM	1679-1686	**C-3021**
BMD	1751-1757	**C-3021**

comprend :

    Chipoudy (Hopewell), N.-B.
B	1755-1756	**C-3021**
M	1756	**C-3021**

    comprend : Petitcoudiac (Hillsborough), N.-B.

    Petitcoudiac (Hopewell), N.-B.
BMD	1753-1755	**C-3021**

Jemseg (Rivière Saint-Jean), comté de Queens

Registres d'état civil d'Acadie et Gaspésie, N.-É.
BM	1679-1686	**C-3021**
BMD	1751-1757	**C-3021**

comprend :

    Jemsek (Rivière St-Jean), N.-B.
B	1681	**C-3021**

Kings County

L. Allison's Cemetery Recordings, Kings Co.
B	1725-1890	**H-1806**
D	1793-1895	**H-1806**

comprises:

    Kings County Cemetery Recordings
B	1730-1890	**H-1806**
D	1793-1893	**H-1806**

    includes: Apohaqui, Hampton, Lester [Brook], Milliken [Milligan Brook], Penobsquis, Smiths Creek, Sussex, and Wards Creek, Kings Co.

    Coates [Mills] Old Triangular Burying Ground, [Kent Co.]
B	1763-1856	**H-1806**
D	1829-1882	**H-1806**

    Fredericton Cemetery, York Co.
B	1754-1853	**H-1806**
D	1821-1879	**H-1806**

(cont.)

St. John Rural Cemetery, St. John Co.
B	1735-1874	**H-1806**
D	1821-1895	**H-1806**

Salisbury Cemeteries, Westmorland Co.
B	1725-1887	**H-1806**
D	18[1]0-1889	**H-1806**

Kingsclear, comté d'York

Ste-Anne-d'Ekoupahag, en la Rivière St-Jean (Mission catholique)
BMD	1767-1768	**M-4604** (originaux)
	1767-1768	**H-1806** (copies)
	1767-1768 extraits	**C-3109**

Ste-Anne-de-Fredericton, ou des Pays-Bas (Mission catholique)
BMD	1806-1824	**M-4604** (originaux)
	1806-1824	**C-3019** (copies)
	1806-1824 extraits	**C-3109**

Ste-Anne-de-Fredericton, ou Kingsclear (Église catholique)
BMD	1824-1859	**M-4604** (originaux, index)
	1824-1859	**C-3019** (copies, index)

Kingsclear Parish, York Co.

S.P.G. Anglican Mission of Woodstock, etc., Carleton Co.
BMD	1791-1816	**H-1806**
communicants,	1803-1820	**H-1806**

includes:

    Prince William Parish, York Co.
BMD	1792-1815	**H-1806**
communicants,	1803-1820	**H-1806**

    includes: the Parishes of Dumfries, Kingsclear, and Queensbury, York Co.

    Queensbury Parish, York Co.
BMD	1792-1814	**H-1806**

    includes: Kingsclear Parish, York Co.

Kingston, Kings Co.

Trinity Anglican Church, memorials and epitaphs
B	1697-1874	**H-1806**
D	1793-1906	**H-1806**

S.P.G. Anglican Mission of Gagetown, Queens Co.
BM	1786-1792	**H-1806**

includes: Carleton Parish, Kent Co.; Kingston, and Sussex, Kings Co.; Hampstead, Long Island, Waterborough, and Wickham, Queens Co.; Lancaster, and St. John, St. John Co.; Maugerville, Sunbury Co.; Fredericton, York Co.; and Woodbury, Connecticut, U.S.A.

Lancaster, St. John Co.

S.P.G. Anglican Mission of Gagetown, Queens Co.
BM   1786-1792   **H-1806**
includes: Carleton Parish, Kent Co.; Kingston, and Sussex, Kings Co.; Hampstead, Long Island, Waterborough, and Wickham, Queens Co.; Lancaster, and St. John, St. John Co.; Maugerville, Sunbury Co.; Fredericton, York Co.; and Woodbury, Connecticut, U.S.A.

L'Ardoine, comté de Kent

St-Charles-de-L'Ardoine (Église catholique)
BD	1800-1870	**C-3019**
M	1801-1870	**C-3019**

Lester [Brook], Kings Co.

L. Allison's Cemetery Recordings, Kings Co.
B	1725-1890	**H-1806**
D	1793-1895	**H-1806**

includes:

    Kings County Cemetery Recordings
B	1730-1890	**H-1806**
D	1793-1893	**H-1806**

    includes: Apohaqui, Hampton, Lester [Brook], Milliken [Milligan Brook], Penobsquis, Smiths Creek, Sussex, and Wards Creek, Kings Co.

Long Island, [Queens Co.]

S.P.G. Anglican Mission of Gagetown
BM   1786-1792   **H-1806**
includes: Carleton Parish, Kent Co.; Kingston, and Sussex, Kings Co.; Hampstead, Long Island, Waterborough, and Wickham, Queens Co.; Lancaster, and St. John, St. John Co.; Maugerville, Sunbury Co.; Fredericton, York Co.; and Woodbury, Connecticut, U.S.A.

Maugerville, Sunbury Co.

Civil registers of Sheffield, Sunbury Co.
B	1750-1829	**C-3020**
M	1766-1835	**C-3020**
D	1766-1845, n.d., 1894	**C-3020**

includes:

    Maugerville
B	1763-1786	**C-3020**

(cont.)

S.P.G. Anglican Mission of Gagetown, Queens Co.
BM   1786-1792   **H-1806**
includes: Carleton Parish, Kent Co.; Kingston, and Sussex, Kings Co.; Hampstead, Long Island, Waterborough, and Wickham, Queens Co.; Lancaster, and St. John, St. John Co.; Maugerville, Sunbury Co.; Fredericton, York Co.; and Woodbury, Connecticut, U.S.A.

S.P.G. Anglican Mission of Maugerville, Burton, etc.
BM	1787-1803	**H-1806**
D	1788-1801	**H-1806**

Memramcook, comté de Westmorland

St-Thomas-de-Memramcook (Église catholique)
BM	1806-1870	**C-3018**
D	1807-1870	**C-3018**

Milligan Brook, Kings Co.

L. Allison's Cemetery Recordings, Kings Co.
B	1725-1890	**H-1806**
D	1793-1895	**H-1806**

includes:

    Kings County Cemetery Recordings
B	1730-1890	**H-1806**
D	1793-1893	**H-1806**

    includes: Apohaqui, Hampton, Lester [Brook], Milliken [Milligan Brook], Penobsquis, Smiths Creek, Sussex, and Wards Creek, Kings Co.

Milliken [Milligan Brook], Kings Co.

L. Allison's Cemetery Recordings, Kings Co.
B	1725-1890	**H-1806**
D	1793-1895	**H-1806**

includes:

    Kings County Cemetery Recordings
B	1730-1890	**H-1806**
D	1793-1893	**H-1806**

    includes: Apohaqui, Hampton, Lester [Brook], Milliken [Milligan Brook], Penobsquis, Smiths Creek, Sussex, and Wards Creek, Kings Co.

Naboiyagan (Naboujagan), comté de Westmorland

St-Henri-de-Barachois (Église catholique)
BD	1812-1870	**C-3016**
M	1820-1870	**C-3016** (index)

comprend : Didiche, Naboiyagan (Naboujagan), et Haute-Aboujagane

Néguac, comté de Northumberland

St-Bernard-de-Néguac (Église catholique)
BM	1796-1848	**C-3018**
D	1796-1846	**C-3018**

Northampton Parish, Carleton Co.

S.P.G. Anglican Mission of Woodstock, etc.
BMD	1791-1816	**H-1806**
communicants,	1803-1820	**H-1806**

includes:

    Northampton Parish
BMD	1792-1815	**H-1806**
communicants,	1803-1819	**H-1806**

    includes: Southampton Parish, York Co.

Nouveau-Brunswick, Missions du

Registres d'état civil d'Acadie et Gaspésie, N.-É.
BM	1679-1686	**C-3021**
BMD	1751-1757	**C-3021**

comprend :

    Missions catholiques du Nouveau-Brunswick
B	1755-1757	**C-3021**

Penobsquis, Kings Co.

L. Allison's Cemetery Recordings, Kings Co.
B	1725-1890	**H-1806**
D	1793-1895	**H-1806**

includes:

    Kings County Cemetery Recordings
B	1730-1890	**H-1806**
D	1793-1893	**H-1806**

    includes: Apohaqui, Hampton, Lester [Brook], Milliken [Milligan Brook], Penobsquis, Smiths Creek, Sussex, and Wards Creek, Kings Co.

Petitcodiac/Petitcoudiac, comté de Westmorland/Westmorland Co.

Registres d'état civil d'Acadie et Gaspésie, N.-É.
BM	1679-1686	**C-3021**
BMD	1751-1757	**C-3021**

comprend :

    Petitcoudiac (Hopewell), N.-B.
BMD	1753-1755	**C-3021**

    Petitcoudiac (Hillsborough), N.-B.
B	1755-1756	**C-3021**
M	1756	**C-3021**

    comprend : Chipoudy (Hopewell), N.-B.

St. Martin's-in-the-Woods Anglican Church, Shediac Cape
B	1825-1835	**C-3020**
M	1829-1834	**C-3020**
	1868-1874	**H-1806**
D	1830-1833	**C-3020**

includes:

    Register for the Parish of Shediac
B	1825-1835	**C-3020**
M	1829-1834	**C-3020**
D	1830-1833	**C-3020**

    includes: Shediac, Shediac River, [Shemogue], and Petitcodiac, Westmorland Co.; and Buctouche, and Cocagne, Kent Co.

Petitcodiac River, Westmorland Co.

St. Martin's-in-the-Woods Anglican Church, Shediac Cape
B	1825-1835	**C-3020**
M	1829-1834	**C-3020**
	1868-1874	**H-1806**
D	1830-1833	**C-3020**

includes:

    Register for the Parish of Richibucto, Kent Co.
B	1833-1835	**C-3020**

    includes: Richibucto Harbour, Richibucto River, and Buctouche, Kent Co.; and Petitcodiac River, Westmorland Co.

Pointe-Sapin, comté de Kent

St-Joseph-de-Pointe-Sapin (Église catholique)
B	1821-1868	**C-3018**
M	1821-1825, 1835-1836, 1843-1869	**C-3018**
D	1822, 1837-1855	**C-3018**

Prince William Parish, York Co.

S.P.G. Anglican Mission of Woodstock, etc., Carleton Co.
BMD	1791-1816	**H-1806**
communicants,	1803-1820	**H-1806**

includes:

    Prince William Parish
BMD	1792-1815	**H-1806**
communicants,	1803-1820	**H-1806**

    includes: the Parishes of Dumfries, Kingsclear, and Queensbury, York Co.

(cont.)

Queensbury Parish, York Co.

S.P.G. Anglican Mission of Woodstock, etc., Carleton Co.
BMD	1791-1816	**H-1806**
communicants, 1803-1820		**H-1806**

includes:

Prince William Parish, York Co.
BMD	1792-1815	**H-1806**
communicants, 1803-1820		**H-1806**

includes: the Parishes of Dumfries, Kingsclear, and Queensbury, York Co.

Queensbury Parish
BMD	1792-1814	**H-1806**

includes: Kingsclear Parish, York Co.

Richibucto, comté de Kent

St-Antoine-de-Richibouctou (Mission catholique)
B	1796-1823	**C-3018**
	1823-1870	**C-3019**
M	1800-1871	**C-3019**
D	1796-1870	**C-3019**

Richibucto Harbour, Kent Co.

St. Martin's-in-the-Woods Anglican Church, Shediac Cape, Westmorland Co.
B	1825-1835	**C-3020**
M	1829-1834	**C-3020**
	1868-1874	**H-1806**
D	1830-1833	**C-3020**

includes:

Register for the Parish of Richibucto
B	1833-1835	**C-3020**

includes: Richibucto Harbour, Richibucto River, and Buctouche, Kent Co.; and Petitcodiac River, Westmorland Co.

Richibucto Parish, Kent Co.

St. Martin's-in-the-Woods Anglican Church, Shediac Cape, Westmorland Co.
B	1825-1835	**C-3020**
M	1829-1834	**C-3020**
	1868-1874	**H-1806**
D	1830-1833	**C-3020**

includes:

Register for the Parish of Richibucto
B	1833-1835	**C-3020**

includes: Richibucto Harbour, Richibucto River, and Buctouche, Kent Co.; and Petitcodiac River, Westmorland Co.

Richibucto River, Kent Co.

St. Martin's-in-the-Woods Anglican Church, Shediac Cape, Westmorland Co.
B	1825-1835	**C-3020**
M	1829-1834	**C-3020**
	1868-1874	**H-1806**
D	1830-1833	**C-3020**

includes:

Register for the Parish of Richibucto
B	1833-1835	**C-3020**

includes: Richibucto Harbour, Richibucto River, and Buctouche, Kent Co.; and Petitcodiac River, Westmorland Co.

Rivière Saint-Jean (Jemseg), comté de Queens

Registres d'état civil d'Acadie et Gaspésie, N.-É.
BM	1679-1686	**C-3021**
BMD	1751-1757	**C-3021**

comprend :

Jemsek (Rivière Saint-Jean), N.-B.
B	1681	**C-3021**

Rivière Saint-Jean, comté d'York

Ste-Anne-d'Ekoupahag, en la Rivière St-Jean (Mission catholique)
BMD	1767-1768	**M-4604** (originaux)
	1767-1768	**H-1806** (copies)
	1767-1768 extraits	**C-3109**

Ste-Anne-de-Fredericton, ou des Pays-Bas (Mission catholique)
BMD	1806-1824	**M-4604** (originaux)
	1806-1824	**C-3019** (copies)
	1806-1824 extraits	**C-3109**

Ste-Anne-de-Fredericton, ou Kingsclear (Église catholique)
BMD	1824-1859	**M-4604** (originaux, index)
	1824-1859	**C-3019** (copies, index)

Sackville, Westmorland Co.

Civil registers
BD	1768-1822	**C-3201**

Saint-Anselme, comté de Westmorland

St-Anselme (Église catholique)
B	1832-1870	**C-3019**
M	1832-1833, 1848-1870	**C-3019**
D	1833, 1853-1870	**C-3019**

Saint-Basile, comté de Madawaska

St-Basile-de-Madawaska (Église catholique)
BMD	1792-1839	**C-3017**
	1839-1850	**C-3018**
	1792-1799 extraits	**C-3109***
	1792-1835 extraits	**C-3109***

*Cette bobine contient des extraits de plusieurs autres registres pour le comté de Madawaska.

Saint-Charles-de-Kent, comté de Kent

St-Charles-de-L'Ardoine (Église catholique)
BD	1800-1870	**C-3019**
M	1801-1870	**C-3019**

Saint-Henri-de-Barachois, comté de Westmorland

St-Henri-de-Barachois (Église catholique)
BD	1812-1870	**C-3016**
M	1820-1870	**C-3016** (index)

comprend : Didiche, Naboiyagan (Naboujagan), et Sacré-Cœur-de-Haute-Aboujagane

St. John, St. John Co.

L. Allison's Cemetery Recordings, Kings Co.
B	1725-1890	**H-1806**
D	1793-1895	**H-1806**

includes:

St. John Rural Cemetery, St. John Co.
B	1735-1874	**H-1806**
D	1821-1895	**H-1806**

S.P.G. Anglican Mission of Gagetown, Queens Co.
BM	1786-1792	**H-1806**

includes: Carleton Parish, Kent Co.; Kingston, and Sussex, Kings Co.; Hampstead, Long Island, Waterborough, and Wickham, Queens Co.; Lancaster, and St. John, St. John Co.; Maugerville, Sunbury Co.; Fredericton, York Co.; and Woodbury, Connecticut, U.S.A.

Saint-Louis, comté de Kent

St-Louis-de-Kent (Église catholique)
B	1800-1870	**C-3020**
MD	1802-1870	**C-3020**
BMD	1805-1816	**C-3019**

Salisbury, Westmorland Co.

L. Allison's Cemetery Recordings, Kings Co.
B	1725-1890	**H-1806**
D	1793-1895	**H-1806**

includes:

Salisbury Cemeteries, Westmorland Co.
B	1725-1887	**H-1806**
D	18[1]0-1889	**H-1806**

Scoudouc, comté de Westmorland

St-Jacques-de-Scoudouc (Église catholique)
B	1850-1870	**C-3020**
M	1852-1870	**C-3020**
D	1855-1870	**C-3020**

Shediac, Westmorland Co.

St. Martin's-in-the-Woods Anglican Church, Shediac Cape
B	1825-1835	**C-3020**
M	1829-1834	**C-3020**
	1868-1874	**H-1806**
D	1830-1833	**C-3020**

includes:

Register for the Parish of Shediac
B	1825-1835	**C-3020**
M	1829-1834	**C-3020**
D	1830-1833	**C-3020**

includes: Shediac, Shediac River, [Shemogue], and Petitcodiac, Westmorland Co.; and Buctouche, and Cocagne, Kent Co.

Shediac Cape, Westmorland Co.

St. Martin's-in-the-Woods Anglican Church
B	1825-1835	**C-3020**
M	1829-1834	**C-3020**
	1868-1874	**H-1806**
D	1830-1833	**C-3020**

comprises:

Register for the Parish of Shediac
B	1825-1835	**C-3020**
M	1829-1834	**C-3020**
D	1830-1833	**C-3020**

includes: Shediac, Shediac River, [Shemogue], and Petitcodiac, Westmorland Co.; and Buctouche, and Cocagne, Kent Co.

(cont.)

Register for the Parish of Richibucto, Kent Co.
B   1833-1835   **C-3020**
includes: Richibucto Harbour, Richibucto River, and Buctouche, Kent Co.; and Petitcodiac River, Westmorland Co.

Register for the Parishes of Dundas and Wellington, Kent Co.
M   1868, 1870-1872, 1874   **H-1806**
includes: Buctouche, and the Parishes of Wellington, and Dundas

Shediac Parish, Westmorland Co.

St. Martin's-in-the-Woods Anglican Church, Shediac Cape
B	1825-1835	**C-3020**
M	1829-1834	**C-3020**
	1868-1874	**H-1806**
D	1830-1833	**C-3020**

includes:

Register for the Parish of Shediac
B	1825-1835	**C-3020**
M	1829-1834	**C-3020**
D	1830-1833	**C-3020**

includes: Shediac, Shediac River, [Shemogue], and Petitcodiac, Westmorland Co.; and Buctouche, and Cocagne, Kent Co.

Shediac River, Westmorland Co.

St. Martin's-in-the-Woods Anglican Church, Shediac Cape
B	1825-1835	**C-3020**
M	1829-1834	**C-3020**
	1868-1874	**H-1806**
D	1830-1833	**C-3020**

includes:

Register for the Parish of Shediac
B	1825-1835	**C-3020**
M	1829-1834	**C-3020**
D	1830-1833	**C-3020**

includes: Shediac, Shediac River, [Shemogue], and Petitcodiac, Westmorland Co.; and Buctouche, and Cocagne, Kent Co.

Sheffield, Sunbury Co.

Civil registers
B	1750-1829	**C-3020**
M	1766-1835	**C-3020**
D	1766-1845, n.d., 1894	**C-3020**

includes:

Maugerville
B   1763-1786   **C-3020**

Shemogue, comté de Westmorland / Westmorland Co.

St-Timothée-de-Shemogue (Église catholique)
BD	1813-1899	**C-3020**
M	1818-1899	**C-3020**

St. Martin's-in-the-Woods Anglican Church, Shediac Cape
B	1825-1835	**C-3020**
M	1829-1834	**C-3020**
	1868-1874	**H-1806**
D	1830-1833	**C-3020**

includes:

Register for the Parish of Shediac
B	1825-1835	**C-3020**
M	1829-1834	**C-3020**
D	1830-1833	**C-3020**

includes: Shediac, Shediac River, [Shemogue], and Petitcodiac, Westmorland Co.; and Buctouche, and Cocagne, Kent Co.

Shepody (Chipoudie), comté d'Albert

Registres d'état civil d'Acadie et Gaspésie, N.-É.
BM	1679-1686	**C-3021**
BMD	1751-1757	**C-3021**

comprend :

Chipoudy (Hopewell), N.-B.
B	1755-1756	**C-3021**
M	1756	**C-3021**

comprend : Petitcoudiac (Hillsborough), N.-B.

Petitcoudiac (Hopewell), N.-B.
BMD   1753-1755   **C-3021**

Smiths Creek, Kings Co.

L. Allison's Cemetery Recordings, Kings Co.
B	1725-1890	**H-1806**
D	1793-1895	**H-1806**

includes:

Kings County Cemetery Recordings
B	1730-1890	**H-1806**
D	1793-1893	**H-1806**

includes: Apohaqui, Hampton, Lester [Brook], Milliken [Milligan Brook], Penobsquis, Smiths Creek, Sussex, and Wards Creek, Kings Co.

Southampton Parish, York Co.

S.P.G. Anglican Mission of Woodstock, etc., Carleton Co.
BMD   1791-1816   **H-1806**
communicants, 1803-1820   **H-1806**
includes:

   Northampton Parish, Carleton Co.
   BMD   1792-1815   **H-1806**
   communicants, 1803-1819   **H-1806**
   includes: Southampton Parish, York Co.

Sussex, Kings Co.

L. Allison's Cemetery Recordings, Kings Co.
B   1725-1890   **H-1806**
D   1793-1895   **H-1806**
includes:

   Kings County Cemetery Recordings
   B   1730-1890   **H-1806**
   D   1793-1893   **H-1806**
   includes: Apohaqui, Hampton, Lester [Brook], Milliken [Milligan Brook], Penobsquis, Smiths Creek, Sussex, and Wards Creek, Kings Co.

S.P.G. Anglican Mission of Gagetown, Queens Co.
BM   1786-1792   **H-1806**
includes: Carleton Parish, Kent Co.; Kingston, and Sussex, Kings Co.; Hampstead, Long Island, Waterborough, and Wickham, Queens Co.; Lancaster, and St. John, St. John Co.; Maugerville, Sunbury Co.; Fredericton, York Co.; and Woodbury, Connecticut, U.S.A.

Wards Creek, Kings Co.

L. Allison's Cemetery Recordings, Kings Co.
B   1725-1890   **H-1806**
D   1793-1895   **H-1806**
includes:

   Kings County Cemetery Recordings
   B   1730-1890   **H-1806**
   D   1793-1893   **H-1806**
   includes: Apohaqui, Hampton, Lester [Brook], Milliken [Milligan Brook], Penobsquis, Smiths Creek, Sussex, and Wards Creek, Kings Co.

Waterborough, Queens Co.

S.P.G. Anglican Mission of Gagetown
BM   1786-1792   **H-1806**
includes: Carleton Parish, Kent Co.; Kingston, and Sussex, Kings Co.; Hampstead, Long Island, Waterborough, and Wickham, Queens Co.; Lancaster, and St. John, St. John Co.; Maugerville, Sunbury Co.; Fredericton, York Co.; and Woodbury, Connecticut, U.S.A.

Wellington Parish, Kent Co.

St. Martin's-in-the-Woods Anglican Church, Shediac Cape, Westmorland Co.
B   1825-1835   **C-3020**
M   1829-1834   **C-3020**
       1868-1874   **H-1806**
D   1830-1833   **C-3020**
includes:

   Register for the Parishes of Dundas and Wellington
   M   1868, 1870-1872, 1874   **H-1806**
   includes: Buctouche, and the Parishes of Wellington, and Dundas

Westmorland County

Civil registers
M   1790-1835   **M-828**   (index)

Wickham, Queens Co.

S.P.G. Anglican Mission of Gagetown
BM   1786-1792   **H-1806**
includes: Carleton Parish, Kent Co.; Kingston, and Sussex, Kings Co.; Hampstead, Long Island, Waterborough, and Wickham, Queens Co.; Lancaster, and St. John, St. John Co.; Maugerville, Sunbury Co.; Fredericton, York Co.; and Woodbury, Connecticut, U.S.A.

Woodstock Parish, Carleton Co.

S.P.G. Anglican Mission of Woodstock, etc.
BMD   1791-1816   **H-1806**
communicants, 1803-1820   **H-1806**
comprises:

   Woodstock Parish
   BMD   1791-1816   **H-1806**
   communicants, 1803-1820   **H-1806**

   Northampton Parish
   BMD   1792-1815   **H-1806**
   communicants, 1803-1819   **H-1806**
   includes: Southampton Parish, York Co.

   Prince William Parish, York Co.
   BMD   1792-1815   **H-1806**
   communicants, 1803-1820   **H-1806**
   includes: the Parishes of Dumfries, Kingsclear, and Queensbury, York Co.

   Queensbury Parish, York Co.
   BMD   1792-1814   **H-1806**
   includes: Kingsclear Parish, York Co.

Hebron, Lab.

Moravian Mission
M   1904-1933   **H-1806**
includes:

    Moravian Mission, Nain
    M   1904   **H-1806**

    Moravian Mission, Ramah
    M   1904-1908   **H-1806**
(In Eskimo and English)

Nain, Lab.

Moravian Mission, Hebron
M   1904-1933   **H-1806**
includes:

    Moravian Mission, Nain
    M   1904   **H-1806**
(In Eskimo and English)

Okak, Lab.

Moravian Mission
B   1777-1919   **M-518**
BMD   1899-1919   **M-518**
(Pages 54183-54228 and 54229-54364.
Registers are in German and English.)

Ramah, Lab.

Moravian Mission
BMD   1874-1929   **M-521**
(Pages 57936-57949. Registers are in German.)

Moravian Mission, Hebron
M   1904-1933   **H-1806**
includes:

    Moravian Mission, Ramah
    M   1904-1908   **H-1806**
(In Eskimo and English)

St. John's, Nfld.

St. John's Anglican Cathedral
BMD   1752-1790   **M-1904**
includes:

    St. John's District
    B   1786-1803, 1849   **M-1904**
    M   1784-1795   **M-1904**
    D   1795-1803   **M-1904**

St. John's Congregational Church
B   1780-1816   **M-720**
M   1802-1817, 1834-1844   **M-720**
D   1837-1838   **M-720**
membership lists 1809-1843   **M-720**
ministers' list 1775-1932   **M-720**

St. John's District, Nfld.

St. John's Anglican Cathedral
BMD   1752-1790   **M-1904**
includes:

    St. John's District
    B   1786-1803, 1849   **M-1904**
    M   1784-1795   **M-1904**
    D   1795-1803   **M-1904**

Trinity, Nfld.

St. Paul's Anglican Church
B   1753-1867   **M-1947**
MD   1757-1867   **M-1947**

Zoar, Lab.

Moravian Mission
BMD   1825-1939   **M-519**
(Pages 55761-55912. Registers are in German.)

Fort McPherson, District of Mackenzie
See: Hudson's Bay Company returns (page 3)

Fort Simpson, District of Mackenzie
See: Hudson's Bay Company returns (page 3)

Peel's River Fort (Fort McPherson), District of Mackenzie
See: Hudson's Bay Company returns (page 3)

Acadie* et Gaspésie

Registres d'état civil
BM	1679-1686	**C-3021**
BMD	1751-1757	**C-3021**

comprend :

Beaubassin, N.-É.
B	1680-1686	**C-3021**
M	1679-1682	**C-3021**

Chipoudy (Hopewell), N.-B.
B	1755-1756	**C-3021**
M	1756	**C-3021**

comprend : Petitcoudiac (Hillsborough), N.-B.

Jemsek (Rivière-Saint-Jean), N.-B.
B	1681	**C-3021**

Mines, Les, N.-É.
B	1686	**C-3021**

Mines, Rivière-des-, N.-É.
B	1684	**C-3021**

Missions du Nouveau-Brunswick
B	1755-1757	**C-3021**

Pabos, Qué.
Ste-Famille-de-Pabos (Église catholique)
BMD	1751-1757	**C-3021**

Petitcoudiac (Hopewell), N.-B.
BMD	1753-1755	**C-3021**

Rivière-des-Mines, N.-É.
B	1684	**C-3021**

*Voir aussi : GUYANE FRANÇAISE pour des extraits de l'état civil de la Guyane concernant les habitants de l'Acadie, de l'Île Royale, et de l'Île Saint-Jean, etc., réfugiés en France, puis envoyés dans la Guyane. Voir, également, ÉTATS-UNIS pour les habitants de l'Acadie réfugiés en Louisiane à la Nouvelle-Acadie.

Ste-Anne-de-Ristigouche, comté de Bonaventure, Qué.
(Église catholique)
BMD	1759-1795	**C-3024** (originaux)
	1759-1795	**C-1449** (copies, index)

comprend : autres missions environnantes, dont certaines de l'Acadie

Annapolis, Annapolis Co.

Civil registers
BMD	1747, 1774-1874, 1884	**C-3026** (index)

Annapolis Methodist Circuit
B	1835-1854	**C-3021**
M	1834-1852	**C-3021**

(cont.)

St. Luke's Anglican Church
B	1782-1800, 1808-1817, 1833-1888	**C-3021**
M	1782-1794, 1807-1817	**C-3021**
	1806, 1813, 1817-1834	**C-3021**
D	1808-1817	**C-3021**
confirmations 1791, 1885		**C-3021**

includes: Clements, Dalhousie, Granville, Graywood, Lake La Rose, Perotte, and Rosette

Antigonish County

St. John's Presbyterian Church, Belfast, Queens Co., P.E.I.
B	1823-1849	**C-3028**

includes: Charlottetown, Pinette, and Rustico, Queens Co., and Murray Harbour, Kings Co., with their environs, P.E.I.; as well as many places in all the counties of Cape Breton Island, and a few in the counties of Pictou and Antigonish, N.S.

Aylesford, Kings Co.

St. Mary's Anglican Church
B	1817-1861, 1773	**C-3021**
	1792-1861	**C-3021**

St. John's Anglican Church, Cornwallis, Annapolis Co.
B	1783-1902	**C-3021**
M	1783-1911	**C-3021**
D	1830-1920	**C-3021**

includes: Wilmot, and Aylesford, B 1784-1789; and Horton

Trinity Anglican Church, Wilmot Township, Annapolis Co.
BMD	1789-1909	**C-3026**
confirmations 1842-1909		**C-3026**

includes: Aylesford, and Bridgetown

Baie Sainte-Marie (Church Point), comté de Digby

Ste-Marie (Église catholique)
BMD	1799-1801	**C-3026**

Baleine, Havre de la, comté du Cap-Breton

Registres d'état civil de l'Île Royale (Île du Cap-Breton)
BMD	1714-1758	**F-592 à F-594** (originaux)
	1715-1758 Index*	**F-596** (originaux)
	1714-1758	**C-2573** (copies)
	1722-1754	**C-3111** et **C-3112** (copies)

comprend :

* Cet index donne le lieu de résidence mais non les dates des BMD. Il est très difficile de se servir de cet index pour trouver les entrées dans les registres, dont plusieurs sont perdus.

(cont.)

Havre de la Baleine, comté du Cap-Breton
Notre-Dame-de-Bon-Secours (Église catholique)

Havre du Petit-Laurent-le-Bec, comté du Cap-Breton
Ste-Claire-de-Lorembec (Église catholique)
BMD	1714-1745, 1750-1757	F-594	(originaux)
	1715-1758 Index*	F-596	(originaux)
	1714-1745, 1750-1757	C-2573	(copies)

* Cet index donne le lieu de résidence mais non les dates des BMD. Il est très difficile de se servir de cet index pour trouver les entrées dans les registres, dont plusieurs sont perdus.

Beaubassin, comté de Cumberland

Registres d'état civil d'Acadie et Gaspésie
BM	1679-1686	C-3021
BMD	1751-1757	C-3021

comprend :

Beaubassin, N.-É.
B	1680-1686	C-3021
M	1679-1682	C-3021

Notre-Dame-de-l'Assomption-de-Beaubassin (Église catholique)
BMD	1712-1723, 1732-1735, 1740-1746	F-696	(originaux)
	1712-1723, 1732-1735, 1740-1746	C-1207	(copies)
BM	1746-1748	F-696	(originaux)
	1746-1748	C-1207	(copies)

Bridgetown, Annapolis Co.

Trinity Anglican Church, Wilmot
BMD	1789-1909	C-3026
confirmations	1842-1909	C-3026

includes: Aylesford

with:

St. James' Anglican Church, Bridgetown
BMD	1830-1854	C-3026

includes: Upper Granville

Cape Breton Island/Île du Cap-Breton*

Registres d'état civil de l'Île Royale (Île du Cap-Breton)
BMD	1714-1758	F-592 à F-594	(originaux)
	1715-1758 Index**	F-596	(originaux)
	1714-1758	C-2573	(copies)
	1722-1754	C-3111 et C-3112	(copies)

comprend :

(cont.)

Havre de la Baleine, comté du Cap-Breton
Notre-Dame-de-Bon-Secours (Église catholique)

Havre du Petit-Laurent-le-Bec, comté du Cap-Breton
Ste-Claire-de-Lorembec (Église catholique)
BMD	1714-1745, 1750-1757	F-594	(originaux)
	1715-1758 Index**	F-596	(originaux)
	1714-1745, 1750-1757	C-2573	(copies)

Havre du Saint-Esprit, comté de Richmond
BMD	1726-1737, 1741-1745, 1749	F-594	(originaux)
	1715-1758 Index**	F-596	(originaux)
	1726-1737, 1741-1745, 1749	C-2573	(copies)

Louisbourg, comté du Cap-Breton
BMD	1722-1745	F-592	(originaux)
	1749-1758	F-593	(originaux)
	1715-1758 Index**	F-596	(originaux)
	1722-1744	C-3111	(copies)
	1744-1745, 1749-1754	C-3112	(copies)
	1754-1758	C-2573	(copies)

Petit-Nord (Port Fourché et Port-au-Basque), comté de Richmond
BMD	1740-1745	F-594	(originaux)
	1715-1758 Index**	F-596	(originaux)
	1740-1745	C-2573	(copies)

* Voir aussi : GUYANE FRANÇAISE pour des extraits de l'état civil de la Guyane concernant les habitants de l'Acadie, de l'Île Royale, et de l'Île Saint-Jean, etc., réfugiés en France, puis envoyés dans la Guyane.

** Cet index donne le lieu de résidence mais non les dates des BMD. Il est très difficile de se servir de cet index pour trouver les entrées dans les registres, dont plusieurs sont perdus.

St. George's Anglican Church, Sydney
BMD	1785-1813	C-3026
banns	1824-1845	C-3026

St. John's Presbyterian Church, Belfast, Queens Co., P.E.I.
B	1823-1849	C-3028

includes: Charlottetown, Pinette, and Rustico, Queens Co., and Murray Harbour, Kings Co., with their environs, P.E.I.; as well as many places in all the counties of Cape Breton Island, and a few in the counties of Pictou and Antigonish, Nova Scotia.

Chester, Lunenburg Co.

Civil registers
B	1762-1829	C-3027
M	1763-1817	C-3027
D	1763-1818	C-3027

St. Stephen's Anglican Church
B	1762-1841	C-3021

Church Point, (Baie Sainte-Marie), comté de Digby

Ste-Marie (Église catholique)
BMD   1799-1801   **C-3026**

Clements, Annapolis Co.

St. Luke's Anglican Church, Annapolis
B	1782-1800, 1808-1817,	
	1833-1888	**C-3021**
M	1782-1794, 1807-1817	**C-3021**
	1806, 1813, 1817-1834	**C-3021**
D	1808-1817	**C-3021**
confirmations 1791, 1885		**C-3021**

includes: Clements, Dalhousie, Granville, Graywood, Lake La Rose, Perotte, and Rosette

St. Edward's (or St. Edmund's) Anglican Church
B	1841-1873	**C-3021** (index)
M	1841-1911	**C-3021**
confirmations 1841-1879		**C-3021**

Cornwallis, Annapolis Co.

Cornwallis Baptist Church
M   1801, 1804-1822   **C-3021**

Cornwallis Methodist Church
B   1814-1827   **C-3021**

St. John's Anglican Church
B	1783-1902	**C-3021**
M	1783-1911	**C-3021**
D	1830-1920	**C-3021**

includes: Wilmot, and Horton

Cornwallis Township, Annapolis Co.

Civil registers
BMD   1720-1885   **C-3027**

Cumberland, Cumberland Co.

Civil registers
BM   1774-1813   **M-843**
includes: Fort Lawrence

Cumberland County

Civil registers
BMD   1746-1817, 1832-1837   **M-843**
includes: District of Francklin Manor, Elysian Fields, Maccan, and Nappan

Civil registers, Fort Lawrence District
BMD   1766-1891   **M-843**

Dalhousie, Annapolis Co.

St. Luke's Anglican Church, Annapolis
B	1782-1800, 1808-1817,	
	1833-1888	**C-3021**
M	1782-1794, 1807-1817	**C-3021**
	1806, 1813, 1817-1834	**C-3021**
D	1808-1817	**C-3021**
confirmations 1791, 1885		**C-3021**

includes: Clements, Dalhousie, Granville, Graywood, Lake La Rose, Perotte, and Rosette

Digby, Digby Co.

Trinity Anglican Church
B	1786-1830	**C-2217**
M	1786-1834	**C-2217**
D	1786-1845	**C-2217**

Douglas, [Hants] Co.

St. Paul's Anglican Church, Rawdon
B	1793, 1809, 1815-1880	**C-3026**
M	1814-1889	**C-3026**
D	1815-1920	**C-3026**

includes: Parish of St. James, Newport, and Douglas

Douglas Township, Hants Co.

Civil registers
BMD   1715-1873   **H-1806** (index)

Elysian Fields (Minudie Marsh), Cumberland Co.

Civil registers of Cumberland County
BMD   1746-1817, 1832-1837   **M-843**
includes: District of Francklin Manor, Elysian Fields, Maccan, and Nappan

Falmouth, Hants Co.

Civil registers
BMD   1747-1825   **C-3027**

Fort Lawrence, Cumberland Co.

Civil registers
BMD   1766-1891   **M-843**

(cont.)

Civil registers of Cumberland
BM 1774-1813 **M-843**
includes: Fort Lawrence

Fourchu (Petit-Nord), comté de Richmond

Registres d'état civil de l'Île Royale (Île du Cap-Breton)
BMD 1714-1758 **F-592 à F-594**
(originaux)
1715-1758 Index* **F-596** (originaux)
1714-1758 **C-2573** (copies)
1722-1754 **C-3111 et C-3112**
(copies)

comprend :

Petit-Nord (Port-Fourché et Port-au-Basque), etc.
BMD 1740-1745 **F-594** (originaux)
1715-1758 Index* **F-596** (originaux)
1740-1745 **C-2573** (copies)

* Cet index donne le lieu de résidence mais non les dates des BMD. Il est très difficile de se servir de cet index pour trouver les entrées dans les registres, dont plusieurs sont perdus.

Franklin Manor, Cumberland Co.

Civil registers of Cumberland County
BMD 1746-1817, 1832-1837 **M-843**
includes: District of Francklin Manor, Elysian Fields, Maccan, and Nappan

Grand-Pré, comté de Kings

St-Charles-des-Mines (Église catholique)
B 1707-1748 **C-1869**
MD 1709-1748 **C-1869**

Granville, Annapolis Co.

Civil registers
BMD 1720-1881 **C-3027** (index)

St. Luke's Anglican Church, Annapolis
B 1782-1800, 1808-1817,
 1833-1888 **C-3021**
M 1782-1794, 1807-1817 **C-3021**
 1806, 1813, 1817-1834 **C-3021**
D 1808-1817 **C-3021**
confirmations 1791, 1885 **C-3021**
includes: Clements, Dalhousie, Granville, Graywood, Lake La Rose, Perotte, and Rosette

(cont.)

Anglican Churches of Granville
B 1790-1801, 1829-1918 **C-3021**
M 1790-1801, 1814-1831 **C-3021**
 1831-1882 **C-3022**
D 1828-1918 **C-3022**
confirmations 1876-1901 **C-3021**
includes: All Saints Anglican Church, Christ Church Anglican Church, Trinity Anglican Church

Trinity Anglican Church, Wilmot
BMD 1789-1909 **C-3026**
confirmations 1842-1909 **C-3026**
includes: Aylesford

with:

St. James' Anglican Church, Bridgetown
BMD 1830-1854 **C-3026**
includes: Upper Granville

Graywood (Greywood), Annapolis Co.

St. Luke's Anglican Church, Annapolis
B 1782-1800, 1808-1817,
 1833-1888 **C-3021**
M 1782-1794, 1807-1817 **C-3021**
 1806, 1813, 1817-1834 **C-3021**
D 1808-1817 **C-3021**
confirmations 1791, 1885 **C-3021**
includes: Clements, Dalhousie, Granville, Graywood, Lake La Rose, Perotte, and Rosette

Havre de la Baleine, comté du Cap-Breton

Registres d'état civil de l'Île Royale (Île du Cap-Breton)
BMD 1714-1758 **F-592 à F-594**
(originaux)
1715-1758 Index* **F-596** (originaux)
1714-1758 **C-2573** (copies)
1722-1754 **C-3111 et C-3112**
(copies)

comprend :

Havre de la Baleine, comté du Cap-Breton
 Notre-Dame-de-Bon-Secours (Église catholique)
Havre du Petit-Laurent-le-Bec, comté du Cap-Breton
 Ste-Claire-de-Lorembec (Église catholique)
 BMD 1714-1745, 1750-1757 **F-594** (originaux)
 1715-1758 Index* **F-596** (originaux)
 1714-1745, 1750-1757 **C-2573** (copies)

* Cet index donne le lieu de résidence mais non les dates des BMD. Il est très difficile de se servir de cet index pour trouver les entrées dans les registres, dont plusieurs sont perdus.

NOVA SCOTIA / NOUVELLE-ÉCOSSE

Havre du Petit-Laurent-le-Bec (Lorembec), comté du Cap-Breton

Registres d'état civil de l'Île Royale (Île du Cap-Breton)
BMD	1714-1758	**F-592** à **F-594**	(originaux)
	1715-1758 Index*	**F-596**	(originaux)
	1714-1758	**C-2573**	(copies)
	1722-1754	**C-3111** et **C-3112**	(copies)

comprend :

Havre de la Baleine, comté du Cap-Breton
Notre-Dame-de-Bon-Secours (Église catholique)
Havre du Petit-Laurent-le-Bec, comté du Cap-Breton
Ste-Claire-de-Lorembec (Église catholique)
BMD	1714-1745, 1750-1757	**F-594**	(originaux)
	1715-1758 Index*	**F-596**	(originaux)
	1714-1745, 1750-1757	**C-2573**	(copies)

Havre du Saint-Esprit, comté de Richmond

Registres d'état civil de l'Île Royale (Île du Cap-Breton)
BMD	1714-1758	**F-592** à **F-594**	(originaux)
	1715-1758 Index*	**F-596**	(originaux)
	1714-1758	**C-2573**	(copies)
	1722-1754	**C-3111** et **C-3112**	(copies)

comprend :

Havre du Saint-Esprit, etc.
BMD	1726-1737, 1741-1745, 1749	**F-594**	(originaux)
	1715-1758 Index*	**F-596**	(originaux)
	1726-1737, 1741-1745, 1749	**C-2573**	(copies)

Horton, Kings Co.

Civil registers
BMD	1751-1895	**C-3027**

St. John's Anglican Church, Cornwallis, Annapolis Co.
B	1783-1902	**C-3021**
M	1783-1911	**C-3021**
D	1830-1920	**C-3021**

includes: Horton, and Wilmot

St. John's Anglican Church
B	1823-1877	**C-3022**

* Cet index donne le lieu de résidence mais non les dates des BMD. Il est très difficile de se servir de cet index pour trouver les entrées dans les registres, dont plusieurs sont perdus.

Horton Township, Kings Co.

Eagles' Compilation of Township Registers, etc.
BMD	1751-1895	**H-1806** (index)

Eagles' Cemetery Recordings for 19 Horton Township cemeteries
BD	1767-1873	**H-1806** (index)

Île du Cap-Breton*/Cape Breton Island

Registres d'état civil de l'Île Royale (Île du Cap-Breton)
BMD	1714-1758	**F-592** à **F-594**	(originaux)
	1715-1758 Index**	**F-596**	(originaux)
	1714-1758	**C-2573**	(copies)
	1722-1754	**C-3111** et **C-3112**	(copies)

comprend :

Havre de la Baleine, comté du Cap-Breton
Notre-Dame-de-Bon-Secours (Église catholique)
Havre du Petit-Laurent-le-Bec, comté du Cap-Breton
Ste-Claire-de-Lorembec (Église catholique)
BMD	1714-1745, 1750-1757	**F-594**	(originaux)
	1715-1758 Index**	**F-596**	(originaux)
	1714-1745, 1750-1757	**C-2573**	(copies)

Havre du Saint-Esprit, comté de Richmond
BMD	1726-1737, 1741-1745, 1749	**F-594**	(originaux)
	1715-1758 Index**	**F-596**	(originaux)
	1726-1737, 1741-1745, 1749	**C-2573**	(copies)

Louisbourg, comté du Cap-Breton
BMD	1722-1745	**F-592**	(originaux)
	1749-1758	**F-593**	(originaux)
	1715-1758 Index**	**F-596**	(originaux)
	1722-1744	**C-3111**	(copies)
	1744-1745, 1749-1754	**C-3112**	(copies)
	1754-1758	**C-2573**	(copies)

Petit-Nord (Port Fourché et Port-au-Basque), comté de Richmond
BMD	1740-1745	**F-594**	(originaux)
	1715-1758 Index**	**F-596**	(originaux)
	1740-1745	**C-2573**	(copies)

* Voir aussi : GUYANE FRANÇAISE pour des extraits de l'état civil de la Guyane concernant les habitants de l'Acadie, de l'Île Royale, et de l'Île Saint-Jean, etc., réfugiés en France, puis envoyés dans la Guyane.

** Cet index donne le lieu de résidence mais non les dates des BMD. Il est très difficile de se servir de cet index pour trouver les entrées dans les registres, dont plusieurs sont perdus.

(cont.)

St. George's Anglican Church, Sydney, Cape Breton Co.
BMD   1785-1813   **C-3026**
banns   1824-1845   **C-3026**

St. John's Presbyterian Church, Belfast, Queens Co., P.E.I.
B   1823-1849   **C-3028**
includes: Charlottetown, Pinette, and Rustico, Queens Co., and Murray Harbour, Kings Co., with their environs, P.E.I.; as well as many places in all the counties of Cape Breton Island, and a few in the counties of Pictou and Antigonish, N.S.

Île Royale (Île du Cap-Breton)*

Registres d'état civil de l'Île Royale (Île du Cap-Breton)
BMD   1714-1758   **F-592 à F-594**
                                (originaux)
          1715-1758 Index**   **F-596** (originaux)
          1714-1758   **C-2573** (copies)
          1722-1754   **C-3111 et C-3112**
                                (copies)
comprend :

Havre de la Baleine, comté du Cap-Breton
    Notre-Dame-de-Bon-Secours (Église catholique)
Havre du Petit-Laurent-le-Bec, comté du Cap-Breton
    Ste-Claire-de-Lorembec (Église catholique)
    BMD   1714-1745, 1750-1757 **F-594** (originaux)
          1715-1758 Index**   **F-596** (originaux)
          1714-1745, 1750-1757 **C-2573** (copies)

Havre du Saint-Esprit, comté de Richmond
BMD   1726-1737, 1741-1745,
          1749   **F-594** (originaux)
          1715-1758 Index**   **F-596** (originaux)
          1726-1737, 1741-1745,
          1749   **C-2573** (copies)

Louisbourg, comté du Cap-Breton
BMD   1722-1745   **F-592** (originaux)
          1749-1758   **F-593** (originaux)
          1715-1758 Index**   **F-596** (originaux)
          1722-1744   **C-3111** (copies)
          1744-1745, 1749-1754 **C-3112** (copies)
          1754-1758   **C-2573** (copies)

Petit-Nord (Port Fourché et Port-au-Basque), comté de Richmond
BMD   1740-1745   **F-594** (originaux)
          1715-1758 Index**   **F-596** (originaux)
          1740-1745   **C-2573** (copies)

* Voir aussi : GUYANE FRANÇAISE pour des extraits de l'état civil de la Guyane concernant les habitants de l'Acadie, de l'Île Royale, et de l'Île Saint-Jean, etc., réfugiés en France, puis envoyés dans la Guyane.

** Cet index donne le lieu de résidence mais non les dates des BMD. Il est très difficile de se servir de cet index pour trouver les entrées dans les registres, dont plusieurs sont perdus.

Lake La Rose, Annapolis Co.

St. Luke's Anglican Church, Annapolis
B   1782-1800, 1808-1817,
          1833-1888   **C-3021**
M   1782-1794, 1807-1817 **C-3021**
          1806, 1813, 1817-1834 **C-3021**
D   1808-1817   **C-3021**
confirmations 1791, 1885   **C-3021**
includes: Clements, Dalhousie, Granville, Graywood, Lake La Rose, Perotte, and Rosette

Liverpool, Queens Co.

Liverpool Methodist Church
B   1796-1889   **C-3022**
M   1816-1886   **C-3022**

Trinity Anglican Church
B   1819-1869   **C-3022**
M   1820-1869   **C-3022**
D   1821-1869   **C-3022**

Milton Baptist Church of Queens County
B   1821-1870   **H-1806**
comprises:

    Liverpool Baptist Church
    B   1821-1851   **H-1806**
    members, 1829   **H-1806**

    First Liverpool Baptist Church
    B   1851-1853   **H-1806**

    Milton Baptist Church of Queens County
    B   1853-1870   **H-1806**

Liverpool Township, Queens Co.

Milton Baptist Church of Queens County
B   1821-1870   **H-1806**
comprises:

    Liverpool Baptist Church
    B   1821-1851   **H-1806**
    members, 1829   **H-1806**

    First Liverpool Baptist Church
    B   1851-1853   **H-1806**

    Milton Baptist Church of Queens County
    B   1853-1870   **H-1806**

NOVA SCOTIA / NOUVELLE-ÉCOSSE

Londonderry, Colchester Co.

St. Paul's Anglican Church
B/M	1873-1889	**C-3022**
D	1874-1889	**C-3022**

Lorembec (Lorraine Head), comté du Cap-Breton

Registres d'état civil de l'Île Royale (Île du Cap-Breton)
BMD	1714-1758	**F-592** à **F-594**	(originaux)
	1715-1758 Index*	**F-596**	(originaux)
	1714-1758	**C-2573**	(copies)
	1722-1754	**C-3111** et **C-3112**	(copies)

comprend :

Havre de la Baleine, comté du Cap-Breton
Notre-Dame-de-Bon-Secours (Église catholique)
Havre du Petit-Laurent-le-Bec, comté du Cap-Breton
Ste-Claire-de-Lorembec (Église catholique)
BMD	1714-1745, 1750-1757	**F-594**	(originaux)
	1715-1758 Index*	**F-596**	(originaux)
	1714-1745, 1750-1757	**C-2573**	(copies)

* Cet index donne le lieu de résidence mais non les dates des BMD. Il est très difficile de se servir de cet index pour trouver les entrées dans les registres, dont plusieurs sont perdus.

Lorraine Head (Lorembec), comté du Cap-Breton

Registres d'état civil de l'Île Royale (Île du Cap-Breton)
BMD	1714-1758	**F-592** à **F-594**	(originaux)
	1715-1758 Index*	**F-596**	(originaux)
	1714-1758	**C-2573**	(copies)
	1722-1754	**C-3111** et **C-3112**	(copies)

comprend :

Havre de la Baleine, comté du Cap-Breton
Notre-Dame-de-Bon-Secours (Église catholique)
Havre du Petit-Laurent-le-Bec, comté du Cap-Breton
Ste-Claire-de-Lorembec (Église catholique)
BMD	1714-1745, 1750-1757	**F-594**	(originaux)
	1715-1758 Index*	**F-596**	(originaux)
	1714-1745, 1750-1757	**C-2573**	(copies)

* Cet index donne le lieu de résidence mais non les dates des BMD. Il est très difficile de se servir de cet index pour trouver les entrées dans les registres, dont plusieurs sont perdus.

Louisbourg, comté du Cap-Breton

Registres d'état civil de l'Île Royale (Île du Cap-Breton)
BMD	1714-1758	**F-592** à **F-594**	(originaux)
	1715-1758 Index*	**F-596**	(originaux)
	1714-1758	**C-2573**	(copies)
	1722-1754	**C-3111** et **C-3112**	(copies)

comprend :

Louisbourg
BMD	1722-1745	**F-592**	(originaux)
	1749-1758	**F-593**	(originaux)
	1715-1758 Index*	**F-596**	(originaux)
	1722-1744	**C-3111**	(copies)
	1744-1745, 1749-1754	**C-3112**	(copies)
	1754-1758	**C-2573**	(copies)

* Cet index donne le lieu de résidence mais non les dates des BMD. Il est très difficile de se servir de cet index pour trouver les entrées dans les registres, dont plusieurs sont perdus.

Lunenburg, Lunenburg Co.

Lunenburg Baptist Church
B	1792-1872	**C-3022**
M	1819-1856	**C-3022**
D	1817-1894	**C-3022**

Dutch Reformed Congregation (later, Presbyterian Church)
B	1770-1833	**M-2210** (originals)
	1835-1927	**M-2211** (originals)
M	1770-1834	**M-2210** (originals)
	1835-1855, 1880-1927	**M-2211** (originals)
D	1771-1834	**M-2210** (originals)
	1835-1854, 1880-1927	**M-2211** (originals)
communion rolls 1782-1794, 1818-1834		**M-2210** (originals)
confirmations	1835-1842	**M-2211** (originals)
B	1770-1819, 1837-1870	**C-3022** (copies)
M	1770-1818, 1837-1855	**C-3022** (copies)
D	1771-1818, 1837-1854	**C-3022** (copies)
communion rolls 1780-1816		**C-3022** (copies)

Note: Prior to 1837 the Dutch Reformed Congregation kept its records in German. The copies on Reel C-3022 include translations into English of these earlier registers.

Lunenburg Methodist Church
B	1813-1837	**C-3022**
M	1815-1836	**C-3022**

St. John's Anglican Church
B	1752-1869	**C-3022**
	1761-1773	**C-3022**
MD	1752-1869	**C-3022**

Maccan, Cumberland Co.

Civil registers of Cumberland County
BMD   1746-1817, 1832-1837   **M-843**
includes: District of Francklin Manor, Elysian Fields,
    Maccan, and Nappan

Mahone Bay, Lunenburg Co.

St. James' Anglican Church
B   1845-1870   **C-3026**
M   1844-1875   **C-3026**
D   1844-1870   **C-3026**

Milton, Queens Co.

Milton Baptist Church of Queens County
B   1821-1870   **H-1806**
comprises:

   Liverpool Baptist Church
   B   1821-1851   **H-1806**
   members, 1829   **H-1806**

   First Liverpool Baptist Church
   B   1851-1853   **H-1806**

   Milton Baptist Church of Queens County
   B   1853-1870   **H-1806**

Mines, Les, comté de Kings

Registres d'état civil d'Acadie et Gaspésie
BM   1679-1686   **C-3021**
BMD   1751-1757   **C-3021**
comprend :

   Les Mines
   B   1686   **C-3021**

St-Charles-des-Mines (Église catholique), Grand-Pré
B   1707-1748   **C-1869**
MD   1709-1748   **C-1869**

Mines, Rivière-des-, comté de Cumberland

Registres d'état civil d'Acadie et Gaspésie
BM   1679-1686   **C-3021**
BMD   1751-1757   **C-3021**
comprend :

   Rivière-des-Mines
   B   1684   **C-3021**

Minudie Marsh (Elysian Fields), Cumberland Co.

Civil registers of Cumberland County
BMD   1746-1817, 1832-1837   **M-843**
includes: District of Francklin Manor, Elysian Fields,
    Maccan, and Nappan

Nappan, Cumberland Co.

Civil registers of Cumberland County
BMD   1746-1817, 1832-1837   **M-843**
includes: District of Francklin Manor, Elysian Fields,
    Maccan, and Nappan

Newport, Hants Co.

Civil registers
B   1752-1845   **C-3027**
M   1762-1856   **C-3027**
D   1762-1858   **C-3027**

St. Paul's Anglican Church, Rawdon
B   1793, 1809, 1815-1880   **C-3026**
M   1814-1889   **C-3026**
D   1815-1920   **C-3026**
includes: Parish of St. James, Newport, and Douglas

Onslow, Colchester Co.

Civil registers
BMD   1761-1855, 1896   **C-3027** (index)

Perotte, Annapolis Co.

St. Luke's Anglican Church, Annapolis
B   1782-1800, 1808-1817,
        1833-1888   **C-3021**
M   1782-1794, 1807-1817   **C-3021**
        1806, 1813, 1817-1834   **C-3021**
D   1808-1817   **C-3021**
confirmations 1791, 1885   **C-3021**
includes: Clements, Dalhousie, Granville, Graywood,
    Lake La Rose, Perotte, and Rosette

Petit-Laurent-le-Bec, Havre du (Lorembec ou Lorraine Head), comté du Cap-Breton

Registres d'état civil de l'Île Royale (Île du Cap-Breton)
BMD	1714-1758	**F-592** à **F-594** (originaux)
	1715-1758 Index*	**F-596** (originaux)
	1714-1758	**C-2573** (copies)
	1722-1754	**C-3111** et **C-3112** (copies)

comprend :

Havre de la Baleine, comté du Cap-Breton
Notre-Dame-de-Bon-Secours (Église catholique)
Havre du Petit-Laurent-le-Bec, comté du Cap-Breton
Ste-Claire-de-Lorembec (Église catholique)
BMD	1714-1745, 1750-1757	**F-594** (originaux)
	1715-1758 Index*	**F-596** (originaux)
	1714-1745, 1750-1757	**C-2573** (copies)

* Cet index donne le lieu de résidence mais non les dates des BMD. Il est très difficile de se servir de cet index pour trouver les entrées dans les registres, dont plusieurs sont perdus.

Petit-Nord (Port Fourchu et Port-au-Basque), comté de Richmond

Registres d'état civil de l'Île Royale (Île du Cap-Breton)
BMD	1714-1758	**F-592** à **F-594** (originaux)
	1715-1758 Index*	**F-596** (originaux)
	1714-1758	**C-2573** (copies)
	1722-1754	**C-3111** et **C-3112** (copies)

comprend :

Petit-Nord (Port Fourché et Port-au-Basque)
BMD	1740-1745	**F-594** (originaux)
	1715-1758 Index*	**F-596** (originaux)
	1740-1745	**C-2573** (copies)

* Cet index donne le lieu de résidence mais non les dates des BMD. Il est très difficile de se servir de cet index pour trouver les entrées dans les registres, dont plusieurs sont perdus.

Pictou County

St. John's Presbyterian Church, Belfast, Queens Co., P.E.I.
B	1823-1849	**C-3028**

includes: Charlottetown, Pinette, and Rustico, Queens Co., and Murray Harbour, Kings Co., with their environs, P.E.I.; as well as many places in all the counties of Cape Breton Island, and a few in the counties of Pictou and Antigonish, N.S.

Port-au-Basque (Petit-Nord), comté de Richmond

Registres d'état civil de l'Île Royale (Île du Cap-Breton)
BMD	1714-1758	**F-592** à **F-594** (originaux)
	1715-1758 Index*	**F-596** (originaux)
	1714-1758	**C-2573** (copies)
	1722-1754	**C-3111** et **C-3112** (copies)

comprend :

Petit-Nord (Port Fourché et Port-au-Basque)
BMD	1740-1745	**F-594** (originaux)
	1715-1758 Index*	**F-596** (originaux)
	1740-1745	**C-2573** (copies)

* Cet index donne le lieu de résidence mais non les dates des BMD. Il est très difficile de se servir de cet index pour trouver les entrées dans les registres, dont plusieurs sont perdus.

Port-Fourchu (Petit-Nord), comté de Richmond

Registres d'état civil de l'Île Royale (Île du Cap-Breton)
BMD	1714-1758	**F-592** à **F-594** (originaux)
	1715-1758 Index*	**F-596** (originaux)
	1714-1758	**C-2573** (copies)
	1722-1754	**C-3111** et **C-3112** (copies)

comprend :

Petit-Nord (Port Fourché et Port-au-Basque)
BMD	1740-1745	**F-594** (originaux)
	1715-1758 Index*	**F-596** (originaux)
	1740-1745	**C-2573** (copies)

* Cet index donne le lieu de résidence mais non les dates des BMD. Il est très difficile de se servir de cet index pour trouver les entrées dans les registres, dont plusieurs sont perdus.

Port-Royal, comté d'Annapolis

St-Jean-Baptiste-du-Port-Royal (Église catholique)
B	1702-1717	**C-1869**
	1717-1724	**C-1870**
BMD	1724-1727	**C-1870**
M	1702-1724	**C-1870**
D	1702-1728	**C-1870**
BMD	1727-1755	**C-1870**

Rawdon, Hants Co.

St. Paul's Anglican Church
B	1793, 1809, 1815-1880	**C-3026**
M	1814-1889	**C-3026**
D	1815-1920	**C-3026**

includes: Parish of St. James, Newport, and Douglas

Rivière-des-Mines, comté de Cumberland

Registres d'état civil d'Acadie et Gaspésie
BM	1679-1686	**C-3021**
BMD	1751-1757	**C-3021**

comprend :

Rivière-des-Mines		
B	1684	**C-3021**

Rosette, Queens Co.

St. Luke's Anglican Church, Annapolis, Annapolis Co.
B	1782-1800, 1808-1817, 1833-1888	**C-3021**
M	1782-1794, 1807-1817	**C-3021**
	1806, 1813, 1817-1834	**C-3021**
D	1808-1817	**C-3021**
confirmations 1791, 1885		**C-3021**

includes: Clements, Dalhousie, Granville, Graywood, Lake La Rose, Perotte, and Rosette

Saint-Esprit, Havre du, comté de Richmond

Registres d'état civil de l'Île Royale (Île du Cap-Breton)
BMD	1714-1758	**F-592** à **F-594**	(originaux)
	1715-1758 Index*	**F-596**	(originaux)
	1714-1758	**C-2573**	(copies)
	1722-1754	**C-3111** et **C-3112**	(copies)

comprend :

Havre du Saint-Esprit, etc.			
BMD	1726-1737, 1741-1745, 1749	**F-594**	(originaux)
	1715-1758 Index*	**F-596**	(originaux)
	1726-1737, 1741-1745, 1749	**C-2573**	(copies)

* Cet index donne le lieu de résidence mais non les dates des BMD. Il est très difficile de se servir de cet index pour trouver les entrées dans les registres, dont plusieurs sont perdus.

Sainte-Marie, Baie (Church Point), comté de Digby

Ste-Marie (Église catholique)
BMD	1799-1801	**C-3026**

Shelburne, Shelburne Co.

Christ Church Anglican Church
BMD	1783-1869	**C-3026**

Sydney, Cape Breton Co.

St. George's Anglican Church
BMD	1785-1813	**C-3026**
banns	1824-1845	**C-3026**

Truro, Colchester Co.

Civil registers
BMD	1761-1851	**C-3027**

Wilmot, Annapolis Co.

St. John's Anglican Church, Cornwallis
B	1783-1902	**C-3021**
M	1783-1911	**C-3021**
D	1830-1920	**C-3021**

includes: Wilmot, and Aylesford, B 1784-1789; and Horton

Trinity Anglican Church
BMD	1789-1909	**C-3026**
confirmations 1842-1909		**C-3026**

includes: Aylesford

with:

St. James' Anglican Church, Bridgetown
BMD	1830-1854	**C-3026**

Wilmot Township, Annapolis Co.

Civil registers
BMD	1749-1894	**C-1346**

Adolphustown Township, Lennox and Addington Co.

St. John's Anglican Church, Bath
B	1787-1813	**H-1810**
M	1787-1816	**H-1810**
D	1787-1813	**H-1810**

comprises:

St. Thomas' Anglican Church, Ernestown Township
B	1788-1813	**H-1810**
M	1787-1813, 1814, 1816	**H-1810**
D	1788-1813	**H-1810**

includes: Amherst Island, and the Townships of Adolphustown, Camden, and Fredericksburg, Lennox and Addington Co.; the Townships of Ameliasburg, Marysburgh, and Sophiasburgh, Prince Edward Co.; the Townships of Sidney, and Thurlow, Hastings Co.; and Kingston, Frontenac Co.; as well as Oswego, New York, U.S.A.

St. Paul's Anglican Church, Fredericksburg Township
B	1787-1813	**H-1810**
M	1788-1812	**H-1810**
D	1787-1813	**H-1810**

includes: Amherst Island, and the Townships of Adolphustown, Camden, Ernestown, and Richmond, Lennox and Addington Co.; the Townships of Ameliasburg, Hallowell, Marysburgh, and Sophiasburgh, Prince Edward Co.; the Townships of Sidney, and Thurlow, Hastings Co.; and the Townships of Cramahé, and Percy, Northumberland Co.; as well as Oswego, New York, U.S.A.

Presbyterian Mission of Ernestown, Fredericksburg, Adolphustown, and the Bay of Quinté region
B	1800-1841	**H-1810**
M	1800-1836	**H-1810**
D	1841	**H-1810**

comprises:

Adolphustown Township, Lennox and Addington Co.
B	1800-1811	**H-1810**
M	1800-1821, 1831-1835	**H-1810**

Amherst Island Township, Lennox and Addington Co.
B	1834-1840	**H-1810**
M	1802, 1816, 1819	**H-1810**

Camden Township, Lennox and Addington Co.
B	1800-1813, 1820, 1835-1839	**H-1810**
M	1805-1821, 1832-1833	**H-1810**

Ernestown Township, Lennox and Addington Co.
B	1800-1813, 1819-1821, 1827, 1830, 1832, 1835	**H-1810**
M	1800-1822, 1831-1835	**H-1810**

(cont.)

Fredericksburg Township, Lennox and Addington Co.
B	1800-1813, 1815, 1827, 1832, 1837-1840	**H-1810**
M	1800-1822, 1831-1836	**H-1810**

Richmond Township, Lennox and Addington Co.
B	1800-1811, 1813-1814, 1824-1825, 1832-1833, 1838-1839	**H-1810**
M	1802-1803, 1807-1821, 1832-1835	**H-1810**

Sheffield Township, Lennox and Addington Co.
B	1831, 1836, 1839	**H-1810**

Rawdon Township, Hastings Co.
B	1803	**H-1810**

Sidney Township, Hastings Co.
B	1800-1820, 1837, 1839	**H-1810**
M	1803, 1806-1818	**H-1810**

Thurlow Township, Hastings Co.
B	1802-1816, 1821, 1839	**H-1810**
M	1807, 1812, 1816, 1822	**H-1810**

Tyendinaga Township, Hastings Co.
B	1826-1837	**H-1810**

Cramahé Township, Northumberland Co.
B	1800-1806, 1811, 1818, 1820	**H-1810**

Hamilton Township, Northumberland Co.
B	1800-1803	**H-1810**

Murray Township, Northumberland Co.
B	1800-1821	**H-1810**
M	1803, 1812	**H-1810**

Ameliasburg Township, Prince Edward Co.
B	1800-1822, 1827, 1829, 1833-1840	**H-1810**
M	1807-1808, 1812, 1820	**H-1810**

Hallowell Township, Prince Edward Co.
B	1800-1810, 1812, 1820, 1826	**H-1810**
M	1800-1820, 1831-1835	**H-1810**

Marysburgh Township, Prince Edward Co.
B	1800-1812, 1820, 1835, 1837	**H-1810**
M	1800-1822, 1831-1835	**H-1810**

Sophiasburgh Township, Prince Edward Co.
B	1806-1822, 1828	**H-1810**
M	1801-1822, 1831-1834	**H-1810**

Kingston, Frontenac Co.
B	1802-1811, 1820, 1822	**H-1810**
M	1802, 1805-1822, 1831-1832, 1835	**H-1810**

(cont.)

Loughborough Township, Frontenac Co.
B   1804-1805, 1809-1811,
        1830-1838   **H-1810**
M   1809, 1812, 1818-1820   **H-1810**

Pittsburg Township, Frontenac Co.
B   1800-1809   **H-1810**

Portland Township, Frontenac Co.
B   1800-1811   **H-1810**
M   1810, 1816   **H-1810**

Alderville, Northumberland Co.

Civil register of Alnwick Township
M   1858-1864, 1867,
        1869-1872, 1875-1882   **H-1810**
includes: Alderville, and the Townships of Hamilton, and Haldimand

Alexandria, Glengarry Co.

Civil registers for the Eastern District
M   1858-1869   **M-3205**
includes:

    St. Finnan's Roman Catholic Cathedral, Alexandria
    M   1858-1869   **M-3205**

Farmer's Almanac diaries of Angus Alexander McMillan and Family of Glengarry County
BMD   1862-1910   **H-1808**
includes:

    Lochiel Township, Glengarry Co.
    BMD   1862-1910   **H-1808**

    as well as, among others:

        Alexandria, Lochiel Township
        BMD   1862-1902   **H-1808**

Almonte, Lanark Co.

Almonte United Church
BMD   1833-1962   **M-2217**
M   1896-1926   **M-2229**
comprises:

    Ramsay "Auld Kirk" (later, St. Andrew's Presbyterian Church), Almonte
    B   1833-1902   **M-2217**
    M   1834-1857   **M-2217**
    D   1848-1869, 1873, 1877,
           1889-1894   **M-2217**
    communicants 1834-1869   **M-2217**
    membership lists c. 1890,
           1892-1894   **M-2217**

    St. Andrew's Presbyterian Church (formerly, Ramsay "Auld Kirk") Almonte
    B   1902-1911   **M-2217**
    M   1858-1901, 1937   **M-2217**
        1896-1911   **M-2217**
        1898-1926   **M-2229**

    St. John's Presbyterian Church, Almonte
    B   1877-1905   **M-2217**
    M   1859-1912   **M-2217**

    United Presbyterian Church (formerly, St. Andrew's and St. John's), Almonte
    B   1906-1925   **M-2217**
    M   1912-1925   **M-2217**

    Bethany United Church, Almonte
    B   1925-1953   **M-2217**
    M   1925-1937   **M-2217**

    Carleton Place Wesleyan Methodist Circuit, Carleton Place
    B   1905-1906, 1915   **M-2217**
    M   1858-1872, 1879,
           1889-1890   **M-2217**
    D   1905-1907   **M-2217**

    Almonte Methodist Circuit, Almonte
    B   1915-1921   **M-2217**

    St. Andrew's (Presbyterian) Church, Appleton
    B   1908-1962   **M-2217**
    communion rolls c. 1889-1917   **M-2229**

    Trinity United Church, Almonte
    B   1928-1953   **M-2217**
    M   1918-1943   **M-2217**
    D   1917-1953   **M-2217**
    includes: Appleton Pastoral Charge

    Almonte and Appleton United Church
    B   1953-1962   **M-2217**

    Ashton Presbyterian Church, Ashton
    M   1896-1911   **M-2229**
    communion rolls c. 1889-1917   **M-2229**

Alnwick Township, Northumberland Co.

Civil register
M   1858-1864, 1867,
        1869-1872, 1875-1882   **H-1810**
includes: Alderville, and the Townships of Hamilton, and Haldimand

(cont.)

Ameliasburgh Township, Prince Edward Co.

St. John's Anglican Church, Bath, Lennox and Addington Co.
B	1787-1813	**H-1810**
M	1787-1816	**H-1810**
D	1787-1813	**H-1810**

comprises:

St. Thomas' Anglican Church, Ernestown Township
B	1788-1813	**H-1810**
M	1787-1813, 1814, 1816	**H-1810**
D	1788-1813	**H-1810**

includes: Amherst Island, and the Townships of Adolphustown, Camden, and Fredericksburg, Lennox and Addington Co.; the Townships of Ameliasburg, Marysburgh, and Sophiasburgh, Prince Edward Co.; the Townships of Sidney, and Thurlow, Hastings Co.; and Kingston, Frontenac Co.; as well as Oswego, New York, U.S.A.

St. Paul's Anglican Church, Fredericksburg Township
B	1787-1813	**H-1810**
M	1788-1812	**H-1810**
D	1787-1813	**H-1810**

includes: Amherst Island, and the Townships of Adolphustown, Camden, Ernestown, and Richmond, Lennox and Addington Co.; the Townships of Ameliasburg, Hallowell, Marysburgh, and Sophiasburgh, Prince Edward Co.; the Townships of Sidney, and Thurlow, Hastings Co.; and the Townships of Cramahé, and Percy, Northumberland Co.; as well as Oswego, New York, U.S.A.

Presbyterian Mission of Ernestown, Fredericksburg, Adolphustown, and the Bay of Quinté region
B	1800-1841	**H-1810**
M	1800-1836	**H-1810**
D	1841	**H-1810**

includes:

Ameliasburgh Township
B	1800-1822, 1827, 1829, 1833-1840	**H-1810**
M	1807-1808, 1812, 1820	**H-1810**

Amherst Island Township, Lennox and Addington Co.

St. John's Anglican Church, Bath
B	1787-1813	**H-1810**
M	1787-1816	**H-1810**
D	1787-1813	**H-1810**

comprises:

St. Thomas' Anglican Church, Ernestown Township
B	1788-1813	**H-1810**
M	1787-1813, 1814, 1816	**H-1810**
D	1788-1813	**H-1810**

includes: Amherst Island, and the Townships of Adolphustown, Camden, and Fredericksburg, Lennox and Addington Co.; the Townships of Ameliasburg, Marysburgh, and Sophiasburgh, Prince Edward Co.; the Townships of Sidney, and Thurlow, Hastings Co.; and Kingston, Frontenac Co.; as well as Oswego, New York, U.S.A.

St. Paul's Anglican Church, Fredericksburg Township
B	1787-1813	**H-1810**
M	1788-1812	**H-1810**
D	1787-1813	**H-1810**

includes: Amherst Island, and the Townships of Adolphustown, Camden, Ernestown, and Richmond, Lennox and Addington Co.; the Townships of Ameliasburg, Hallowell, Marysburgh, and Sophiasburgh, Prince Edward Co.; the Townships of Sidney, and Thurlow, Hastings Co.; and the Townships of Cramahé, and Percy, Northumberland Co.; as well as Oswego, New York, U.S.A.

Presbyterian Mission of Ernestown, Fredericksburg, Adolphustown, and the Bay of Quinté Region
B	1800-1841	**H-1810**
M	1800-1836	**H-1810**
D	1841	**H-1810**

includes:

Amherst Island Township
B	1834-1840	**H-1810**
M	1802, 1816, 1819	**H-1810**

Amherstburg, Essex Co.

Civil registers of Essex County
B	1826, 1845-1862	**C-15758**

includes:

Christ Church [Anglican Church], Amherstburg
B	1861	**C-15758**

St. John the Baptist [Roman Catholic] Church, Amherstburg
B	1847, c. 1852, 1855-1861	**C-15758**

Ancaster Township, Wentworth Co.

Dundas and Ancaster Presbyterian Church
M	1848-1852	**C-3028**

comprises:

Dundas
M	1848-1852	**C-3028**

Ancaster, and West Flamboro
M	1848-1852	**C-3028**

with:

L'Orignal and Plantagenet Presbyterian Church, Prescott Co.
M	1854-1856	**C-3028**
	1852-1856	**H-1807**

comprises:

L'Orignal, Prescott Co.
M	1852-1856	**H-1807**
	1855-1856	**C-3028**

Hawkesbury, Prescott Co.
M	1853	**H-1807**

West Hawkesbury Township, Prescott Co.
M	1853	**H-1807**

Caledonia Township, Prescott Co.
M	1853, 1856	**H-1807**

North Plantagenet Township, Prescott Co.
M	1853-1854	**H-1807**

Plantagenet, Prescott Co.
M	1854	**C-3028**

Lochiel, Glengarry Co.
M	1854	**H-1807**

Antrim, Carleton Co.

St. Andrew's United Church of Canada, Pakenham, Lanark Co.
B	1891-1966	**M-7761**
M	1840-1973	**M-7761**
D	1901-1985	**M-7761**

includes:

Pakenham United Church of Canada Pastoral Charge, Lanark Co.
B	1909-1966	**M-7761**
M	1909-1973	**M-7761**
D	1909-1985	**M-7761**

includes: Cedar Hill, Lanark Co.; Antrim, and Fitzroy Township, Carleton Co.

Appleton, Lanark Co.

Zion Memorial United Church, Carleton Place
BMD	1878-1933	**M-2209**

includes:

Carleton Place and Appleton Methodist Circuit
BD	1901-1926	**M-2209**
M	1898-1912	**M-2209**

(cont.)

Almonte United Church, Almonte
BMD	1833-1962	**M-2217**
M	1896-1926	**M-2229**

includes:

St. Andrew's (Presbyterian) Church, Appleton
B	1908-1962	**M-2217**
communion rolls c. 1889-1917		**M-2229**

Trinity United Church, Almonte
B	1928-1953	**M-2217**
M	1918-1943	**M-2217**
D	1917-1953	**M-2217**

includes: Appleton Pastoral Charge

Almonte and Appleton United Church
B	1953-1962	**M-2217**

Artemesia Township, Grey Co.

Returns of coroners' inquests for the Counties of Grey, Wellington, Bruce [and Dufferin]
D	1873	**C-15758**

includes: Durham, Owen Sound, and the Townships of Artemesia, Egremont, Euphrasia, Keppel, Normanby, Osprey, Proton, St. Vincent, and Sydenham, Grey Co.; and Melancthon Township, Dufferin Co.

Ashbury, Lanark Co.

St. Paul's United Church of Canada Church, Perth
B	1896-1945	**M-2232**
M	1858-1958	**M-2232**
D	1902-1968	**M-2232**

includes:

Perth Wesleyan Methodist Church (later, Ashbury Methodist Church)
M	1858-1896	**M-2232**

Ashbury Methodist Church (formerly, Perth Wesleyan Methodist Church)
BD	1902-1927	**M-2232**
M	1858-1949	**M-2232**

Ashton, Lanark and Carleton Cos.

Almonte United Church, Almonte, Lanark Co.
BMD	1833-1962	**M-2217**
M	1896-1926	**M-2229**

includes:

Ashton Presbyterian Church, Ashton
M	1896-1911	**M-2229**
communion rolls c. 1889-1917		**M-2229**

Aspdin, Muskoka District

Register of the Rev. John Becket (1838-1921), Presbyterian missionary at Aspdin, 1905-1908
M   1905-1908, 1910, 1913,
          1915   **H-1810**
comprises:

    Elmhill, Peterborough Co.
    M   1905   **H-1810**

    McMurrich Township, Parry Sound District
    M   1906-1907   **H-1810**

    Stephenson Township, Muskoka District
    M   1905-1908   **H-1810**

    Stisted Township, Muskoka District
    M   1907-1908   **H-1810**

    Chinguacousy Township, Peel Co.
    M   1910   **H-1810**

    Orford Township, Kent Co.
    M   1910   **H-1810**

    Chatham, Kent Co.
    M   1913   **H-1810**

    Toronto, York Co.
    M   1915   **H-1810**

Asphodel Township, Peterborough Co.

St. Paul's Presbyterian Church, Peterborough
M   1834-1857   **H-1810**
includes: Townships of Asphodel, Douro, Dummer, Ennismore, Harvey, North Monaghan, Otonabee, and Smith, Peterborough Co.; the Townships of Hamilton, and South Monaghan in Northumberland Co.; the Township of Cavan, Durham Co.; and the Townships of Emily, and Ops, Victoria Co.

Augusta Township, Grenville Co.

Returns of coroners' inquests for the Counties of Leeds, and Grenville
D   1873   **C-15758**
includes: Townships of Augusta, and Wolford, Grenville Co.; as well as Brockville, Gananoque, and Elizabethtown Township, Leeds Co.

Aylmer, Elgin Co.

Personal registers of the Rev. J. Nelson Gould of Sarnia, Methodist and United Church of Canada minister
B   1916-1960   **H-1811**

(cont.)

M   1916-1961   **H-1811**
D   1916-1959   **H-1811**
includes:

    Richmond-Corinth United Church of Canada Charge, Elgin Co.
    B   1947-1960   **H-1811**
    M   1947-1961   **H-1811**
    D   1947-1959   **H-1811**
    includes: Aylmer West, Corinth, Fairview, North Bayham, Richmond Village (Bayham), and Summers Corners, Elgin Co.

Ayr, Waterloo Co.

Civil registers of Waterloo County
B   1836-1861   **C-15758**
M   1854-1855   **C-15758**
D   1854-1855, 1858, 1860   **C-15758**
includes:

    Presbyterian Church of Canada, Ayr
    M   1855   **C-15758**

Baden, Waterloo Co.

Civil registers of Waterloo County
B   1836-1861   **C-15758**
M   1854-1855   **C-15758**
D   1854-1855, 1858, 1860   **C-15758**
includes:

    German Evangelical Lutheran Congregations, Phillipsburg, Wellesley Village, and New Baden
    B   1836-1855, 1858, 1860   **C-15758**
    D   1858, 1860   **C-15758**
    includes: places in the Townships of Waterloo, Wellesley, and Wilmot, Waterloo Co.; Ellice, Mornington, and North Easthope Townships, Perth Co.; Normanby Township, Grey Co.

See also: Wilmot Township, and Waterloo County

Bastard Township, Leeds Co.

St. Andrew's Presbyterian (Church of Scotland) Church, Toledo (formerly, Presbyterian Congregation of Kitley Township)
B   1846-1852, 1863-1913   **H-1810**
M   1863-1864, 1880-1881,
          1890-1893, 1903, 1907 **H-1810**
D   1894, 1897-1902, 1911 **H-1810**
members, 1847, 1850, 1854,
          1863-1913   **H-1810**
includes: Townships of Bastard, Elizabethtown, Front of Yonge, and Kitley, Leeds Co.; as well as Montague Township, Lanark Co.; and Wolford Township, Grenville Co.

Bath, Lennox and Addington Co.

St. John's Anglican Church, Bath
B	1787-1813	**H-1810**
M	1787-1816	**H-1810**
D	1787-1813	**H-1810**

comprises:

St. Thomas' Anglican Church, Ernestown Township
B	1788-1813	**H-1810**
M	1787-1813, 1814, 1816	**H-1810**
D	1788-1813	**H-1810**

includes: Amherst Island, and the Townships of Adolphustown, Camden, and Fredericksburg, Lennox and Addington Co.; the Townships of Ameliasburg, Marysburgh, and Sophiasburgh, Prince Edward Co.; the Townships of Sidney, and Thurlow, Hastings Co.; and Kingston, Frontenac Co.; as well as Oswego, New York, U.S.A.

St. Paul's Anglican Church, Fredericksburg Township
B	1787-1813	**H-1810**
M	1788-1812	**H-1810**
D	1787-1813	**H-1810**

includes: Amherst Island, and the Townships of Adolphustown, Camden, Ernestown, and Richmond, Lennox and Addington Co.; the Townships of Ameliasburg, Hallowell, Marysburgh, and Sophiasburgh, Prince Edward Co.; the Townships of Sidney, and Thurlow, Hastings Co.; and the Townships of Cramahé, and Percy, Northumberland Co.; as well as Oswego, New York, U.S.A.

Bathurst District (later, Carleton and Lanark Counties)

Civil registers of Ontario
M	1816-1869	**M-5497**
	1858-1869	**M-7092**

includes:

Bathurst District
M	1831-1848	**M-5497**

Bathurst Township, Lanark Co.

St. Paul's United Church of Canada Church, Perth
B	1896-1945	**M-2232**
M	1858-1958	**M-2232**
D	1902-1968	**M-2232**

includes:

Calvin Presbyterian Church, Bathurst Township
M	1899-1958	**M-2232**

Bay of Quinté Region

St. John's Anglican Church, Bath, Lennox and Addington Co.
B	1787-1813	**H-1810**
M	1787-1816	**H-1810**
D	1787-1813	**H-1810**

comprises:

St. Thomas' Anglican Church, Ernestown Township
B	1788-1813	**H-1810**
M	1787-1813, 1814, 1816	**H-1810**
D	1788-1813	**H-1810**

includes: Amherst Island, and the Townships of Adolphustown, Camden, and Fredericksburg, Lennox and Addington Co.; the Townships of Ameliasburg, Marysburgh, and Sophiasburgh, Prince Edward Co.; the Townships of Sidney, and Thurlow, Hastings Co.; and Kingston, Frontenac Co.; as well as Oswego, New York, U.S.A.

St. Paul's Anglican Church, Fredericksburg Township
B	1787-1813	**H-1810**
M	1788-1812	**H-1810**
D	1787-1813	**H-1810**

includes: Amherst Island, and the Townships of Adolphustown, Camden, Ernestown, and Richmond, Lennox and Addington Co.; the Townships of Ameliasburg, Hallowell, Marysburgh, and Sophiasburgh, Prince Edward Co.; the Townships of Sidney, and Thurlow, Hastings Co.; and the Townships of Cramahé, and Percy, Northumberland Co.; as well as Oswego, New York, U.S.A.

Presbyterian Mission of Ernestown, Fredericksburg, Adolphustown, and the Bay of Quinté region
B	1800-1841	**H-1810**
M	1800-1836	**H-1810**
D	1841	**H-1810**

comprises:

Adolphustown Township, Lennox and Addington Co.
B	1800-1811	**H-1810**
M	1800-1821, 1831-1835	**H-1810**

Amherst Island Township, Lennox and Addington Co.
B	1834-1840	**H-1810**
M	1802, 1816, 1819	**H-1810**

Camden Township, Lennox and Addington Co.
B	1800-1813, 1820, 1835-1839	**H-1810**
M	1805-1821, 1832-1833	**H-1810**

Ernestown Township, Lennox and Addington Co.
B	1800-1813, 1819-1821, 1827, 1830, 1832, 1835	**H-1810**
M	1800-1822, 1831-1835	**H-1810**

(cont.)

Fredericksburg Township, Lennox and Addington Co.
B   1800-1813, 1815, 1827,
          1832, 1837-1840   **H-1810**
M   1800-1822, 1831-1836   **H-1810**

Richmond Township, Lennox and Addington Co.
B   1800-1811, 1813-1814,
          1824-1825, 1832-1833,
          1838-1839   **H-1810**
M   1802-1803, 1807-1821,
         1832-1835   **H-1810**

Sheffield Township, Lennox and Addington Co.
B   1831, 1836, 1839   **H-1810**

Rawdon Township, Hastings Co.
B   1803   **H-1810**

Sidney Township, Hastings Co.
B   1800-1820, 1837, 1839   **H-1810**
M   1803, 1806-1818   **H-1810**

Thurlow Township, Hastings Co.
B   1802-1816, 1821, 1839   **H-1810**
M   1807, 1812, 1816, 1822   **H-1810**

Tyendinaga Township, Hastings Co.
B   1826-1837   **H-1810**

Cramahé Township, Northumberland Co.
B   1800-1806, 1811, 1818,
          1820   **H-1810**

Hamilton Township, Northumberland Co.
B   1800-1803   **H-1810**

Murray Township, Northumberland Co.
B   1800-1821   **H-1810**
M   1803, 1812   **H-1810**

Ameliasburg Township, Prince Edward Co.
B   1800-1822, 1827, 1829,
         1833-1840   **H-1810**
M   1807-1808, 1812, 1820   **H-1810**

Hallowell Township, Prince Edward Co.
B   1800-1810, 1812, 1820,
         1826   **H-1810**
M   1800-1820, 1831-1835   **H-1810**

Marysburgh Township, Prince Edward Co.
B   1800-1812, 1820, 1835,
         1837   **H-1810**
M   1800-1822, 1831-1835   **H-1810**

Sophiasburgh Township, Prince Edward Co.
B   1806-1822, 1828   **H-1810**
M   1801-1822, 1831-1834   **H-1810**

Kingston, Frontenac Co.
B   1802-1811, 1820, 1822   **H-1810**
M   1802, 1805-1822,
         1831-1832, 1835   **H-1810**

(cont.)

Loughborough Township, Frontenac Co.
B   1804-1805, 1809-1811,
         1830-1838   **H-1810**
M   1809, 1812, 1818-1820   **H-1810**

Pittsburg Township, Frontenac Co.
B   1800-1809   **H-1810**

Portland Township, Frontenac Co.
B   1800-1811   **H-1810**
M   1810, 1816   **H-1810**

Bayham (Richmond Village), Elgin Co.

Personal registers of the Rev. J. Nelson Gould of Sarnia, Methodist and United Church of Canada minister
B   1916-1960   **H-1811**
M   1916-1961   **H-1811**
D   1916-1959   **H-1811**
includes:

    Richmond-Corinth United Church of Canada Charge, Elgin Co.
    B   1947-1960   **H-1811**
    M   1947-1961   **H-1811**
    D   1947-1959   **H-1811**
    includes: Aylmer West, Corinth, Fairview, North Bayham, Richmond Village (Bayham), and Summers Corners, Elgin Co.

Beausoleil Island, Muskoka District

Journals of the Rev. Allen Salt, a Methodist Indian missionary in western Ontario
BMD   1854-1855, 1874-1899,
           1904   **C-15709**
includes:

    Christian and Beausoleil Islands Methodist Indian Mission, Georgian Bay
    BMD   1875-1882   **C-15709**

Beckwith Township, Lanark Co.

Mississippi Circuit of the Methodist Episcopal (later, the Wesleyan Methodist) Church
B   1829-1843   **H-1809**
includes: places in the Townships of Beckwith, Lanark, Pakenham, and Ramsay, Lanark Co.; in the Townships of Horton, McNab, Pembroke, and Westmeath, Renfrew Co.; and Fitzroy Township, Carleton Co.

Zion Memorial United Church, Carleton Place
BMD   1878-1933   **M-2209**
includes:

    Beckwith and Franktown Presbyterian Church
    B   1914-1922   **M-2209**

(cont.)

Beckwith, Drummond and Montague Methodist Circuit
M   1896-1922   **M-2209**

Bellamy Pond, Leeds Co.

St. Francis-Xavier Roman Catholic Church, Brockville
B   1835-1859   **M-4613**
       1854-1860   **M-4613** (index)
       1882-1893   **M-4613**
M   1841-1847   **M-4613**
       1855-1856   **M-4613** (index)
confirmations 1847   **M-4613**
includes: records of the Bellamy Pond and Toledo area of Kitley Township, Leeds Co.

Bells Corners, Carleton Co.

Carp United Church, Carp
BMD   1858-1929   **M-816** and **M-817**
includes:

  Bell's Corners Wesleyan Methodist Church
  M   1858-1895   **M-816**

Burials in Hazeldean Cemeteries
D   1835-1939   **M-7718**
includes:

  Bells Corners Anglican Church (including the Anglican Churches of Hazeldean, Stittsville, and Fallowfield, at various dates)
  D   1883-1939 extracts   **M-7718**

Berlin (later, Kitchener), Waterloo Co.

Civil registers of Waterloo County
B   1836-1861   **C-15758**
M   1854-1855   **C-15758**
D   1854-1855, 1858, 1860   **C-15758**
includes:

  German Baptist Church of the Rev. Henry Schneider
  B   1861   **C-15758**
  M   1855*   **C-15758**
  D   1855*, 1860   **C-15758**
  includes: Berlin (later, Kitchener), as well as other places in the Townships of Waterloo, Wilmot, and Woolwich, Waterloo Co.; and in South Easthope Township, Perth Co.

  * In German

  Evangelical Association
  BD   1860   **C-15758**
  includes: Berlin (later, Kitchener), and other places in the Township of Waterloo, as well as Heidelberg, in the Townships of Wellesley, and Woolwich

  [Unorthodox Evangelical Lutheran] Congregation of the Rev. Frederick W. Bindemann, Waterloo Township
  M   1855   **C-15758**
  includes: Berlin (later, Kitchener), and places in the Townships of North Dumfries, Waterloo, Wellesley, Wilmot, and Woolwich, Waterloo Co.; Carrick Township, Bruce Co.; Normanby Township, Grey Co.; the Townships of Blandford, and Blenheim, Oxford Co.; Hay Township, Huron Co.; the Townships of North Easthope, South Easthope, and Wallace, Perth Co.; the Townships of Peel, Guelph, Nichol, and Puslinch, Wellington Co.; and Hamilton, Wentworth Co.

  Wesleyan Methodist Church, Berlin (later, Kitchener)
  B   1860   **C-15758**
  includes: places in the Townships of Waterloo, and Wellesley

  New Jerusalem (Swedenborgian) Church, Berlin (later, Kitchener)
  B   1855-1860   **C-15758**
  D   1860   **C-15758**
  includes: Waterloo Township, and various places in the Townships of Wilmot and Wellesley

  Roman Catholic Mission, Berlin (later, Kitchener)
  BD   1860   **C-15758**
  includes: places in the Townships of Waterloo and Wilmot

Beverly Township, Wentworth Co.

Civil registers of Waterloo Co.
B   1836-1861   **C-15758**
M   1854-1855   **C-15758**
D   1854-1855, 1858, 1860   **C-15758**
includes:

  German Evangelical Lutheran Church, Preston (later, Cambridge), Waterloo Co.
  B   1853-1855, 1860   **C-15758**
  M   1855   **C-15758**
  D   1860   **C-15758**
  includes: places in the Townships of North Dumfries, Waterloo, Wilmot, and Woolwich, Waterloo Co.; in the Townships of Brantford, Burford, and South Dumfries, Brant Co.; as well as Blenheim Township, Oxford Co.; Puslinch Township, Wellington Co.; and Beverly Township, Wentworth Co.

(cont.)

Biddulph Township, Middlesex Co.

Anglican Parish of Kirkton with Granton and Saintsbury (including the Anglican Churches of: St. Paul's, Kirkton; Trinity, Prospect Hill; St. Patrick's, Saintsbury; and St. Thomas', Granton)
B	1862-1971	**M-2227**
MD	1863-1971	**M-2227**

includes: Township of Usborne, Huron Co.; Township of Blanshard, Perth Co.; and Township of Biddulph, Middlesex Co.

Blakeney, Lanark Co.

St. Andrew's United Church of Canada, Pakenham
B	1891-1966	**M-7761**
M	1840-1973	**M-7761**
D	1901-1985	**M-7761**

includes:

Blakeney and Clayton Presbyterian (later, United Church of Canada) Church
M	1896-1946	**M-7761**

Clayon United Church, Clayton
BMD	1805-1965	**M-3687** and **M-3688**
	1876-1965	**M-3243**

includes:

Blakeney and Clayton Presbyterian Congregations
B	1901-1951	**M-3687**
D	1908-1946	**M-3687**
communion rolls 1907-1957		**M-3687**

includes: Guthrie

Blandford Township, Oxford Co.

Civil registers of Waterloo County
B	1836-1861	**C-15758**
M	1854-1855	**C-15758**
D	1854-1855, 1858, 1860	**C-15758**

includes:

St. James' Anglican Church, Wilmot Township, Waterloo Co.
BD	1860	**C-15758**

includes: other places in Wilmot Township, as well as St. George, Brant Co.; and the Townships of Blandford and East Zorra, Oxford Co.

[Unorthodox Evangelical Lutheran] Congregation of the Rev. Frederick W. Bindemann, Waterloo Township, Waterloo Co.
M	1855	**C-15758**

includes: Berlin (later, Kitchener), and other places in the Townships of North Dumfries, Waterloo, Wellesley, Wilmot, and Woolwich, Waterloo Co.;

(cont.)

Carrick Township, Bruce Co.; Normanby Township, Grey Co.; the Townships of Blandford, and Blenheim, Oxford Co.; Hay Township, Huron Co.; the Townships of North Easthope, South Easthope, and Wallace, Perth Co.; the Townships of Peel, Guelph, Nichol, and Puslinch, Wellington Co.; and Hamilton, Wentworth Co.

Returns of coroners' inquests for Oxford County
D	1873	**C-15758**

includes: Woodstock, and the Townships of Blandford, and Blenheim

Blanshard Township, Perth Co.

Anglican Parish of Kirkton with Granton and Saintsbury (including the Anglican Churches of: St. Paul's, Kirkton; Trinity, Prospect Hill; St. Patrick's, Saintsbury; and St. Thomas', Granton)
B	1862-1971	**M-2227**
MD	1863-1971	**M-2227**

includes: Township of Usborne, Huron Co.; Township of Blanshard, Perth Co.; and Township of Biddulph, Middlesex Co.

Blenheim Township, Oxford Co.

Civil registers of Waterloo County
B	1836-1861	**C-15758**
M	1854-1855	**C-15758**
D	1854-1855, 1858, 1860	**C-15758**

includes:

Evangelical Lutheran Church, Mannheim, New Dundee, and New Hamburg, Waterloo Co.
B	1858, 1860	**C-15758**
D	1860	**C-15758**

includes: places in Wilmot Township, Waterloo Co.; in Brant and Carrick Townships, Bruce Co.; in Hay, Stanley, and Tuckersmith Townships, Huron Co.; and Blenheim Township, Oxford Co.; as well as Hanover, [Grey Co.]; and Williamsburgh [Township], Dundas Co.

German Evangelical Lutheran Church, Preston (later, Cambridge), Waterloo Co.
B	1853-1855, 1860	**C-15758**
M	1855	**C-15758**
D	1860	**C-15758**

includes: places in the Townships of North Dumfries, Waterloo, Wilmot, and Woolwich, Waterloo Co.; in the Townships of Brantford, Burford, and South Dumfries, Brant Co.; as well as Blenheim Township, Oxford Co.; Puslinch Township, Wellington Co.; and Beverly Township, Wentworth Co.

(cont.)

[Unorthodox Evangelical Lutheran] Congregation of the Rev. Frederick W. Bindemann, Waterloo Township, Waterloo Co.
M   1855   **C-15758**
includes: Berlin (later, Kitchener), and other places in the Townships of North Dumfries, Waterloo, Wellesley, Wilmot, and Woolwich, Waterloo Co.; Carrick Township, Bruce Co.; Normanby Township, Grey Co.; the Townships of Blandford, and Blenheim, Oxford Co.; Hay Township, Huron Co.; the Townships of North Easthope, South Easthope, and Wallace, Perth Co.; the Townships of Peel, Guelph, Nichol, and Puslinch, Wellington Co.; and Hamilton, Wentworth Co.

Returns of coroners' inquests for Oxford County
D   1873   **C-15758**
includes: Woodstock, and the Townships of Blandford, and Blenheim

Boyd, Renfrew Co.

Zion Memorial United Church, Carleton Place, Lanark Co.
BMD   1878-1933   **M-2209**
includes:

    Clayton Methodist Circuit, Clayton, Lanark Co.
    B   1890-1899   **M-2209**
    D   1896-1899   **M-2209**
    membership 1893-1902   **M-2209**
    includes: Boyd and Prestonvale

    Lanark and Clayton Methodist Circuit
    B   1884-1933   **M-2209**
    M   1903-1931   **M-2209**
    D   1902-1931   **M-2209**
    circuit register 1903-1924   **M-2209**
    includes: Boyd, Erwins, Harper, Playfair, and Prestonvale

Brant Township, Bruce Co.

Civil registers of Waterloo County
B   1836-1861   **C-15758**
M   1854-1855   **C-15758**
D   1854-1855, 1858, 1860   **C-15758**
includes:

    Evangelical Lutheran Church, Mannheim, New Dundee, and New Hamburg, Waterloo Co.
    B   1858, 1860   **C-15758**
    D   1860   **C-15758**
    includes: places in Wilmot Township, Waterloo Co.; in Brant and Carrick Townships, Bruce Co.; in Hay, Stanley, and Tuckersmith Townships, Huron Co.; and Blenheim Township, Oxford Co.; as well as Hanover, [Grey Co.]; and Williamsburgh [Township], Dundas Co.

Brantford Township, Brant Co.

Civil registers of Waterloo County
B   1836-1861   **C-15758**
M   1854-1855   **C-15758**
D   1854-1855, 1858, 1860   **C-15758**
includes:

    German Evangelical Lutheran Church, Preston (later, Cambridge), Waterloo Co.
    B   1853-1855, 1860   **C-15758**
    M   1855   **C-15758**
    D   1860   **C-15758**
    includes: places in the Townships of North Dumfries, Waterloo, Wilmot, and Woolwich, Waterloo Co.; in the Townships of Brantford, Burford, and South Dumfries, Brant Co.; as well as Blenheim Township, Oxford Co.; Puslinch Township, Wellington Co.; and Beverly Township, Wentworth Co.

    Wesleyan Methodist Congregation, Galt (later, Cambridge), Waterloo Co.
    B   1860   **C-15758**
    M   1854-1855   **C-15758**
    includes: places in the Township of Waterloo, Waterloo Co.; Paris, and the Township of Brantford, Brant Co.; Esquesing Township, Halton Co.; and Chinguacousy Township, Peel Co.

Breadalbane, Glengarry Co.

Breadalbane Cemetery recordings by Ann MacLaurin, 1970
D   1810-1970   **H-1807**

Breadalbane Cemetery recordings by Eleanor Forbes, 1970
D   1837-1969   **H-1807**

[Baptist] Congregation of Breadalbane and its connections. Deaths recorded in the Handbook of Peter Stewart
D   1857-1887, 1908-1910   **H-1807**

Baptist Congregation of Breadalbane
M   1858-1886   **H-1807**
includes: places in the Township of Lochiel, Glengarry Co.; as well as in the Townships of East Hawkesbury, and West Hawkesbury, Prescott Co.

Civil registers of the Surrogate Court for the Eastern and Johnstown Districts
B   1831, 1859, 1862-1865   **C-3030**
M   1831-1857, 1863, 1865   **C-3030** (index)
includes:

    Baptist Congregation, Breadalbane
    M   1834-1850   **C-3030** (index)
    includes: places in the Townships of Kenyon, and Lochiel, Glengarry Co.; as well as in the

(cont.)

Townships of Caledonia, East Hawkesbury, West Hawkesbury, and North Plantagenet, Prescott Co.

Civil registers for the Eastern District
M	1858-1869	**M-3205**

includes:

Baptist Congregation, Bradalan [Breadalbane]
M	1862-1864	**M-3205**

Farmer's Almanac diaries of Angus Alexander McMillan and Family of Glengarry County
BMD	1862-1910	**H-1808**

includes:

Lochiel Township
BMD	1862-1910	**H-1808**

as well as, among others:

Breadalbane, Lochiel Township
MD	1867-1868	**H-1808**

Breslau, Waterloo Co.

Civil registers of Waterloo County
B	1836-1861	**C-15758**
M	1854-1855	**C-15758**
D	1854-1855, 1858, 1860	**C-15758**

includes:

Mennonite Congregation of [Bishop] Joseph Hagey, [Hagey, or Breslau]
BD	1860	**C-15758**

Brockville, Leeds Co.

Civil registers of the Surrogate Court for the Eastern and Johnstown Districts
B	1831, 1859, 1862-1865	**C-3030**
M	1831-1857, 1863, 1865	**C-3030** (index)

includes:

Wesleyan Methodist Church in Canada, Circuits in the Eastern District
B	1859	**C-3030**
M	1833-1857	**C-3030** (index)

includes: Townships of Matilda, Mountain, Williamsburgh, and Winchester, Dundas Co.; the Townships of Edwardsburgh, and Oxford, Grenville Co.; Sheek Island, and the Townships of Cornwall, Finch, Osnabruck, and Roxborough, Stormont Co.; as well as the Brockville district, Leeds Co.; and other places in the Counties of Dundas, Stormont, and Glengarry

St. Francis-Xavier Roman Catholic Church
B	1835-1859	**M-4613**
	1854-1860	**M-4613** (index)
	1882-1893	**M-4613**
M	1841-1847	**M-4613**
	1855-1856	**M-4613** (index)
confirmations 1847		**M-4613**

includes: records of the Bellamy Pond and Toledo area of Kitley Township, Leeds Co.

Returns of coroners' inquests for the Counties of Leeds, and Grenville
D	1873	**C-15758**

includes: Townships of Augusta, and Wolford, Grenville Co.; as well as Brockville, Gananoque, and Elizabethtown Township, Leeds Co.

Bruce County

Returns of coroners' inquests for Grey, Wellington, Bruce, [and Dufferin] Counties
D	1873	**C-15758**

includes: Durham, Owen Sound, and the Townships of Artemesia, Egremont, Euphrasia, Keppel, Normanby, Osprey, Proton, St. Vincent, and Sydenham, Grey Co.; and Melancthon Township, Dufferin Co.

Brudenell Township, Renfrew Co.

Our Lady of Czestochowa, Queen of Poland (Roman Catholic) Church (formerly, St. Stanislaus Kostka Roman Catholic Church, Hagarty Township), Wilno
BMD	1880-1884	**H-1456** (partial index)
B	1877-1880	**H-1456**
	1888-1940	**H-1456** (partial index)
M	1885-1937	**H-1456** (partial index)
	1928-1960	**H-1457**
D	1885-1928	**H-1456** (partial index)
	1928-1943, 1945	**H-1457**
	1961-1975	**H-1457**
ordinations, 1910, 1923-1924		**H-1456**
confirmations, 1912-1913		**H-1456**
	1947-1948, 1950, 1953, 1956, 1959	**H-1457**
first communions, 1946-1947, 1951, 1958-1959		**H-1457**

includes: Townships of Brudenell, Burns, Hagarty, Radcliffe, and Sherwood

(The registers are in French, Latin, and English. Miscellaneous related items are in Polish.)

(cont.)

Burford Township, Brant Co.

Civil registers of Waterloo County
B	1836-1861	**C-15758**
M	1854-1855	**C-15758**
D	1854-1855, 1858, 1860	**C-15758**

includes:

German Evangelical Lutheran Church, Preston (later, Cambridge), Waterloo County
B	1853-1855, 1860	**C-15758**
M	1855	**C-15758**
D	1855, 1860	**C-15758**

includes: places in the Townships of North Dumfries, Waterloo, Wilmot, and Woolwich, Waterloo Co.; in the Townships of Brantford, Burford, and South Dumfries, Brant Co.; as well as Blenheim Township, Oxford Co.; Puslinch Township, Wellington Co.; and Beverly Township, Wentworth Co.

Burns Township, Renfrew Co.

Our Lady of Czestochowa, Queen of Poland (Roman Catholic) Church (formerly, St. Stanislaus Kostka Roman Catholic Church, Hagarty Township), Wilno
BMD	1880-1884	**H-1456** (partial index)
B	1877-1880	**H-1456**
	1888-1940	**H-1456** (partial index)
M	1885-1937	**H-1456** (partial index)
	1928-1960	**H-1457**
D	1885-1928	**H-1456** (partial index)
	1928-1943, 1945	**H-1457**
	1961-1975	**H-1457**
ordinations, 1910, 1923-1924		**H-1456**
confirmations, 1912-1913		**H-1456**
	1947-1948, 1950, 1953, 1956, 1959	**H-1457**
first communions, 1946-1947, 1951, 1958-1959		**H-1457**

includes: Townships of Brudenell, Burns, Hagarty, Radcliffe, and Sherwood

(The registers are in French, Latin, and English. Miscellaneous related items are in Polish.)

Bytown, Carleton Co.
See: Ottawa

Caledonia Township, Prescott Co.

Civil registers of the Surrogate Court for the Eastern and Johnstown Districts
B	1831, 1859, 1862-1865	**C-3030**
M	1831-1857, 1863, 1865	**C-3030** (index)

includes:

Baptist Congregation, Breadalbane, Glengarry Co.
M	1834-1850	**C-3030** (index)

includes: places in the Townships of Kenyon, and Lochiel, Glengarry Co.; as well as in the Townships of Caledonia, East Hawkesbury, West Hawkesbury, and North Plantagenet, Prescott Co.

Congregational Church, 9th Concession, Lochiel Township, Glengarry Co.
M	1833-1835, 1838-1840, 1843-1844	**C-3030** (index)

includes: places in the Townships of Kenyon (including the Indian Lands) and Lochiel, Glengarry Co.; and in the Townships of Caledonia, East Hawkesbury, and West Hawkesbury, Prescott Co.

L'Orignal and Plantagenet Presbyterian Church
M	1854-1856	**C-3028**
	1852-1856	**H-1807**

includes:

Caledonia Township
M	1853, 1856	**H-1807**

Farmer's Almanac diaries of Angus Alexander McMillan and Family of Glengarry County
BMD	1862-1910	**H-1808**

includes:

Prescott County
MD	1863-1902	**H-1808**

as well as:

Caledonia Township
BMD	1862-1903	**H-1808**

Cambridge (formerly, Galt, Preston, and Hespeler), Waterloo Co.

St. Peter's Lutheran Church
B	1834-1942	**M-3241**
M	1834-1847, 1856-1951	**M-3241**
D	1839-1942	**M-3241**
confirmations 1835-1942		**M-3241**
communion rolls 1835, 1853-1942		**M-3241**

(cont.)

Civil registers of Waterloo County
B   1836-1861   **C-15758**
M   1854-1855   **C-15758**
D   1854-1855, 1858, 1860   **C-15758**
includes:

   German Evangelical Lutheran Church, Preston (later, Cambridge)
   B   1853-1855, 1860   **C-15758**
   M   1855   **C-15758**
   D   1855, 1860   **C-15758**
   includes: places in the Townships of North Dumfries, Waterloo, Wilmot, and Woolwich, Waterloo Co.; in the Townships of Brantford, Burford, and South Dumfries, Brant Co.; as well as Blenheim Township, Oxford Co.; Puslinch Township, Wellington Co.; and Beverly Township, Wentworth Co.

   Wesleyan Methodist Congregation, Galt (later, Cambridge)
   B   1860   **C-15758**
   M   1854-1855   **C-15758**
   includes: places in the Township of Waterloo, Waterloo Co.; Paris, and the Township of Brantford, Brant Co.; Esquesing Township, Halton Co.; and Chinguacousy Township, Peel Co.

   St. Andrew's Presbyterian (Church of Scotland) Church, Galt (later, Cambridge)
   B   1837, 1839, 1852-1855,
            1860   **C-15758**

   Associate Presbyterian Church of the Rev. James Strang, Galt (later, Cambridge)
   BD   1855   **C-15758**

   Roman Catholic Mission, Preston (later, Cambridge)
   B   1860   **C-15758**
   includes: places in the Townships of North Dumfries, and Waterloo

Cambridge Township, Russell Co.

Civil registers of the Surrogate Court for the Eastern and Johnstown Districts
B   1831, 1859, 1862-1865   **C-3030**
M   1831-1857, 1863, 1865   **C-3030** (index)
includes:

   Presbyterian (Church of Scotland) Church, Kenyon Township, Glengarry Co.
   M   1865   **C-3030** (index)
   includes: Cambridge Township, Russell Co.; and Roxborough Township, Stormont Co.

Camden Township, Lennox and Addington Co.

St. John's Anglican Church, Bath
B   1787-1813   **H-1810**
M   1787-1816   **H-1810**
D   1787-1813   **H-1810**
comprises:

   St. Thomas' Anglican Church, Ernestown Township
   B   1788-1813   **H-1810**
   M   1787-1813, 1814, 1816   **H-1810**
   D   1788-1813   **H-1810**
   includes: Amherst Island, and the Townships of Adolphustown, Camden, and Fredericksburg, Lennox and Addington Co.; the Townships of Ameliasburg, Marysburgh, and Sophiasburgh, Prince Edward Co.; the Townships of Sidney, and Thurlow, Hastings Co.; and Kingston, Frontenac Co.; as well as Oswego, New York, U.S.A.

   St. Paul's Anglican Church, Fredericksburg Township
   B   1787-1813   **H-1810**
   M   1788-1812   **H-1810**
   D   1787-1813   **H-1810**
   includes: Amherst Island, and the Townships of Adolphustown, Camden, Ernestown, and Richmond, Lennox and Addington Co.; the Townships of Ameliasburg, Hallowell, Marysburgh, and Sophiasburgh, Prince Edward Co.; the Townships of Sidney, and Thurlow, Hastings Co.; and the Townships of Cramahé, and Percy, Northumberland Co.; as well as Oswego, New York, U.S.A.

Presbyterian Mission of Ernestown, Fredericksburg, Adolphustown, and the Bay of Quinté Region
B   1800-1841   **H-1810**
M   1800-1836   **H-1810**
D   1841   **H-1810**
includes:

   Camden Township
   B   1800-1813, 1820,
            1835-1839   **H-1810**
   M   1805-1821, 1832-1833   **H-1810**

Carleton County

Civil registers for the Johnstown District, Grenville Co.
M   1801-1845   **C-3030** (index)
            1844-1851   **C-3031** (index, on
                                           C-3030)
includes: Leeds, Grenville, and Carleton Counties

(cont.)

Civil registers of Ontario
M   1816-1869   **M-5497**
          1858-1869   **M-7092**
includes:

     Bathurst District (later, Carleton and Lanark Counties)
     M   1831-1848   **M-5497**

     Carleton County
     M   1865-1869   **M-5497**

Carleton Place, Lanark Co.

Almonte United Church, Almonte
BMD   1833-1962   **M-2217**
M   1896-1926   **M-2229**
includes:

     Carleton Place Wesleyan Methodist Circuit
     B   1905-1906, 1915   **M-2217**
     M   1858-1872, 1879,
              1889-1890   **M-2217**
     D   1905-1907   **M-2217**

Zion Memorial United Church, Carleton Place
BMD   1878-1933   **M-2209**
comprises:

     Certificates registered mainly at Carleton Place
     M   1878-1894   **M-2209**

     Carleton Place and Appleton Methodist Circuit
     BD   1901-1926   **M-2209**
     M   1898-1912   **M-2209**

     Carleton Place Methodist Church
     M   1910-1921   **M-2209**

     Zion Presbyterian Church, Carleton Place
     B   1878-1921   **M-2209**
     M   1896-1921   **M-2209**

     St. Andrew's Presbyterian Church, Carleton Place
     B   1910-1922   **M-2209**
     M   1910-1921   **M-2209**

                with:

     St. Paul's Presbyterian Church, Franktown
     M   1897-1921   **M-2209**

     Beckwith and Franktown Presbyterian Church
     B   1914-1921   **M-2209**

     Beckwith, Drummond and Montague Methodist Circuit
     M   1896-1922   **M-2209**

     Montague Methodist Circuit, Montague
     BD   1899-1922   **M-2209**

     Clayton Methodist Circuit, Clayton
     B   1890-1899   **M-2209**
     D   1896-1899   **M-2209**
     membership lists 1893-1902   **M-2209**
     includes: Boyd, and Prestonvale

     Lanark and Clayton Methodist Circuit
     B   1884-1933   **M-2209**
     M   1903-1931   **M-2209**
     D   1902-1931   **M-2209**
     circuit register 1903-1924   **M-2209**
     includes: Boyd, Erwins, Harper, Playfair, and Prestonvale

Carp, Carleton Co.

Carp United Church
BMD   1858-1929   **M-816** and
                                      M-817
comprises:

     Carp, Lowry, and Kinburn Presbyterian Congregations
     B   1860-1929   **M-817**
     M   1880-1903   **M-817**
     D   1880-1927   **M-817**
     membership rolls 1880-1929   **M-817**

     St. Andrew's Presbyterian Church, Carp
     M   1897-1928   **M-816** (index)

     St. Paul's Methodist Church, Carp
     M   1898-1928   **M-816**
     membership roll 1893-1929   **M-816**
     includes: Hazeldean, Huntley, Marchhurst, Stittsville

     Carp Methodist Circuit
     B   1887-1929   **M-816**
     M   1901-1928   **M-816**
     D   1901-1929   **M-816**

                with:

Bell's Corners Wesleyan Methodist Church
M   1858-1895   **M-816**

Carrick Township, Bruce Co.

Civil registers of Waterloo County
B   1836-1861   **C-15758**
M   1854-1855   **C-15758**
D   1854-1855, 1858, 1860   **C-15758**
includes:

     Evangelical Lutheran Church, Mannheim, New Dundee, and New Hamburg, Waterloo Co.
     B   1858, 1860   **C-15758**
     D   1860   **C-15758**
     includes: places in Wilmot Township, Waterloo Co.; in Brant, and Carrick Townships, Bruce Co.; in Hay, Stanley, and Tuckersmith Townships, Huron Co.; and Blenheim Township, Oxford

(cont.)

Co.; as well as Hanover, [Grey Co.]; and Williamsburgh [Township], Dundas Co.

[Unorthodox Evangelical Lutheran] Congregation of the Rev. Frederick W. Bindemann, Waterloo Township, Waterloo Co.
M	1855	**C-15758**

includes: Berlin (later, Kitchener), and places in the Townships of North Dumfries, Waterloo, Wellesley, Wilmot, and Woolwich, Waterloo Co.; Carrick Township, Bruce Co.; Normanby Township, Grey Co.; the Townships of Blandford, and Blenheim, Oxford Co.; Hay Township, Huron Co.; the Townships of North Easthope, South Easthope, and Wallace, Perth Co.; the Townships of Peel, Guelph, Nichol, and Puslinch, Wellington Co.; and Hamilton, Wentworth Co.

Castleford, Renfrew Co.

Lochwinnoch Presbyterian Church, Loch Winnoch
B	1867-1919	**M-2368**
M	1883-1906	**M-2368**
communion rolls 1887-1918		**M-2368**

includes: Castleford, Dewar's Settlement, and Stewartville

Cavan Township, Durham Co.

St. Paul's Presbyterian Church, Peterborough, Peterborough Co.
M	1834-1857	**H-1810**

includes: Townships of Asphodel, Douro, Dummer, Ennismore, Harvey, North Monaghan, Otonabee, and Smith, Peterborough Co.; the Townships of Hamilton, and South Monaghan in Northumberland Co.; the Township of Cavan, Durham Co.; and the Townships of Emily, and Ops, Victoria Co.

Cedar Hill, Lanark Co.

St. Andrew's United Church of Canada, Pakenham
B	1891-1966	**M-7761**
M	1840-1973	**M-7761**
D	1901-1985	**M-7761**

includes:

St. Andrew's Presbyterian Church, Pakenham, and Zion Presbyterian Church, Cedar Hill
B	1891-1921	**M-7761**
M	1896-1920	**M-7761**

Pakenham United Church of Canada Pastoral Charge
B	1909-1966	**M-7761**
M	1909-1973	**M-7761**
D	1909-1985	**M-7761**

includes: Cedar Hill, Lanark Co.; Antrim, and Fitzroy Township, Carleton Co.

Centreville, Lennox and Addington County

St. Anthony de Padua Roman Catholic Church
BMD	1846-1902	**M-3196**

Charlottenburg Township, Glengarry Co.

Civil registers of the Surrogate Court for the Eastern and Johnstown Districts
B	1831, 1859, 1862-1865	**C-3030**
M	1831-1857, 1863, 1865	**C-3030** (index)

includes:

Lutheran Congregation, Williamsburgh Township, Dundas Co.
M	1832-1843, 1847-1848	**C-3030** (index)

includes: Townships of Matilda, Williamsburgh, and Winchester, Dundas Co.; the Townships of Cornwall, and Osnabruck, Stormont Co.; and Charlottenburg Township, Glengarry Co.

Evangelical Lutheran Congregations, Williamsburgh Township, Dundas Co.
M	1842-1844, 1846-1857	**C-3030** (index)

includes: Townships of Matilda, Williamsburgh, and Winchester, Dundas Co.; the Townships of Cornwall, and Osnabruck, Stormont Co.; and Charlottenburg Township, Glengarry Co.

St. John's Presbyterian (Church of Scotland) Church, Cornwall, Stormont Co.
M	1831-1850, 1855-1857	**C-3030** (index)

includes: Townships of Charlottenburg, Kenyon (including the Indian Lands), and Lancaster, Glengarry Co.; and Roxborough Township, Stormont Co.

St. Andrew's (Presbyterian) Church of the Rev. Peter McVicar, Martintown, Glengarry Co.
M	1857	**C-3030** (index)

includes: Townships of Charlottenburg, and Kenyon, Glengarry Co.; and Roxborough Township, Stormont Co.

[Presbyterian] Congregation of the Rev. Peter Watson, Williamstown, Glengarry Co.
M	1865	**C-3030** (index)

includes: Martintown, and Williamstown, and other places in Charlottenburg Township, as well as the Townships of Lancaster, and Lochiel, Glengarry Co.; Cornwall Township, Stormont Co.; and the Townships of North Plantagenet, and South Plantagenet, Prescott Co.

Civil registers for the Eastern District
M	1858-1869	**M-3205**

includes:

Presbyterian (Free Church) Congregation, Charlottenburg Township
M	1861-1863	**M-3205**

(cont.)

Farmer's Almanac diaries of Angus Alexander McMillan and Family of Glengarry County
BMD   1862-1910   **H-1808**
includes:

    Charlottenburg Township
    MD   1862-1865   **H-1808**

Charlotteville Township, Norfolk Co.

Norfolk County Historical Society Collections
B	1783-1863	**M-283**
M	1807-1835	**M-274, M-275** and **M-277**
	1858-1897	**M-283**
D	1840-1899	**M-283**

includes:

    Civil registers for Norfolk County
M	1807-1813	**M-274**
	1807-1815	**M-274**
	1826-1828	**M-275**
	1831-1835	**M-277**

    includes: Townships of Charlotteville, and Woodhouse in the London District
    (Pages 829-837, 1040-1041, 2121-2123, 3940-3991)

Chatham, Kent Co.

Register of the Rev. John Becket (1838-1921), Presbyterian missionary at Aspdin, Muskoka District, 1905-1908
M   1905-1908, 1910, 1913, 1915   **H-1810**
includes:

    Chatham
    M   1913   **H-1810**

Chinguacousy Township, Peel Co.

Civil registers of Waterloo County
B	1836-1861	**C-15758**
M	1854-1855	**C-15758**
D	1854-1855, 1858, 1860	**C-15758**

includes:

    Wesleyan Methodist Congregation, Galt, (later, Cambridge), Waterloo Co.
B	1860	**C-15758**
M	1854-1855	**C-15758**

    includes: places in the Township of Waterloo, Waterloo Co.; Paris, and the Township of Brantford, Brant Co.; Esquesing Township, Halton Co.; and Chinguacousy Township, Peel Co.

(cont.)

Register of the Rev. John Becket (1838-1921), Presbyterian missionary at Aspdin, Muskoka District, 1905-1908
M   1905-1908, 1910, 1913, 1915   **H-1810**
includes:

    Chinguacousy Township
    M   1910   **H-1810**

Christian Island, Simcoe County

Journals of the Rev. Allen Salt, a Methodist Indian missionary in western Ontario
BMD   1854-1855, 1874-1899, 1904   **C-15709**
includes:

    Christian and Beausoleil Islands Methodist Indian Mission, Georgian Bay
    BMD   1875-1882   **C-15709**

Clayton, Lanark Co.

Zion Memorial United Church, Carleton Place
BMD   1878-1933   **M-2209**
includes:

    Clayton Methodist Circuit
B	1890-1899	**M-2209**
D	1896-1899	**M-2209**
membership 1893-1902		**M-2209**

    includes: Boyd, and Prestonvale

    Lanark and Clayton Methodist Circuit
B	1884-1933	**M-2209**
M	1903-1931	**M-2209**
D	1902-1931	**M-2209**
circuit register 1903-1924		**M-2209**

    includes: Boyd, Erwins, Harper, Playfair, and Prestonvale

    St. Andrew's United Church of Canada, Pakenham
B	1891-1966	**M-7761**
M	1840-1973	**M-7761**
D	1901-1985	**M-7761**

    includes:

    Blakeney and Clayton Presbyterian (later, United Church of Canada) Church
    M   1896-1946   **M-7761**

Clayton United Church
BMD   1805-1965   **M-3687** and **M-3688**
    1876-1965   **M-3243**
comprises:

    Clayton Methodist Circuit
    M   1896-1899   **M-3243**

(cont.)

Clayton and Blakeney Presbyterian Congregations
B 1901-1951 **M-3687**
D 1908-1946 **M-3687**
communion rolls 1907-1957 **M-3687**
includes: Guthrie

Clayton-Middleville Presbyterian Charge (later, Middleville United Church)
B 1881-1950 **M-3243**
D 1942-1957 **M-3688**
communion rolls 1942-1957 **M-3688**
includes: Hopetown, Rosetta, Darling, and Tatlock

with:

St. Paul's Presbyterian Charge, Middleville
B 1805-1879 **M-3687**

[St. James'] Presbyterian Charge, Dalhousie (later, Dalhousie-Playfair United Church)
B 1847-1880 **M-3687**
1908-1965 **M-3243**

St. Paul's, Middleville, and St. James', Dalhousie, United (Presbyterian) Pastoral Charge
B 1858-1864 **M-3687**
M 1859-1896, 1909-1910 **M-3687**
communion rolls 1858-1865 **M-3687**
1872-1954 **M-3688**
includes: St. John's United Church, Hopetown, 1925-1941; and Rosetta United Church, 1935-1942

St. Peter's Presbyterian Church, Darling Township
B 1871-1878 **M-3687**
communion rolls 1890-1942 **M-3688**
includes: St. John's, Hopetown; Rosetta Presbyterian Congregation; and St. Peter's, Tatlock

St. Paul's, Middleville, and St. Peter's, Darling, Presbyterian Congregations
BD 1893-1965 **M-3688**
M 1897-1919 **M-3243**
includes: Hopetown, Rosetta, and Tatlock

St. Paul's Presbyterian (later, United) Church, Middleville
M 1919-1943 **M-3243**

Poland Presbyterian Congregation, Poland
B 1876-1907, 1912 **M-3243**
includes: Clyde Forks, Flower Station, South Lavant, South Poland, Lanark Co.; and Thurlow, Hastings Co.

Watson's Corners Presbyterian Church, Watsons Corners
M 1896-1926 **M-3243**
includes: Flower Station, Poland, Lavant, Dalhousie Township

Dalhousie-Playfair Presbyterian Charge (including the Presbyterian Churches of: St. James', Dalhousie; and Zion, Watsons Corners; as well as the Poland Presbyterian Congregation, Poland; and the Playfair Presbyterian

(cont.)

Congregation, Playfair) (later, the Dalhousie-Playfair United Church)
communion rolls 1907-1964 **M-3688**

Dalhousie-Playfair United Church
M 1931-1964 **M-3243**
D 1929-1965 **M-3243**

Middleville Congregational Church, Middleville
B 1913-1928 **M-3243**
M 1858-1871 **M-3687**
1896-1925 **M-3243**
D 1910-1964 **M-3243**
includes: Rosetta

Lanark Methodist Church
M 1896-1926 **M-3243**

Clyde Forks, Lanark Co.

Clayton United Church, Clayton
BMD 1805-1965 **M-3687** and
M-3688
1876-1965 **M-3243**
includes:

Poland Presbyterian Congregation, Poland
B 1876-1907, 1912 **M-3243**
includes: Clyde Forks, Flower Station, South Lavant, South Poland, Lanark Co.; and Thurlow, Hastings Co.

Colchester, Essex Co.

Civil registers of Essex County
B 1826, 1845-1862 **C-15758**
includes:

Congregation of the Rev. I.F. Elliott, Colchester
B 1845, 1848, 1854, 1856,
1858, 1860-1861 **C-15758**

Corinth, Elgin Co.

Personal registers of the Rev. J. Nelson Gould of Sarnia, Methodist and United Church of Canada minister
B 1916-1960 **H-1811**
M 1916-1961 **H-1811**
D 1916-1959 **H-1811**
includes:

Richmond-Corinth United Church of Canada Charge
B 1947-1960 **H-1811**
M 1947-1961 **H-1811**
D 1947-1959 **H-1811**
includes: Aylmer West, Corinth, Fairview, North Bayham, Richmond Village (Bayham), and Summers Corners, Elgin Co.

Cornwall, Stormont Co.

Trinity Anglican Church
B	1803-1846	**C-3028** (index)
M	1803-1845	**C-3028** (index)
D	1813-1846	**C-3028** (index)

Civil registers of the Surrogate Court for the Eastern and Johnstown Districts
B	1831, 1859, 1862-1865	**C-3030**
M	1831-1857, 1863, 1865	**C-3030** (index)

includes:

St. John's Presbyterian (Church of Scotland) Church, Cornwall
M   1831-1850, 1855-1857   **C-3030** (index)
includes: Townships of Charlottenburg, Kenyon (including the Indian Lands), and Lancaster, Glengarry Co.; and Roxborough Township, Stormont Co.

Presbyterian (Free Church) Congregation of the Rev. Hugh Campbell, Cornwall
M   1854, [1855]   **C-3030** (index)

Cornwall Township, Stormont Co.

Civil registers of the Surrogate Court for the Eastern and Johnstown Districts
B	1831, 1859, 1862-1865	**C-3030**
M	1831-1857, 1863, 1865	**C-3030** (index)

includes:

[Anglican] Parish, Cornwall Township
M   1854-1857   **C-3030** (index)

Lutheran Congregation, Williamsburgh Township, Dundas Co.
M   1832-1843, 1847-1848   **C-3030** (index)
includes: Townships of Matilda, Williamsburgh, and Winchester, Dundas Co.; the Townships of Cornwall, and Osnabruck, Stormont Co.; and Charlottenburg Township, Glengarry Co.

Evangelical Lutheran Congregations, Williamsburgh Township, Dundas Co.
M   1842-1844, 1846-1857   **C-3030** (index)
includes: Townships of Matilda, Williamsburgh, and Winchester, Dundas Co.; the Townships of Cornwall, and Osnabruck, Stormont Co.; and Charlottenburg Township, Glengarry Co.

(cont.)

Methodist Episcopal Church in Canada, Circuits in the Eastern District
B	1831, 1862-1865	**C-3030**
M	1831-1833, 1839-1841, 1843-1844, 1846-1857, 1863	**C-3030** (index)

includes: Townships of Matilda, Mountain, Williamsburgh, and Winchester, Dundas Co.; Lochiel Township, Glengarry Co.; the Townships of Cornwall, Finch, and Osnabruck, Stormont Co.; and West Hawkesbury Township, Prescott Co.

Wesleyan Methodist Church in Canada, Circuits in the Eastern District
B	1859	**C-3030**
M	1833-1857	**C-3030** (index)

includes: Townships of Matilda, Mountain, Williamsburgh, and Winchester, Dundas Co.; the Townships of Edwardsburgh, and Oxford, Grenville Co.; Sheek Island, and the Townships of Cornwall, Finch, Osnabruck, and Roxborough, Stormont Co.; as well as the Brockville district, Leeds Co.; and other places in the Counties of Dundas, Stormont, and Glengarry

St. John's Presbyterian (Church of Scotland) Church, Cornwall
M   1831-1850, 1855-1857   **C-3030** (index)
includes: Townships of Charlottenburg, Kenyon (including the Indian Lands), and Lancaster, Glengarry Co.; and Roxborough Township, Stormont Co.

Presbyterian (Free Church) Congregation of the Rev. Hugh Campbell, Cornwall
M   1854, [1855]   **C-3030** (index)

Presbyterian (Free Church) Congregation of the Rev. Robert Lyle
M   1831-1837   **C-3030** (index)
includes: Townships of Matilda, and Williamsburgh, Dundas Co.; and the Townships of Cornwall, and Osnabruck, Stormont Co.

Presbyterian Church of the Rev. Isaac Purkis, Osnabruck Township
M   1840, 1842-1849   **C-3030** (index)

[Presbyterian] Congregation of the Rev. Peter Watson, Williamstown, Glengarry Co.
M   1865   **C-3030** (index)
includes: Martintown, and Williamstown, and other places in Charlottenburg Township, as well as the Townships of Lancaster, and Lochiel, Glengarry Co.; Cornwall Township, Stormont Co.; and the Townships of North Plantagenet, and South Plantagenet, Prescott Co.

Congregation of the Rev. John W. Sills
M   1850-1851   **C-3030** (index)
includes: Williamsburgh Township, Dundas Co.; and the Townships of Cornwall, and Osnabruck, Stormont Co.

(cont.)

St. Andrew's Roman Catholic Parish, St. Andrew's
M   1848   **C-3030** (index)

Roman Catholic Mission of Cornwall
M   [1848]   **C-3030** (index)

Farmer's Almanac diaries of Angus Alexander McMillan and Family of Glengarry County
BMD   1862-1910   **H-1808**
includes:

    Cornwall Township
    D   1864-1886   **H-1808**

Osnabruck and Lunenburg Presbyterian Congregations
B   1848-1909   **C-3030**
M   1860-1900   **C-3030**
D   1907-1909   **C-3030**
includes:

    Canada Presbyterian Church of Lunenburg and Osnabruck
    M   1860-1900   **C-3030**
    includes: Cornwall Township, Finch, Newington, Osnabruck, and Roxborough Township, Stormont Co.; the Indian Lands, Glengarry Co.; and the Townships of Williamsburgh, and Winchester, Dundas Co.

Cramahé Township, Northumberland Co.

St. John's Anglican Church, Bath, Lennox and Addington Co.
B   1787-1813   **H-1810**
M   1787-1816   **H-1810**
D   1787-1813   **H-1810**
includes:

    St. Paul's Anglican Church, Fredericksburg Township
    B   1787-1813   **H-1810**
    M   1788-1812   **H-1810**
    D   1787-1813   **H-1810**
    includes: Amherst Island, and the Townships of Adolphustown, Camden, Ernestown, and Richmond, Lennox and Addington Co.; the Townships of Ameliasburg, Hallowell, Marysburgh, and Sophiasburgh, Prince Edward Co.; the Townships of Sidney, and Thurlow, Hastings Co.; and the Townships of Cramahé, and Percy, Northumberland Co.; as well as Oswego, New York, U.S.A.

(cont.)

Presbyterian Mission of Ernestown, Fredericksburg, Adolphustown, and the Bay of Quinté region
B   1800-1841   **H-1810**
M   1800-1836   **H-1810**
D   1841   **H-1810**
includes:

    Cramahé Township
    B   1800-1806, 1811, 1818,
            1820   **H-1810**

Dalhousie Mills, Glengarry Co.

Presbyterian Church of Côte St. George (Soulanges Co., Quebec) and Dalhousie Mills
B   1843-1867, 1870-1874,
        1883   **M-3187**
M   1843-1850, 1862-1873   **M-3187**
BMD   1862-1875, 1882   **M-2228**
communion rolls 1862-1867, n.d.,
        1888-1889   **M-2228**

Civil registers of the Surrogate Court for the Eastern and Johnstown Districts
B   1831, 1859, 1862-1865   **C-3030**
M   1831-1857, 1863, 1865   **C-3030** (index)
includes:

    Congregation of the Rev. Aeneas McLean, Dalhousie Mills
    M   1848   **C-3030** (index)

Civil registers for the Eastern District
M   1858-1869   **M-3205**
includes:

    Canada Presbyterian Church, Lancaster and Dalhousie Mills
    M   1860-1861, 1863-1864,
            1866-1868   **M-3205**

Dalhousie Township, Lanark Co.

Clayton United Church, Clayton
BMD   1805-1965   **M-3687** and
                                M-3688
        1876-1965   **M-3243**
includes:

    [St. James'] Presbyterian Charge (later, Dalhousie-Playfair United Church)
    B   1847-1880   **M-3687**
            1908-1965   **M-3243**

(cont.)

St. James', Dalhousie, and St. Paul's, Middleville, United
(Presbyterian) Pastoral Charge
B	1858-1864	**M-3687**
M	1859-1896, 1909-1910	**M-3687**
communion rolls 1858-1865		**M-3687**
	1872-1954	**M-3688**

includes: St. John's United Church, Hopetown,
1925-1941, and Rosetta United Church,
1935-1942

Watson's Corners Presbyterian Church, Watsons Corners
M	1896-1926	**M-3243**

includes: Flower Station, Poland, Lavant, Dalhousie
Township

Dalhousie-Playfair Presbyterian Charge (including the
Presbyterian Churches of: St. James', Dalhousie; and
Zion, Watsons Corners; as well as the Poland
Presbyterian Congregation, Poland; and the Playfair
Presbyterian Congregation, Playfair) (later, the Dalhousie-
Playfair United Church)
communion rolls 1907-1964		**M-3688**

Dalhousie-Playfair United Church
M	1931-1964	**M-3243**
D	1929-1965	**M-3243**

Knox Presbyterian Church, McDonalds Corners
B	1847-1857	**M-4614**

includes: Elphin, and Snow Road, Frontenac Co.; and the
Townships of Dalhousie, and North Sherbrooke,
Lanark Co.

Dalkeith, Glengarry Co.

Farmer's Almanac diaries of Angus Alexander McMillan
and Family of Glengarry County
BMD	1862-1910	**H-1808**

includes:

Lochiel Township
BMD	1862-1910	**H-1808**

as well as, among others:

Dalkeith, Lochiel Township
MD	1863-1902	**H-1808**

Darling Township, Lanark Co.

Clayton United Church, Clayton
BMD	1805-1965	**M-3687** and
		M-3688
	1876-1965	**M-3243**

includes:

[St. Peter's] Presbyterian Church, Darling Township
B	1871-1878	**M-3687**
communion rolls 1890-1942		**M-3688**

includes: St. John's, Hopetown; Rosetta Presbyterian
Congregation; and St. Peter's, Tatlock

Clayton-Middleville Presbyterian Charge (later, Middleville
United Church)
B	1881-1950	**M-3243**
D	1942-1957	**M-3688**
communion rolls 1942-1957		**M-3688**

includes: Hopetown, Rosetta, Darling, and Tatlock

St. Peter's, Darling, and St. Paul's, Middleville,
Presbyterian Congregations
BD	1893-1965	**M-3688**
M	1897-1919	**M-3243**

includes: Hopetown, Rosetta, and Tatlock

Delhi (Fredericksburg), Norfolk Co.

Norfolk County Historical Society Collections
B	1783-1863	**M-283**
M	1807-1835	**M-274, M-275** and
		M-277
	1858-1897	**M-283**
D	1840-1899	**M-283**

includes:

Hartford and Fredericksburg (Delhi) Regular Baptist
Congregations
B	1783-1863	**M-283**
M	1858-1897	**M-283**
D	1840-1899	**M-283**

includes: Townships of Middleton, South Walsingham,
Townsend, and Windham, Norfolk Co.; and
Walpole Township, Haldimand Co.

(Pages 12941-12987)

Dewars Settlement, Renfrew Co.

Lochwinnoch Presbyterian Church, Loch Winnoch
B	1867-1919	**M-2368**
M	1883-1906	**M-2368**
communion rolls 1887-1918		**M-2368**

includes: Castleford, Dewar's Settlement, and Stewartville

Dexter, Elgin Co.

Personal registers of the Rev. J. Nelson Gould of Sarnia,
Methodist and United Church of Canada minister
B	1916-1960	**H-1811**
M	1916-1961	**H-1811**
D	1916-1959	**H-1811**

includes:

Sparta-Dexter Methodist Charge
BMD	1916-1921	**H-1811**

(cont.)

ONTARIO

Douro Township, Peterborough Co.

St. Paul's Presbyterian Church, Peterborough
M   1834-1857   **H-1810**
includes: Townships of Asphodel, Douro, Dummer, Ennismore, Harvey, North Monaghan, Otonabee, and Smith, Peterborough Co.; the Townships of Hamilton, and South Monaghan in Northumberland Co.; the Township of Cavan, Durham Co.; and the Townships of Emily, and Ops, Victoria Co.

Civil registers of Peterborough County
M   1859-1873   **H-1810**
consists of:

     Christ Church Anglican Church, Lakefield
     M   1859-1873   **H-1810**
     includes: Lakefield (North Douro), and Peterborough, as well as the Townships of Douro, Dummer, Otonabee, and Smith, Peterborough Co.; and Lindsay, Victoria Co.

Drummond Township, Lanark Co.

Zion Memorial United Church, Carleton Place
BMD   1878-1933   **M-2209**
includes:

     Beckwith, Drummond and Montague Methodist Circuit
     M   1896-1922   **M-2209**

Dufferin County

Returns of coroners' inquests for Grey, Wellington, Bruce, [and Dufferin] Counties
D   1873   **C-15758**
includes: Durham, Owen Sound, and the Townships of Artemesia, Egremont, Euphrasia, Keppel, Normanby, Osprey, Proton, St. Vincent, and Sydenham, Grey Co.; and Melancthon Township, Dufferin Co.

Dummer Township, Peterborough Co.

St. Paul's Presbyterian Church, Peterborough
M   1834-1857   **H-1810**
includes: Townships of Asphodel, Douro, Dummer, Ennismore, Harvey, North Monaghan, Otonabee, and Smith, Peterborough Co.; the Townships of Hamilton, and South Monaghan in Northumberland Co.; the Township of Cavan, Durham Co.; and the Townships of Emily, and Ops, Victoria Co.

(cont.)

Civil registers of Peterborough County
M   1859-1873   **H-1810**
consists of:

     Christ Church Anglican Church, Lakefield
     M   1859-1873   **H-1810**
     includes: Lakefield (North Douro), and Peterborough, as well as the Townships of Douro, Dummer, Otonabee, and Smith, Peterborough Co.; and Lindsay, Victoria Co.

Dundas, Wentworth Co.

Dundas and Ancaster Presbyterian Church
M   1848-1852   **C-3028**
comprises:

     Dundas
     M   1848-1852   **C-3028**

     Ancaster, and West Flamboro
     M   1848-1852   **C-3028**

     with:

L'Orignal and Plantagenet Presbyterian Church, Prescott Co.
M   1854-1856   **C-3028**
               1852-1856   **H-1807**
comprises:

     L'Orignal, Prescott Co.
     M   1852-1856   **H-1807**
               1855-1856   **C-3028**

     Hawkesbury, Prescott Co.
     M   1853   **H-1807**

     West Hawkesbury Township, Prescott Co.
     M   1853   **H-1807**

     Caledonia Township, Prescott Co.
     M   1853, 1856   **H-1807**

     North Plantagenet Township, Prescott Co.
     M   1853-1854   **H-1807**

     Plantagenet, Prescott Co.
     M   1854   **C-3028**

     Lochiel, Glengarry Co.
     M   1854   **H-1807**

Dundas County

Civil registers of the Surrogate Court for the Eastern and Johnstown Districts

B	1831, 1859, 1862-1865	**C-3030**
M	1831-1857, 1863, 1865	**C-3030** (index)

includes:

Wesleyan Methodist Church in Canada, Circuits in the Eastern District

B	1859	**C-3030**
M	1833-1857	**C-3030** (index)

includes: Townships of Matilda, Mountain, Williamsburgh, and Winchester, Dundas Co.; the Townships of Edwardsburgh, and Oxford, Grenville Co.; Sheek Island, and the Townships of Cornwall, Finch, Osnabruck, and Roxborough, Stormont Co.; as well as the Brockville district, Leeds Co.; and other places in the Counties of Dundas, Stormont, and Glengarry

Affidavits for marriage licences

M	1877-1896	**M-2179** (index)

Dungannon, Huron Co.

Journal of the Rev. Jabez Waters Sims (1831-1869), Anglican Missionary

BMD	1863-1865	**H-1812** (index)

comprises:

St. Paul's Anglican Church, Dungannon

BMD	1863-1864	**H-1812** (index)

Manitoulin Island Anglican Mission

BD	1865	**H-1812** (index)
M	1864-1865	**H-1812** (index)

Dunvegan, Glengarry Co.

Farmer's Almanac diaries of Angus Alexander McMillan and Family of Glengarry County

BMD	1862-1910	**H-1808**

includes:

Kenyon Township

BMD	1862-1910	**H-1808**

as well as, among others:

Dunvegan, Kenyon Township

BMD	1866-1903	**H-1808**

Durham, Grey Co.

Returns of coroners' inquests for Grey, Wellington, Bruce, [and Dufferin] Counties

D	1873	**C-15758**

includes: Durham, Owen Sound, and the Townships of Artemesia, Egremont, Euphrasia, Keppel, Normanby, Osprey, Proton, St. Vincent, and Sydenham, Grey Co.; and Melancthon Township, Dufferin Co.

Dwyer Hill, Carleton Co.

St. Philip's Roman Catholic Church, Richmond

BMD	1836-1924	**M-2818**

includes:

St. Clare's Roman Catholic Church (Goulbourn Mission), Dwyer Hill

BMD	1891-1924	**M-2818**

East Hawkesbury Township, Prescott Co.

Civil registers of the Surrogate Court for the Eastern and Johnstown Districts

B	1831, 1859, 1862-1865	**C-3030**
M	1831-1857, 1863, 1865	**C-3030** (index)

includes:

Baptist Congregation, Breadalbane, Glengarry Co.

M	1834-1850	**C-3030** (index)

includes: places in the Townships of Kenyon, and Lochiel, Glengarry Co.; as well as in the Townships of Caledonia, East Hawkesbury, West Hawkesbury, and North Plantagenet, Prescott Co.

Congregational Church, 9th Concession, Lochiel Township, Glengarry Co.

M	1833-1835, 1838-1840, 1843-1844	**C-3030** (index)

includes: places in the Townships of Kenyon (including the Indian Lands) and Lochiel, Glengarry Co.; and in the Townships of Caledonia, East Hawkesbury, and West Hawkesbury, Prescott Co.

Baptist Congregation of Breadalbane, Glengarry Co.

M	1858-1886	**H-1807**

includes: places in the Township of Lochiel, Glengarry Co.; as well as in the Townships of East Hawkesbury and West Hawkesbury, Prescott Co.

East Zorra Township, Oxford Co.

Civil registers of Waterloo County
B	1836-1861	**C-15758**
M	1854-1855	**C-15758**
D	1854-1855, 1858, 1860	**C-15758**

includes:

St. James' Anglican Church, Wilmot Township
BD	1860	**C-15758**

includes: other places in Wilmot Township; as well as St. George, Brant Co.; and the Townships of Blandford, and East Zorra, Oxford Co.

Eastern District (later, Counties of Glengarry, Stormont, Dundas, Prescott, and Russell)

Civil registers of the Surrogate Court for the Eastern and Johnstown Districts
B	1831, 1859, 1862-1865	**C-3030**
M	1831-1857, 1863, 1865	**C-3030** (index)

comprises:

[Anglican] Parish, Cornwall Township, Stormont Co.
M	1854-1857	**C-3030** (index)

[Anglican] Parish, Williamsburgh Township, Dundas Co.
M	1855	**C-3030** (index)

Baptist Congregation, Breadalbane, Glengarry Co.
M	1834-1850	**C-3030** (index)

includes: places in the Townships of Kenyon, and Lochiel, Glengarry Co.; as well as in the Townships of Caledonia, East Hawkesbury, West Hawkesbury, and North Plantagenet, Prescott Co.

Lutheran Congregation, Williamsburgh Township, Dundas Co.
M	1832-1843, 1847-1848	**C-3030** (index)

includes: Townships of Matilda, Williamsburgh, and Winchester, Dundas Co.; the Townships of Cornwall, and Osnabruck, Stormont Co.; and Charlottenburg Township, Glengarry Co.

Evangelical Lutheran Congregations, Williamsburgh Township, Dundas Co.
M	1842-1844, 1846-1857	**C-3030** (index)

includes: Townships of Matilda, Williamsburgh, and Winchester, Dundas Co.; the Townships of Cornwall, and Osnabruck, Stormont Co.; and Charlottenburg Township, Glengarry Co.

(cont.)

Methodist Episcopal Church in Canada, Circuits in the Eastern District
B	1831, 1862-1865	**C-3030**
M	1831-1833, 1839-1841, 1843-1844, 1846-1857, 1863	**C-3030** (index)

includes: Townships of Matilda, Mountain, Williamsburgh, and Winchester, Dundas Co.; Lochiel Township, Glengarry Co.; the Townships of Cornwall, Finch, and Osnabruck, Stormont Co.; and West Hawkesbury Township, Prescott Co.

Wesleyan Methodist Church, Matilda Township, Dundas Co.
M	1831-1837, 1839-1844, 1846-1849	**C-3030** (index)

includes: Townships of Matilda, and Mountain, Dundas Co.; and Edwardsburgh Township, Grenville Co.

Wesleyan Methodist Church in Canada, Circuits in the Eastern District
B	1859	**C-3030**
M	1833-1857	**C-3030** (index)

includes: Townships of Matilda, Mountain, Williamsburgh, and Winchester, Dundas Co.; the Townships of Edwardsburgh, and Oxford, Grenville Co.; Sheek Island, and the Townships of Cornwall, Finch, Osnabruck, and Roxborough, Stormont Co.; as well as the Brockville district, Leeds Co.; and other places in the Counties of Dundas, Stormont, and Glengarry

St. John's Presbyterian (Church of Scotland) Church, Cornwall, Stormont Co.
M	1831-1850, 1855-1857	**C-3030** (index)

includes: Townships of Charlottenburg, Kenyon (including the Indian Lands), and Lancaster, Glengarry Co.; and Roxborough Township, Stormont Co.

Presbyterian (Church of Scotland) Church, Lancaster Township, Glengarry Co.
M	1834-1836	**C-3030** (index)

includes: Coteau-du-Lac, and Rivière-Beaudette, Soulanges Co., Que.

Presbyterian (Church of Scotland) Church, Kenyon Township, Glengarry Co.
M	1865	**C-3030** (index)

includes: Cambridge Township, Russell Co.; and Roxborough Township, Stormont Co.

Presbyterian Church of the Rev. John Dickey, Williamsburgh, Matilda, and Winchester Townships, Dundas Co.
M	1836-1849	**C-3030** (index)

includes: Mountain Township, Dundas Co.; and Osnabruck Township, Stormont Co.

(cont.)

Presbyterian (Church of Scotland) Church of the
Rev. T. Scott, Williamsburgh, Matilda, and Winchester
Townships, Dundas Co.
M   1853-1857   **C-3030** (index)
includes: Mountain Township, Dundas Co.; and
      Osnabruck Township, Stormont Co.

Presbyterian (Free Church) Congregation of the
Rev. Hugh Campbell, Cornwall, Stormont Co.
M   1854, [1855]   **C-3030** (index)

Presbyterian (Free Church) Congregation of the
Rev. Robert Lyle
M   1831-1837   **C-3030** (index)
includes: Townships of Matilda, and Williamsburgh,
      Dundas Co.; and the Townships of Cornwall,
      and Osnabruck, Stormont Co.

Presbyterian Church of the Rev. Isaac Purkis, Osnabruck
Township, Stormont Co.
M   1840, 1842-1849   **C-3030** (index)

St. Andrew's (Presbyterian) Church of the Rev. Peter
McVicar, Martintown, Glengarry Co.
M   1857   **C-3030** (index)
includes: Townships of Charlottenburg, and Kenyon,
      Glengarry Co.; and Roxborough Township,
      Stormont Co.

[Presbyterian] Congregation of the Rev. Peter Watson,
Williamstown, Glengarry Co.
M   1865   **C-3030** (index)
includes: Martintown, and Williamstown, and other
      places in Charlottenburg Township, as well as
      the Townships of Lancaster, and Lochiel,
      Glengarry Co.; Cornwall Township, Stormont
      Co.; and the Townships of North Plantagenet,
      and South Plantagenet, Prescott Co.

Congregation of the Rev. Aeneas McLean, Dalhousie
Mills, Glengarry Co.
M   1848   **C-3030** (index)

Congregation of the Rev. John W. Sills
M   1850-1851   **C-3030** (index)
includes: Williamsburgh Township, Dundas Co.; and the
      Townships of Cornwall, and Osnabruck,
      Stormont Co.

Congregation of the Rev. E. Sallows
M   1851   **C-3030** (index)
includes: Townships of Osnabruck, and Roxborough,
      Stormont Co.

Congregational Church, 9th Concession, Lochiel
Township, Glengarry Co.
M   1833-1835, 1838-1840,
      1843-1844   **C-3030** (index)
includes: places in the Townships of Kenyon (including
      the Indian Lands) and Lochiel, Glengarry Co.;
      and in the townships of Caledonia, East
      Hawkesbury, and West Hawkesbury, Prescott
      Co.

(cont.)

Congregational Church, Martintown, Glengarry Co.
M   1854   **C-3030** (index)

St. Andrew's Roman Catholic Parish, St. Andrew's,
Stormont Co.
M   1848   **C-3030** (index)

Roman Catholic Mission of Cornwall, Stormont Co.
M   [1848]   **C-3030** (index)

Civil registers
M   1858-1869   **M-3205**
comprises:

    St. Finnan's Roman Catholic Cathedral Church,
    Alexandria, Glengarry Co.
    M   1858-1869   **M-3205**

    Baptist Congregation, Bradalan [Breadalbane,
    Glengarry Co.]
    M   1862-1864   **M-3205**

    Presbyterian (Free Church) Congregation,
    Charlottenburg Township, Glengarry Co.
    M   1861-1863   **M-3205**

    Regular Baptist Church, Indian Lands, [Kenyon
    Township, Glengarry Co.]
    M   1862-1863   **M-3205**

    Congregational Church, Indian Lands, [Kenyon
    Township, Glengarry Co.]
    M   1859, 1862   **M-3205**

    Presbyterian Church of Canada Congregation,
    Kenyon Township, Glengarry Co.
    M   1859-1869   **M-3205**

    Canada Presbyterian Church, Lancaster and Dalhousie
    Mills, Glengarry Co.
    M   1860-1861, 1863-1864,
            1866-1868   **M-3205**

    Presbyterian (Church of Scotland) Church, Lochiel
    Township, Glengarry Co.
    M   1858, 1860-1869   **M-3205**

    Presbyterian (Church of Scotland) Church, Martintown,
    Glengarry Co.
    M   1858, 1861-[1867]   **M-3205**

    Baptist Church, Notfield, Glengarry Co.
    M   1869   **M-3205**

    Baptist Church, Roxborough Township, Stormont Co.
    M   1867   **M-3205**

    St. Andrew's Presbyterian (Church of Scotland) Church,
    Williamstown, Glengarry Co.
    M   1858-1860, 1862-1869   **M-3205**

(cont.)

Presbyterian (Free Church) Congregation, Williamstown, Glengarry Co.
M   1867-1869   **M-3205**

St. Mary's Roman Catholic Church, Williamstown, Glengarry Co.
M   1858-1861, 1863-1864   **M-3205**

Edwardsburgh Township, Grenville Co.

Zion Lutheran Church, Williamsburg, Dundas Co.
BM   1790-1814   **M-1496** (index)
D   1790-1814   **M-1496**
communicants and confirmations,
     1808-1814   **M-1496**
includes: Morrisburg, and the Townships of Matilda, and Williamsburgh, Dundas Co.; and the Township of Osnabruck, Stormont Co.

with:

United Anglican Mission of Williamsburgh, Matilda, and Edwardsburgh
BM   1814-1886   **M-1496** (partial index)
D   1814-1886   **M-1496**
communicants and confirmations,
     1814-1819, 1829,
     1846-1886   **M-1496**
includes: Morrisburg, Williamsburg, and the Townships of Matilda, and Williamsburgh, Dundas Co.; the Township of Osnabruck, Stormont Co.; and the Township of Edwardsburgh, Grenville Co.
(The early registers are in Latin.)

Civil registers of the Surrogate Court for the Eastern and Johnstown Districts
B   1831, 1859, 1862-1865   **C-3030**
M   1831-1857, 1863, 1865   **C-3030** (index)
includes:

Wesleyan Methodist Church, Matilda Township, Dundas Co.
M   1831-1837, 1839-1844,
     1846-1849   **C-3030** (index)
includes: Townships of Matilda, and Mountain, Dundas Co.; and Edwardsburgh Township, Grenville Co.

Wesleyan Methodist Church in Canada, Circuits in the Eastern District
B   1859   **C-3030**
M   1833-1857   **C-3030** (index)
includes: Townships of Matilda, Mountain, Williamsburgh, and Winchester, Dundas Co.; the Townships of Edwardsburgh, and Oxford, Grenville Co.; Sheek Island, and the Townships of Cornwall, Finch, Osnabruck, and Roxborough, Stormont Co.; as well as the Brockville district, Leeds Co.; and other places in the Counties of Dundas, Stormont, and Glengarry

Egremont Township, Grey Co.

Returns of coroners' inquests for Grey, Wellington, Bruce, [and Dufferin] Counties
D   1873   **C-15758**
includes: Durham, Owen Sound, and the Townships of Artemesia, Egremont, Euphrasia, Keppel, Normanby, Osprey, Proton, St. Vincent, and Sydenham, Grey Co.; and Melancthon Township, Dufferin Co.

Elizabethtown Township, Leeds Co.

St. Andrew's Presbyterian (Church of Scotland) Church, Toledo (formerly, Presbyterian Congregation of Kitley Township)
B   1846-1852, 1863-1913   **H-1810**
M   1863-1864, 1880-1881,
     1890-1893, 1903, 1907   **H-1810**
D   1894, 1897-1902, 1911   **H-1810**
members, 1847, 1850, 1854,
     1863-1913   **H-1810**
includes: Townships of Bastard, Elizabethtown, Front of Yonge, and Kitley, Leeds Co.; as well as Montague Township, Lanark Co.; and Wolford Township, Grenville Co.

Returns of coroners' inquests for the Counties of Leeds, and Grenville
D   1873   **C-15758**
includes: Brockville, Gananoque, and Elizabethtown Township, Leeds Co.; as well as the Townships of Augusta, and Wolford, Grenville Co.

Ellice Township, Perth Co.

Civil registers of Waterloo County
B   1836-1861   **C-15758**
M   1854-1855   **C-15758**
D   1854-1855, 1858, 1860   **C-15758**
includes:

German Evangelical Lutheran Congregations, Phillipsburg, Wellesley Village, and New Baden, Waterloo Co.
B   1836-1855, 1858, 1860   **C-15758**
D   1858, 1860   **C-15758**
includes: places in the Townships of Waterloo, Wellesley, and Wilmot, Waterloo Co.; Ellice, Mornington, and North Easthope Townships, Perth Co.; Normanby Township, Grey Co.

Elmhill, Peterborough Co.

Register of the Rev. John Becket (1838-1921), Presbyterian missionary at Aspdin, Muskoka District, 1905-1908
M	1905-1908, 1910, 1913, 1915	**H-1810**

includes:

Elmhill
M	1905	**H-1810**

Elmira, Waterloo Co.

Civil registers of Waterloo County
B	1836-1861	**C-15758**
M	1854-1855	**C-15758**
D	1854-1855, 1858, 1860	**C-15758**

includes:

[St. James' Evangelical Lutheran Church, Elmira]
B	1853-1860	**C-15758**
D	1860	**C-15758**

Elphin, Frontenac Co.

Knox Presbyterian Church, McDonalds Corners, Lanark Co.
B	1847-1857	**M-4614**

includes: Elphin, and Snow Road, Frontenac Co.; and the Townships of Dalhousie, and North Sherbrooke, Lanark Co.

Embrun, comté de Russell

Missions du comté de Wright, Aylmer et Gatineau, comté de Gatineau, Qué. (Église catholique)
B/M/D	1841-1848	**C-2978**
M	1841-1853 Index	**C-2978**

comprend : St-Jacques-de-Bytown (ou d'Embrun), etc.

St-Jacques-d'Embrun (Église catholique)
B/M/D	1855-1883	**M-3124** (index)
	1884-1902	**M-3125** (index)
	1902-1905	**M-3126** (index)
	1905-1926	**M-3127** (index)
	1926-1959	**M-3128** (index)
	1960-1974	**M-3201** (index)
	1858-1973 Index	**M-3201**
M	1908-1915	**M-3129** (index)

Emily Township, Victoria Co.

St. Paul's Presbyterian Church, Peterborough, Peterborough Co.
M	1834-1857	**H-1810**

includes: Townships of Asphodel, Douro, Dummer, Ennismore, Harvey, North Monaghan, Otonabee, and Smith, Peterborough Co.; the Townships of Hamilton, and South Monaghan in Northumberland Co.; the Township of Cavan, Durham Co.; and the Townships of Emily, and Ops, Victoria Co.

Ennismore Township, Peterborough Co.

St. Paul's Presbyterian Church, Peterborough
M	1834-1857	**H-1810**

includes: Townships of Asphodel, Douro, Dummer, Ennismore, Harvey, North Monaghan, Otonabee, and Smith, Peterborough Co.; the Townships of Hamilton, and South Monaghan in Northumberland Co.; the Township of Cavan, Durham Co.; and the Townships of Emily, and Ops, Victoria Co.

Ernestown Township, Lennox and Addington Co.

St. John's Anglican Church, Bath
B	1787-1813	**H-1810**
M	1787-1816	**H-1810**
D	1787-1813	**H-1810**

comprises:

St. Thomas' Anglican Church, Ernestown Township
B	1788-1813	**H-1810**
M	1787-1813, 1814, 1816	**H-1810**
D	1788-1813	**H-1810**

includes: Amherst Island, and the Townships of Adolphustown, Camden, and Fredericksburg, Lennox and Addington Co.; the Townships of Ameliasburg, Marysburgh, and Sophiasburgh, Prince Edward Co.; the Townships of Sidney, and Thurlow, Hastings Co.; and Kingston, Frontenac Co.; as well as Oswego, New York, U.S.A.

St. Paul's Anglican Church, Fredericksburg Township
B	1787-1813	**H-1810**
M	1788-1812	**H-1810**
D	1787-1813	**H-1810**

includes: Amherst Island, and the Townships of Adolphustown, Camden, Ernestown, and Richmond, Lennox and Addington Co.; the Townships of Ameliasburg, Hallowell, Marysburgh, and Sophiasburgh, Prince Edward Co.; the Townships of Sidney, and Thurlow, Hastings Co.; and the Townships of Cramahé, and Percy, Northumberland Co.; as well as Oswego, New York, U.S.A.

(cont.)

Presbyterian Mission of Ernestown, Fredericksburg, Adolphustown, and the Bay of Quinté region
B	1800-1841	**H-1810**
M	1800-1836	**H-1810**
D	1841	**H-1810**

comprises:

Adolphustown Township, Lennox and Addington Co.
B	1800-1811	**H-1810**
M	1800-1821, 1831-1835	**H-1810**

Amherst Island Township, Lennox and Addington Co.
B	1834-1840	**H-1810**
M	1802, 1816, 1819	**H-1810**

Camden Township, Lennox and Addington Co.
B	1800-1813, 1820, 1835-1839	**H-1810**
M	1805-1821, 1832-1833	**H-1810**

Ernestown Township, Lennox and Addington Co.
B	1800-1813, 1819-1821, 1827, 1830, 1832, 1835	**H-1810**
M	1800-1822, 1831-1835	**H-1810**

Fredericksburg Township, Lennox and Addington Co.
B	1800-1813, 1815, 1827, 1832, 1837-1840	**H-1810**
M	1800-1822, 1831-1836	**H-1810**

Richmond Township, Lennox and Addington Co.
B	1800-1811, 1813-1814, 1824-1825, 1832-1833, 1838-1839	**H-1810**
M	1802-1803, 1807-1821, 1832-1835	**H-1810**

Sheffield Township, Lennox and Addington Co.
B	1831, 1836, 1839	**H-1810**

Rawdon Township, Hastings Co.
B	1803	**H-1810**

Sidney Township, Hastings Co.
B	1800-1820, 1837, 1839	**H-1810**
M	1803, 1806-1818	**H-1810**

Thurlow Township, Hastings Co.
B	1802-1816, 1821, 1839	**H-1810**
M	1807, 1812, 1816, 1822	**H-1810**

Tyendinaga Township, Hastings Co.
B	1826-1837	**H-1810**

Cramahé Township, Northumberland Co.
B	1800-1806, 1811, 1818, 1820	**H-1810**

Hamilton Township, Northumberland Co.
B	1800-1803	**H-1810**

Murray Township, Northumberland Co.
B	1800-1821	**H-1810**
M	1803, 1812	**H-1810**

Ameliasburg Township, Prince Edward Co.
B	1800-1822, 1827, 1829, 1833-1840	**H-1810**
M	1807-1808, 1812, 1820	**H-1810**

Hallowell Township, Prince Edward Co.
B	1800-1810, 1812, 1820, 1826	**H-1810**
M	1800-1820, 1831-1835	**H-1810**

Marysburgh Township, Prince Edward Co.
B	1800-1812, 1820, 1835, 1837	**H-1810**
M	1800-1822, 1831-1835	**H-1810**

Sophiasburgh Township, Prince Edward Co.
B	1806-1822, 1828	**H-1810**
M	1801-1822, 1831-1834	**H-1810**

Kingston, Frontenac Co.
B	1802-1811, 1820, 1822	**H-1810**
M	1802, 1805-1822, 1831-1832, 1835	**H-1810**

Loughborough Township, Frontenac Co.
B	1804-1805, 1809-1811, 1830-1838	**H-1810**
M	1809, 1812, 1818-1820	**H-1810**

Pittsburg Township, Frontenac Co.
B	1800-1809	**H-1810**

Portland Township, Frontenac Co.
B	1800-1811	**H-1810**
M	1810, 1816	**H-1810**

Esquesing Township, Halton Co.

Civil registers of Waterloo County
B	1836-1861	**C-15758**
M	1854-1855	**C-15758**
D	1854-1855, 1858, 1860	**C-15758**

includes:

Wesleyan Methodist Congregation, Galt (later, Cambridge)
B	1860	**C-15758**
M	1854-1855	**C-15758**

includes: places in the Township of Waterloo, Waterloo Co.; Paris, and the Township of Brantford, Brant Co.; Esquesing Township, Halton Co.; and Chinguacousy Township, Peel Co.

(cont.)

Essex County

Civil registers of Essex County
B   1826, 1845-1862   **C-15758**
comprises:

    Christ Church [Anglican Church], Amherstburg
    B   1861   **C-15758**

    Congregation of the Rev. R.R. Disney
    B   1861   **C-15758**

    Congregation of the Rev. P.D. Laurent, Maidstone
    B   1861   **C-15758**

    Congregation of the Rev. Isaac Christian
    B   1861   **C-15758**

    Congregation of the Rev. I.F. Elliott, Colchester
    B   1845, 1848, 1854, 1856,
              1858, 1860-1861   **C-15758**

    Rev. Mr. Fauteux
    B   1861   **C-15758**

    St. John the Baptist [Roman Catholic] Church, Amherstburg
    B   1847, c. 1852, 1855-1861   **C-15758**

    Congregation of the Rev. John [H.] John, Sandwich Township
    B   1826, 1847, 1849-1851,
              1855-1856, 1859-1862   **C-15758**

    Wesleyan Methodist Church, Sandwich Township
    B   1860-1861   **C-15758**

Euphrasia Township, Grey Co.

Returns of coroners' inquests for Grey, Wellington, Bruce, [and Dufferin] Counties
D   1873   **C-15758**
includes: Durham, Owen Sound, and the Townships of Artemesia, Egremont, Euphrasia, Keppel, Normanby, Osprey, Proton, St. Vincent, and Sydenham, Grey Co.; and Melancthon Township, Dufferin Co.

Fairview, Elgin Co.

Personal Registers of the Rev. J. Nelson Gould of Sarnia, Methodist and United Church of Canada minister
B   1916-1960   **H-1811**
M   1916-1961   **H-1811**
D   1916-1959   **H-1811**
includes:

    Richmond-Corinth United Church of Canada Charge
    B   1947-1960   **H-1811**
    M   1947-1961   **H-1811**
    D   1947-1959   **H-1811**
    includes: Aylmer West, Corinth, Fairview, North Bayham, Richmond Village (Bayham), and Summers Corners, Elgin Co.

Fallowfield, Carleton Co.

St. Patrick's Roman Catholic Church
BMD   1851-1882   **M-1954**
           1882-1926   **M-1954** (index)
confirmations   **M-1954**

Burials in Hazeldean Cemeteries
D   1835-1939   **M-7718**
includes:

    Bells Corners Anglican Church (including the Anglican Churches of Hazeldean, Stittsville, and Fallowfield at various dates)
    D   1883-1939 extracts   **M-7718**

Finch Township, Stormont Co.

Civil registers of the Surrogate Court for the Eastern and Johnstown Districts
B   1831, 1859, 1862-1865   **C-3030**
M   1831-1857, 1863, 1865   **C-3030** (index)
includes:

    Methodist Episcopal Church in Canada, Circuits in the Eastern District
    B   1831, 1862-1865   **C-3030**
    M   1831-1833, 1839-1841,
              1843-1844, 1846-1857,
              1863   **C-3030** (index)
    includes: Townships of Matilda, Mountain, Williamsburgh, and Winchester, Dundas Co.; Lochiel Township, Glengarry Co.; the Townships of Cornwall, Finch, and Osnabruck, Stormont Co.; and West Hawkesbury Township, Prescott Co.

(cont.)

Wesleyan Methodist Church in Canada, Circuits in the Eastern District
B   1859   **C-3030**
M   1833-1857   **C-3030** (index)
includes: Townships of Matilda, Mountain, Williamsburgh, and Winchester, Dundas Co.; the Townships of Edwardsburgh, and Oxford, Grenville Co.; Sheek Island, and the Townships of Cornwall, Finch, Osnabruck, and Roxborough, Stormont Co.; as well as the Brockville district, Leeds Co.; and other places in the Counties of Dundas, Stormont, and Glengarry

Presbyterian Church of the Rev. Isaac Purkis, Osnabruck Township
M   1840, 1842-1849   **C-3030** (index)

Osnabruck and Lunenburg Presbyterian Congregations
B   1848-1909   **C-3030**
M   1860-1900   **C-3030**
D   1907-1909   **C-3030**
includes:

Canada Presbyterian Church of Lunenburg and Osnabruck
M   1860-1900   **C-3030**
includes: Cornwall Township, Finch, Newington, Osnabruck, and Roxborough Township, Stormont Co.; the Indian Lands, Glengarry Co.; and the Townships of Williamsburgh, and Winchester, Dundas Co.

Civil registers of Stormont County
M   1866   **C-15758**
consists of:

Wesleyan Methodist Mission, Roxborough
M   1866   **C-15758**
includes: Townships of Finch, Osnabruck, and Roxborough

Farmer's Almanac diaries of Angus Alexander McMillan and Family of Glengarry County
BMD   1862-1910   **H-1808**
includes:

Finch Township
D   1862-1902   **H-1808**

Fitzroy Harbour, Carleton Co.

United Presbyterian Congregation
M   1852-1922   **M-1955**
includes: members who later joined congregations in Kilmaurs, Kinburn, Torbolton Township, Woodlawn, etc.

Fitzroy Township, Carleton Co.

Mississippi Circuit of the Methodist Episcopal (later, the Wesleyan Methodist) Church
B   1829-1843   **H-1809**
includes: places in the Townships of Beckwith, Lanark, Pakenham, and Ramsay, Lanark Co.; in the Townships of Horton, McNab, Pembroke, and Westmeath, Renfrew Co.; and Fitzroy Township, Carleton Co.

Civil registration lists and slips
BD   1870-1895   **H-1809**
M   1886, 1888-1889, 1891-1892, 1894   **H-1809**

St. Andrew's United Church of Canada, Pakenham, Lanark Co.
B   1891-1966   **M-7761**
M   1840-1973   **M-7761**
D   1901-1985   **M-7761**
includes:

Pakenham Wesleyan Methodist Circuit (later, Pakenham United Church of Canada), Lanark Co.
BD   1901-1918   **M-7761**
M   1858-1931   **M-7761**
membership (with some D),
    1864-1920   **M-7761**
includes: Fitzroy Township, Carleton Co.

St. Andrew's Presbyterian Church, Pakenham, Lanark Co.
M   1840-1883   **M-7761**
includes: Townships of Fitzroy, and Torbolton, Carleton Co.; Townships of Horton, and McNab, Renfrew Co.; and neighbouring settlements

St. Andrew's Presbyterian Church, Pakenham, Lanark Co., and Zion Presbyterian Church, Cedar Hill, Lanark Co.
B   1891-1921   **M-7761**
M   1896-1920   **M-7761**

Pakenham United Church of Canada Pastoral Charge, Lanark Co.
B   1909-1966   **M-7761**
M   1909-1973   **M-7761**
D   1909-1985   **M-7761**
includes: Cedar Hill, Lanark Co.; Antrim, and Fitzroy Township, Carleton Co.

Flamborough (West) Township, Wentworth Co.

Dundas Presbyterian Church, Dundas
M   1848-1852   **C-3028**
includes:

Ancaster, and West Flamboro
M   1848-1852   **C-3028**

Flower Station, Lanark Co.

Clayton United Church, Clayton
BMD   1805-1965   **M-3687** and **M-3688**
              1876-1965   **M-3243**
includes:

    Poland Presbyterian Church, Poland
    B   1876-1907, 1912   **M-3243**
    includes: Clyde Forks, Flower Station, South Lavant, South Poland, Lanark Co.; and Thurlow, Hastings Co.

    Watson's Corners Presbyterian Church, Watsons Corners
    M   1896-1926   **M-3243**
    includes: Flower Station, Poland, Lavant, and Dalhousie

Fort Frances (Fort Rainy Lake), Rainy River District
See: Hudson's Bay Company returns (page 3)

Fort Hope, Patricia District (later, Patricia portion of the Kenora District)

Fort Hope Anglican Church
BD   1895-1899   **C-3028**
M   1895-1896   **C-3028**

Fort Lac-la-Pluie (Fort Rainy Lake, Fort Frances), Rainy River District
See: Hudson's Bay Company returns (page 3)

Fort Rainy Lake (Fort Lac-la-Pluie, Fort Frances), Rainy River District
See: Hudson's Bay Company returns (page 3)

Fort William (later, Thunder Bay), Thunder Bay District

St. John the Evangelist Anglican Church, Thunder Bay
B   1873-1911   **M-2820**
        1911-1926   **M-2821**
M   1872-1913   **M-2820**
        1913-1917   **M-2821**
        1917-1925   **M-2820** (index)
        1925-1926   **M-2821**
D   1877-1911   **M-2820**
        1911-1926   **M-2821**
confirmations 1874-1910   **M-2820**
                  1911-1925   **M-2821**
parish list   1877, c. 1903   **M-2820**
includes:

    St. Ansgarius' Lutheran Church, Port Arthur
    BMD   1906-1912   **M-2821**
    confirmations 1911-1912   **M-2821**
    parish list c. 1907   **M-2821**

Franktown, Lanark Co.

Zion Memorial United Church, Carleton Place
BMD   1878-1933   **M-2209**
includes:

    St. Paul's Presbyterian Church, Franktown
    M   1897-1921   **M-2209**

    Beckwith and Franktown Presbyterian Church
    B   1914-1921   **M-2209**

Fredericksburg (Delhi), Norfolk Co.

Norfolk County Historical Society Collections
B   1783-1863   **M-283**
M   1807-1835   **M-274, M-275** and **M-277**
        1858-1897   **M-283**
D   1840-1899   **M-283**
includes:

    Hartford and Fredericksburg Regular Baptist Congregations
    B   1783-1863   **M-283**
    M   1858-1897   **M-283**
    D   1840-1899   **M-283**
    includes: Townships of Middleton, South Walsingham, Townsend, and Windham, Norfolk Co.; and Walpole Township, Haldimand Co.

(Pages 12941-12987)

Fredericksburgh Township, Lennox and Addington Co.

St. John's Anglican Church, Bath
B   1787-1813   **H-1810**
M   1787-1816   **H-1810**
D   1787-1813   **H-1810**
comprises:

    St. Thomas' Anglican Church, Ernestown Township
    B   1788-1813   **H-1810**
    M   1787-1813, 1814, 1816   **H-1810**
    D   1788-1813   **H-1810**
    includes: Amherst Island, and the Townships of Adolphustown, Camden, and Fredericksburg, Lennox and Addington Co.; the Townships of Ameliasburg, Marysburgh, and Sophiasburgh, Prince Edward Co.; the Townships of Sidney, and Thurlow, Hastings Co.; and Kingston, Frontenac Co.; as well as Oswego, New York, U.S.A.

(cont.)

ONTARIO

St. Paul's Anglican Church, Fredericksburg Township
B   1787-1813   **H-1810**
M   1788-1812   **H-1810**
D   1787-1813   **H-1810**
includes: Amherst Island, and the Townships of Adolphustown, Camden, Ernestown, and Richmond, Lennox and Addington Co.; the Townships of Ameliasburg, Hallowell, Marysburgh, and Sophiasburgh, Prince Edward Co.; the Townships of Sidney, and Thurlow, Hastings Co.; and the Townships of Cramahé, and Percy, Northumberland Co.; as well as Oswego, New York, U.S.A.

Presbyterian Mission of Ernestown, Fredericksburg, Adolphustown, and the Bay of Quinté region
B   1800-1841   **H-1810**
M   1800-1836   **H-1810**
D   1841   **H-1810**
comprises:

    Adolphustown Township, Lennox and Addington Co.
    B   1800-1811   **H-1810**
    M   1800-1821, 1831-1835   **H-1810**

    Amherst Island Township, Lennox and Addington Co.
    B   1834-1840   **H-1810**
    M   1802, 1816, 1819   **H-1810**

    Camden Township, Lennox and Addington Co.
    B   1800-1813, 1820, 1835-1839   **H-1810**
    M   1805-1821, 1832-1833   **H-1810**

    Ernestown Township, Lennox and Addington Co.
    B   1800-1813, 1819-1821, 1827, 1830, 1832, 1835   **H-1810**
    M   1800-1822, 1831-1835   **H-1810**

    Fredericksburg Township, Lennox and Addington Co.
    B   1800-1813, 1815, 1827, 1832, 1837-1840   **H-1810**
    M   1800-1822, 1831-1836   **H-1810**

    Richmond Township, Lennox and Addington Co.
    B   1800-1811, 1813-1814, 1824-1825, 1832-1833, 1838-1839   **H-1810**
    M   1802-1803, 1807-1821, 1832-1835   **H-1810**

    Sheffield Township, Lennox and Addington Co.
    B   1831, 1836, 1839   **H-1810**

    Rawdon Township, Hastings Co.
    B   1803   **H-1810**

    Sidney Township, Hastings Co.
    B   1800-1820, 1837, 1839   **H-1810**
    M   1803, 1806-1818   **H-1810**

    Thurlow Township, Hastings Co.
    B   1802-1816, 1821, 1839   **H-1810**
    M   1807, 1812, 1816, 1822   **H-1810**

    Tyendinaga Township, Hastings Co.
    B   1826-1837   **H-1810**

    Cramahé Township, Northumberland Co.
    B   1800-1806, 1811, 1818, 1820   **H-1810**

    Hamilton Township, Northumberland Co.
    B   1800-1803   **H-1810**

    Murray Township, Northumberland Co.
    B   1800-1821   **H-1810**
    M   1803, 1812   **H-1810**

    Ameliasburg Township, Prince Edward Co.
    B   1800-1822, 1827, 1829, 1833-1840   **H-1810**
    M   1807-1808, 1812, 1820   **H-1810**

    Hallowell Township, Prince Edward Co.
    B   1800-1810, 1812, 1820, 1826   **H-1810**
    M   1800-1820, 1831-1835   **H-1810**

    Marysburgh Township, Prince Edward Co.
    B   1800-1812, 1820, 1835, 1837   **H-1810**
    M   1800-1822, 1831-1835   **H-1810**

    Sophiasburgh Township, Prince Edward Co.
    B   1806-1822, 1828   **H-1810**
    M   1801-1822, 1831-1834   **H-1810**

    Kingston, Frontenac Co.
    B   1802-1811, 1820, 1822   **H-1810**
    M   1802, 1805-1822, 1831-1832, 1835   **H-1810**

    Loughborough Township, Frontenac Co.
    B   1804-1805, 1809-1811, 1830-1838   **H-1810**
    M   1809, 1812, 1818-1820   **H-1810**

    Pittsburg Township, Frontenac Co.
    B   1800-1809   **H-1810**

    Portland Township, Frontenac Co.
    B   1800-1811   **H-1810**
    M   1810, 1816   **H-1810**

(cont.)

French River, Parry Sound District

Journals of the Rev. Allen Salt, a Methodist Indian missionary in western Ontario
BMD   1854-1855, 1874-1899,
               1904   **C-15709**
includes:

    Parry Island Methodist Indian Mission, Georgian Bay
    BMD   1883-1899, 1904   **C-15709**
    includes: French River, Henvey Inlet, and Shawanaga Township in the Parry Sound District, as well as other Indian reserves in the region

Front of Yonge Township, Leeds Co.

St. Andrew's Presbyterian (Church of Scotland) Church, Toledo (formerly, Presbyterian Congregation of Kitley Township)
B   1846-1852, 1863-1913   **H-1810**
M   1863-1864, 1880-1881,
         1890-1893, 1903, 1907   **H-1810**
D   1894, 1897-1902, 1911   **H-1810**
members, 1847, 1850, 1854,
         1863-1913   **H-1810**
includes: Townships of Bastard, Elizabethtown, Front of Yonge, and Kitley, Leeds Co.; as well as Montague Township, Lanark Co.; and Wolford Township, Grenville Co.

Galt (later, Cambridge), Waterloo Co.

Civil registers of Waterloo County
B   1836-1861   **C-15758**
M   1854-1855   **C-15758**
D   1854-1855, 1858, 1860   **C-15758**
includes:

    Wesleyan Methodist Congregation, Galt (later, Cambridge)
    B   1860   **C-15758**
    M   1854-1855   **C-15758**
    includes: places in the Township of Waterloo, Waterloo Co.; Paris, and the Township of Brantford, Brant Co.; Esquesing Township, Halton Co.; and Chinguacousy Township, Peel Co.

    St. Andrew's Presbyterian (Church of Scotland) Church, Galt (later, Cambridge)
    B   1837, 1839, 1852-1855,
           1860   **C-15758**

    Associate Presbyterian Church of the Rev. James Strang, Galt (later, Cambridge)
    BD   1855   **C-15758**

Gananoque, Leeds Co.

Returns of coroners' inquests for the Counties of Leeds, and Grenville
D   1873   **C-15758**
includes: Townships of Augusta, and Wolford, Grenville Co.; as well as Brockville, Gananoque, and Elizabethtown Township, Leeds Co.

Georgian Bay Region, western Ontario

Journals of the Rev. Allen Salt, a Methodist Indian missionary in western Ontario
BMD   1854-1855, 1874-1899,
               1904   **C-15709**
includes:

    Christian and Beausoleil Islands Methodist Indian Mission, Georgian Bay
    BMD   1875-1882   **C-15709**

    Parry Island Methodist Indian Mission, Georgian Bay
    BMD   1883-1899, 1904   **C-15709**
    includes: French River, Henvey Inlet, and Shawanaga Township in the Parry Sound District, as well as other Indian reserves in the region

Glengarry County

Civil registers of the Surrogate Court for the Eastern and Johnstown Districts
B   1831, 1859, 1862-1865   **C-3030**
M   1831-1857, 1863, 1865   **C-3030** (index)
includes:

    Wesleyan Methodist Church in Canada, Circuits in the Eastern District
    B   1859   **C-3030**
    M   1833-1857   **C-3030** (index)
    includes: Townships of Matilda, Mountain, Williamsburgh, and Winchester, Dundas Co.; the Townships of Edwardsburgh, and Oxford, Grenville Co.; Sheek Island, and the Townships of Cornwall, Finch, Osnabruck, and Roxborough, Stormont Co.; as well as the Brockville district, Leeds Co.; and other places in the Counties of Dundas, Stormont, and Glengarry

Civil register for the Eastern District
M   1858-1869   **M-3205**
includes: Charlottenburg, Kenyon, Lancaster, and Lochiel Townships, Glengarry Co.; and Roxborough Township, Stormont Co.

(cont.)

Farmer's Almanac diaries of Angus Alexander McMillan and Family of Glengarry County
BMD   1862-1910   **H-1808**
comprises:

   Charlottenburg Township, Glengarry Co.
   MD   1862-1865   **H-1808**

   Kenyon Township, Glengarry Co.
   BMD   1862-1910   **H-1808**

        as well as, among others:

     Dunvegan, Kenyon Township
     BMD   1866-1903   **H-1808**

     Indian Lands, Kenyon Township
     BMD   1862-1886   **H-1808**

     Maxville, Kenyon Township
     MD   1885-1902   **H-1808**

   Lancaster Township, Glengarry Co.
   D   1868-1902   **H-1808**

   Lochiel Township, Glengarry Co.
   BMD   1862-1910   **H-1808**

        as well as, among others:

     Alexandria, Lochiel Township
     BMD   1862-1902   **H-1808**

     Breadalbane, Lochiel Township
     MD   1867-1868   **H-1808**

     Dalkeith, Lochiel Township
     MD   1863-1902   **H-1808**

     Laggan, Lochiel Township
     BMD   1874-1885   **H-1808**

     McCrimmon, Kenyon and Lochiel Townships
     BMD   1887-1902   **H-1808**

        and

   Prescott County
   MD   1863-1902   **H-1808**

        as well as:

     Caledonia Township, Prescott Co.
     BMD   1862-1903   **H-1808**

        and

   Cornwall Township, Stormont Co.
   D   1864-1886   **H-1808**

   Finch Township, Stormont Co.
   D   1862-1902   **H-1808**

   Roxborough Township, Stormont Co.
   D   1864-1902   **H-1808**

        also

   Sundry entries for other parts of Canada and the U.S.A.
   MD   1862-1903   **H-1808**

Goulbourn Township, Carleton Co.

St. Philip's Roman Catholic Church, Richmond
BMD   1836-1924   **M-2818**
includes:

   St. Clare's Roman Catholic Church (Goulbourn Mission), Dwyer Hill
   BMD   1891-1924   **M-2818**

Granton, Middlesex Co.

Anglican Parish of Kirkton with Granton and Saintsbury (including the Anglican Churches of: St. Paul's, Kirkton; Trinity, Prospect Hill; St. Patrick's, Saintsbury; and St. Thomas', Granton)
B   1862-1971   **M-2227**
MD   1863-1971   **M-2227**
includes: Township of Usborne, Huron Co.; Township of Blanshard, Perth Co.; and Township of Biddulph, Middlesex Co.

Grenville County

Civil registers for the Johnstown District, Grenville Co.
M   1801-1845   **C-3030** (index)
       1844-1851   **C-3031** (index, on **C-3030**)
includes: Leeds, Grenville, and Carleton Counties

Rideau Methodist Circuit
B   1814-1843   **C-3030**
includes: Lanark, and Grenville Counties; and Smith's Falls Methodist Circuit

Returns of coroners' inquests for the Counties of Leeds, and Grenville
D   1873   **C-15758**
includes: Townships of Augusta, and Wolford, Grenville Co.; as well as Brockville, Gananoque, and Elizabethtown Township, Leeds Co.

(cont.)

Grey County

Returns of coroners' inquests for Grey, Wellington, Bruce, [and Dufferin] Counties
D   1873   **C-15758**
includes: Durham, Owen Sound, and the Townships of Artemesia, Egremont, Euphrasia, Keppel, Normanby, Osprey, Proton, St. Vincent, and Sydenham, Grey Co.; and Melancthon Township, Dufferin Co.

Guelph Township, Wellington Co.

Civil registers of Waterloo County
B	1836-1861	**C-15758**
M	1854-1855	**C-15758**
D	1854-1855, 1858, 1860	**C-15758**

includes:

[Unorthodox Evangelical Lutheran] Congregation of the Rev. Frederick W. Bindemann, Waterloo Township, Waterloo Co.
M   1855   **C-15758**
includes: Berlin (later, Kitchener), and places in the Townships of North Dumfries, Waterloo, Wellesley, Wilmot, and Woolwich, Waterloo Co.; Carrick Township, Bruce Co.; Normanby Township, Grey Co.; the Townships of Blandford, and Blenheim, Oxford Co.; Hay Township, Huron Co.; the Townships of North Easthope, South Easthope, and Wallace, Perth Co.; the Townships of Peel, Guelph, Nichol, and Puslinch, Wellington Co.; and Hamilton, Wentworth Co.

[Mennonite] Congregation in New Germany [near Guelph]
BMD   1855   **C-15758**

Roman Catholic Mission, New Germany [near Guelph]
BD   1860   **C-15758**
includes: places in the Townships of Waterloo, and Woolwich, Waterloo Co.; and the Townships of Guelph, and Pilkington, Wellington Co.

Hagarty Township, Renfrew Co.

Our Lady of Czestochowa, Queen of Poland (Roman Catholic) Church (formerly, St. Stanislaus Kostka Roman Catholic Church, Hagarty Township), Wilno

BMD	1880-1884	**H-1456** (partial index)
B	1877-1880	**H-1456**
	1888-1940	**H-1456** (partial index)
M	1885-1937	**H-1456** (partial index)
	1928-1960	**H-1457**
D	1885-1928	**H-1456** (partial index)
	1928-1943, 1945	**H-1457**
	1961-1975	**H-1457**
ordinations, 1910, 1923-1924		**H-1456**
confirmations, 1912-1913		**H-1456**
	1947-1948, 1950, 1953, 1956, 1959	**H-1457**
first communions, 1946-1947, 1951, 1958-1959		**H-1457**

includes: Townships of Brudenell, Burns, Hagarty, Radcliffe, and Sherwood

(The registers are in French, Latin, and English. Miscellaneous related items are in Polish.)

Hagey, Waterloo Co.

Civil registers of Waterloo County
B	1836-1861	**C-15758**
M	1854-1855	**C-15758**
D	1854-1855, 1858, 1860	**C-15758**

includes:

Mennonite Congregation of [Bishop] Joseph Hagey, [Hagey or Breslau]
BD   1860   **C-15758**

Haldimand Township, Northumberland Co.

Civil register of Alnwick Township
M   1858-1864, 1867, 1869-1872, 1875-1882   **H-1810**
includes: Alderville, and the Townships of Hamilton, and Haldimand

Hallowell Township, Prince Edward Co.

St. John's Anglican Church, Bath, Lennox and Addington Co.
B	1787-1813	**H-1810**
M	1787-1816	**H-1810**
D	1787-1813	**H-1810**

includes:

St. Paul's Anglican Church, Fredericksburg Township
B	1787-1813	**H-1810**
M	1788-1812	**H-1810**
D	1787-1813	**H-1810**

includes: Amherst Island, and the Townships of Adolphustown, Camden, Ernestown, and Richmond, Lennox and Addington Co.; the Townships of Ameliasburg, Hallowell, Marysburgh, and Sophiasburgh, Prince Edward Co.; the Townships of Sidney, and Thurlow, Hastings Co.; and the Townships of Cramahé, and Percy, Northumberland Co.; as well as Oswego, New York, U.S.A.

(cont.)

Presbyterian Mission of Ernestown, Fredericksburg, Adolphustown, and the Bay of Quinté region
B	1800-1841	**H-1810**
M	1800-1836	**H-1810**
D	1841	**H-1810**

includes:

    Hallowell Township
B	1800-1810, 1812, 1820, 1826	**H-1810**
M	1800-1820, 1831-1835	**H-1810**

Hamilton, Wentworth Co.

Civil registers of Waterloo County
B	1836-1861	**C-15758**
M	1854-1855	**C-15758**
D	1854-1855, 1858, 1860	**C-15758**

includes:

    [Unorthodox Evangelical Lutheran] Congregation of the Rev. Frederick W. Bindemann, Waterloo Township, Waterloo Co.
M	1855	**C-15758**

    includes: Berlin (later, Kitchener), and places in the Townships of North Dumfries, Waterloo, Wellesley, Wilmot, and Woolwich, Waterloo Co.; Carrick Township, Bruce Co.; Normanby Township, Grey Co.; the Townships of Blandford, and Blenheim, Oxford Co.; Hay Township, Huron Co.; the Townships of North Easthope, South Easthope, and Wallace, Perth Co.; the Townships of Peel, Guelph, Nichol, and Puslinch, Wellington Co.; and Hamilton, Wentworth Co.

Returns of coroners' inquests for Wentworth County
D	1873	**C-15758**

includes: Hamilton

Personal record of marriages performed by the Reverend Dr. Isaac Tovell, of the Methodist Church of Canada and the United Church of Canada, Toronto
M	1875-1935 Index	**H-1810**

includes:

    Hamilton
M	1891-1897, 1904-1906 Index	**H-1810**

Hamilton Township, Northumberland Co.

Presbyterian Mission of Ernestown, Fredericksburg, Adolphustown, and the Bay of Quinté region
B	1800-1841	**H-1810**
M	1800-1836	**H-1810**
D	1841	**H-1810**

includes:

    Hamilton Township
B	1800-1803	**H-1810**

St. Paul's Presbyterian Church, Peterborough, Peterborough Co.
M	1834-1857	**H-1810**

includes: Townships of Asphodel, Douro, Dummer, Ennismore, Harvey, North Monaghan, Otonabee, and Smith, Peterborough Co.; the Townships of Hamilton, and South Monaghan in Northumberland Co.; the Township of Cavan, Durham Co.; and the Townships of Emily, and Ops, Victoria Co.

Civil register of Alnwick Township
M	1858-1864, 1867, 1869-1872, 1875-1882	**H-1810**

includes: Alderville, and the Townships of Hamilton, and Haldimand

Hanover, Grey Co.

Civil registers of Waterloo County
B	1836-1861	**C-15758**
M	1854-1855	**C-15758**
D	1854-1855, 1858, 1860	**C-15758**

includes:

    Evangelical Lutheran Church, Mannheim, New Dundee, and New Hamburg, Waterloo Co.
B	1858, 1860	**C-15758**
D	1860	**C-15758**

    includes: places in Wilmot Township, Waterloo Co.; in Brant, and Carrick Townships, Bruce Co.; in Hay, Stanley, and Tuckersmith Townships, Huron Co.; and Blenheim Township, Oxford Co.; as well as Hanover, Grey Co.; and Williamsburgh [Township], Dundas Co.

Harper, Lanark Co.

Zion Memorial United Church, Carleton Place
BMD	1878-1933	**M-2209**

includes:

    Lanark and Clayton Methodist Circuit
B	1884-1933	**M-2209**
M	1903-1931	**M-2209**
D	1902-1931	**M-2209**
circuit register 1903-1924		**M-2209**

    includes: Boyd, Erwins, Harper, Playfair, and Prestonvale

Hartford, Norfolk, and Haldimand Cos.

Norfolk County Historical Society Collections
B	1783-1863	**M-283**
M	1807-1835	**M-274, M-275** and **M-277**
	1858-1897	**M-283**
D	1840-1899	**M-283**

includes:

    Hartford and Fredericksburg (Delhi) Regular Baptist Congregations
B	1783-1863	**M-283**
M	1858-1897	**M-283**
D	1840-1899	**M-283**

    includes: Townships of Middleton, South Walsingham, Townsend, and Windham, Norfolk Co.; and Walpole Township, Haldimand Co.

(Pages 12941-12987)

Harvey Township, Peterborough Co.

St. Paul's Presbyterian Church, Peterborough
M	1834-1857	**H-1810**

includes: Townships of Asphodel, Douro, Dummer, Ennismore, Harvey, North Monaghan, Otonabee, and Smith, Peterborough Co.; the Townships of Hamilton, and South Monaghan in Northumberland Co.; the Township of Cavan, Durham Co.; and the Townships of Emily, and Ops, Victoria Co.

Hawkesbury, Prescott Co.

L'Orignal and Plantagenet Presbyterian Church
M	1854-1856	**C-3028**
	1852-1856	**H-1807**

includes:

    Hawkesbury
M	1853	**H-1807**

Hay Township, Huron Co.

Civil registers of Waterloo County
B	1836-1861	**C-15758**
M	1854-1855	**C-15758**
D	1854-1855, 1858, 1860	**C-15758**

includes:

    Evangelical Lutheran Church, Mannheim, New Dundee, and New Hamburg, Waterloo Co.
B	1858, 1860	**C-15758**
D	1860	**C-15758**

    includes: places in Wilmot Township, Waterloo Co.; in Brant and Carrick Townships, Bruce Co.; in Hay, Stanley, and Tuckersmith Townships, Huron Co.; and Blenheim Township, Oxford Co.; as well as Hanover, Grey Co.; and Williamsburgh [Township], Dundas Co.

    [Unorthodox Evangelical Lutheran] Congregation of the Rev. Frederick W. Bindemann, Waterloo Township, Waterloo Co.
M	1855	**C-15758**

    includes: Berlin (later, Kitchener), and places in the Townships of North Dumfries, Waterloo, Wellesley, Wilmot, and Woolwich, Waterloo Co.; Carrick Township, Bruce Co.; Normanby Township, Grey Co.; the Townships of Blandford, and Blenheim, Oxford Co.; Hay Township, Huron Co.; the Townships of North Easthope, South Easthope, and Wallace, Perth Co.; the Townships of Peel, Guelph, Nichol, and Puslinch, Wellington Co.; and Hamilton, Wentworth Co.

Hazeldean, Carleton Co.

Burials in Hazeldean Cemeteries
D	1835-1939	**M-7718**

comprises:

    Anglican Parish of March (including: St. Mary's Anglican Church, North March, and St. John's Anglican Church, South March)
D	1835-1862 extracts	**M-7718**

    Christ Church Anglican Church, Huntley Township
D	1852-1883 extracts	**M-7718**

    Bells Corners Anglican Church (including the Anglican Churches of Hazeldean, Stittsville, and Fallowfield, at various dates)
D	1883-1939 extracts	**M-7718**

    St. John the Baptist's Anglican Church, Richmond
D	1892, 1894 extracts	**M-7718**

    Maple Grove Cemetery Burial Permits
D	1897-1951	**M-7718**

Carp United Church, Carp
BMD	1858-1929	**M-816** and **M-817**

includes:

    St. Paul's Methodist Church, Carp
M	1898-1928	**M-816**
membership roll, 1893-1929		**M-816**

    includes: Hazeldean, Huntley, Marchhurst, and Stittsville

(cont.)

Heidelberg, Waterloo Co.

Civil registers of Waterloo County
B	1836-1861	**C-15758**
M	1854-1855	**C-15758**
D	1854-1855, 1858, 1860	**C-15758**

includes:

    Evangelical Association
    BD   1860   **C-15758**
    includes: Berlin (later, Kitchener), and other places in the Township of Waterloo, as well as Heidelberg, in the Townships of Wellesley, and Woolwich

Henvey Inlet, Parry Sound District

Journals of the Rev. Allen Salt, a Methodist Indian missionary in western Ontario
BMD   1854-1855, 1874-1899,
           1904   **C-15709**
includes:

    Parry Island Methodist Indian Mission, Georgian Bay
    BMD   1883-1899, 1904   **C-15709**
    includes: French River, Henvey Inlet, and Shawanaga Township in the Parry Sound District, as well as other Indian reserves in the region

Hillier Township, Prince Edward Co.

Civil registers
BMD   1880-1898   **H-1810**

Hopetown, Lanark Co.

Clayton United Church, Clayton
BMD	1805-1965	**M-3687** and **M-3688**
	1876-1965	**M-3243**

includes:

    St. Paul's, Middleville, and St. James', Dalhousie, United (Presbyterian) Pastoral Charge
B	1858-1864	**M-3687**
M	1859-1896, 1909-1910	**M-3687**
communion rolls	1858-1865,	**M-3687**
	1872-1954	**M-3688**

    includes: St. John's United Church, Hopetown, 1925-1941; and Rosetta United Church, 1935-1942

    St. Peter's Presbyterian Church, Darling Township
    B   1871-1878   **M-3687**
    communion rolls 1890-1942   **M-3688**
    includes: St. John's, Hopetown; Rosetta Presbyterian Congregation; and St. Peter's, Tatlock

    Clayton-Middleville Presbyterian Charge (later, Middleville United Church)
B	1881-1950	**M-3243**
D	1942-1957	**M-3688**
communion rolls 1942-1957		**M-3688**

    includes: Hopetown, Rosetta, Darling, and Tatlock

    St. Paul's, Middleville, and St. Peter's, Darling, Presbyterian Congregations
BD	1893-1965	**M-3688**
M	1897-1919	**M-3243**

    includes: Hopetown, Rosetta, and Tatlock

Horton Township, Renfrew Co.

Clarendon Anglican Mission (later, St. Paul's Anglican Church, Shawville, etc.), Pontiac Co., Que.
BM	1823-1842 extracts	**M-1303**
BMD	1842-1898	**M-1303** and **M-1304** (partial index)
	1864-1873	**M-2819** (index)
	1875-1916	**M-3114** (partial index)

includes:

    St. Paul's Anglican Church, Shawville, Pontiac Co., Que.
BMD	1842-1888	**M-1303** (partial index)
	1888-1898	**M-1304** (index)

    includes: Calumet-Island, and the Townships of Bristol, Clarendon, Leslie, Litchfield, Mansfield, Onslow, and Thorne, Pontiac Co.; and Eardley Township, Gatineau Co., Que.; as well as Horton Township, Renfrew Co., Ont.

Mississippi Circuit, of the Methodist Episcopal (later, the Wesleyan Methodist) Church
B   1829-1843   **H-1809**
includes: places in the Townships of Beckwith, Lanark, Pakenham, and Ramsay, Lanark Co.; in the Townships of Horton, McNab, Pembroke, and Westmeath, Renfrew Co.; and Fitzroy Township, Carleton Co.

St. Andrew's United Church of Canada, Pakenham, Lanark Co.
B	1891-1966	**M-7761**
M	1840-1973	**M-7761**
D	1901-1985	**M-7761**

includes:

    St. Andrew's Presbyterian Church, Pakenham, Lanark Co.
    M   1840-1883   **M-7761**
    includes: Townships of Fitzroy, and Torbolton, Carleton Co.; Townships of Horton, and McNab, Renfrew Co.; and neighbouring settlements

(cont.)

Huntley, Carleton Co.

Carp United Church, Carp
BMD 1858-1929 **M-816** and **M-817**
includes:

   St. Paul's Methodist Church, Carp
   M 1898-1928 **M-816**
   membership roll 1893-1929 **M-816**
   includes: Hazeldean, Huntley, Marchhurst, and Stittsville

Huntley Township, Carleton Co.

Burials in Hazeldean Cemeteries
D 1835-1939 **M-7718**
includes:

   Christ Church Anglican Church, Huntley Township
   D 1852-1883 extracts **M-7718**

Indian Lands, Glengarry Co.

Civil registers of the Surrogate Court for the Eastern and Johnstown Districts
B 1831, 1859, 1862-1865 **C-3030**
M 1831-1857, 1863, 1865 **C-3030** (index)
includes:

   Congregational Church, 9th Concession, Lochiel Township
   M 1833-1835, 1838-1840,
       1843-1844 **C-3030** (index)
   includes: places in the Townships of Kenyon (including the Indian Lands) and Lochiel, Glengarry Co.; and in the Townships of Caledonia, East Hawkesbury, and West Hawkesbury, Prescott Co.

   St. John's Presbyterian (Church of Scotland) Church, Cornwall, Stormont Co.
   M 1831-1850, 1855-1857 **C-3030** (index)
   includes: Townships of Charlottenburg, Kenyon (including the Indian Lands), and Lancaster, Glengarry Co.; and Roxborough Township, Stormont Co.

Civil registers for the Eastern District
M 1858-1869 **M-3205**
includes:

   Regular Baptist Church, Indian Lands, [Kenyon Township]
   M 1862-1863 **M-3205**

   Congregational Church, Indian Lands, [Kenyon Township]
   M 1859, 1862 **M-3205**

Osnabruck and Lunenburg Presbyterian Congregations, Stormont Co.
B 1848-1909 **C-3030**
M 1860-1900 **C-3030**
D 1907-1909 **C-3030**
includes:

   Canada Presbyterian Church of Lunenburg and Osnabruck, Stormont Co.
   M 1860-1900 **C-3030**
   includes: Cornwall Township, Finch, Newington, Osnabruck, and Roxborough Township, Stormont Co.; the Indian Lands, Glengarry Co.; and the Townships of Williamsburgh, and Winchester, Dundas Co.

Farmer's Almanac diaries of Angus Alexander McMillan and Family of Glengarry County
BMD 1862-1910 **H-1808**
includes:

   Kenyon Township
   BMD 1862-1910 **H-1808**

   as well as, among others:

   Indian Lands, Kenyon Township
   BMD 1862-1886 **H-1808**

Indian Lands, western Ontario

Journals of the Rev. Allen Salt, a Methodist Indian missionary in western Ontario
BMD 1854-1855, 1874-1899,
       1904 **C-15709**
comprises:

   Lac-La-Pluie Wesleyan Methodist Indian Mission, Rainy River District
   BMD 1854-1855 **C-15709**

   Muncey Methodist Indian Mission, Middlesex County
   BMD 1874 **C-15709**

   Christian and Beausoleil Islands Methodist Indian Mission, Georgian Bay
   BMD 1875-1882 **C-15709**

   Parry Island Methodist Indian Mission, Georgian Bay
   BMD 1883-1899, 1904 **C-15709**
   includes: French River, Henvey Inlet, and Shawanaga Township in the Parry Sound District, as well as other Indian reserves in the region

(cont.)

ONTARIO

Inkerman, Dundas Co.

Wesleyan Methodist Church of America
B	1898-1909 **MG 9, D 7-67,**	Fiche 5
M	1904-1919	Fiche 4
	1922-1943	Fiche 5
MD	1896-1938 (notes)	Fiche 3
members	1896-1938	Fiches 3 and 4

includes: Mountain Township

Johnstown District (later, Counties of Grenville, Leeds, and Carleton)

Civil registers
M	1801-1845	**C-3030** (index)
	1844-1851	**C-3031** (index on **C-3030**)

includes: Leeds, Grenville, and Carleton Counties

Civil registers of the Surrogate Court for the Eastern and Johnstown Districts
B	1831, 1859, 1862-1865	**C-3030**
M	1831-1857, 1863, 1865	**C-3030** (index)

comprises:

[Anglican] Parish, Cornwall Township, Stormont Co.
M 1854-1857 **C-3030** (index)

[Anglican] Parish, Williamsburgh Township, Dundas Co.
M 1855 **C-3030** (index)

Baptist Congregation, Breadalbane, Glengarry Co.
M 1834-1850 **C-3030** (index)
includes: places in the Townships of Kenyon, and Lochiel, Glengarry Co.; as well as in the Townships of Caledonia, East Hawkesbury, West Hawkesbury, and North Plantagenet, Prescott Co.

Lutheran Congregation, Williamsburgh Township, Dundas Co.
M 1832-1843, 1847-1848 **C-3030** (index)
includes: Townships of Matilda, Williamsburgh, and Winchester, Dundas Co.; the Townships of Cornwall, and Osnabruck, Stormont Co.; and Charlottenburg Township, Glengarry Co.

Evangelical Lutheran Congregations, Williamsburg Township, Dundas Co.
M 1842-1844, 1846-1857 **C-3030** (index)
includes: Townships of Matilda, Williamsburgh, and Winchester, Dundas Co.; the Townships of Cornwall, and Osnabruck, Stormont Co.; and Charlottenburg Township, Glengarry Co.

(cont.)

Methodist Episcopal Church in Canada, Circuits in the Eastern District
B	1831, 1862-1865	**C-3030**
M	1831-1833, 1839-1841, 1843-1844, 1846-1857, 1863	**C-3030** (index)

includes: Townships of Matilda, Mountain, Williamsburgh, and Winchester, Dundas Co.; Lochiel Township, Glengarry Co.; the Townships of Cornwall, Finch, and Osnabruck, Stormont Co.; and West Hawkesbury Township, Prescott Co.

Presbyterian (Free Church) Congregation of the Rev. Hugh Campbell, Cornwall, Stormont Co.
M 1854, [1855] **C-3030** (index)

Presbyterian (Free Church) Congregation of the Rev. Robert Lyle
M 1831-1837 **C-3030** (index)
includes: Townships of Matilda, and Williamsburgh, Dundas Co.; and the Townships of Cornwall, and Osnabruck, Stormont Co.

Presbyterian Church of the Rev. Isaac Purkis, Osnabruck Township, Stormont Co.
M 1840, 1842-1849 **C-3030** (index)

St. Andrew's (Presbyterian) Church of the Rev. Peter McVicar, Martintown, Glengarry Co.
M 1857 **C-3030** (index)
includes: Townships of Charlottenburg, and Kenyon, Glengarry Co.; and Roxborough Township, Stormont Co.

[Presbyterian] Congregation of the Rev. Peter Watson, Williamstown, Glengarry Co.
M 1865 **C-3030** (index)
includes: Martintown, and Williamstown, and other places in Charlottenburg Township, as well as the Townships of Lancaster, and Lochiel, Glengarry Co.; Cornwall Township, Stormont Co.; and the Townships of North Plantagenet, and South Plantagenet, Prescott Co.

Congregation of the Rev. Aeneas McLean, Dalhousie Mills, Glengarry Co.
M 1848 **C-3030** (index)

Congregation of the Rev. John W. Sills
M 1850-1851 **C-3030** (index)
includes: Williamsburgh Township, Dundas Co.; and the Townships of Cornwall, and Osnabruck, Stormont Co.

Congregation of the Rev. E. Sallows
M 1851 **C-3030** (index)
includes: Townships of Osnabruck, and Roxborough, Stormont Co.

(cont.)

Congregational Church, 9th Concession, Lochiel Township, Glengarry Co.
M   1833-1835, 1838-1840,
1843-1844   **C-3030** (index)
includes: places in the Townships of Kenyon (including the Indian Lands) and Lochiel, Glengarry Co.; and in the Townships of Caledonia, East Hawkesbury, and West Hawkesbury, Prescott Co.

Wesleyan Methodist Church, Matilda Township, Dundas Co.
M   1831-1837, 1839-1844,
1846-1849   **C-3030** (index)
includes: Townships of Matilda, and Mountain, Dundas Co.; and Edwardsburgh Township, Grenville Co.

Wesleyan Methodist Church in Canada, Circuits in the Eastern District
B   1859   **C-3030**
M   1833-1857   **C-3030** (index)
includes: Townships of Matilda, Mountain, Williamsburgh, and Winchester, Dundas Co.; the Townships of Edwardsburgh, and Oxford, Grenville Co.; Sheek Island, and the Townships of Cornwall, Finch, Osnabruck, and Roxborough, Stormont Co.; as well as the Brockville district, Leeds Co.; and other places in the Counties of Dundas, Stormont, and Glengarry

St. John's Presbyterian (Church of Scotland) Church, Cornwall, Stormont Co.
M   1831-1850, 1855-1857   **C-3030** (index)
includes: Townships of Charlottenburg, Kenyon (including the Indian Lands), and Lancaster, Glengarry Co.; and Roxborough Township, Stormont Co.

Presbyterian (Church of Scotland) Church, Lancaster Township, Glengarry Co.
M   1834-1836   **C-3030** (index)
includes: Coteau-du-Lac, and Rivière-Beaudette, Soulanges Co., Que.

Presbyterian (Church of Scotland) Church, Kenyon Township, Glengarry Co.
M   1865   **C-3030** (index)
includes: Cambridge Township, Russell Co.; and Roxborough Township, Stormont Co.

Presbyterian Church of the Rev. John Dickey, Williamsburgh, Matilda, and Winchester Townships, Dundas Co.
M   1836-1849   **C-3030** (index)
includes: Mountain Township, Dundas Co.; and Osnabruck Township, Stormont Co.

Presbyterian (Church of Scotland) Church of the Rev. T. Scott, Williamsburgh, Matilda, and Winchester Townships, Dundas Co.
M   1853-1857   **C-3030** (index)
includes: Mountain Township, Dundas Co.; and Osnabruck Township, Stormont Co.

Congregational Church, Martintown, Glengarry Co.
M   1854   **C-3030** (index)

St. Andrew's Roman Catholic Parish, St. Andrew's, Stormont Co.
M   1848   **C-3030** (index)

Roman Catholic Mission of Cornwall, Stormont Co.
M   [1848]   **C-3030** (index)

Kemptville, comté de Grenville

Exaltation-de-la-Ste-Croix (Église catholique)
BMD   1844-1874   **C-3029** (index)

Kenyon Township, Glengarry Co.

Civil registers of the Surrogate Court for the Eastern and Johnstown Districts
B   1831, 1859, 1862-1865   **C-3030**
M   1831-1857, 1863, 1865   **C-3030** (index)
includes:

Baptist Congregation, Breadalbane, Glengarry Co.
M   1834-1850   **C-3030** (index)
includes: places in the Townships of Kenyon, and Lochiel, Glengarry Co.; as well as in the Townships of Caledonia, East Hawkesbury, West Hawkesbury, and North Plantagenet, Prescott Co.

Congregational Church, 9th Concession, Lochiel Township, Glengarry Co.
M   1833-1835, 1838-1840,
1843-1844   **C-3030** (index)
includes: places in the Townships of Kenyon (including the Indian Lands) and Lochiel, Glengarry Co.; and in the Townships of Caledonia, East Hawkesbury, and West Hawkesbury, Prescott Co.

St. John's Presbyterian (Church of Scotland) Church, Cornwall, Stormont Co.
M   1831-1850, 1855-1857   **C-3030** (index)
includes: Townships of Charlottenburg, Kenyon (including the Indian Lands), and Lancaster, Glengarry Co.; and Roxborough Township, Stormont Co.

Presbyterian (Church of Scotland) Church, Kenyon Township, Glengarry Co.
M   1865   **C-3030** (index)
includes: Cambridge Township, Russell Co.; and Roxborough Township, Stormont Co.

St. Andrew's (Presbyterian) Church of the Rev. Peter McVicar, Martintown, Glengarry Co.
M   1857   **C-3030** (index)
includes: Townships of Charlottenburg, and Kenyon, Glengarry Co.; and Roxborough Township, Stormont Co.

(cont.)

Civil registers for the Eastern District
M   1858-1869   **M-3205**
includes:

   Regular Baptist Church, Indian Lands, [Kenyon Township]
   M   1862-1863   **M-3205**

   Congregational Church, Indian Lands, [Kenyon Township]
   M   1859, 1862   **M-3205**

   Presbyterian Church of Canada Congregation, Kenyon Township
   M   1859-1869   **M-3205**

Farmer's Almanac diaries of Angus Alexander McMillan and Family of Glengarry County
BMD   1862-1910   **H-1808**
includes:

   Kenyon Township, Glengarry Co.
   BMD   1862-1910   **H-1808**

          as well as, among others:

   Dunvegan, Kenyon Township
   BMD   1866-1903   **H-1808**

   Indian Lands, Kenyon Township
   BMD   1862-1886   **H-1808**

   Maxville, Kenyon Township
   MD   1885-1902   **H-1808**

   McCrimmon, Kenyon and Lochiel Townships
   BMD   1887-1902   **H-1808**

Keppel Township, Grey Co.

Returns of coroners' inquests for Grey, Wellington, Bruce, [and Dufferin] Counties
D   1873   **C-15758**
includes: Durham, Owen Sound, and the Townships of Artemesia, Egremont, Euphrasia, Keppel, Normanby, Osprey, Proton, St. Vincent, and Sydenham, Grey Co.; and Melancthon Township, Dufferin Co.

Kilmaurs, Carleton Co.

United Presbyterian Congregation, Fitzroy Harbour
M   1852-1922   **M-1955**
includes: members who later joined congregations in Kilmaurs, Kinburn, Torbolton Township, Woodlawn, etc.

Kinburn, Carleton Co.

United Presbyterian Congregation, Fitzroy Harbour
M   1852-1922   **M-1955**
includes: members who later joined congregations in Kilmaurs, Kinburn, Torbolton Township, Woodlawn, etc.

Carp United Church, Carp
BMD   1858-1929   **M-816** and **M-817**
includes:

   Carp, Lowry, and Kinburn Presbyterian Congregations
   B   1860-1929   **M-817**
   M   1880-1903   **M-817**
   D   1880-1927   **M-817**
   membership rolls 1880-1929   **M-817**

Kingston, Frontenac Co.

St. John's Anglican Church, Bath, Lennox and Addington Co.
B   1787-1813   **H-1810**
M   1787-1816   **H-1810**
D   1787-1813   **H-1810**
includes:

   St. Thomas' Anglican Church, Ernestown Township
   B   1788-1813   **H-1810**
   M   1787-1813, 1814, 1816   **H-1810**
   D   1788-1813   **H-1810**
   includes: Amherst Island, and the Townships of Adolphustown, Camden, and Fredericksburg, Lennox and Addington Co.; the Townships of Ameliasburg, Marysburgh, and Sophiasburgh, Prince Edward Co.; the Townships of Sidney, and Thurlow, Hastings Co.; and Kingston, Frontenac Co.; as well as Oswego, New York, U.S.A.

Presbyterian Mission of Ernestown, Fredericksburg, Adolphustown, and the Bay of Quinté region
B   1800-1841   **H-1810**
M   1800-1836   **H-1810**
D   1841   **H-1810**
includes:

   Kingston
   B   1802-1811, 1820, 1822   **H-1810**
   M   1802, 1805-1822,
            1831-1832, 1835   **H-1810**

Register of the Royal Canadian Artillery (Army Book 91) — non-commissioned officers and men
B   1871-1911   **C-11775** (index)
M   1870-1915   **C-11775** (index)
D   1895-1905   **C-11775** (index)
includes: Kingston, Ont.; as well as a few entries for Lévis, and Québec, Que.; and for Aldershot, and Barntfield, [England]; and Benares, and Cawnpore, [India]

Kirkhill, Glengarry Co.

Lochiel Church of Scotland Parish (later, St. Columba's Presbyterian Church, Kirkhill)
B/M	1820-1848, 1850-1857	**M-2246** (originals)
	1820-1848, 1850-1857	**H-1807** (copies, index)
B	1858-1872, 1881-1884	**M-2246** (originals)
	1858-1872, 1881-1884	**H-1807** (copies, index)
	1909-1911	**M-2246** (originals)
	1909-1911	**H-1807** (copies, index)

Kirkton, Huron, and Perth Cos.

Anglican Parish of Kirkton with Granton and Saintsbury (including the Anglican Churches of: St. Paul's, Kirkton; Trinity, Prospect Hill; St. Patrick's, Saintsbury; and St. Thomas', Granton)
B	1862-1971	**M-2227**
MD	1863-1971	**M-2227**

includes: Township of Usborne, Huron Co.; Township of Blanshard, Perth Co.; and Township of Biddulph, Middlesex Co.

Kitchener (formerly, Berlin), Waterloo Co.

Civil registers of Waterloo County
B	1836-1861	**C-15758**
M	1854-1855	**C-15758**
D	1854-1855, 1858, 1860	**C-15758**

includes:

German Baptist Church of the Rev. Henry Schneider
B	1861	**C-15758**
M	1855*	**C-15758**
D	1855*, 1860	**C-15758**

includes: Berlin (later, Kitchener), as well as other places in the Townships of Waterloo, Wilmot, and Woolwich, Waterloo Co.; and in South Easthope Township, Perth Co.

*In German

Evangelical Association
BD	1860	**C-15758**

includes: Berlin (later, Kitchener), and other places in the Township of Waterloo, as well as Heidelberg, in the Townships of Wellesley, and Woolwich

[Unorthodox Evangelical Lutheran] Congregation of the Rev. Frederick W. Bindemann, Waterloo Township
M	1855	**C-15758**

includes: Berlin (later, Kitchener), and places in the Townships of North Dumfries, Waterloo, Wellesley, Wilmot, and Woolwich, Waterloo Co.; Carrick Township, Bruce Co.; Normanby Township, Grey Co.; the Townships of Blandford, and Blenheim, Oxford Co.; Hay Township, Huron Co.; the Townships of North Easthope, South Easthope, and Wallace, Perth Co.; the Townships of Peel, Guelph, Nichol, and Puslinch, Wellington Co.; and Hamilton, Wentworth Co.

Wesleyan Methodist Church, Berlin (later, Kitchener)
B	1860	**C-15758**

includes: places in the Townships of Waterloo, and Wellesley

New Jerusalem (Swedenborgian) Church, Berlin (later, Kitchener)
B	1855-1860	**C-15758**
D	1860	**C-15758**

includes: Waterloo Township, and various places in the Townships of Wilmot and Wellesley

Roman Catholic Mission, Berlin (later, Kitchener)
BD	1860	**C-15758**

includes: places in the Townships of Waterloo and Wilmot

Kitley Township, Leeds Co.

St. Francis-Xavier Roman Catholic Church, Brockville
B	1835-1859	**M-4613**
	1854-1860	**M-4613** (index)
	1882-1893	**M-4613**
M	1841-1847	**M-4613**
	1855-1856	**M-4613** (index)
confirmations	1847	**M-4613**

includes: records of the Bellamy Pond and Toledo area of Kitley Township, Leeds Co.

St. Andrew's Presbyterian (Church of Scotland) Church, Toledo (formerly, Presbyterian Congregation of Kitley Township)
B	1846-1852, 1863-1913	**H-1810**
M	1863-1864, 1880-1881, 1890-1893, 1903, 1907	**H-1810**
D	1894, 1897-1902, 1911	**H-1810**
members,	1847, 1850, 1854, 1863-1913	**H-1810**

includes: Townships of Bastard, Elizabethtown, Front of Yonge, and Kitley, Leeds Co.; as well as Montague Township, Lanark Co.; and Wolford Township, Grenville Co.

Lac-La-Pluie, Rainy River District

Journals of the Rev. Allen Salt, a Methodist Indian missionary in western Ontario
BMD	1854-1855, 1874-1899, 1904	**C-15709**

includes:

Lac-La-Pluie Wesleyan Methodist Indian Mission
BMD	1854-1855	**C-15709**

(cont.)

Lac-la-Pluie, Fort (Fort Rainy Lake, Fort Frances), Rainy River District
See: Hudson's Bay Company returns (page 3)

Laggan, Glengarry Co.

Farmer's Almanac diaries of Angus Alexander McMillan and Family of Glengarry County
BMD	1862-1910	**H-1808**

includes:

Lochiel Township
BMD	1862-1910	**H-1808**

as well as, among others:

Laggan, Lochiel Township
BMD	1874-1885	**H-1808**

Lakefield (North Douro), Peterborough Co.

Civil registers of Peterborough County
M	1859-1873	**H-1810**

consists of:

Christ Church Anglican Church, Lakefield
M	1859-1873	**H-1810**

includes: Lakefield (North Douro), and Peterborough, as well as the Townships of Douro, Dummer, Otonabee, and Smith, Peterborough Co.; and Lindsay, Victoria Co.

Lanark, Lanark Co.

Zion Memorial United Church, Carleton Place
BMD	1878-1933	**M-2209**

includes:

Lanark and Clayton Methodist Circuit
B	1890-1933	**M-2209**
M	1903-1931	**M-2209**
D	1902-1931	**M-2209**
circuit register	1903-1921	**M-2209**

Clayton United Church, Clayton
BMD	1805-1965	**M-3687** and **M-3688**
	1876-1965	**M-3243**

includes:

Lanark Methodist Church
M	1896-1926	**M-3243**

Lanark County

Rideau Methodist Circuit
B	1814-1843	**C-3030**

includes: Lanark, and Grenville Counties; and Smith's Falls Methodist Circuit

(cont.)

Civil registers of Ontario
M	1816-1869	**M-5497**
	1858-1869	**M-7092**

includes:

Bathurst District (later, Carleton and Lanark Counties)
M	1831-1848	**M-5497**

Lanark County
M	1858-1869	**M-5497**

Lanark Township, Lanark Co.

Mississippi Circuit of the Methodist Episcopal (later, the Wesleyan Methodist) Church
B	1829-1843	**H-1809**

includes: places in the Townships of Beckwith, Lanark, Pakenham, and Ramsay, Lanark Co.; in the Townships of Horton, McNab, Pembroke, and Westmeath, Renfrew Co.; and Fitzroy Township, Carleton Co.

Lancaster, Glengarry Co.

Civil registers of the Surrogate Court for the Eastern and Johnstown Districts
B	1831, 1859, 1862-1865	**C-3030**
M	1831-1857, 1863, 1865	**C-3030** (index)

includes:

St. John's Presbyterian (Church of Scotland) Church, Cornwall, Stormont Co.
M	1831-1850, 1855-1857	**C-3030** (index)

includes: Townships of Charlottenburg, Kenyon (including the Indian Lands), and Lancaster, Glengarry Co.; and Roxborough Township, Stormont Co.

Presbyterian (Church of Scotland) Church, Lancaster Township
M	1834-1836	**C-3030** (index)

includes: Coteau-du-Lac, and Rivière-Beaudette, Soulanges Co., Que.

[Presbyterian] Congregation of the Rev. Peter Watson, Williamstown
M	1865	**C-3030** (index)

includes: Martintown, and Williamstown, and other places in Charlottenburg Township, as well as the Townships of Lancaster, and Lochiel, Glengarry Co.; Cornwall Township, Stormont Co.; and the Townships of North Plantagenet, and South Plantagenet, Prescott Co.

(cont.)

Civil registers for the Eastern District
M 1858-1869 **M-3205**
includes:

 Canada Presbyterian Church, Lancaster and Dalhousie
 Mills
 M 1860-1861, 1863-1864,
    1866-1868 **M-3205**

Lancaster Township, Glengarry Co.

Farmer's Almanac diaries of Angus Alexander McMillan
and Family of Glengarry Co.
BMD 1862-1910 **H-1808**
includes:

 Lancaster Township
 D 1868-1902 **H-1808**

L'Assomption-de-la-Pointe-de-Montréal-du-Détroit (par
après, Sandwich), comté d'Essex
Voir: Sandwich

Latshaws, Waterloo Co.

Civil registers of Waterloo County
B 1836-1861 **C-15758**
M 1854-1855 **C-15758**
D 1854-1855, 1858, 1860 **C-15758**
includes:

 Mennonite Congregation of the Rev. Moses S. Bowman,
 Latshaws, Wilmot Township
 BD 1860 **C-15758**

Lavant Township, Lanark Co.

Clayton United Church, Clayton
BMD 1805-1965 **M-3687** and
        M-3688
   1876-1965 **M-3243**
includes:

 Poland Presbyterian Congregation, Poland
 B 1876-1907, 1912 **M-3243**
 includes: Clyde Forks, Flower Station, South Lavant,
    South Poland, Lanark Co.; and Thurlow,
    Hastings Co.

 Watson's Corners Presbyterian Church, Watsons Corners
 M 1896-1926 **M-3243**
 includes: Flower Station, Poland, Lavant, and Dalhousie
    Township

Leeds County

Civil registers for the Johnstown District, Grenville Co.
M 1801-1845 **C-3030** (index)
   1844-1851 **C-3031** (index on
         C-3030)
includes: Leeds, Grenville, and Carleton Counties

Returns of coroners' inquests for the Counties of Leeds,
and Grenville
D 1873 **C-15758**
includes: Brockville, Gananoque, and Elizabethtown
    Township, Leeds Co.; as well as the Townships of
    Augusta, and Wolford, Grenville Co.

Lindsay, Victoria Co.

Civil registers of Peterborough County
M 1859-1873 **H-1810**
consists of:

 Christ Church Anglican Church, Lakefield
 M 1859-1873 **H-1810**
 includes: Lakefield (North Douro), and Peterborough, as
    well as the Townships of Douro, Dummer,
    Otonabee, and Smith, Peterborough Co.; and
    Lindsay, Victoria Co.

Loch Winnoch, Renfrew Co.

Lochwinnoch Presbyterian Church
B 1867-1919 **M-2368**
M 1883-1906 **M-2368**
communion rolls 1887-1918 **M-2368**
includes: Castleford, Dewar's Settlement, and Stewartville

Lochiel, Glengarry Co.

L'Orignal and Plantagenet Presbyterian Church,
Prescott Co.
M 1854-1856 **C-3028**
   1852-1856 **H-1807**
includes:

 Lochiel
 M 1854 **H-1807**

Lochiel Township, Glengarry Co.

Lochiel Church of Scotland Parish (later, St. Columba's
Presbyterian Church, Kirkhill)
BM 1820-1848, 1850-1857 **M-2246** (originals)
    1820-1848, 1850-1857 **H-1807** (copies,
          index)
B   1858-1872, 1881-1884 **M-2246** (originals)
    1858-1872, 1881-1884 **H-1807** (copies,
          index)

(cont.)

B	1909-1911	**M-2246** (originals)
	1909-1911	**H-1807** (copies, index)

Civil registers of the Surrogate Court for the Eastern and Johnstown Districts

B	1831, 1859, 1862-1865	**C-3030**
M	1831-1857, 1863, 1865	**C-3030** (index)

includes:

Baptist Congregation, Breadalbane
M	1834-1850	**C-3030** (index)

includes: places in the Townships of Kenyon, and Lochiel, Glengarry Co.; as well as in the Townships of Caledonia, East Hawkesbury, West Hawkesbury, and North Plantagenet, Prescott Co.

Congregational Church, 9th Concession, Lochiel Township
M	1833-1835, 1838-1840, 1843-1844	**C-3030** (index)

includes: places in the Townships of Kenyon (including the Indian Lands) and Lochiel, Glengarry Co.; and in the Townships of Caledonia, East Hawkesbury, and West Hawkesbury, Prescott Co.

Methodist Episcopal Church in Canada, Circuits in the Eastern District
B	1831, 1862-1865	**C-3030**
M	1831-1833, 1839-1841, 1843-1844, 1846-1857, 1863	**C-3030** (index)

includes: Townships of Matilda, Mountain, Williamsburgh, and Winchester, Dundas Co.; Lochiel Township, Glengarry Co.; the Townships of Cornwall, Finch, and Osnabruck, Stormont Co.; and West Hawkesbury Township, Prescott Co.

[Presbyterian] Congregation of the Rev. Peter Watson, Williamstown, Glengarry Co.
M	1865	**C-3030** (index)

includes: Martintown, and Williamstown, and other places in Charlottenburg Township, as well as the Townships of Lancaster, and Lochiel, Glengarry Co.; Cornwall Township, Stormont Co.; and the Townships of North Plantagenet, and South Plantagenet, Prescott Co.

Civil registers for the Eastern District
M	1858-1869	**M-3205**

includes:

Presbyterian Church (Church of Scotland), Lochiel Township
M	1858, 1861, 1863-1865, 1869	**M-3205**

Presbyterian (Free Church) Congregation, Lochiel Township
M	1858, 1860-1869	**M-3205**

(cont.)

Baptist Congregation of Breadalbane
M	1858-1886	**H-1807**

includes: places in the Township of Lochiel, Glengarry Co.; as well as in the Townships of East Hawkesbury, and West Hawkesbury, Prescott Co.

Farmer's Almanac diaries of Angus Alexander McMillan and Family of Glengarry County
BMD	1862-1910	**H-1808**

includes:

Lochiel Township
BMD	1862-1910	**H-1808**

as well as, among others:

Alexandria, Lochiel Township
BMD	1862-1902	**H-1808**

Breadalbane, Lochiel Township
MD	1867-1868	**H-1808**

Dalkeith, Lochiel Township
MD	1863-1902	**H-1808**

Laggan, Lochiel Township
BMD	1874-1885	**H-1808**

McCrimmon, Kenyon and Lochiel Townships
BMD	1887-1902	**H-1808**

London District (later, Counties of Norfolk, Oxford, Middlesex, and Huron)

Civil registers
M	1784-1833	**C-3031** (index)

includes: Norfolk, Oxford, and Middlesex Counties

Norfolk County Historical Society Collections
B	1783-1863	**M-283**
M	1807-1835	**M-274, M-275** and **M-277**
	1858-1897	**M-283**
D	1840-1899	**M-283**

includes:

Civil registers of Norfolk County
M	1807-1813	**M-274**
	1807-1815	**M-274**
	1826-1828	**M-275**
	1831-1835	**M-277**

includes: Townships of Charlotteville, and Woodhouse, in the London District

(Pages 829-837, 1040-1041, 2121-2123, 3940-3991)

London Township, Middlesex Co.

St. Paul's Anglican Church
BM	1829-1834	**C-3029**

L'Orignal, Prescott Co.

L'Orignal and Plantagenet Presbyterian Church
M	1854-1856	**C-3028**
	1852-1856	**H-1807**

comprises:

L'Orignal
M	1852-1856	**H-1807**
	1855-1856	**C-3028**

Hawkesbury
M	1853	**H-1807**

West Hawkesbury Township
M	1853	**H-1807**

Caledonia Township
M	1853, 1856	**H-1807**

North Plantagenet Township
M	1853-1854	**H-1807**

Plantagenet
M	1854	**C-3028**

Lochiel, Glengarry Co.
M	1854	**H-1807**

with:

Dundas and Ancaster Presbyterian Church, Wentworth Co.
M	1848-1852	**C-3028**

comprises:

Dundas, Wentworth Co.
M	1848-1852	**C-3028**

Ancaster, and West Flamboro, Wentworth Co.
M	1848-1852	**C-3028**

Loughborough Township, Frontenac Co.

Presbyterian Mission of Ernestown, Fredericksburg, Adolphustown, and the Bay of Quinté Region
B	1800-1841	**H-1810**
M	1800-1836	**H-1810**
D	1841	**H-1810**

includes:

Loughborough Township
B	1804-1805, 1809-1811, 1830-1838	**H-1810**
M	1809, 1812, 1818-1820	**H-1810**

Lowry, Carleton Co.

Carp United Church, Carp
BMD	1858-1929	**M-816** and **M-817**

includes:

Carp, Lowry, and Kinburn Presbyterian Congregation
BMD	1880-1929	**M-817**

Lunenburg, Stormont Co.

Osnabruck and Lunenburg Presbyterian Congregations
B	1848-1909	**C-3030**
M	1860-1900	**C-3030**
D	1907-1909	**C-3030**

comprises:

Osnabruck Free Presbyterian Congregation
B	1852-1909	**C-3030**

Lunenburg Presbyterian Church
B	1848-1896	**C-3030**

Canada Presbyterian Church of Lunenburg and Osnabruck
M	1860-1900	**C-3030**

includes: Cornwall Township, Finch, Newington, Osnabruck, and Roxborough Township, Stormont Co.; the Indian Lands, Glengarry Co.; and the Townships of Williamsburgh, and Winchester, Dundas Co.

Lunenburg and Pleasant Valley Presbyterian Church
B	1882-1902	**C-3030**

North Lunenburg and Newington Presbyterian Church
B	1879-1909	**C-3030**

North Lunenburg Presbyterian Church
D	1907-1909	**C-3030**

McCrimmon, Glengarry Co.

Farmer's Almanac diaries of Angus Alexander McMillan and Family of Glengarry County
BMD	1862-1910	**H-1808**

includes:

Kenyon Township
BMD	1862-1910	**H-1808**

and

Lochiel Township
BMD	1862-1910	**H-1808**

as well as, among others:

McCrimmon, Kenyon and Lochiel Townships
BMD	1887-1902	**H-1808**

McDonalds Corners, Lanark Co.

Knox Presbyterian Church
B   1847-1857   **M-4614**
includes: congregations in Elphin, and Snow Road, Frontenac Co.; and Dalhousie, and North Sherbrooke Townships, Lanark Co.

McMurrich Township, Parry Sound District

Register of the Rev. John Becket (1838-1921), Presbyterian missionary at Aspdin, Muskoka District, 1905-1908
M   1905-1908, 1910, 1913,
          1915   **H-1810**
includes:

     McMurrich Township
     M   1906-1907   **H-1810**

McNab Township, Renfrew Co.

Mississippi Circuit, of the Methodist Episcopal (later, the Wesleyan Methodist) Church
B   1829-1843   **H-1809**
includes: places in the Townships of Beckwith, Lanark, Pakenham, and Ramsay, Lanark Co.; in the Townships of Horton, McNab, Pembroke, and Westmeath, Renfrew Co.; and Fitzroy Township, Carleton Co.

St. Andrew's United Church of Canada, Pakenham, Lanark Co.
B   1891-1966   **M-7761**
M   1840-1973   **M-7761**
D   1901-1985   **M-7761**
includes:

     St. Andrew's Presbyterian Church, Pakenham, Lanark Co.
     M   1840-1883   **M-7761**
     includes: Townships of Fitzroy, and Torbolton, Carleton Co.; Townships of Horton, and McNab, Renfrew Co.; and neighbouring settlements

Maidstone, Essex Co.

Civil registers of Essex County
B   1826, 1845-1862   **C-15758**
includes:

     Congregation of the Rev. P.D. Laurent, Maidstone
     B   1861   **C-15758**

Manitoulin Island, Manitoulin District

Journal of the Rev. Jabez Waters Sims (1831-1869), Anglican Missionary
BMD   1863-1865   **H-1812** (index)
comprises:

     St. Paul's Anglican Church, Dungannon, Huron Co.
     BMD   1863-1864   **H-1812** (index)

     Manitoulin Island Anglican Mission
     BD   1865   **H-1812** (index)
     M   1864-1865   **H-1812** (index)

Mannheim, Waterloo Co.

Civil registers of Waterloo County
B   1836-1861   **C-15758**
M   1854-1855   **C-15758**
D   1854-1855, 1858, 1860   **C-15758**
includes:

     Evangelical Lutheran Church, Mannheim, New Dundee, and New Hamburg
     B   1858, 1860   **C-15758**
     D   1860   **C-15758**
     includes: places in Wilmot Township, Waterloo Co.; in Brant, and Carrick Townships, Bruce Co.; in Hay, Stanley, and Tuckersmith Townships, Huron Co.; and Blenheim Township, Oxford Co.; as well as Hanover, Grey Co.; and Williamsburgh [Township], Dundas Co.

March Township, Carleton Co.

Burials in Hazeldean Cemeteries
D   1835-1939   **M-7718**
includes:

     Anglican Parish of March (including: St. Mary's Anglican Church, North March, and St. John's Anglican Church, South March)
     D   1835-1862   extracts   **M-7718**

Marchhurst, Carleton Co.

Carp United Church, Carp
BMD   1858-1929   **M-816** and **M-817**
includes:

     St. Paul's Methodist Church, Carp
     M   1898-1928   **M-816**
     membership roll 1893-1929   **M-816**
     includes: Hazeldean, Huntley, Marchhurst, and Stittsville

Martintown, Glengarry Co.

Civil registers of the Surrogate Court for the Eastern and Johnstown Districts
B	1831, 1859, 1862-1865	**C-3030**
M	1831-1857, 1863, 1865	**C-3030** (index)

includes:

St. Andrew's (Presbyterian) Church of the Rev. Peter McVicar, Martintown
M	1857	**C-3030** (index)

includes: Townships of Charlottenburg, and Kenyon, Glengarry Co.; and Roxborough Township, Stormont Co.

[Presbyterian] Congregation of the Rev. Peter Watson, Williamstown
M	1865	**C-3030** (index)

includes: Martintown, and Williamstown, and other places in Charlottenburg Township, as well as the Townships of Lancaster, and Lochiel, Glengarry Co.; Cornwall Township, Stormont Co.; and the Townships of North Plantagenet, and South Plantagenet, Prescott Co.

Congregational Church, Martintown
M	1854	**C-3030** (index)

Civil registers for the Eastern District
M	1858-1869	**M-3205**

includes:

Presbyterian Church (Church of Scotland), Martintown
M	1858, 1861-[1867]	**M-3205**

Marysburgh Township, Prince Edward Co.

St. John's Anglican Church, Bath, Lennox and Addington Co.
B	1787-1813	**H-1810**
M	1787-1816	**H-1810**
D	1787-1813	**H-1810**

comprises:

St. Thomas' Anglican Church, Ernestown Township, Lennox and Addington Co.
B	1788-1813	**H-1810**
M	1787-1813, 1814, 1816	**H-1810**
D	1788-1813	**H-1810**

includes: Amherst Island, and the Townships of Adolphustown, Camden, and Fredericksburg, Lennox and Addington Co.; the Townships of Ameliasburg, Marysburgh, and Sophiasburgh, Prince Edward Co.; the Townships of Sidney, and Thurlow, Hastings Co.; and Kingston, Frontenac Co.; as well as Oswego, New York, U.S.A.

St. Paul's Anglican Church, Fredericksburg Township, Lennox and Addington Co.
B	1787-1813	**H-1810**
M	1788-1812	**H-1810**
D	1787-1813	**H-1810**

includes: Amherst Island, and the Townships of Adolphustown, Camden, Ernestown, and Richmond, Lennox and Addington Co.; the Townships of Ameliasburg, Hallowell, Marysburgh, and Sophiasburgh, Prince Edward Co.; the Townships of Sidney, and Thurlow, Hastings Co.; and the Townships of Cramahé, and Percy, Northumberland Co.; as well as Oswego, New York, U.S.A.

Presbyterian Mission of Ernestown, Fredericksburg, Adolphustown, and the Bay of Quinté region
B	1800-1841	**H-1810**
M	1800-1836	**H-1810**
D	1841	**H-1810**

includes:

Marysburgh Township
B	1800-1812, 1820, 1835, 1837	**H-1810**
M	1800-1822, 1831-1835	**H-1810**

Matilda Township, Dundas Co.

Zion Lutheran Church, Williamsburg
BM	1790-1814	**M-1496** (index)
D	1790-1814	**M-1496**
communicants and confirmations, 1808-1814		**M-1496**

includes: Morrisburg, and the Townships of Matilda, and Williamsburgh, Dundas Co.; and the Township of Osnabruck, Stormont Co.

with:

United Anglican Mission of Williamsburgh, Matilda, and Edwardsburgh
BM	1814-1886	**M-1496** (partial index)
D	1814-1886	**M-1496**
communicants and confirmations, 1814-1819, 1829, 1846-1886		**M-1496**

includes: Morrisburg, Williamsburg, and the Townships of Matilda, and Williamsburgh, Dundas Co.; the Township of Osnabruck, Stormont Co.; and the Township of Edwardsburgh, Grenville Co.

(The early registers are in Latin.)

(cont.)

ONTARIO

Civil registers of the Surrogate Court for the Eastern and Johnstown Districts
B   1831, 1859, 1862-1865   **C-3030**
M   1831-1857, 1863, 1865   **C-3030** (index)
includes:

    Lutheran Congregation, Williamsburgh Township
    M   1832-1843, 1847-1848   **C-3030** (index)
    includes: Townships of Matilda, Williamsburgh, and Winchester, Dundas Co.; the Townships of Cornwall, and Osnabruck, Stormont Co.; and Charlottenburg Township, Glengarry Co.

    Evangelical Lutheran Congregations, Williamsburgh Township
    M   1842-1844, 1846-1857   **C-3030** (index)
    includes: Townships of Matilda, Williamsburgh, and Winchester, Dundas Co.; the Townships of Cornwall, and Osnabruck, Stormont Co.; and Charlottenburg Township, Glengarry Co.

    Methodist Episcopal Church in Canada, Circuits in the Eastern District
    B   1831, 1862-1865   **C-3030**
    M   1831-1833, 1839-1841, 1843-1844, 1846-1857, 1863   **C-3030** (index)
    includes: Townships of Matilda, Mountain, Williamsburgh, and Winchester, Dundas Co.; Lochiel Township, Glengarry Co.; the Townships of Cornwall, Finch, and Osnabruck, Stormont Co.; and West Hawkesbury Township, Prescott Co.

    Wesleyan Methodist Church, Matilda Township
    M   1831-1837, 1839-1844, 1846-1849   **C-3030** (index)
    includes: Townships of Matilda, and Mountain, Dundas Co.; and Edwardsburgh Township, Grenville Co.

    Wesleyan Methodist Church in Canada, Circuits in the Eastern District
    B   1859   **C-3030**
    M   1833-1857   **C-3030** (index)
    includes: Townships of Matilda, Mountain, Williamsburgh, and Winchester, Dundas Co.; the Townships of Edwardsburgh, and Oxford, Grenville Co.; Sheek Island, and the Townships of Cornwall, Finch, Osnabruck, and Roxborough, Stormont Co.; as well as the Brockville district, Leeds Co.; and other places in the Counties of Dundas, Stormont, and Glengarry

    Presbyterian (Church of Scotland) Church of the Rev. T. Scott, Williamsburgh, Matilda, and Winchester Townships
    M   1853-1857   **C-3030** (index)
    includes: Mountain Township, Dundas Co.; and Osnabruck Township, Stormont Co.

    Presbyterian (Free Church) Congregation of the Rev. Robert Lyle
    M   1831-1837   **C-3030** (index)
    includes: Townships of Matilda, and Williamsburgh, Dundas Co.; and the Townships of Cornwall, and Osnabruck, Stormont Co.

    Presbyterian Church of the Rev. John Dickey, Williamsburgh, Matilda, and Winchester Townships
    M   1836-1849   **C-3030** (index)
    includes: Mountain Township, Dundas Co.; and Osnabruck Township, Stormont Co.

Maxville, Glengarry Co.

Farmer's Almanac diaries of Angus Alexander McMillan and Family of Glengarry County
BMD   1862-1910   **H-1808**
includes:

    Kenyon Township
    BMD   1862-1910   **H-1808**

        as well as, among others:

    Maxville, Kenyon Township
    MD   1885-1902   **H-1808**

Mecklenburg (from 1792, Midland) **District** (later, Counties of Lennox and Addington, Frontenac, Hastings, and Prince Edward)

St. John's Anglican Church, Bath, Lennox and Addington Co.
B   1787-1813   **H-1810**
M   1787-1816   **H-1810**
D   1787-1813   **H-1810**
comprises:

    St. Thomas' Anglican Church, Ernestown Township, Lennox and Addington Co.
    B   1788-1813   **H-1810**
    M   1787-1813, 1814, 1816   **H-1810**
    D   1788-1813   **H-1810**
    includes: Amherst Island, and the Townships of Adolphustown, Camden, and Fredericksburg, Lennox and Addington Co.; the Townships of Ameliasburg, Marysburgh, and Sophiasburgh, Prince Edward Co.; the Townships of Sidney, and Thurlow, Hastings Co.; and Kingston, Frontenac Co.; as well as Oswego, New York, U.S.A.

(cont.)

St. Paul's Anglican Church, Fredericksburg Township, Lennox and Addington Co.
B   1787-1813   **H-1810**
M   1788-1812   **H-1810**
D   1787-1813   **H-1810**
includes: Amherst Island, and the Townships of Adolphustown, Camden, Ernestown, and Richmond, Lennox and Addington Co.; the Townships of Ameliasburg, Hallowell, Marysburgh, and Sophiasburgh, Prince Edward Co.; the Townships of Sidney, and Thurlow, Hastings Co.; and the Townships of Cramahé, and Percy, Northumberland Co.; as well as Oswego, New York, U.S.A.

Presbyterian Mission of Ernestown, Fredericksburg, Adolphustown, and the Bay of Quinté region
B   1800-1841   **H-1810**
M   1800-1836   **H-1810**
D   1841   **H-1810**
comprises:

Adolphustown Township, Lennox and Addington Co.
B   1800-1811   **H-1810**
M   1800-1821, 1831-1835   **H-1810**

Amherst Island Township, Lennox and Addington Co.
B   1834-1840   **H-1810**
M   1802, 1816, 1819   **H-1810**

Camden Township, Lennox and Addington Co.
B   1800-1813, 1820, 1835-1839   **H-1810**
M   1805-1821, 1832-1833   **H-1810**

Ernestown Township, Lennox and Addington Co.
B   1800-1813, 1819-1821, 1827, 1830, 1832, 1835   **H-1810**
M   1800-1822, 1831-1835   **H-1810**

Fredericksburg Township, Lennox and Addington Co.
B   1800-1813, 1815, 1827, 1832, 1837-1840   **H-1810**
M   1800-1822, 1831-1836   **H-1810**

Richmond Township, Lennox and Addington Co.
B   1800-1811, 1813-1814, 1824-1825, 1832-1833, 1838-1839   **H-1810**
M   1802-1803, 1807-1821, 1832-1835   **H-1810**

Sheffield Township, Lennox and Addington Co.
B   1831, 1836, 1839   **H-1810**

Rawdon Township, Hastings Co.
B   1803   **H-1810**

Sidney Township, Hastings Co.
B   1800-1820, 1837, 1839   **H-1810**
M   1803, 1806-1818   **H-1810**

Thurlow Township, Hastings Co.
B   1802-1816, 1821, 1839   **H-1810**
M   1807, 1812, 1816, 1822   **H-1810**

Tyendinaga Township, Hastings Co.
B   1826-1837   **H-1810**

Cramahé Township, Northumberland Co.
B   1800-1806, 1811, 1818, 1820   **H-1810**

Hamilton Township, Northumberland Co.
B   1800-1803   **H-1810**

Murray Township, Northumberland Co.
B   1800-1821   **H-1810**
M   1803, 1812   **H-1810**

Ameliasburg Township, Prince Edward Co.
B   1800-1822, 1827, 1829, 1833-1840   **H-1810**
M   1807-1808, 1812, 1820   **H-1810**

Hallowell Township, Prince Edward Co.
B   1800-1810, 1812, 1820, 1826   **H-1810**
M   1800-1820, 1831-1835   **H-1810**

Marysburgh Township, Prince Edward Co.
B   1800-1812, 1820, 1835, 1837   **H-1810**
M   1800-1822, 1831-1835   **H-1810**

Sophiasburgh Township, Prince Edward Co.
B   1806-1822, 1828   **H-1810**
M   1801-1822, 1831-1834   **H-1810**

Kingston, Frontenac Co.
B   1802-1811, 1820, 1822   **H-1810**
M   1802, 1805-1822, 1831-1832, 1835   **H-1810**

Loughborough Township, Frontenac Co.
B   1804-1805, 1809-1811, 1830-1838   **H-1810**
M   1809, 1812, 1818-1820   **H-1810**

Pittsburg Township, Frontenac Co.
B   1800-1809   **H-1810**

Portland Township, Frontenac Co.
B   1800-1811   **H-1810**
M   1810, 1816   **H-1810**

(cont.)

ONTARIO

Melancthon Township, Dufferin Co.

Returns of coroners' inquests for Grey, Wellington, Bruce, [and Dufferin] Counties
D   1873   **C-15758**
includes: Durham, Owen Sound, and the Townships of Artemesia, Egremont, Euphrasia, Keppel, Normanby, Osprey, Proton, St. Vincent, and Sydenham, Grey Co.; and Melancthon Township, Dufferin Co.

Middlesex County

Civil registers
M   1784-1833   **C-3031** (index)
includes: Norfolk, Oxford, and Middlesex Counties

Middleton Township, Norfolk Co.

Norfolk County Historical Society Collections
B	1783-1863	**M-283**
M	1807-1835	**M-274, M-275** and **M-277**
	1858-1897	**M-283**
D	1840-1899	**M-283**

includes:

    Hartford and Fredericksburg (Delhi) Regular Baptist Congregations
B	1783-1863	**M-283**
M	1858-1897	**M-283**
D	1840-1899	**M-283**

    includes: Townships of Middleton, South Walsingham, Townsend, and Windham, Norfolk Co.; and Walpole Township, Haldimand Co.

(Pages 12941-12987)

Middleville, Lanark Co.

Clayton United Church, Clayton
BMD	1805-1965	**M-3687** and **M-3688**
	1876-1965	**M-3243**

includes:

    Middleville Congregational Church
B	1913-1928	**M-3243**
M	1858-1871	**M-3687**
	1896-1925	**M-3243**
D	1910-1964	**M-3243**

    includes: Rosetta

    St. Paul's Presbyterian Charge, Middleville
B	1805-1879	**M-3687**

(cont.)

St. Paul's, Middleville, and St. James', Dalhousie, United (Presbyterian) Pastoral Charge
B	1858-1864	**M-3687**
M	1859-1896, 1909-1910	**M-3687**
communion rolls 1858-1865		**M-3687**
	1872-1954	**M-3688**

includes: St. John's United Church, Hopetown, 1925-1941; and Rosetta United Church, 1935-1942

Clayton-Middleville Presbyterian Charge (later, Middleville United Church)
B	1881-1950	**M-3243**
D	1942-1957	**M-3688**
communion rolls 1942-1957		**M-3688**

includes: Hopetown, Rosetta, Darling, and Tatlock

St. Paul's, Middleville, and St. Peter's, Darling, Presbyterian Congregations
BD	1893-1965	**M-3688**
M	1897-1919	**M-3243**

includes: Hopetown, Rosetta, and Tatlock

St. Paul's Presbyterian (later, United) Church, Middleville
M	1919-1943	**M-3243**

Midland (prior to 1792, Mecklenburg) **District** (later, Counties of Lennox and Addington, Frontenac, Hastings, and Prince Edward)

St. John's Anglican Church, Bath, Lennox and Addington Co.
B	1787-1813	**H-1810**
M	1787-1816	**H-1810**
D	1787-1813	**H-1810**

comprises:

    St. Thomas' Anglican Church, Ernestown Township, Lennox and Addington Co.
B	1788-1813	**H-1810**
M	1787-1813, 1814, 1816	**H-1810**
D	1788-1813	**H-1810**

    includes: Amherst Island, and the Townships of Adolphustown, Camden, and Fredericksburg, Lennox and Addington Co.; the Townships of Ameliasburg, Marysburgh, and Sophiasburgh, Prince Edward Co.; the Townships of Sidney, and Thurlow, Hastings Co.; and Kingston, Frontenac Co.; as well as Oswego, New York, U.S.A.

    St. Paul's Anglican Church, Fredericksburg Township, Lennox and Addington Co.
B	1787-1813	**H-1810**
M	1788-1812	**H-1810**
D	1787-1813	**H-1810**

    includes: Amherst Island, and the Townships of Adolphustown, Camden, Ernestown, and Richmond, Lennox and Addington Co.; the Townships of Ameliasburg, Hallowell, Marysburgh, and Sophiasburgh, Prince Edward

(cont.)

Co.; the Townships of Sidney, and Thurlow, Hastings Co.; and the Townships of Cramahé, and Percy, Northumberland Co.; as well as Oswego, New York, U.S.A.

Presbyterian Mission of Ernestown, Fredericksburg, Adolphustown, and the Bay of Quinté region

B	1800-1841	**H-1810**
M	1800-1836	**H-1810**
D	1841	**H-1810**

comprises:

Adolphustown Township, Lennox and Addington Co.
B	1800-1811	**H-1810**
M	1800-1821, 1831-1835	**H-1810**

Amherst Island Township, Lennox and Addington Co.
B	1834-1840	**H-1810**
M	1802, 1816, 1819	**H-1810**

Camden Township, Lennox and Addington Co.
B	1800-1813, 1820, 1835-1839	**H-1810**
M	1805-1821, 1832-1833	**H-1810**

Ernestown Township, Lennox and Addington Co.
B	1800-1813, 1819-1821, 1827, 1830, 1832, 1835	**H-1810**
M	1800-1822, 1831-1835	**H-1810**

Fredericksburg Township, Lennox and Addington Co.
B	1800-1813, 1815, 1827, 1832, 1837-1840	**H-1810**
M	1800-1822, 1831-1836	**H-1810**

Richmond Township, Lennox and Addington Co.
B	1800-1811, 1813-1814, 1824-1825, 1832-1833, 1838-1839	**H-1810**
M	1802-1803, 1807-1821, 1832-1835	**H-1810**

Sheffield Township, Lennox and Addington Co.
B	1831, 1836, 1839	**H-1810**

Rawdon Township, Hastings Co.
B	1803	**H-1810**

Sidney Township, Hastings Co.
B	1800-1820, 1837, 1839	**H-1810**
M	1803, 1806-1818	**H-1810**

Thurlow Township, Hastings Co.
B	1802-1816, 1821, 1839	**H-1810**
M	1807, 1812, 1816, 1822	**H-1810**

Tyendinaga Township, Hastings Co.
B	1826-1837	**H-1810**

Cramahé Township, Northumberland Co.
B	1800-1806, 1811, 1818, 1820	**H-1810**

(cont.)

Hamilton Township, Northumberland Co.
B	1800-1803	**H-1810**

Murray Township, Northumberland Co.
B	1800-1821	**H-1810**
M	1803, 1812	**H-1810**

Ameliasburg Township, Prince Edward Co.
B	1800-1822, 1827, 1829, 1833-1840	**H-1810**
M	1807-1808, 1812, 1820	**H-1810**

Hallowell Township, Prince Edward Co.
B	1800-1810, 1812, 1820, 1826	**H-1810**
M	1800-1820, 1831-1835	**H-1810**

Marysburgh Township, Prince Edward Co.
B	1800-1812, 1820, 1835, 1837	**H-1810**
M	1800-1822, 1831-1835	**H-1810**

Sophiasburgh Township, Prince Edward Co.
B	1806-1822, 1828	**H-1810**
M	1801-1822, 1831-1834	**H-1810**

Kingston, Frontenac Co.
B	1802-1811, 1820, 1822	**H-1810**
M	1802, 1805-1822, 1831-1832, 1835	**H-1810**

Loughborough Township, Frontenac Co.
B	1804-1805, 1809-1811, 1830-1838	**H-1810**
M	1809, 1812, 1818-1820	**H-1810**

Pittsburg Township, Frontenac Co.
B	1800-1809	**H-1810**

Portland Township, Frontenac Co.
B	1800-1811	**H-1810**
M	1810, 1816	**H-1810**

Mississippi Lake, Lanark Co.

Mississippi Circuit, of the Methodist Episcopal (later, the Wesleyan Methodist) Church

B	1829-1843	**H-1809**

includes: places in the Townships of Beckwith, Lanark, Pakenham, and Ramsay, Lanark Co.; in the Townships of Horton, McNab, Pembroke, and Westmeath, Renfrew Co.; and Fitzroy Township, Carleton Co.

ONTARIO

Montague Township, Lanark Co.

St. Andrew's Presbyterian (Church of Scotland) Church, Toledo (formerly, Presbyterian Congregation of Kitley Township)
B	1846-1852, 1863-1913	**H-1810**
M	1863-1864, 1880-1881, 1890-1893, 1903, 1907	**H-1810**
D	1894, 1897-1902, 1911	**H-1810**
members,	1847, 1850, 1854, 1863-1913	**H-1810**

includes: Townships of Bastard, Elizabethtown, Front of Yonge, and Kitley, Leeds Co.; as well as Montague Township, Lanark Co.; and Wolford Township, Grenville Co.

Zion Memorial United Church, Carleton Place
BMD	1878-1933	**M-2209**

includes:

Beckwith, Drummond, and Montague Methodist Circuit
M	1896-1922	**M-2209**

Montague Methodist Circuit
BD	1899-1922	**M-2209**

Mornington Township, Perth Co.

Civil registers of Waterloo County
B	1836-1861	**C-15758**
M	1854-1855	**C-15758**
D	1854-1855, 1858, 1860	**C-15758**

includes:

German Evangelical Lutheran Congregations, Phillipsburg, Wellesley Village, and New Baden, Waterloo Co.
B	1836-1855, 1858, 1860	**C-15758**
D	1858, 1860	**C-15758**

includes: places in the Townships of Waterloo, Wellesley, and Wilmot, Waterloo Co.; Ellice, Mornington, and North Easthope Townships, Perth Co.; and Normanby Township, Grey Co.

[Amish Mennonite Congregation of Bishop] Peter Litwiller, [Wilmot Township, Waterloo Co.]
BD	1860	**C-15758**
M	1855*	**C-15758**

includes: places in the Townships of Wellesley, and Wilmot, Waterloo Co.; and Mornington Township, Perth Co.

*In German

St. Agatha's Roman Catholic Church, Wilmot Township, Waterloo Co.
BD	1860	**C-15758**

includes: places in the Townships of Waterloo, Wellesley, Wilmot, and Woolwich, Waterloo Co.; and Mornington, and South Easthope Townships, Perth Co.

Morrisburg, Dundas Co.

Zion Lutheran Church, Williamsburg
BM	1790-1814	**M-1496** (index)
D	1790-1814	**M-1496**
communicants and confirmations,	1808-1814	**M-1496**

includes: Morrisburg, and the Townships of Matilda, and Williamsburgh, Dundas Co.; and the Township of Osnabruck, Stormont Co.

with:

United Anglican Mission of Williamsburgh, Matilda, and Edwardsburgh
BM	1814-1886	**M-1496** (partial index)
D	1814-1886	**M-1496**
communicants and confirmations,	1814-1819, 1829, 1846-1886	**M-1496**

includes: Morrisburg, Williamsburg, and the Townships of Matilda, and Williamsburgh, Dundas Co.; the Township of Osnabruck, Stormont Co.; and the Township of Edwardsburgh, Grenville Co.

(The early registers are in Latin.)

St. Lawrence Evangelical Lutheran Church, Morrisburg
BMD	1826-1972	**M-2981**

comprises:

St. George's (later, St. John's) Evangelical Lutheran Congregation, Williamsburg
BMD	1826-1840	**M-2981**
confirmations	1827-1840	**M-2981**

St. John's Lutheran Congregation, Osnabruck, Stormont Co.
BD	1837-1853	**M-2981**

St. John's, Riverside, and St. Paul's, Morrisburg, Evangelical Lutheran Church
BMD	1840-1895	**M-2981**
confirmations	1841-1863	**M-2981**
communicants n.d.		**M-2981**

St. John's, Riverside, and St. Peter's, North Williamsburg, Evangelical Lutheran Church
M	1858-1914	**M-2981**

St. John's Evangelical Lutheran Church, Williamsburg, and St. Paul's Lutheran Church, Morrisburg
B	1872-1972	**M-2981**
M	1873-1936	**M-2981**
D	1873-1972	**M-2981**
communicants n.d., 1876-1901		**M-2981**

St. Paul's Evangelical Lutheran Church, Morrisburg
B	1887-1894	**M-2981**
M	1887-1895	**M-2981**
D	1890-1895, 1908-1972	**M-2981**
confirmations	1887-1895	**M-2981**
communicants	1887-1899	**M-2981**

Mountain Township, Dundas Co.

Civil registers of the Surrogate Court for the Eastern and Johnstown Districts
B   1831, 1859, 1862-1865   **C-3030**
M   1831-1857, 1863, 1865   **C-3030** (index)
includes:

    Methodist Episcopal Church in Canada, Circuits in the Eastern District
    B   1831, 1862-1865   **C-3030**
    M   1831-1833, 1839-1841,
            1843-1844, 1846-1857,
            1863   **C-3030** (index)
    includes: Townships of Matilda, Mountain, Williamsburgh, and Winchester, Dundas Co.; Lochiel Township, Glengarry Co.; the Townships of Cornwall, Finch, and Osnabruck, Stormont Co.; and West Hawkesbury Township, Prescott Co.

    Wesleyan Methodist Church, Matilda Township
    M   1831-1837, 1839-1844,
            1846-1849   **C-3030** (index)
    includes: Townships of Matilda, and Mountain, Dundas Co.; and Edwardsburgh Township, Grenville Co.

    Wesleyan Methodist Church in Canada, Circuits in the Eastern District
    B   1859   **C-3030**
    M   1833-1857   **C-3030** (index)
    includes: Townships of Matilda, Mountain, Williamsburgh, and Winchester, Dundas Co.; the Townships of Edwardsburgh, and Oxford, Grenville Co.; Sheek Island, and the Townships of Cornwall, Finch, Osnabruck, and Roxborough, Stormont Co.; as well as the Brockville district, Leeds Co.; and other places in the Counties of Dundas, Stormont, and Glengarry

    Presbyterian Church of the Rev. John Dickey, Williamsburgh, Matilda, and Winchester Townships
    M   1836-1849   **C-3030** (index)
    includes: Mountain Township, Dundas Co.; and Osnabruck Township, Stormont Co.

    Presbyterian (Church of Scotland) Church of the Rev. T. Scott, Williamsburgh, Matilda, and Winchester Townships
    M   1853-1857   **C-3030** (index)
    includes: Mountain Township, Dundas Co.; and Osnabruck Township, Stormont Co.

Wesleyan Methodist Church of America, Inkerman
B   1898-1909 **MG 9, D 7-67,** Fiche 5
M   1904-1919   Fiche 4
           1922-1943   Fiche 5
MD   1896-1938 (notes)   Fiche 3
members 1896-1938   Fiches 3 and 4
includes: Mountain Township

Muncey, Middlesex County

Journals of the Rev. Allen Salt, a Methodist Indian missionary in western Ontario
BMD   1854-1855, 1874-1899,
              1904   **C-15709**
includes:

    Muncey Methodist Indian Mission
    BMD   1874   **C-15709**

Murray Township, Northumberland Co.

Presbyterian Mission of Ernestown, Fredericksburg, Adolphustown, and the Bay of Quinté region
B   1800-1841   **H-1810**
M   1800-1836   **H-1810**
D   1841   **H-1810**
includes:

    Murray Township
    B   1800-1821   **H-1810**
    M   1803, 1812   **H-1810**

[New] Baden, Waterloo Co.

Civil registers of Waterloo County
B   1836-1861   **C-15758**
M   1854-1855   **C-15758**
D   1854-1855, 1858, 1860   **C-15758**
includes:

    German Evangelical Lutheran Congregations, Phillipsburg, Wellesley Village, and New Baden
    B   1836-1855, 1858, 1860   **C-15758**
    D   1858, 1860   **C-15758**
    includes: places in the Townships of Waterloo, Wellesley, and Wilmot, Waterloo Co.; Ellice, Mornington, and North Easthope Townships, Perth Co.; and Normanby Township, Grey Co.

See also: Wilmot Township, and Waterloo County

New Dundee, Waterloo Co.

Civil registers of Waterloo County
B   1836-1861   **C-15758**
M   1854-1855   **C-15758**
D   1854-1855, 1858, 1860   **C-15758**
includes:

    Evangelical Lutheran Church, Mannheim, New Dundee, and New Hamburg
    B   1858, 1860   **C-15758**
    D   1860   **C-15758**
    includes: places in Wilmot Township, Waterloo Co.; in Brant, and Carrick Townships, Bruce Co.; in Hay, Stanley, and Tuckersmith Townships,

(cont.)

Huron Co.; and Blenheim Township, Oxford Co.; as well as Hanover, Grey Co.; and Williamsburgh Township, Dundas Co.

New Germany, [Wellington Co.]

Civil registers of Waterloo County
B	1836-1861	**C-15758**
M	1854-1855	**C-15758**
D	1854-1855, 1858, 1860	**C-15758**

includes:

Roman Catholic Mission, New Germany [near Guelph]
BD	1860	**C-15758**

includes: places in the Townships of Waterloo, and Woolwich, Waterloo Co.; and the Townships of Guelph, and Pilkington, Wellington Co.

[Mennonite] Congregation in New Germany [near Guelph]
BMD	1855	**C-15758**

New Hamburg, Waterloo Co.

Civil registers of Waterloo County
B	1836-1861	**C-15758**
M	1854-1855	**C-15758**
D	1854-1855, 1858, 1860	**C-15758**

includes:

Evangelical Lutheran Church, Mannheim, New Dundee, and New Hamburg
B	1858, 1860	**C-15758**
D	1860	**C-15758**

includes: places in Wilmot Township, , Waterloo Co.; in Brant, and Carrick Townships, Bruce Co.; in Hay, Stanley, and Tuckersmith Townships, Huron Co.; and Blenheim Township, Oxford Co.; as well as Hanover, Grey Co.; and Williamsburgh [Township], Dundas Co.

Congregation of the Rev. David Fisher, New Hamburg
B	1852-1860	**C-15758**
D	1860	**C-15758**

Newington, Stormont Co.

Osnabruck and Lunenburg Presbyterian Congregations
B	1848-1909	**C-3030**
M	1860-1900	**C-3030**
D	1907-1909	**C-3030**

includes:

North Lunenburg and Newington Presbyterian Church
B	1879-1909	**C-3030**

(cont.)

Canada Presbyterian Church of Lunenburg and Osnabruck
M	1860-1900	**C-3030**

includes: Cornwall Township, Finch, Newington, Osnabruck, and Roxborough Township, Stormont Co.; the Indian Lands, Glengarry Co.; and the Townships of Williamsburgh, and Winchester, Dundas Co.

Nichol Township, Wellington Co.

Civil registers of Waterloo County
B	1836-1861	**C-15758**
M	1854-1855	**C-15758**
D	1854-1855, 1858, 1860	**C-15758**

includes:

[Unorthodox Evangelical Lutheran] Congregation of the Rev. Frederick W. Bindemann, Waterloo Township, Waterloo Co.
M	1855	**C-15758**

includes: Berlin (later, Kitchener), and places in the Townships of North Dumfries, Waterloo, Wellesley, Wilmot, and Woolwich, Waterloo Co.; Carrick Township, Bruce Co.; Normanby Township, Grey Co.; the Townships of Blandford, and Blenheim, Oxford Co.; Hay Township, Huron Co.; the Townships of North Easthope, South Easthope, and Wallace, Perth Co.; the Townships of Peel, Guelph, Nichol, and Puslinch, Wellington Co.; and Hamilton, Wentworth Co.

Norfolk County

Civil registers for the London District
M	1784-1833	**C-3031** (index)

includes: Norfolk, Oxford, and Middlesex Counties

Norfolk County Historical Society Collections
B	1783-1863	**M-283**
M	1807-1835	**M-274, M-275** and **M-277**
	1858-1897	**M-283**
D	1840-1899	**M-283**

comprises:

Hartford and Fredericksburg (Delhi) Regular Baptist Congregations
B	1783-1863	**M-283**
M	1858-1897	**M-283**
D	1840-1899	**M-283**

includes: Townships of Middleton, South Walsingham, Townsend, and Windham, Norfolk Co.; and Walpole Township, Haldimand Co.

(Pages 12941-12987)

(cont.)

Civil registers for Norfolk County
M	1807-1813	**M-274**
	1807-1815	**M-274**
	1826-1828	**M-275**
	1831-1835	**M-277**

includes: Townships of Charlotteville, and Woodhouse, in the London District

(Pages 829-837, 1040-1041, 2121-2123, 3940-3991)

Normanby Township, Grey Co.

Civil registers of Waterloo County
B	1836-1861	**C-15758**
M	1854-1855	**C-15758**
D	1854-1855, 1858, 1860	**C-15758**

includes:

German Evangelical Lutheran Congregations, Phillipsburg, Wellesley Village, and New Baden, Waterloo Co.
B	1836-1855, 1858, 1860	**C-15758**
D	1858, 1860	**C-15758**

includes: places in the Townships of Waterloo, Wellesley, and Wilmot, Waterloo Co.; Ellice, Mornington, and North Easthope Townships, Perth Co.; and Normanby Township, Grey Co.

[Unorthodox Evangelical Lutheran] Congregation of the Rev. Frederick W. Bindemann, Waterloo Township, Waterloo Co.
M	1855	**C-15758**

includes: Berlin (later, Kitchener), and places in the Townships of North Dumfries, Waterloo, Wellesley, Wilmot, and Woolwich, Waterloo Co.; Carrick Township, Bruce Co.; Normanby Township, Grey Co.; the Townships of Blandford, and Blenheim, Oxford Co.; Hay Township, Huron Co.; the Townships of North Easthope, South Easthope, and Wallace, Perth Co.; the Townships of Peel, Guelph, Nichol, and Puslinch, Wellington Co.; and Hamilton, Wentworth Co.

Returns of coroners' inquests for Grey, Wellington, Bruce, [and Dufferin] Counties
D	1873	**C-15758**

includes: Durham, Owen Sound, and the Townships of Artemesia, Egremont, Euphrasia, Keppel, Normanby, Osprey, Proton, St. Vincent, and Sydenham, Grey Co.; and Melancthon Township, Dufferin Co.

North Bayham, Elgin Co.

Personal registers of the Rev. J. Nelson Gould of Sarnia, Methodist and United Church of Canada minister
B	1916-1960	**H-1811**
M	1916-1961	**H-1811**
D	1916-1959	**H-1811**

includes:

Richmond-Corinth United Church of Canada Charge
B	1947-1960	**H-1811**
M	1947-1961	**H-1811**
D	1947-1959	**H-1811**

includes: Aylmer West, Corinth, Fairview, North Bayham, Richmond Village (Bayham), and Summers Corners, Elgin Co.

North Douro [Lakefield], Peterborough Co.

Civil registers of Peterborough County
M	1859-1873	**H-1810**

consists of:

Christ Church Anglican Church, Lakefield
M	1859-1873	**H-1810**

includes: Lakefield (North Douro), and Peterborough, as well as the Townships of Douro, Dummer, Otonabee, and Smith, Peterborough Co.; and Lindsay, Victoria Co.

North Dumfries Township, Waterloo Co.

Civil registers of Waterloo County
B	1836-1861	**C-15758**
M	1854-1855	**C-15758**
D	1854-1855, 1858, 1860	**C-15758**

includes:

German Evangelical Lutheran Church, Preston (later, Cambridge)
B	1853-1855, 1860	**C-15758**
M	1855	**C-15758**
D	1855, 1860	**C-15758**

includes: places in the Townships of North Dumfries, Waterloo, Wilmot, and Woolwich, Waterloo Co.; in the Townships of Brantford, Burford, and South Dumfries, Brant Co.; as well as Blenheim Township, Oxford Co.; Puslinch Township, Wellington Co.; and Beverley Township, Wentworth Co.

[Unorthodox Evangelical Lutheran] Congregation of the Rev. Frederick W. Bindemann, Waterloo Township
M	1855	**C-15758**

includes: Berlin (later, Kitchener), and places in the Townships of North Dumfries, Waterloo, Wellesley, Wilmot, and Woolwich, Waterloo Co.; Carrick Township, Bruce Co.; Normanby Township, Grey Co.; the Townships of

(cont.)

Blandford, and Blenheim, Oxford Co.; Hay Township, Huron Co.; the Townships of North Easthope, South Easthope, and Wallace, Perth Co.; the Townships of Peel, Guelph, Nichol, and Puslinch, Wellington Co.; and Hamilton, Wentworth Co.

Roman Catholic Mission, Preston (later, Cambridge)
B   1860   **C-15758**
includes: places in the Townships of North Dumfries, and Waterloo

North Easthope Township, Perth Co.

Civil registers of Waterloo County
B   1836-1861   **C-15758**
M   1854-1855   **C-15758**
D   1854-1855, 1858, 1860   **C-15758**
includes:

German Evangelical Lutheran Congregations, Phillipsburg, Wellesley Village, and New Baden, Waterloo Co.
B   1836-1855, 1858, 1860   **C-15758**
D   1858, 1860   **C-15758**
includes: places in the Townships of Waterloo, Wellesley, and Wilmot, Waterloo Co.; Ellice, Mornington, and North Easthope Townships, Perth Co.; and Normanby Township, Grey Co.

[Unorthodox Evangelical Lutheran] Congregation of the Rev. Frederick W. Bindemann, Waterloo Township, Waterloo Co.
M   1855   **C-15758**
includes: Berlin (later, Kitchener), and places in the Townships of North Dumfries, Waterloo, Wellesley, Wilmot, and Woolwich, Waterloo Co.; Carrick Township, Bruce Co.; Normanby Township, Grey Co.; the Townships of Blandford, and Blenheim, Oxford Co.; Hay Township, Huron Co.; the Townships of North Easthope, South Easthope, and Wallace, Perth Co.; the Townships of Peel, Guelph, Nichol, and Puslinch, Wellington Co.; and Hamilton, Wentworth Co.

North Fredericksburgh Township, Lennox and Addington Co.
See: Fredericksburgh Township

North Lunenburg, Stormont Co.

Osnabruck and Lunenburg Presbyterian Congregations
B   1848-1909   **C-3030**
M   1860-1900   **C-3030**
D   1907-1909   **C-3030**
includes:

(cont.)

North Lunenburg and Newington Presbyterian Church
B   1879-1909   **C-3030**

North Lunenburg Presbyterian Church
D   1907-1909   **C-3030**

North Monaghan Township, Peterborough Co.

St. Paul's Presbyterian Church, Peterborough
M   1834-1857   **H-1810**
includes: Townships of Asphodel, Douro, Dummer, Ennismore, Harvey, North Monaghan, Otonabee, and Smith, Peterborough Co.; the Townships of Hamilton, and South Monaghan in Northumberland Co.; the Township of Cavan, Durham Co.; and the Townships of Emily, and Ops, Victoria Co.

North Plantagenet Township, Prescott Co.

Civil registers of the Surrogate Court for the Eastern and Johnstown Districts
B   1831, 1859, 1862-1865   **C-3030**
M   1831-1857, 1863, 1865   **C-3030** (index)
includes:

Baptist Congregation, Breadalbane, Glengarry Co.
M   1834-1850   **C-3030** (index)
includes: places in the Townships of Kenyon, and Lochiel, Glengarry Co.; as well as in the Townships of Caledonia, East Hawkesbury, West Hawkesbury, and North Plantagenet, Prescott Co.

[Presbyterian] Congregation of the Rev. Peter Watson, Williamstown, Glengarry Co.
M   1865   **C-3030** (index)
includes: Martintown, and Williamstown, and other places in Charlottenburg Township, as well as the Townships of Lancaster, and Lochiel, Glengarry Co.; Cornwall Township, Stormont Co.; and the Townships of North Plantagenet, and South Plantagenet, Prescott Co.

L'Orignal and Plantagenet Presbyterian Church
M   1854-1856   **C-3028**
           1852-1856   **H-1807**
includes:

North Plantagenet Township
M   1853-1854   **H-1807**

Plantagenet
M   1854   **C-3028**

North Sherbrooke Township, Lanark Co.

Knox Presbyterian Church, McDonalds Corners
B   1847-1857   **M-4614**
includes: Elphin, and Snow Road, Frontenac Co.; and Dalhousie, and North Sherbrooke Townships, Lanark Co.

Norwich, Oxford Co.

Pelham Monthly Meeting of Friends (Hicksite Quakers), Pelham Township, Welland Co.
BD   1789-1847   **M-3838**
         1727-1867   **M-3838**
M   1790-1843   **M-3838**
         1807-1906   **M-3838**
includes: Norwich, Oxford Co.

(Records of the Religious Society of Friends, Volumes C-3-53 and C-3-54)

Norwich Monthly Meeting of Friends (Hicksite Quakers), Norwich
M   1859-1973   **M-3843**
includes: Pelham Township, Welland Co.

(Records of the Religious Society of Friends, Volume C-3-94)

Pelham Monthly Meeting of Friends (Conservative Quakers), Pelham Township, Welland Co.
B   1734-1841   **M-3800**
BD   1765-1830   **M-3800**
M etc.   1819-1842   **M-3800**
separation list 1830   **M-3800**
includes: Norwich, Oxford Co.

(Records of the Religious Society of Friends, Volume A-2-1)

Pelham Monthly Meeting of Friends (Orthodox Quakers), Pelham Township, Welland Co.
M   1897-1908   **M-3814**
includes: Norwich, Oxford Co.

(Records of the Religious Society of Friends, Volume B-2-24)

Notfield, Glengarry Co.

Civil registers for the Eastern District
M   1858-1869   **M-3205**
includes:

    Baptist Church, Notfield
    M   1869   **M-3205**

Ontario County

Civil registers of Ontario
M   1816-1869   **M-5497**
         1858-1869   **M-7092**
includes:

    Ontario County
    M   1858-1869   **M-7092**

Ontario Province

Civil registers of Ontario
M   1816-1869   **M-5497**
         1858-1869   **M-7092**
comprises:

    Ottawa District (later, Prescott and Russell Counties)
    M   1816-1853   **M-5497**
    includes: Hull, Gatineau Co., Que.; as well as extracts of
         B   1822-1836 for the districts of Montreal, and Quebec, Que.

    Ottawa City
    M   1859-1869   **M-7092**

    Bathurst District (later, Carleton and Lanark Counties)
    M   1831-1848   **M-5497**

    Carleton County
    M   1865-1869   **M-5497**

    Lanark County
    M   1858-1869   **M-5497**

    Ontario County
    M   1858-1869   **M-7092**

    Oxford County
    M   1858-1869   **M-7092**

    Renfrew County
    M   1858-1869   **M-5497**

    Russell County
    M   1855-1869   **M-5497**

Ops Township, Victoria Co.

St. Paul's Presbyterian Church, Peterborough, Peterborough Co.
M   1834-1857   **H-1810**
includes: Townships of Asphodel, Douro, Dummer, Ennismore, Harvey, North Monaghan, Otonabee, and Smith, Peterborough Co.; the Townships of Hamilton, and South Monaghan in Northumberland Co.; the Township of Cavan, Durham Co.; and the Townships of Emily, and Ops, Victoria Co.

ONTARIO

Orford Township, Kent Co.

Register of the Rev. John Becket (1838-1921), Presbyterian missionary at Aspdin, Muskoka District, 1905-1908
M   1905-1908, 1910, 1913,
          1915   **H-1810**
includes:

    Orford Township
    M   1910   **H-1810**

Osnabruck Township, Stormont Co.

Zion Lutheran Church, Williamsburg, Dundas Co.
BM   1790-1814   **M-1496** (index)
D   1790-1814   **M-1496**
communicants and confirmations,
       1808-1814   **M-1496**
includes: Morrisburg, and the Townships of Matilda, and Williamsburgh, Dundas Co.; and the Township of Osnabruck, Stormont Co.

            with:

United Anglican Mission of Williamsburgh, Matilda, and Edwardsburgh
BM   1814-1886   **M-1496** (partial
                                       index)
D   1814-1886   **M-1496**
communicants and confirmations,
      1814-1819, 1829,
      1846-1886   **M-1496**
includes: Morrisburg, Williamsburg, and the Townships of Matilda, and Williamsburgh, Dundas Co.; the Township of Osnabruck, Stormont Co.; and the Township of Edwardsburgh, Grenville Co.
(The early registers are in Latin.)

St. Lawrence Lutheran Church, Morrisburg, Dundas Co.
BMD   1826-1972   **M-2981**
includes:

    St. John's Lutheran Congregation, Osnabruck
    BD   1837-1853   **M-2981**

Civil registers of the Surrogate Court for the Eastern and Johnstown Districts
B   1831, 1859, 1862-1865   **C-3030**
M   1831-1857, 1863, 1865   **C-3030** (index)
includes:

    Lutheran Congregation, Williamsburgh Township, Dundas Co.
    M   1832-1843, 1847-1848   **C-3030** (index)
    includes: Townships of Matilda, Williamsburgh, and Winchester, Dundas Co.; the Townships of Cornwall, and Osnabruck, Stormont Co.; and Charlottenburg Township, Glengarry Co.

    Evangelical Lutheran Congregations, Williamsburgh Township, Dundas Co.
    M   1842-1844, 1846-1857   **C-3030** (index)
    includes: Townships of Matilda, Williamsburgh, and Winchester, Dundas Co.; the Townships of Cornwall, and Osnabruck, Stormont Co.; and Charlottenburg Township, Glengarry Co.

    Methodist Episcopal Church in Canada, Circuits in the Eastern District
    B   1831, 1862-1865   **C-3030**
    M   1831-1833, 1839-1841,
           1843-1844, 1846-1857,
           1863   **C-3030** (index)
    includes: Townships of Matilda, Mountain, Williamsburgh, and Winchester, Dundas Co.; Lochiel Township, Glengarry Co.; the Townships of Cornwall, Finch, and Osnabruck, Stormont Co.; and West Hawkesbury Township, Prescott Co.

    Wesleyan Methodist Church in Canada, Circuits in the Eastern District
    B   1859   **C-3030**
    M   1833-1857   **C-3030** (index)
    includes: Townships of Matilda, Mountain, Williamsburgh, and Winchester, Dundas Co.; the Townships of Edwardsburgh, and Oxford, Grenville Co.; Sheek Island, and the Townships of Cornwall, Finch, Osnabruck, and Roxborough, Stormont Co.; as well as the Brockville district, Leeds Co.; and other places in the Counties of Dundas, Stormont, and Glengarry

    Presbyterian Church of the Rev. John Dickey, Williamsburgh, Matilda, and Winchester Townships, Dundas Co.
    M   1836-1849   **C-3030** (index)
    includes: Mountain Township, Dundas Co.; and Osnabruck Township, Stormont Co.

    Presbyterian (Church of Scotland) Church of the Rev. T. Scott, Williamsburgh, Matilda, and Winchester Townships, Dundas Co.
    M   1853-1857   **C-3030** (index)
    includes: Mountain Township, Dundas Co.; and Osnabruck Township, Stormont Co.

    Presbyterian (Free Church) Congregation of the Rev. Robert Lyle
    M   1831-1837   **C-3030** (index)
    includes: Townships of Matilda, and Williamsburgh, Dundas Co.; and the Townships of Cornwall, and Osnabruck, Stormont Co.

    Presbyterian Church of the Rev. Isaac Purkis, Osnabruck Township
    M   1840, 1842-1849   **C-3030** (index)

    Congregation of the Rev. John W. Sills
    M   1850-1851   **C-3030** (index)
    includes: Williamsburgh Township, Dundas Co.; and the Townships of Cornwall, and Osnabruck, Stormont Co.

            (cont.)   (cont.)

Congregation of the Rev. E. Sallows
M   1851   C-3030 (index)
includes: Townships of Osnabruck, and Roxborough, Stormont Co.

Civil registers of Stormont Co.
M   1866   C-15758
consists of:

Wesleyan Methodist Mission, Roxborough
M   1866   C-15758
includes: Townships of Finch, Osnabruck, and Roxborough

Osnabruck and Lunenburg Presbyterian Congregations
B   1848-1909   C-3030
M   1860-1900   C-3030
D   1907-1909   C-3030
comprises:

Osnabruck Free Presbyterian Congregation
B   1852-1909   C-3030

Lunenburg Presbyterian Church
B   1848-1896   C-3030

Canada Presbyterian Church of Lunenburg and Osnabruck
M   1860-1900   C-3030
includes: Cornwall Township, Finch, Newington, Osnabruck, and Roxborough Township, Stormont Co.; the Indian Lands, Glengarry Co.; and the Townships of Williamsburgh, and Winchester, Dundas Co.

Lunenburg and Pleasant Valley Presbyterian Church
B   1882-1902   C-3030

North Lunenburg and Newington Presbyterian Church
B   1879-1909   C-3030

North Lunenburg Presbyterian Church
D   1907-1909   C-3030

Osprey Township, Grey Co.

Returns of coroners' inquests for Grey, Wellington, Bruce, [and Dufferin] Counties
D   1873   C-15758
includes: Durham, Owen Sound, and the Townships of Artemesia, Egremont, Euphrasia, Keppel, Normanby, Osprey, Proton, St. Vincent, and Sydenham, Grey Co.; and Melancthon Township, Dufferin Co.

Otonabee Township, Peterborough Co.

St. Paul's Presbyterian Church, Peterborough
M   1834-1857   H-1810
includes: Townships of Asphodel, Douro, Dummer,

(cont.)

Ennismore, Harvey, North Monaghan, Otonabee, and Smith, Peterborough Co.; the Townships of Hamilton, and South Monaghan in Northumberland Co.; the Township of Cavan, Durham Co.; and the Townships of Emily, and Ops, Victoria Co.

Civil registers of Peterborough County
M   1859-1873   H-1810
consists of:

Christ Church Anglican Church, Lakefield
M   1859-1873   H-1810
includes: Lakefield (North Douro), and Peterborough, as well as the Townships of Douro, Dummer, Otonabee, and Smith, Peterborough Co.; and Lindsay, Victoria Co.

Ottawa (formerly, Bytown), Carleton Co.

Civil registers of Ontario
M   1816-1869   M-5497
       1858-1869   M-7092
includes:

City of Ottawa
M   1859-1869   M-7092

Anglican Missions of Ottawa Co., Que., which became:
St. James' Anglican Church, Hull, Que.
St. George's Anglican Church, Gatineau, Que.
St. Mary Magdalen Anglican Church, Chelsea, Que.
BMD   1831-1853   M-299
       1854-1940   M-3689
comprises:

St. James' Anglican Church, Hull, Gatineau Co., Que.
BMD   1831-1853   M-299
includes: Townships of Bristol, and Clarendon, Pontiac Co.; and the Townships of Eardley, and Hull, Gatineau Co.; Que.

St. James' Hull, and Christ Church, Aylmer, Gatineau Co., Que.
BMD   1854-1886   M-3689
includes: Townships of Eardley, and Hull, Gatineau Co.; and Onslow Township, Pontiac Co., Que.; as well as Ottawa, Carleton Co., Ont.

St. James' Anglican Church, Hull, Gatineau Co., Que.
BMD   1886-1919   M-3689
includes: Ottawa, Carleton Co., Ont.

Anglican Mission of Chelsea and Gatineau (later, St. George's Church, Gatineau, Hull Co., and St. Mary Magdalen Church, Chelsea, Gatineau Co.), Que.
BMD   1899-1938   M-3689
       1934-1940   M-3689
confirmations 1888-1912   M-3689

(cont.)

ONTARIO

communicants 1888-1913 **M-3689**
members 1925-1932 **M-3689**
includes: census of the parish of Chelsea, etc., c. 1818-1933, as well as entries for Hull, Gatineau Co., Que.; and for Ottawa, Carleton Co., Ont.

Christ Church (Anglican) Cathedral, Ottawa

Banns	1837-1858	**M-588**
M	1858-1876	**M-588**

St. Andrew's Presbyterian Church, Ottawa

B	1829-1943	**M-2365**
	1863-1942	**M-16**
M	1830-1949	**M-2365**
	1949-1964	**M-2366**
	1964-1979	**M-5566**
D	1836-1869	**M-2365**
	1866-1892, 1926-1929	**M-2366**
	1961-1980	**M-5566**

Missions du comté de Wright, Qué. (Église catholique)

B/M/D	1841-1852	**C-2978**
M	1841-1852 Index	**C-2978**

comprend :

St-Jacques-de-Bytown (ou St-Jacques d'Embrun)

B/M/D	1841-1848	**C-2978**
M	1841-1852 Index	**C-2978**

St-Jacques-d'Embrun (Église catholique), Embrun, comté de Russell

B/M/D	1855-1883	**M-3124** (index)
	1884-1902	**M-3125** (index)
	1902-1905	**M-3126** (index)
	1905-1926	**M-3127** (index)
	1926-1959	**M-3128** (index)
	1960-1974	**M-3201** (index)
	1858-1973 Index	**M-3201**
M	1908-1915	**M-3129** (index)

St. Joseph's Roman Catholic Church, Ottawa

B/M/D	1858-1901	**M-3191**
	1902-1927	**M-3192**
	1927-1935	**M-3193**

Ottawa District (later, Counties of Prescott and Russell)

Civil registers of Ontario

M	1816-1869	**M-5497**
	1858-1869	**M-7092**

includes:

Ottawa District
M   1816-1853   **M-5497**
includes: Hull, Gatineau Co., Que.; as well as extracts of
B 1822-1836, for the districts of Montreal, and Quebec, Que.

Owen Sound, Grey Co.

Returns of coroners' inquests for Grey, Wellington, Bruce, [and Dufferin] Counties

D	1873	**C-15758**

includes: Durham, Owen Sound, and the Townships of Artemesia, Egremont, Euphrasia, Keppel, Normanby, Osprey, Proton, St. Vincent, and Sydenham, Grey Co.; and Melancthon Township, Dufferin Co.

Oxford County

Civil registers for the London District

M	1784-1833	**C-3031** (index)

includes: Norfolk, Oxford, and Middlesex Counties

Civil registers of Ontario

M	1816-1869	**M-5497**
	1858-1869	**M-7092**

includes:

Oxford County

M	1858-1869	**M-7092**

Returns of coroners' inquests for Oxford County

D	1873	**C-15758**

includes: Woodstock, and the Townships of Blandford, and Blenheim

Oxford Township, Grenville Co.

Civil registers of the Surrogate Court for the Eastern and Johnstown Districts

B	1831, 1859, 1862-1865	**C-3030**
M	1831-1857, 1863, 1865	**C-3030** (index)

includes:

Wesleyan Methodist Church in Canada, Circuits in the Eastern District

B	1859	**C-3030**
M	1833-1857	**C-3030** (index)

includes: Townships of Matilda, Mountain, Williamsburgh, and Winchester, Dundas Co.; the Townships of Edwardsburgh, and Oxford, Grenville Co.; Sheek Island, and the Townships of Cornwall, Finch, Osnabruck, and Roxborough, Stormont Co.; as well as the Brockville district, Leeds Co.; and other places in the Counties of Dundas, Stormont, and Glengarry

Pakenham, Lanark Co.

St. Andrew's United Church of Canada, Pakenham

B	1891-1966	**M-7761**
M	1840-1973	**M-7761**
D	1901-1985	**M-7761**

comprises:

(cont.)

Pakenham Wesleyan Methodist Circuit (later, Pakenham United Church of Canada)
BD   1901-1918   **M-7761**
M   1858-1931   **M-7761**
membership (with some D),
       1864-1920   **M-7761**
includes: Fitzroy Township, Carleton Co.

Blakeney and Clayton Presbyterian (later, United Church of Canada) Church
M   1896-1946   **M-7761**

St. Andrew's Presbyterian Church, Pakenham
M   1840-1883   **M-7761**
includes: Townships of Fitzroy, and Torbolton, Carleton Co.; Townships of Horton, and McNab, Renfrew Co.; and neighbouring settlements

St. Andrew's Presbyterian Church, Pakenham, and Zion Presbyterian Church, Cedar Hill
B   1891-1921   **M-7761**
M   1896-1920   **M-7761**

Pakenham United Church of Canada Pastoral Charge
B   1909-1966   **M-7761**
M   1909-1973   **M-7761**
D   1909-1985   **M-7761**
includes: Cedar Hill, Lanark Co.; Antrim, and Fitzroy Township, Carleton Co.

Pakenham Township, Lanark Co.

Mississippi Circuit of the Methodist Episcopal (later, the Wesleyan Methodist) Church
B   1829-1843   **H-1809**
includes: places in the Townships of Beckwith, Lanark, Pakenham, and Ramsay, Lanark Co.; in the Townships of Horton, McNab, Pembroke, and Westmeath, Renfrew Co.; and Fitzroy Township, Carleton Co.

Paris, Brant Co.

Civil registers of Waterloo County
B   1836-1861   **C-15758**
M   1854-1855   **C-15758**
D   1854-1855, 1858, 1860   **C-15758**
includes:

Wesleyan Methodist Congregation, Galt (later, Cambridge)
B   1860   **C-15758**
M   1854-1855   **C-15758**
includes: places in the Township of Waterloo, Waterloo Co.; Paris, and the Township of Brantford, Brant Co.; Esquesing Township, Halton Co.; and Chinguacousy Township, Peel Co.

Parry Island, Parry Sound District

Journals of the Rev. Allen Salt, a Methodist Indian missionary in western Ontario
BMD   1854-1855, 1874-1899,
       1904   **C-15709**
includes:

Parry Island Methodist Indian Mission, Georgian Bay
BMD   1883-1899, 1904   **C-15709**
includes: French River, Henvey Inlet, and Shawanaga Township in the Parry Sound District, as well as other Indian reserves in the region

Parry Sound District

Journals of the Rev. Allen Salt, a Methodist Indian missionary in western Ontario
BMD   1854-1855, 1874-1899,
       1904   **C-15709**
includes:

Parry Island Methodist Indian Mission, Georgian Bay
BMD   1883-1899, 1904   **C-15709**
includes: French River, Henvey Inlet, and Shawanaga Township in the Parry Sound District, as well as other Indian reserves in the region

Patricia District (later, Patricia portion of the Kenora District)

Fort Hope Anglican Church [on the Albany River, north of Lake Nepigon]
BD   1895-1899   **C-3028**
M   1895-1896   **C-3028**

Peel Township, Wellington Co.

Civil registers of Waterloo County
B   1836-1861   **C-15758**
M   1854-1855   **C-15758**
D   1854-1855, 1858, 1860   **C-15758**
includes:

[Unorthodox Evangelical Lutheran] Congregation of the Rev. Frederick W. Bindemann, Waterloo Township, Waterloo Co.
M   1855   **C-15758**
includes: Berlin (later, Kitchener), and places in the Townships of North Dumfries, Waterloo, Wellesley, Wilmot, and Woolwich, Waterloo Co.; Carrick Township, Bruce Co.; Normanby Township, Grey Co.; the Townships of Blandford, and Blenheim, Oxford Co.; Hay Township, Huron Co.; the Townships of North Easthope, South Easthope, and Wallace, Perth Co.; the Townships of Peel, Guelph, Nichol, and Puslinch, Wellington Co.; and Hamilton, Wentworth Co.

(cont.)

Primitive Methodist Church, Peel Township,
Wellington Co.; and Wellesley Station, Waterloo Co.
B	1845-1858	**C-15758**
D	1858	**C-15758**

Pelham Township, Welland Co.

Pelham Monthly Meeting of Friends (Hicksite Quakers)
BD	1789-1847	**M-3838**
	1727-1867	**M-3838**
M	1790-1843	**M-3838**
	1807-1906	**M-3838**

includes: Norwich, Oxford Co.

(Records of the Religious Society of Friends, Volumes C-3-53 and C-3-54)

Norwich Monthly Meeting of Friends (Hicksite Quakers), Norwich, Oxford Co.
M	1859-1973	**M-3843**

includes: Pelham Township, Welland Co.

(Records of the Religious Society of Friends, Volume C-3-94)

Pelham Monthly Meeting of Friends (Conservative Quakers)
B	1734-1841	**M-3800**
BD	1765-1830	**M-3800**
M etc.	1819-1842	**M-3800**
separation list 1830		**M-3800**

includes: Norwich, Oxford Co.

(Records of the Religious Society of Friends, Volume A-2-1)

Pelham Monthly Meeting of Friends (Orthodox Quakers)
M	1897-1908	**M-3814**

includes: Norwich, Oxford Co.

(Records of the Religious Society of Friends, Volume B-2-24)

Pembroke Township, Renfrew Co.

Mississippi Circuit of the Methodist Episcopal (later, the Wesleyan Methodist) Church
B	1829-1843	**H-1809**

includes: places in the Townships of Beckwith, Lanark, Pakenham, and Ramsay, Lanark Co.; in the Townships of Horton, McNab, Pembroke, and Westmeath, Renfrew Co.; and Fitzroy Township, Carleton Co.

Pembroke Circuit of the Wesleyan Methodist Church
B	1841-1843	**H-1809**

includes: Townships of Pembroke, and Westmeath, Renfrew Co., Ont.; as well as Allumette Island, Pontiac Co., Que.

Percy Township, Northumberland Co.

St. John's Anglican Church, Bath, Lennox and Addington Co.
B	1787-1813	**H-1810**
M	1787-1816	**H-1810**
D	1787-1813	**H-1810**

includes:

St. Paul's Anglican Church, Fredericksburg Township, Lennox and Addington Co.
B	1787-1813	**H-1810**
M	1788-1812	**H-1810**
D	1787-1813	**H-1810**

includes: Amherst Island, and the Townships of Adolphustown, Camden, Ernestown, and Richmond, Lennox and Addington Co.; the Townships of Ameliasburg, Hallowell, Marysburgh, and Sophiasburgh, Prince Edward Co.; the Townships of Sidney, and Thurlow, Hastings Co.; and the Townships of Cramahé, and Percy, Northumberland Co.; as well as Oswego, New York, U.S.A.

Perth, Lanark Co.

St. Andrew's Presbyterian Church
BM	1817-1839	**C-3029** (partial index)
	1840-1857	**C-3030** (partial index on **C-3029**)
B	1830-1881	**M-196**
M	1831-1887	**M-196**
D	1848-1881	**M-196**

St. John the Baptist Roman Catholic Church
BMD	1823-1859	**M-3197** (partial index)
B	1860-1870	**M-3197**
	1870-1878	**M-3198**
BMD	1879-1899	**M-3198**
M	1858-1872, 1879-1899	**M-3198**
D	1885-1899, 1904	**M-3198**
confirmations	1861	**M-3197**
	1867-1941	**M-3198**

St. Paul's United Church of Canada Church
B	1896-1945	**M-2232**
M	1858-1958	**M-2232**
D	1902-1968	**M-2232**

comprises:

Presbyterian (Free Church) Congregation, Perth
M	1858-1895	**M-2232**

Knox Presbyterian Church, Perth
B	1896-1945	**M-2232**
M	1896-1917	**M-2232**

(cont.)

Perth Wesleyan Methodist Church (later, Ashbury Methodist Church)
M   1858-1896   **M-2232**

Ashbury Methodist Church (formerly, Perth Wesleyan Methodist Church)
BD   1902-1927   **M-2232**
M   1858-1949   **M-2232**

Calvin Presbyterian Church, Bathurst Township
M   1899-1958   **M-2232**

St. Paul's United Church of Canada Church, Perth
M   1918-1935   **M-2232**
D   1940-1968   **M-2232**
communion rolls 1928-1938   **M-2232**

Peterborough, Peterborough Co.

St. Paul's Presbyterian Church
M   1834-1857   **H-1810**
includes: Townships of Asphodel, Douro, Dummer, Ennismore, Harvey, North Monaghan, Otonabee, and Smith, Peterborough Co.; the Townships of Hamilton, and South Monaghan in Northumberland Co.; the Township of Cavan, Durham Co.; and the Townships of Emily, and Ops, Victoria Co.

Civil registers of Peterborough County
M   1859-1873   **H-1810**
consists of:

Christ Church Anglican Church, Lakefield
M   1859-1873   **H-1810**
includes: Lakefield (North Douro), and Peterborough, as well as the Townships of Douro, Dummer, Otonabee, and Smith, Peterborough Co.; and Lindsay, Victoria Co.

Personal record of marriages performed by the Reverend Dr. Isaac Tovell, of the Methodist Church of Canada and the United Church of Canada, Toronto
M   1875-1935 Index   **H-1810**
includes:

Peterborough
M   1877, 1884-1889 Index **H-1810**

Peterborough County

Civil registers of Peterborough County
M   1859-1873   **H-1810**
consists of:

Christ Church Anglican Church, Lakefield
M   1859-1873   **H-1810**
includes: Lakefield (North Douro), and Peterborough, as well as the Townships of Douro, Dummer,
(cont.)

Otonabee, and Smith, Peterborough Co.; and Lindsay, Victoria Co.

Phillipsburg, Waterloo Co.

Civil registers of Waterloo County
B   1836-1861   **C-15758**
M   1854-1855   **C-15758**
D   1854-1855, 1858, 1860 **C-15758**
includes:

German Evangelical Lutheran Congregations, Phillipsburg, Wellesley Village, and New Baden
B   1836-1855, 1858, 1860 **C-15758**
D   1858, 1860   **C-15758**
includes: places in the Townships of Waterloo, Wellesley, and Wilmot, Waterloo Co.; Ellice, Mornington, and North Easthope Townships, Perth Co.; and Normanby Township, Grey Co.

Pickering, Ontario Co.

Pickering Monthly Meeting of Friends (Hicksite Quakers)
BD   1777-1898   **M-3839**
M   1844-1881   **M-3839**

(Records of the Religious Society of Friends, Volumes C-3-61 and C-3-63)

Pickering Monthly Meeting of Friends (Orthodox Quakers)
BD etc. 1804-1908   **M-3814**
M   1851-1869, 1895   **M-3815**
removals 1845-1866, 1878   **M-3815**

(Records of the Religious Society of Friends, Volumes B-2-29 and B-2-32)

Pilkington Township, Wellington Co.

Civil registers of Waterloo County
B   1836-1861   **C-15758**
M   1854-1855   **C-15758**
D   1854-1855, 1858, 1860 **C-15758**
includes:

Roman Catholic Mission, New Germany [near Guelph]
BD   1860   **C-15758**
includes: places in the Townships of Waterloo, and Woolwich, Waterloo Co.; and the Townships of Guelph, and Pilkington, Wellington Co.

Pittsburgh Township, Frontenac Co.

Presbyterian Mission of Ernestown, Fredericksburg, Adolphustown, and the Bay of Quinté Region
B   1800-1841   **H-1810**
M   1800-1836   **H-1810**
D   1841   **H-1810**   (cont.)

includes:

    Pittsburg Township
    B   1800-1809   **H-1810**

Plantagenet, Prescott Co.

L'Orignal and Plantagenet Presbyterian Church
M   1854-1856   **C-3028**
        1852-1856   **H-1807**
comprises:

    L'Orignal
    M   1852-1856   **H-1807**
        1855-1856   **C-3028**

    Hawkesbury
    M   1853   **H-1807**

    West Hawkesbury Township
    M   1853   **H-1807**

    Caledonia Township
    M   1853, 1856   **H-1807**

    North Plantagenet Township
    M   1853-1854   **H-1807**

    Plantagenet
    M   1854   **C-3028**

    Lochiel, Glengarry Co.
    M   1854   **H-1807**

with:

Dundas and Ancaster Presbyterian Church, Wentworth Co.
M   1848-1852   **C-3028**
comprises:

    Dundas, Wentworth Co.
    M   1848-1852   **C-3028**

    Ancaster, and West Flamboro, Wentworth Co.
    M   1848-1852   **C-3028**

Playfair, Lanark Co.

Zion Memorial United Church, Carleton Place
BMD   1878-1933   **M-2209**
includes:

    Lanark and Clayton Methodist Circuit
    B   1884-1933   **M-2209**
    M   1903-1931   **M-2209**
    D   1902-1931   **M-2209**
    circuit register 1903-1924   **M-2209**
    includes: Boyd, Erwins, Harper, Playfair, and Prestonvale

Clayton United Church, Clayton
BMD   1805-1965   **M-3687** and **M-3688**
        1876-1965   **M-3243**
includes:

    Dalhousie-Playfair Presbyterian Charge (including the Presbyterian Churches of: St. James', Dalhousie, and Zion, Watsons Corners; as well as the Poland Presbyterian Congregation, Poland; and the Playfair Presbyterian Congregation, Playfair) (later, the Dalhousie-Playfair United Church)
    communion rolls 1907-1964   **M-3688**

    Dalhousie-Playfair United Church
    M   1931-1964   **M-3243**
    D   1929-1965   **M-3243**

Pleasant Valley, Dundas Co.

Osnabruck and Lunenburg Presbyterian Congregations, Stormont Co.
B   1848-1909   **C-3030**
M   1860-1900   **C-3030**
D   1907-1909   **C-3030**
includes:

    Lunenburg and Pleasant Valley Presbyterian Church
    B   1882-1902   **C-3030**

Pointe-de-Montréal-du-Détroit (par après, Sandwich), comté d'Essex

Sainte-Anne-du-Détroit, Michigan, U.S.A.
(Église catholique)
BMD   1704-1800   **C-2893** à **C-2895**
comprend :

    Missions des Hurons de la Pointe-de-Montréal-du-Détroit
    (Église catholique)
    B   1761-1767   **C-2894**

    L'Assomption-de-la-Pointe-de-Montréal-du-Détroit
    (Église catholique)
    B   1767-1771   **C-2894**
    M   1764-1765, 1768-1771   **C-2894**
    D   1768-1772   **C-2894**
    BMD   1772-1777   **C-2894**
        1777-1783   **C-2895**

    L'Assomption-de-Sandwich-du-Détroit
    (Église catholique)
    BMD   1781-1799   **C-2895**

(cont.)

Poland, Lanark Co.

Clayton United Church, Clayton
BMD	1805-1965	**M-3687** and
		M-3688
	1876-1965	**M-3243**

includes:

Poland Presbyterian Congregation
| B | 1876-1907, 1912 | **M-3243** |

includes: Clyde Forks, Flower Station, South Lavant, South Poland, Lanark Co.; and Thurlow, Hastings Co.

Watson's Corners Presbyterian Church, Watsons Corners
| M | 1896-1926 | **M-3243** |

includes: Flower Station, Poland, Lavant, Dalhousie Township

Dalhousie-Playfair Presbyterian Charge (including the Presbyterian Churches of: St. James', Dalhousie, and Zion, Watsons Corners; as well as the Poland Presbyterian Congregation, Poland; and the Playfair Presbyterian Congregation, Playfair) (later, the Dalhousie-Playfair United Church)
communion rolls 1907-1964 **M-3688**

Port Arthur, Thunder Bay District

St. John the Evangelist Anglican Church, Thunder Bay (formerly, Fort William)
| BMD | 1872-1926 | **M-2820** and |
| | | **M-2821** |

includes:

St. Ansgarius' Lutheran Church, Port Arthur
BMD	1906-1912	**M-2821**
confirmations	1911-1912	**M-2821**
parish list	c. 1907	**M-2821**

Port Stanley, Elgin Co.

Personal registers of the Rev. J. Nelson Gould of Sarnia, Methodist and United Church of Canada minister
B	1916-1960	**H-1811**
M	1916-1961	**H-1811**
D	1916-1959	**H-1811**

includes:

Port Stanley Methodist Charge
| BMD | 1921-1926 | **H-1811** |

Portland Township, Frontenac Co.

Presbyterian Mission of Ernestown, Fredericksburg, Adolphustown, and the Bay of Quinté Region
| B | 1800-1841 | **H-1810** |
| M | 1800-1836 | **H-1810** |

(cont.)

| D | 1841 | **H-1810** |

includes:

Portland Township
| B | 1800-1811 | **H-1810** |
| M | 1810, 1816 | **H-1810** |

Prescott County

Civil registers of Ontario
| M | 1816-1869 | **M-5497** |
| | 1858-1869 | **M-7092** |

includes:

Ottawa District (later, Prescott and Russell Counties)
| M | 1816-1853 | **M-5497** |

includes: Hull, Gatineau Co., Que.; as well as extracts of B 1822-1836, for the districts of Montreal, and Quebec, Que.

Farmer's Almanac diaries of Angus Alexander McMillan and Family of Glengarry County
| BMD | 1862-1910 | **H-1808** |

includes:

Prescott County
| MD | 1863-1902 | **H-1808** |

as well as:

Caledonia Township, Prescott Co.
| BMD | 1862-1903 | **H-1808** |

Preston (later, Cambridge), Waterloo Co.

St. Peter's Evangelical Lutheran Church, Cambridge
B	1834-1942	**M-3241**
M	1834-1847, 1856-1951	**M-3241**
D	1839-1942	**M-3241**
confirmations 1835-1942		**M-3241**
communion rolls 1835, 1853-1942		**M-3241**
church council 1912-1946		**M-3241**

Civil registers of Waterloo County
B	1836-1861	**C-15758**
M	1854-1855	**C-15758**
D	1854-1855, 1858, 1860	**C-15758**

includes:

German Evangelical Lutheran Church, Preston (later, Cambridge)
B	1853-1855, 1860	**C-15758**
M	1855	**C-15758**
D	1855, 1860	**C-15758**

includes: places in the Townships of North Dumfries, Waterloo, Wilmot, and Woolwich, Waterloo Co.; in the Townships of Brantford, Burford, and South Dumfries, Brant Co.; as well as Blenheim Township, Oxford Co.; Puslinch Township,

(cont.)

Wellington Co.; and Beverley Township, Wentworth Co.

Roman Catholic Mission, Preston (later, Cambridge)
B   1860   **C-15758**
includes: places in the Townships of North Dumfries, and Waterloo

Prestonvale, Lanark Co.

Zion Memorial United Church, Carleton Place
BMD   1878-1933   **M-2209**
includes:

    Clayton Methodist Circuit, Clayton
    B   1890-1899   **M-2209**
    D   1896-1899   **M-2209**
    membership rolls 1893-1902   **M-2209**
    includes: Boyd, and Prestonvale

    Lanark and Clayton Methodist Circuit
    B   1884-1933   **M-2209**
    M   1903-1931   **M-2209**
    D   1902-1931   **M-2209**
    circuit register 1903-1924   **M-2209**
    includes: Boyd, Erwins, Harper, Playfair, and Prestonvale

Prospect Hill, Perth Co.

Anglican Parish of Kirkton with Granton and Saintsbury (including the Anglican Churches of: St. Paul's, Kirkton; Trinity, Prospect Hill; St. Patrick's, Saintsbury; and St. Thomas', Granton)
B   1862-1971   **M-2227**
MD   1863-1971   **M-2227**
includes: Township of Usborne, Huron Co.; Township of Blanshard, Perth Co.; and Township of Biddulph, Middlesex Co.

Proton Township, Grey Co.

Returns of coroners' inquests for Grey, Wellington, Bruce, [and Dufferin] Counties
D   1873   **C-15758**
includes: Durham, Owen Sound, and the Townships of Artemesia, Egremont, Euphrasia, Keppel, Normanby, Osprey, Proton, St. Vincent, and Sydenham, Grey Co.; and Melancthon Township, Dufferin Co.

Puslinch Township, Wellington Co.

Civil registers of Waterloo County
B   1836-1861   **C-15758**
M   1854-1855   **C-15758**
D   1854-1855, 1858, 1860   **C-15758**
includes:

(cont.)

German Evangelical Lutheran Church, Preston (later, Cambridge), Waterloo Co.
B   1853-1855, 1860   **C-15758**
M   1855   **C-15758**
D   1855, 1860   **C-15758**
includes: places in the Townships of North Dumfries, Waterloo, Wilmot, and Woolwich, Waterloo Co.; in the Townships of Brantford, Burford, and South Dumfries, Brant Co.; as well as Blenheim Township, Oxford Co.; Puslinch Township, Wellington Co.; and Beverley Township, Wentworth Co.

[Unorthodox Evangelical Lutheran] Congregation of the Rev. Frederick W. Bindemann, Waterloo Township, Waterloo Co.
M   1855   **C-15758**
includes: Berlin (later, Kitchener), and places in the Townships of North Dumfries, Waterloo, Wellesley, Wilmot, and Woolwich, Waterloo Co.; Carrick Township, Bruce Co.; Normanby Township, Grey Co.; the Townships of Blandford, and Blenheim, Oxford Co.; Hay Township, Huron Co.; the Townships of North Easthope, South Easthope, and Wallace, Perth Co.; the Townships of Peel, Guelph, Nichol, and Puslinch, Wellington Co.; and Hamilton, Wentworth Co.

Queenston, Lincoln Co.

Register of 547 marriage licences issued by Robert Grant (d. 1838)
M   1825-1838   **H-1811**

Quinté, Bay of, Region

St. John's Anglican Church, Bath, Lennox and Addington Co.
B   1787-1813   **H-1810**
M   1787-1816   **H-1810**
D   1787-1813   **H-1810**
comprises:

    St. Thomas' Anglican Church, Ernestown Township, Lennox and Addington Co.
    B   1788-1813   **H-1810**
    M   1787-1813, 1814, 1816   **H-1810**
    D   1788-1813   **H-1810**
    includes: Amherst Island, and the Townships of Adolphustown, Camden, and Fredericksburg, Lennox and Addington Co.; the Townships of Ameliasburg, Marysburgh, and Sophiasburgh, Prince Edward Co.; the Townships of Sidney, and Thurlow, Hastings Co.; and Kingston, Frontenac Co.; as well as Oswego, New York, U.S.A.

(cont.)

St. Paul's Anglican Church, Fredericksburg Township,
Lennox and Addington Co.
B   1787-1813   **H-1810**
M   1788-1812   **H-1810**
D   1787-1813   **H-1810**
includes: Amherst Island, and the Townships of Adolphustown, Camden, Ernestown, and Richmond, Lennox and Addington Co.; the Townships of Ameliasburg, Hallowell, Marysburgh, and Sophiasburgh, Prince Edward Co.; the Townships of Sidney, and Thurlow, Hastings Co.; and the Townships of Cramahé, and Percy, Northumberland Co.; as well as Oswego, New York, U.S.A.

Presbyterian Mission of Ernestown, Fredericksburg, Adolphustown, and the Bay of Quinté region
B   1800-1841   **H-1810**
M   1800-1836   **H-1810**
D   1841   **H-1810**
comprises:

Adolphustown Township, Lennox and Addington Co.
B   1800-1811   **H-1810**
M   1800-1821, 1831-1835   **H-1810**

Amherst Island Township, Lennox and Addington Co.
B   1834-1840   **H-1810**
M   1802, 1816, 1819   **H-1810**

Camden Township, Lennox and Addington Co.
B   1800-1813, 1820, 1835-1839   **H-1810**
M   1805-1821, 1832-1833   **H-1810**

Ernestown Township, Lennox and Addington Co.
B   1800-1813, 1819-1821, 1827, 1830, 1832, 1835   **H-1810**
M   1800-1822, 1831-1835   **H-1810**

Fredericksburg Township, Lennox and Addington Co.
B   1800-1813, 1815, 1827, 1832, 1837-1840   **H-1810**
M   1800-1822, 1831-1836   **H-1810**

Richmond Township, Lennox and Addington Co.
B   1800-1811, 1813-1814, 1824-1825, 1832-1833, 1838-1839   **H-1810**
M   1802-1803, 1807-1821, 1832-1835   **H-1810**

Sheffield Township, Lennox and Addington Co.
B   1831, 1836, 1839   **H-1810**

Rawdon Township, Hastings Co.
B   1803   **H-1810**

Sidney Township, Hastings Co.
B   1800-1820, 1837, 1839   **H-1810**
M   1803, 1806-1818   **H-1810**

Thurlow Township, Hastings Co.
B   1802-1816, 1821, 1839   **H-1810**
M   1807, 1812, 1816, 1822   **H-1810**

Tyendinaga Township, Hastings Co.
B   1826-1837   **H-1810**

Cramahé Township, Northumberland Co.
B   1800-1806, 1811, 1818, 1820   **H-1810**

Hamilton Township, Northumberland Co.
B   1800-1803   **H-1810**

Murray Township, Northumberland Co.
B   1800-1821   **H-1810**
M   1803, 1812   **H-1810**

Ameliasburg Township, Prince Edward Co.
B   1800-1822, 1827, 1829, 1833-1840   **H-1810**
M   1807-1808, 1812, 1820   **H-1810**

Hallowell Township, Prince Edward Co.
B   1800-1810, 1812, 1820, 1826   **H-1810**
M   1800-1820, 1831-1835   **H-1810**

Marysburgh Township, Prince Edward Co.
B   1800-1812, 1820, 1835, 1837   **H-1810**
M   1800-1822, 1831-1835   **H-1810**

Sophiasburgh Township, Prince Edward Co.
B   1806-1822, 1828   **H-1810**
M   1801-1822, 1831-1834   **H-1810**

Kingston, Frontenac Co.
B   1802-1811, 1820, 1822   **H-1810**
M   1802, 1805-1822, 1831-1832, 1835   **H-1810**

Loughborough Township, Frontenac Co.
B   1804-1805, 1809-1811, 1830-1838   **H-1810**
M   1809, 1812, 1818-1820   **H-1810**

Pittsburg Township, Frontenac Co.
B   1800-1809   **H-1810**

Portland Township, Frontenac Co.
B   1800-1811   **H-1810**
M   1810, 1816   **H-1810**

(cont.)

Radcliffe Township, Renfrew Co.

Our Lady of Czestochowa, Queen of Poland (Roman Catholic) Church (formerly, St. Stanislaus Kostka Roman Catholic Church, Hagarty Township), Wilno

BMD	1880-1884	**H-1456** (partial index)
B	1877-1880	**H-1456**
	1888-1940	**H-1456** (partial index)
M	1885-1937	**H-1456** (partial index)
	1928-1960	**H-1457**
D	1885-1928	**H-1456** (partial index)
	1928-1943, 1945	**H-1457**
	1961-1975	**H-1457**
ordinations, 1910, 1923-1924		**H-1456**
confirmations, 1912-1913		**H-1456**
	1947-1948, 1950, 1953, 1956, 1959	**H-1457**
first communions, 1946-1947,	1951, 1958-1959	**H-1457**

includes: Townships of Brudenell, Burns, Hagarty, Radcliffe, and Sherwood

(The registers are in French, Latin, and English. Miscellaneous related items are in Polish.)

Ramsay Township, Lanark Co.

Mississippi Circuit of the Methodist Episcopal (later, the Wesleyan Methodist) Church

B	1829-1843	**H-1809**

includes: places in the Townships of Beckwith, Lanark, Pakenham, and Ramsay, Lanark Co.; in the Townships of Horton, McNab, Pembroke, and Westmeath, Renfrew Co.; and Fitzroy Township, Carleton Co.

Almonte United Church, Almonte

BMD	1833-1962	**M-2217**
M	1896-1926	**M-2229**

comprises:

Ramsay "Auld Kirk" (later, St. Andrew's Presbyterian Church), Almonte

B	1833-1902	**M-2217**
M	1834-1857	**M-2217**
D	1848-1869, 1873, 1877, 1889-1894	**M-2217**
communicants 1834-1869		**M-2217**
membership lists c. 1890, 1892-1894		**M-2217**

St. Andrew's Presbyterian Church (formerly, Ramsay "Auld Kirk"), Almonte

B	1902-1911	**M-2217**
M	1858-1901, 1937	**M-2217**
	1896-1911	**M-2217**
	1898-1926	**M-2229**

(cont.)

St. John's Presbyterian Church, Almonte

B	1877-1905	**M-2217**
M	1859-1912	**M-2217**

United Presbyterian Church (formerly, St. Andrew's and St. John's), Almonte

B	1906-1925	**M-2217**
M	1912-1925	**M-2217**

Bethany United Church, Almonte

B	1925-1953	**M-2217**
M	1925-1937	**M-2217**

Carleton Place Wesleyan Methodist Circuit, Carleton Place

B	1905-1906, 1915	**M-2217**
M	1858-1872, 1879, 1889-1890	**M-2217**
D	1905-1907	**M-2217**

Almonte Methodist Circuit, Almonte

B	1915-1921	**M-2217**

St. Andrew's (Presbyterian) Church, Appleton

B	1908-1962	**M-2217**
communion rolls c. 1889-1917		**M-2229**

Trinity United Church, Almonte

B	1928-1953	**M-2217**
M	1918-1943	**M-2217**
D	1917-1953	**M-2217**

includes: Appleton Pastoral Charge

Almonte and Appleton United Church

B	1953-1962	**M-2217**

Ashton Presbyterian Church, Ashton

M	1896-1911	**M-2229**
communion rolls c. 1889-1917		**M-2229**

Rawdon Township, Hastings Co.

Presbyterian Mission of Ernestown, Fredericksburg, Adolphustown, and the Bay of Quinté Region

B	1800-1841	**H-1810**
M	1800-1836	**H-1810**
D	1841	**H-1810**

includes:

Rawdon Township

B	1803	**H-1810**

Renfrew County

Civil registers of Ontario

M	1816-1869	**M-5497**
	1858-1869	**M-7092**

includes:

Renfrew County

M	1858-1869	**M-5497**

Riceville, Prescott Co.

Riceville Cemetery recordings by Ann MacLaurin, 1970
D   1862-1928   **H-1807**

Richmond, Carleton Co.

Burials in Hazeldean Cemeteries
D   1835-1939   **M-7718**
includes:

    St. John the Baptist's Anglican Church, Richmond
    D   1892, 1894 extracts   **M-7718**

St. Philip's Roman Catholic Church
BMD   1836-1924   **M-2818**
includes:

    St. Clare's Roman Catholic Church (Goulbourn Mission), Dwyer Hill
    BMD   1891-1924   **M-2818**

Richmond Township, Lennox and Addington Co.

St. John's Anglican Church, Bath
B   1787-1813   **H-1810**
M   1787-1816   **H-1810**
D   1787-1813   **H-1810**
comprises:

    St. Thomas' Anglican Church, Ernestown Township
    B   1788-1813   **H-1810**
    M   1787-1813, 1814, 1816 **H-1810**
    D   1788-1813   **H-1810**
    includes: Amherst Island, and the Townships of Adolphustown, Camden, and Fredericksburg, Lennox and Addington Co.; the Townships of Ameliasburg, Marysburgh, and Sophiasburgh, Prince Edward Co.; the Townships of Sidney, and Thurlow, Hastings Co.; and Kingston, Frontenac Co.; as well as Oswego, New York, U.S.A.

    St. Paul's Anglican Church, Fredericksburg Township
    B   1787-1813   **H-1810**
    M   1788-1812   **H-1810**
    D   1787-1813   **H-1810**
    includes: Amherst Island, and the Townships of Adolphustown, Camden, Ernestown, and Richmond, Lennox and Addington Co.; the Townships of Ameliasburg, Hallowell, Marysburgh, and Sophiasburgh, Prince Edward Co.; the Townships of Sidney, and Thurlow, Hastings Co.; and the Townships of Cramahé, and Percy, Northumberland Co.; as well as Oswego, New York, U.S.A.

(cont.)

Presbyterian Mission of Ernestown, Fredericksburg, Adolphustown, and the Bay of Quinté region
B   1800-1841   **H-1810**
M   1800-1836   **H-1810**
D   1841   **H-1810**
includes:

    Richmond Township
    B   1800-1811, 1813-1814, 1824-1825, 1832-1833, 1838-1839 **H-1810**
    M   1802-1803, 1807-1821, 1832-1835 **H-1810**

Richmond Village (Bayham), Elgin Co.

Personal registers of the Rev. J. Nelson Gould of Sarnia, Methodist and United Church of Canada minister
B   1916-1960   **H-1811**
M   1916-1961   **H-1811**
D   1916-1959   **H-1811**
includes:

    Richmond-Corinth United Church of Canada Charge
    B   1947-1960   **H-1811**
    M   1947-1961   **H-1811**
    D   1947-1959   **H-1811**
    includes: Aylmer West, Corinth, Fairview, North Bayham, Richmond Village (Bayham), and Summers Corners, Elgin Co.

Rideau District

Rideau Methodist Circuit
B   1781-1843   **C-3030**
includes: Lanark and Grenville Counties; and Smith's Falls Methodist Circuit

Riverside, Dundas Co.

St. Lawrence Evangelical Lutheran Church, Morrisburg
BMD   1823-1972   **M-2981**
includes:

    St. George's (later, St. John's) Evangelical Lutheran Congregation, Williamsburg
    BMD   1823-1840   **M-2981**
    confirmations 1827-1840   **M-2981**

    St. John's, Riverside, and St. Paul's, Morrisburg, Evangelical Lutheran Church
    BMD   1840-1895   **M-2981**
    confirmations 1841-1863   **M-2981**
    communicants n.d.   **M-2981**

    St. John's, Riverside, and St. Peter's, North Williamsburg, Evangelical Lutheran Church
    M   1858-1914   **M-2981**

(cont.)

St. John's Evangelical Lutheran Church, Williamsburg, and St. Paul's Lutheran Church, Morrisburg
B	1872-1972	**M-2981**
M	1873-1936	**M-2981**
D	1873-1972	**M-2981**
communicants n.d., 1876-1901		**M-2981**

Rosetta, Lanark Co.

Clayton United Church, Clayton
BMD	1805-1965	**M-3687** and **M-3688**
	1876-1965	**M-3243**

includes:

Middleville Congregational Church, Middleville
B	1913-1928	**M-3243**
M	1858-1871	**M-3687**
	1896-1925	**M-3243**
D	1910-1964	**M-3243**

includes: Rosetta

St. Peter's Presbyterian Church, Darling Township
B	1871-1878	**M-3687**
communion rolls 1890-1942		**M-3688**

includes: St. John's, Hopetown; Rosetta Presbyterian Congregation; and St. Peter's, Tatlock

St. Peter's, Darling, and St. Paul's, Middleville, Presbyterian Congregations
BD	1893-1965	**M-3688**
M	1897-1919	**M-3243**

includes: Hopetown, Rosetta, and Tatlock

St. Paul's, Middleville, and St. James', Dalhousie, United (Presbyterian) Pastoral Charge
B	1858-1864	**M-3687**
M	1859-1896, 1909-1910	**M-3687**
communion rolls 1858-1865		**M-3687**
	1872-1954	**M-3688**

includes: St. John's United Church, Hopetown, 1925-1941; and Rosetta United Church, 1935-1942

Clayton-Middleville Presbyterian Charge (later, Middleville United Church)
B	1881-1950	**M-3243**
D	1942-1957	**M-3688**
communion rolls 1942-1957		**M-3688**

includes: Hopetown, Rosetta, Darling, and Tatlock

Ross Township, Renfrew Co.

Shawville United Church, Shawville, Pontiac Co., Que.
BMD	1851-1918	**M-2243**
	1877-1939	**M-2374**

includes:

Presbyterian Church (Church of Scotland), Litchfield Township, Pontiac Co., Que.
BMD	1853-1870, 1874-1904, 1918	**M-2243**

includes: Townships of Bristol, Bryson, Calumet-Island, Clarendon, Leslie, and Thorne, Pontiac Co., Que.; as well as Ross, and Westmeath Townships, Renfrew Co., Ont., in the early years

Roxborough Township, Stormont Co.

Civil registers of the Surrogate Court for the Eastern and Johnstown Districts
B	1831, 1859, 1862-1865	**C-3030**
M	1831-1857, 1863, 1865	**C-3030** (index)

includes:

Wesleyan Methodist Church in Canada, Circuits in the Eastern District
B	1859	**C-3030**
M	1833-1857	**C-3030** (index)

includes: Townships of Matilda, Mountain, Williamsburgh, and Winchester, Dundas Co.; the Townships of Edwardsburgh, and Oxford, Grenville Co.; Sheek Island, and the Townships of Cornwall, Finch, Osnabruck, and Roxborough, Stormont Co.; as well as the Brockville district, Leeds Co.; and other places in the Counties of Dundas, Stormont, and Glengarry

St. John's Presbyterian (Church of Scotland) Church, Cornwall, Stormont Co.
M	1831-1850, 1855-1857	**C-3030** (index)

includes: Townships of Charlottenburg, Kenyon (including the Indian Lands), and Lancaster, Glengarry Co.; and Roxborough Township, Stormont Co.

Presbyterian (Church of Scotland) Church, Kenyon Township, Glengarry Co.
M	1865	**C-3030** (index)

includes: Cambridge Township, Russell Co.; and Roxborough Township, Stormont Co.

Presbyterian Church of the Rev. Isaac Purkis, Osnabruck Township, Stormont Co.
M	1840, 1842-1849	**C-3030** (index)

St. Andrew's (Presbyterian) Church of the Rev. Peter McVicar, Martintown, Glengarry Co.
M	1857	**C-3030** (index)

includes: Townships of Charlottenburg, and Kenyon, Glengarry Co.; and Roxborough Township, Stormont Co.

Congregation of the Rev. E. Sallows
M	1851	**C-3030** (index)

includes: Townships of Osnabruck, and Roxborough, Stormont Co.

Civil registers for the Eastern District
M   1858-1869   **M-3205**
includes:

    Baptist Church, Roxborough Township
    M   1867   **M-3205**

Osnabruck and Lunenburg Presbyterian Congregations
B   1848-1909   **C-3030**
M   1860-1900   **C-3030**
D   1907-1909   **C-3030**
includes:

    Canada Presbyterian Church of Lunenburg and Osnabruck
    M   1860-1900   **C-3030**
    includes: Cornwall Township, Finch, Newington, Osnabruck, and Roxborough Township, Stormont Co.; the Indian Lands, Glengarry Co.; and the Townships of Williamsburgh, and Winchester, Dundas Co.

Civil registers of Stormont County
M   1866   **C-15758**
consists of:

    Wesleyan Methodist Mission, Roxborough
    M   1866   **C-15758**
    includes: Townships of Finch, Osnabruck, and Roxborough, Stormont Co.

Farmer's Almanac diaries of Angus Alexander McMillan and Family of Glengarry Co.
BMD   1862-1910   **H-1808**
includes:

    Roxborough Township
    D   1864-1902   **H-1808**

Russell County

Civil registers of Ontario
M   1816-1869   **M-5497**
          1858-1869   **M-7092**
includes:

    Ottawa District (later, Prescott and Russell Counties)
    M   1816-1853   **M-5497**
    includes: Hull, Gatineau Co., Que.; as well as extracts of
        B 1822-1836, for the districts of Montreal, and Quebec, Que.

    Russell County
    M   1855-1869   **M-5497**

St. Agatha, Waterloo Co.

Civil registers of Waterloo County
B   1836-1861   **C-15758**
M   1854-1855   **C-15758**
D   1854-1855, 1858, 1860 **C-15758**
includes:

    St. Agatha's Roman Catholic Church, Wilmot Township
    BD   1860   **C-15758**
    includes: places in the Townships of Waterloo, Wellesley, Wilmot, and Woolwich, Waterloo Co.; and Mornington, and South Easthope Townships, Perth Co.

St. Andrew's, Stormont Co.

Civil registers of the Surrogate Court for the Eastern and Johnstown Districts
B   1831, 1859, 1862-1865 **C-3030**
M   1831-1857, 1863, 1865 **C-3030** (index)
includes:

    St. Andrew's Roman Catholic Parish, St. Andrew's
    M   1848   **C-3030** (index)

St. Catharines, Lincoln Co.

Personal record of marriages performed by the Reverend Dr. Isaac Tovell, of the Methodist Church of Canada and the United Church of Canada, Toronto, York Co.
M   1875-1935 Index   **H-1810**
includes:

    St. Catharines
    M   1888-1892, [1922] Index **H-1810**

St. George, Brant Co.

Civil registers of Waterloo County
B   1836-1861   **C-15758**
M   1854-1855   **C-15758**
D   1854-1855, 1858, 1860 **C-15758**
includes:

    St. James' Anglican Church, Wilmot Township, Waterloo Co.
    BD   1860   **C-15758**
    includes: other places in Wilmot Township; as well as St. George, Brant Co.; and the Townships of Blandford, and East Zorra, Oxford Co.

St. Raphael West, Glengarry Co.

St. Raphael's Roman Catholic Church
B   1805-1818, 1828   **C-3028 & H-1811**
          1818-1825   **C-3029 & H-1811**
          1831   **H-1811**

(cont.)

M	1805-1808, 1815-1823	**C-3028**	
	1805-1815		**H-1811**
	1823-1825	**C-3029**	
D	1805-1810		**H-1811**
	1816-1822	**C-3028**	
BMD	1826-1831	**C-3029**	
	1805-1831 Index	**C-3029**	
	1832-1836		**H-1811**
conversions, 1805-1809			**H-1811**

St. Thomas, Elgin Co.

Personal registers of the Rev. J. Nelson Gould of Sarnia, Methodist and United Church of Canada minister

B	1916-1960	**H-1811**
M	1916-1961	**H-1811**
D	1916-1959	**H-1811**

includes:

    Grace United Church of Canada Church, St. Thomas
    BMD   1926-1933   **H-1811**
    members received, 1926-1932   **H-1811**

St. Vincent Township, Grey Co.

Returns of coroners' inquests for Grey, Wellington, Bruce, [and Dufferin] Counties

D	1873	**C-15758**

includes: Durham, Owen Sound, and the Townships of Artemesia, Egremont, Euphrasia, Keppel, Normanby, Osprey, Proton, St. Vincent, and Sydenham, Grey Co.; and Melancthon Township, Dufferin Co.

Saintsbury, Middlesex Co.

Anglican Parish of Kirkton with Granton and Saintsbury (including the Anglican Churches of: St. Paul's, Kirkton; Trinity, Prospect Hill; St. Patrick's, Saintsbury; and St. Thomas', Granton)

B	1862-1971	**M-2227**
MD	1863-1971	**M-2227**

includes: Township of Usborne, Huron Co.; Township of Blanshard, Perth Co.; and Township of Biddulph, Middlesex Co.

Sandwich (antérieurement, Pointe-de-Montréal-du-Détroit), comté d'Essex

Sainte-Anne-du-Détroit, Michigan, U.S.A.
(Église catholique)

BMD	1704-1800	**C-2893 à C-2895**

comprend :

    Missions des Hurons de la Pointe-de-Montréal-du-Détroit
    (Église catholique)

B	1761-1767	**C-2894**

(cont.)

L'Assomption-de-la-Pointe-de-Montréal-du-Détroit
(Église catholique)

B	1767-1771	**C-2894**
M	1764-1765, 1768-1771	**C-2894**
D	1768-1772	**C-2894**
BMD	1772-1777	**C-2894**
	1777-1783	**C-2895**

L'Assomption-de-Sandwich-du-Détroit
(Église catholique)

BMD	1781-1799	**C-2895**

St. John's Anglican Church

BMD	1802-1827	**C-3030** (index)

Sandwich Township, Essex Co.

Civil registers of Essex County

B	1826, 1845-1862	**C-15758**

includes:

    Congregation of the Rev. John [H.] John,
    Sandwich Township

B	1826, 1847, 1849-1851, 1855-1856, 1859-1862	**C-15758**

    Wesleyan Methodist Church, Sandwich Township

B	1860-1861	**C-15758**

Sarnia, Lambton Co.

Personal registers of the Rev. J. Nelson Gould of Sarnia, Methodist and United Church of Canada minister

B	1916-1960	**H-1811**
M	1916-1961	**H-1811**
D	1916-1959	**H-1811**

comprises:

    Sparta-Dexter Methodist Charge, Elgin Co.
    BMD   1916-1921   **H-1811**

    Port Stanley Methodist Charge, Elgin Co.
    BMD   1921-1926   **H-1811**

    Grace United Church of Canada Church, St. Thomas, Elgin Co.
    BMD   1926-1933   **H-1811**
    members received, 1926-1932   **H-1811**

    Parker Street United Church of Canada, Sarnia
    BMD   1933-1947   **H-1811**

    Richmond-Corinth United Church of Canada Charge, Elgin Co.

B	1947-1960	**H-1811**
M	1947-1961	**H-1811**
D	1947-1959	**H-1811**

    includes: Aylmer West, Corinth, Fairview, North Bayham, Richmond Village (Bayham), and Summers Corners, Elgin Co.

Shawanaga Township, Parry Sound District

Journals of the Rev. Allen Salt, a Methodist Indian missionary in western Ontario
BMD   1854-1855, 1874-1899, 1904   **C-15709**
includes:

    Parry Island Methodist Indian Mission, Georgian Bay
    BMD   1883-1899, 1904   **C-15709**
    includes: French River, Henvey Inlet, and Shawanaga Township in the Parry Sound District, as well as other Indian reserves in the region

Sheek Island, Stormont Co.

Civil registers of the Surrogate Court for the Eastern and Johnstown Districts
B   1831, 1859, 1862-1865   **C-3030**
M   1831-1857, 1863, 1865   **C-3030** (index)
includes:

    Wesleyan Methodist Church in Canada, Circuits in the Eastern District
    B   1859   **C-3030**
    M   1833-1857   **C-3030** (index)
    includes: Townships of Matilda, Mountain, Williamsburgh, and Winchester, Dundas Co.; the Townships of Edwardsburgh, and Oxford, Grenville Co.; Sheek Island, and the Townships of Cornwall, Finch, Osnabruck, and Roxborough, Stormont Co.; as well as the Brockville district, Leeds Co.; and other places in the Counties of Dundas, Stormont, and Glengarry

Sheffield Township, Lennox and Addington Co.

Presbyterian Mission of Ernestown, Fredericksburg, Adolphustown, and the Bay of Quinté region
B   1800-1841   **H-1810**
M   1800-1836   **H-1810**
D   1841   **H-1810**
includes:

    Sheffield Township
    B   1831, 1836, 1839   **H-1810**

Sherbrooke (North) Township, Lanark Co.

Knox Presbyterian Church, McDonalds Corners
B   1847-1857   **M-4614**
includes: Elphin, and Snow Road, Frontenac Co.; and Dalhousie, and North Sherbrooke Townships, Lanark Co.

Sherwood Township, Renfrew Co.

Our Lady of Czestochowa, Queen of Poland (Roman Catholic) Church (formerly, St. Stanislaus Kostka Roman Catholic Church, Hagarty Township), Wilno
BMD   1880-1884   **H-1456** (partial index)
B   1877-1880   **H-1456**
    1888-1940   **H-1456** (partial index)
M   1885-1937   **H-1456** (partial index)
    1928-1960   **H-1457**
D   1885-1928   **H-1456** (partial index)
    1928-1943, 1945   **H-1457**
    1961-1975   **H-1457**
ordinations, 1910, 1923-1924   **H-1456**
confirmations, 1912-1913   **H-1456**
    1947-1948, 1950, 1953, 1956, 1959   **H-1457**
first communions, 1946-1947, 1951, 1958-1959   **H-1457**
includes: Townships of Brudenell, Burns, Hagarty, Radcliffe, and Sherwood

(The registers are in French, Latin, and English. Miscellaneous related items are in Polish.)

Sidney Township, Hastings Co.

St. John's Anglican Church, Bath, Lennox and Addington Co.
B   1787-1813   **H-1810**
M   1787-1816   **H-1810**
D   1787-1813   **H-1810**
comprises:

    St. Thomas' Anglican Church, Ernestown Township, Lennox and Addington Co.
    B   1788-1813   **H-1810**
    M   1787-1813, 1814, 1816   **H-1810**
    D   1788-1813   **H-1810**
    includes: Amherst Island, and the Townships of Adolphustown, Camden, and Fredericksburg, Lennox and Addington Co.; the Townships of Ameliasburg, Marysburgh, and Sophiasburgh, Prince Edward Co.; the Townships of Sidney, and Thurlow, Hastings Co.; and Kingston, Frontenac Co.; as well as Oswego, New York, U.S.A.

    St. Paul's Anglican Church, Fredericksburg Township, Lennox and Addington Co.
    B   1787-1813   **H-1810**
    M   1788-1812   **H-1810**
    D   1787-1813   **H-1810**
    includes: Amherst Island, and the Townships of Adolphustown, Camden, Ernestown, and Richmond, Lennox and Addington Co.; the

(cont.)

Townships of Ameliasburg, Hallowell, Marysburgh, and Sophiasburgh, Prince Edward Co.; the Townships of Sidney, and Thurlow, Hastings Co.; and the Townships of Cramahé, and Percy, Northumberland Co.; as well as Oswego, New York, U.S.A.

Presbyterian Mission of Ernestown, Fredericksburg, Adolphustown, and the Bay of Quinté region
B	1800-1841	**H-1810**
M	1800-1836	**H-1810**
D	1841	**H-1810**

includes:

Sidney Township
B	1800-1820, 1837, 1839	**H-1810**
M	1803, 1806-1818	**H-1810**

Smith's Falls, Lanark and Leeds Cos.

Rideau Methodist Circuit
B	1814-1843	**C-3030**

includes: Lanark, and Grenville Counties; and Smith's Falls Methodist Circuit

Westminster Presbyterian Church
B	1834-1913	**M-5905**
M	1835-1913	**M-5905**
	1897-1915	**M-5906** (index)
D	1860, 1868	**M-5905**

comprises:

St. Andrew's Presbyterian Church
B	1834-1892, 1907-1913	**M-5905**
M	1835-1846, 1850-1913	**M-5905**
D	1860, 1868	**M-5905**
communicants rolls	1835-1867, 1869-1894	**M-5905**

St. Paul's Presbyterian Church (formerly, Union Church)
B	1845-1913	**M-5905**
M	1869-1900	**M-5905**
	1897-1915	**M-5906** (index)
communicants rolls	1869-1890	**M-5906**

Smith Township, Peterborough Co.

St. Paul's Presbyterian Church, Peterborough
M	1834-1857	**H-1810**

includes: Townships of Asphodel, Douro, Dummer, Ennismore, Harvey, North Monaghan, Otonabee, and Smith, Peterborough Co.; the Townships of Hamilton, and South Monaghan in Northumberland Co.; the Township of Cavan, Durham Co.; and the Townships of Emily, and Ops, Victoria Co.

Civil registers of Peterborough County
M	1859-1873	**H-1810**

consists of:

Christ Church Anglican Church, Lakefield
M	1859-1873	**H-1810**

includes: Lakefield (North Douro), and Peterborough, as well as the Townships of Douro, Dummer, Otonabee, and Smith, Peterborough Co.; and Lindsay, Victoria Co.

Snow Road, Frontenac Co.

Knox Presbyterian Church, McDonalds Corners, Lanark Co.
B	1847-1857	**M-4614**

includes: Elphin, and Snow Road, Frontenac Co.; and Dalhousie, and North Sherbrooke Townships, Lanark Co.

Sophiasburgh Township, Prince Edward Co.

St. John's Anglican Church, Bath, Lennox and Addington Co.
B	1787-1813	**H-1810**
M	1787-1816	**H-1810**
D	1787-1813	**H-1810**

comprises:

St. Thomas' Anglican Church, Ernestown Township, Lennox and Addington Co.
B	1788-1813	**H-1810**
M	1787-1813, 1814, 1816	**H-1810**
D	1788-1813	**H-1810**

includes: Amherst Island, and the Townships of Adolphustown, Camden, and Fredericksburg, Lennox and Addington Co.; the Townships of Ameliasburg, Marysburgh, and Sophiasburgh, Prince Edward Co.; the Townships of Sidney, and Thurlow, Hastings Co.; and Kingston, Frontenac Co.; as well as Oswego, New York, U.S.A.

St. Paul's Anglican Church, Fredericksburg Township, Lennox and Addington Co.
B	1787-1813	**H-1810**
M	1788-1812	**H-1810**
D	1787-1813	**H-1810**

includes: Amherst Island, and the Townships of Adolphustown, Camden, Ernestown, and Richmond, Lennox and Addington Co.; the Townships of Ameliasburg, Hallowell, Marysburgh, and Sophiasburgh, Prince Edward Co.; the Townships of Sidney, and Thurlow, Hastings Co.; and the Townships of Cramahé, and Percy, Northumberland Co.; as well as Oswego, New York, U.S.A.

(cont.)

Presbyterian Mission of Ernestown, Fredericksburg, Adolphustown, and the Bay of Quinté region
B	1800-1841	**H-1810**
M	1800-1836	**H-1810**
D	1841	**H-1810**

includes:

    Sophiasburgh Township
B	1806-1822, 1828	**H-1810**
M	1801-1822, 1831-1834	**H-1810**

South Dumfries Township, Brant Co.

Civil registers of Waterloo County
B	1836-1861	**C-15758**
M	1854-1855	**C-15758**
D	1854-1855, 1858, 1860	**C-15758**

includes:

    German Evangelical Lutheran Church, Preston (later, Cambridge)
B	1853-1855, 1860	**C-15758**
M	1855	**C-15758**
D	1855, 1860	**C-15758**

    includes: places in the Townships of North Dumfries, Waterloo, Wilmot, and Woolwich, Waterloo Co.; in the Townships of Brantford, Burford, and South Dumfries, Brant Co.; as well as Blenheim Township, Oxford Co.; Puslinch Township, Wellington Co.; and Beverley Township, Wentworth Co.

South Easthope Township, Perth Co.

Civil registers of Waterloo County
B	1836-1861	**C-15758**
M	1854-1855	**C-15758**
D	1854-1855, 1858, 1860	**C-15758**

includes:

    German Baptist Church of the Rev. Henry Schneider
B	1861	**C-15758**
M	1855*	**C-15758**
D	1855*, 1860	**C-15758**

    includes: Berlin (later, Kitchener), as well as other places in the Townships of Waterloo, Wilmot, and Woolwich, Waterloo Co.; and in South Easthope Township, Perth Co.

    * In German

    [Unorthodox Evangelical Lutheran] Congregation of the Rev. Frederick W. Bindemann, Waterloo Township, Waterloo Co.
M	1855	**C-15758**

    includes: Berlin (later, Kitchener), and places in the Townships of North Dumfries, Waterloo, Wellesley, Wilmot, and Woolwich, Waterloo Co.; Carrick Township, Bruce Co.; Normanby Township, Grey Co.; the Townships of Blandford, and Blenheim, Oxford Co.; Hay Township, Huron Co.; the Townships of North Easthope, South Easthope, and Wallace, Perth Co.; the Townships of Peel, Guelph, Nichol, and Puslinch, Wellington Co.; and Hamilton, Wentworth Co.

St. Agatha's Roman Catholic Church, Wilmot Township, Waterloo Co.
BD	1860	**C-15758**

includes: places in the Townships of Waterloo, Wellesley, Wilmot, and Woolwich, Waterloo Co.; and Mornington, and South Easthope Townships, Perth Co.

South Fredericksburgh Township, Lennox and Addington Co.
See: Fredericksburgh Township

South Monaghan Township, Northumberland Co.

St. Paul's Presbyterian Church, Peterborough, Peterborough Co.
M	1834-1857	**H-1810**

includes: Townships of Asphodel, Douro, Dummer, Ennismore, Harvey, North Monaghan, Otonabee, and Smith, Peterborough Co.; the Townships of Hamilton, and South Monaghan in Northumberland Co.; the Township of Cavan, Durham Co.; and the Townships of Emily, and Ops, Victoria Co.

South Plantagenet Township, Prescott Co.

Civil registers of the Surrogate Court for the Eastern and Johnstown Districts
B	1831, 1859, 1862-1865	**C-3030**
M	1831-1857, 1863, 1865	**C-3030** (index)

includes:

    [Presbyterian] Congregation of the Rev. Peter Watson, Williamstown, Glengarry Co.
M	1865	**C-3030** (index)

    includes: Martintown, and Williamstown, and other places in Charlottenburg Township, as well as the Townships of Lancaster, and Lochiel, Glengarry Co.; Cornwall Township, Stormont Co.; and the Townships of North Plantagenet, and South Plantagenet, Prescott Co.

South Walsingham Township, Norfolk Co.

Norfolk County Historical Society Collections
B	1783-1863	**M-283**
M	1807-1835	**M-274, M-275** and **M-277**
	1858-1897	**M-283**

(cont.)

ONTARIO

D   1840-1899   M-283
includes:

Hartford and Fredericksburg (Delhi) Regular Baptist Congregations
B   1783-1863   M-283
M   1858-1897   M-283
D   1840-1899   M-283
includes: Townships of Middleton, South Walsingham, Townsend, and Windham, Norfolk Co.; and Walpole Township, Haldimand Co.

(Pages 12941-12987)

Sparta, Elgin Co.

Personal registers of the Rev. J. Nelson Gould of Sarnia, Methodist and United Church of Canada minister
B   1916-1960   H-1811
M   1916-1961   H-1811
D   1916-1959   H-1811
includes:

Sparta-Dexter Methodist Charge
BMD   1916-1921   H-1811

Stanley Township, Huron Co.

Civil registers of Waterloo County
B   1836-1861   C-15758
M   1854-1855   C-15758
D   1854-1855, 1858, 1860   C-15758
includes:

Evangelical Lutheran Church, Mannheim, New Dundee, and New Hamburg, Waterloo Co.
B   1858, 1860   C-15758
D   1860   C-15758
includes: places in Wilmot Township, , Waterloo Co.; in Brant, and Carrick Townships, Bruce Co.; in Hay, Stanley, and Tuckersmith Townships, Huron Co.; and Blenheim Township, Oxford Co.; as well as Hanover, Grey Co.; and Williamsburgh [Township], Dundas Co.

Stephenson Township, Muskoka District

Register of the Rev. John Becket (1838-1921), Presbyterian missionary at Aspdin, Muskoka District, 1905-1908
M   1905-1908, 1910, 1913,
         1915   H-1810
includes:

Stephenson Township
M   1905-1908   H-1810

Stewartville, Renfrew Co.

Lochwinnoch Presbyterian Church, Loch Winnoch
B   1867-1919   M-2368
M   1883-1906   M-2368
communion rolls 1887-1918   M-2368
includes: Castleford, Dewar's Settlement, Stewartville

Stisted Township, Muskoka District

Register of the Rev. John Becket (1838-1921), Presbyterian missionary at Aspdin, Muskoka District, 1905-1908
M   1905-1908, 1910, 1913,
         1915   H-1810
includes:

Stisted Township
M   1907-1908   H-1810

Stittsville, Carleton Co.

Burials in Hazeldean Cemeteries
D   1835-1939   M-7718
includes:

Bells Corners Anglican Church (including the Anglican Churches of Hazeldean, Stittsville, and Fallowfield, at various dates)
D   1883-1939 extracts   M-7718

Carp United Church, Carp
BMD   1858-1929   M-816 and M-817
includes:

St. Paul's Methodist Church, Carp
M   1898-1928   M-816
membership rolls 1893-1929   M-816
includes: Hazeldean, Huntley, Marchhurst, and Stittsville

Stormont County

St. Andrew's Presbyterian Church, Williamstown, Glengarry Co.
BM   1779-1810   C-3030 (index)
BMD   1811-1817   C-3030 (index)
includes: Stormont Co., Ont.; Montreal, Que., etc.

Civil registers of the Surrogate Court for the Eastern and Johnstown Districts
B   1831, 1859, 1862-1865   C-3030
M   1831-1857, 1863, 1865   C-3030 (index)
includes:

(cont.)

Wesleyan Methodist Church in Canada, Circuits in the Eastern District
B	1859	**C-3030**
M	1833-1857	**C-3030** (index)

includes: Townships of Matilda, Mountain, Williamsburgh, and Winchester, Dundas Co.; the Townships of Edwardsburgh, and Oxford, Grenville Co.; Sheek Island, and the Townships of Cornwall, Finch, Osnabruck, and Roxborough, Stormont Co.; as well as the Brockville district, Leeds Co.; and other places in the Counties of Dundas, Stormont, and Glengarry

Civil registers for the Eastern District
M	1858-1869	**M-3205**

includes: Charlottenburg, Kenyon, Lancaster, and Lochiel Townships, Glengarry Co.; and Roxborough Township, Stormont Co.

Civil registers of Stormont County
M	1866	**C-15758**

consists of:

Wesleyan Methodist Mission, Roxborough
M	1866	**C-15758**

includes: Townships of Finch, Osnabruck, and Roxborough

Strathroy, Middlesex Co.

St. Mary's Anglican Church
B	1833-1947	**M-2180** (copies)
M	1833-1944	**M-2180** (copies)
D	1833-1971	**M-2180** (copies)
confirmations	1838-1924	**M-2180** (copies)

Summers Corners, Elgin Co.

Personal registers of the Rev. J. Nelson Gould of Sarnia, Methodist and United Church of Canada minister
B	1916-1960	**H-1811**
M	1916-1961	**H-1811**
D	1916-1959	**H-1811**

includes:

Richmond-Corinth United Church of Canada Charge
B	1947-1960	**H-1811**
M	1947-1961	**H-1811**
D	1947-1959	**H-1811**

includes: Aylmer West, Corinth, Fairview, North Bayham, Richmond Village (Bayham), and Summers Corners, Elgin Co.

Sydenham Township, Grey Co.

Returns of coroners' inquests for Grey, Wellington, Bruce, [and Dufferin] Counties
D	1873	**C-15758**

includes: Durham, Owen Sound, and the Townships of Artemesia, Egremont, Euphrasia, Keppel, Normanby, Osprey, Proton, St. Vincent, and Sydenham, Grey Co.; and Melancthon Township, Dufferin Co.

Tatlock, Lanark Co.

Clayton United Church, Clayton
BMD	1805-1965	**M-3687** and **M-3688**
	1876-1965	**M-3243**

includes:

St. Peter's Presbyterian Church, Darling Township
B	1871-1878	**M-3687**
communion rolls	1890-1942	**M-3688**

includes: St. John's, Hopetown; Rosetta Presbyterian Congregation; and St. Peter's, Tatlock

St. Peter's, Darling, and St. Paul's, Middleville, Presbyterian Congregations
BD	1893-1965	**M-3688**
M	1897-1919	**M-3243**

includes: Hopetown, Rosetta, and Tatlock

Clayton-Middleville Presbyterian Charge (later, Middleville United Church)
B	1881-1950	**M-3243**
D	1942-1957	**M-3688**
communion rolls	1942-1957	**M-3688**

includes: Hopetown, Rosetta, Darling, and Tatlock

Thorold, Welland Co.

Register of 873 marriage licences issued by Jacob Keefer (1800-1875)
M	1838-1874	**H-1811**

Thunder Bay (formerly, Fort William), Thunder Bay District

St. John the Evangelist Anglican Church
B	1873-1911	**M-2820**
	1911-1926	**M-2821**
M	1872-1913	**M-2820**
	1913-1917	**M-2821**
	1917-1925	**M-2820** (index)
	1925-1926	**M-2821**
D	1877-1911	**M-2820**
	1911-1926	**M-2821**
confirmations	1874-1910	**M-2820**
	1911-1925	**M-2821**
parish list	1877, c. 1903	**M-2820**

includes:

(cont.)

St. Ansgarius' Lutheran Church, Port Arthur
BMD 1906-1912 **M-2821**
confirmations 1911-1912 **M-2821**
parish list c. 1907 **M-2821**

Thurlow, Hastings Co.

Clayton United Church, Clayton, Lanark Co.
BMD 1805-1965 **M-3687** and **M-3688**
1876-1965 **M-3243**
includes:

Poland Presbyterian Congregation, Poland, Lanark Co.
B 1876-1907, 1912 **M-3243**
includes: Clyde Forks, Flower Station, South Lavant, South Poland, Lanark Co., and Thurlow, Hastings Co.

Thurlow Township, Hastings Co.

St. John's Anglican Church, Bath, Lennox and Addington Co.
B 1787-1813 **H-1810**
M 1787-1816 **H-1810**
D 1787-1813 **H-1810**
comprises:

St. Thomas' Anglican Church, Ernestown Township, Lennox and Addington Co.
B 1788-1813 **H-1810**
M 1787-1813, 1814, 1816 **H-1810**
D 1788-1813 **H-1810**
includes: Amherst Island, and the Townships of Adolphustown, Camden, and Fredericksburg, Lennox and Addington Co.; the Townships of Ameliasburg, Marysburgh, and Sophiasburgh, Prince Edward Co.; the Townships of Sidney, and Thurlow, Hastings Co.; and Kingston, Frontenac Co.; as well as Oswego, New York, U.S.A.

St. Paul's Anglican Church, Fredericksburg Township, Lennox and Addington Co.
B 1787-1813 **H-1810**
M 1788-1812 **H-1810**
D 1787-1813 **H-1810**
includes: Amherst Island, and the Townships of Adolphustown, Camden, Ernestown, and Richmond, Lennox and Addington Co.; the Townships of Ameliasburg, Hallowell, Marysburgh, and Sophiasburgh, Prince Edward Co.; the Townships of Sidney, and Thurlow, Hastings Co.; and the Townships of Cramahé, and Percy, Northumberland Co.; as well as Oswego, New York, U.S.A.

(cont.)

Presbyterian Mission of Ernestown, Fredericksburg, Adolphustown, and the Bay of Quinté region
B 1800-1841 **H-1810**
M 1800-1836 **H-1810**
D 1841 **H-1810**
includes:

Thurlow Township
B 1802-1816, 1821, 1839 **H-1810**
M 1807, 1812, 1816, 1822 **H-1810**

Toledo, Leeds Co.

St. Francis-Xavier Roman Catholic Church, Brockville
B 1835-1859 **M-4613**
1854-1860 **M-4613** (index)
1882-1893 **M-4613**
M 1841-1847 **M-4613**
1855-1856 **M-4613** (index)
confirmations 1847 **M-4613**
includes: records of the Bellamy Pond, and Toledo area of Kitley Township, Leeds Co.

St. Andrew's Presbyterian (Church of Scotland) Church, Toledo (formerly, Presbyterian Congregation of Kitley Township)
B 1846-1852, 1863-1913 **H-1810**
M 1863-1864, 1880-1881, 1890-1893, 1903, 1907 **H-1810**
D 1894, 1897-1902, 1911 **H-1810**
members, 1847, 1850, 1854, 1863-1913 **H-1810**
includes: Townships of Bastard, Elizabethtown, Front of Yonge, and Kitley, Leeds Co.; as well as Montague Township, Lanark Co.; and Wolford Township, Grenville Co.

Torbolton Township, Carleton Co.

St. Andrew's United Church of Canada, Pakenham, Lanark Co.
B 1891-1966 **M-7761**
M 1840-1973 **M-7761**
D 1901-1985 **M-7761**
includes:

St. Andrew's Presbyterian Church, Pakenham, Lanark Co.
M 1840-1883 **M-7761**
includes: Townships of Fitzroy, and Torbolton, Carleton Co.; Townships of Horton, and McNab, Renfrew Co.; and neighbouring settlements

United Presbyterian Congregation, Fitzroy Harbour
M 1852-1922 **M-1955**
includes: members who later joined congregations in Kilmaurs, Kinburn, Torbolton Township, Woodlawn, etc.

Toronto, York Co.

Yonge Street Monthly Meeting of Friends (Hicksite Quakers)
BD	1752-1873	**M-3844**
M	1804-1840	**M-3844**
Sunday School 1861-1871		**M-3845**

includes: Toronto

(Records of the Religious Society of Friends, Volumes C-3-103, C-3-104 and C-3-114)

Toronto Monthly Meeting of Friends (Hicksite Quakers)
M	1941-1942	**M-3839**

(Records of the Religious Society of Friends, Volume C-3-67)

Yonge Street Monthly Meeting of Friends (Orthodox Quakers)
B	1803-1866	**M-3824**
M	1829-1885	**M-3824**
	1859-1897	**M-3824**
D	1811-1873	**M-3824**
removals	1806-1879	**M-3824**

includes: Toronto

(Records of the Religious Society of Friends, Volumes B-2-92, B-2-93, B-2-87, B-2-92, B-2-86)

Civil registers of York County
D	1854	**C-15758**

consists of:

> Return of St. Paul's Roman Catholic Graveyard, Toronto
> | | | |
> |---|---|---|
> | D | 1854 | **C-15758** |

Personal record of marriages performed by the Reverend Dr. Isaac Tovell, of the Methodist Church of Canada and the United Church of Canada, Toronto
M	1875-1935 Index	**H-1810**

comprises:

> Toronto
> | | | |
> |---|---|---|
> | M | 1875-1884, 1888, 1893-1894, 1897-1907, 1909-1931, 1933, 1935 Index | **H-1810** |
>
> Peterborough, Peterborough Co.
> | | | |
> |---|---|---|
> | M | 1877, 1884-1889 Index | **H-1810** |
>
> St. Catharines, Lincoln Co.
> | | | |
> |---|---|---|
> | M | 1888-1892, [1922] Index | **H-1810** |
>
> Hamilton, Wentworth Co.
> | | | |
> |---|---|---|
> | M | 1891-1897, 1904-1906 Index | **H-1810** |

Holy Blossom Hebrew Congregation, Toronto
B	1857-1873	**M-5928**
M	1858-1863, 1871-1873, 1878, 1894	**M-5928**
D	1858-1902	**M-5928**

Register of the Rev. John Becket (1838-1921), Presbyterian missionary at Aspdin, Muskoka District, 1905-1908
M	1905-1908, 1910, 1913, 1915	**H-1810**

includes:

> Toronto
> | | | |
> |---|---|---|
> | M | 1915 | **H-1810** |

Register of the Rev. Dr. Robert J. Douglas Simpson (fl. 1894-1956), clergyman of the Methodist and United Church of Canada Churches, Toronto
M	1923-1956	**H-1810**

Townsend Township, Norfolk Co.

Norfolk County Historical Society Collections
B	1783-1863	**M-283**
M	1807-1835	**M-274, M-275** and **M-277**
	1858-1897	**M-283**
D	1840-1899	**M-283**

includes:

> Hartford and Fredericksburg (Delhi) Regular Baptist Congregations
> | | | |
> |---|---|---|
> | B | 1783-1863 | **M-283** |
> | M | 1858-1897 | **M-283** |
> | D | 1840-1899 | **M-283** |
> includes: Townships of Middleton, South Walsingham, Townsend, and Windham, Norfolk Co.; and Walpole Township, Haldimand Co.

(Pages 12941-12987)

Tuckersmith Township, Huron Co.

Civil registers of Waterloo County
B	1836-1861	**C-15758**
M	1854-1855	**C-15758**
D	1854-1855, 1858, 1860	**C-15758**

includes:

> Evangelical Lutheran Church, Mannheim, New Dundee, and New Hamburg, Waterloo Co.
> | | | |
> |---|---|---|
> | B | 1858, 1860 | **C-15758** |
> | D | 1860 | **C-15758** |
> includes: places in Wilmot Township, , Waterloo Co.; in Brant, and Carrick Townships, Bruce Co.; in Hay, Stanley, and Tuckersmith Townships, Huron Co.; and Blenheim Township, Oxford Co.; as well as Hanover, Grey Co.; and Williamsburgh [Township], Dundas Co.

(cont.)

Tyendinaga Township, Hastings Co.

Presbyterian Mission of Ernestown, Fredericksburg, Adolphustown, and the Bay of Quinté region
B	1800-1841	**H-1810**
M	1800-1836	**H-1810**
D	1841	**H-1810**

includes:

Tyendinaga Township
B	1826-1837	**H-1810**

Usborne Township, Huron Co.

Anglican Parish of Kirkton with Granton and Saintsbury (including the Anglican Churches of: St. Paul's, Kirkton; Trinity, Prospect Hill; St. Patrick's, Saintsbury; and St. Thomas', Granton)
B	1862-1971	**M-2227**
MD	1863-1971	**M-2227**

includes: Township of Usborne, Huron Co.; Township of Blanshard, Perth Co.; and Township of Biddulph, Middlesex Co.

Wallace Township, Perth Co.

Civil registers of Waterloo County
B	1836-1861	**C-15758**
M	1854-1855	**C-15758**
D	1854-1855, 1858, 1860	**C-15758**

includes:

[Unorthodox Evangelical Lutheran] Congregation of the Rev. Frederick W. Bindemann, Waterloo Township, Waterloo Co.
M	1855	**C-15758**

includes: Berlin (later, Kitchener), and places in the Townships of North Dumfries, Waterloo, Wellesley, Wilmot, and Woolwich, Waterloo Co.; Carrick Township, Bruce Co.; Normanby Township, Grey Co.; the Townships of Blandford, and Blenheim, Oxford Co.; Hay Township, Huron Co.; the Townships of North Easthope, South Easthope, and Wallace, Perth Co.; the Townships of Peel, Guelph, Nichol, and Puslinch, Wellington Co.; and Hamilton, Wentworth Co.

Walpole Township, Haldimand Co.

Norfolk County Historical Society Collections
B	1783-1863	**M-283**
M	1807-1835	**M-274, M-275** and **M-277**
	1858-1897	**M-283**
D	1840-1899	**M-283**

includes:

Hartford and Fredericksburg (Delhi) Regular Baptist Congregations
B	1783-1863	**M-283**
M	1858-1897	**M-283**
D	1840-1899	**M-283**

includes: Townships of Middleton, South Walsingham, Townsend, and Windham, Norfolk Co.; and Walpole Township, Haldimand Co.

(Pages 12941-12987)

Waterloo County

Civil registers
B	1836-1861	**C-15758**
M	1854-1855	**C-15758**
D	1854-1855, 1858, 1860	**C-15758**

comprises:

Wilmot Anglican Mission, Wilmot Township
B	1842-1855	**C-15758**
MD	1854-1855	**C-15758**

St. James' Anglican Church, Wilmot Township
BD	1860	**C-15758**

includes: other places in Wilmot Township; as well as St. George, Brant Co.; and the Townships of Blandford, and East Zorra, Oxford Co.

German Baptist Church of the Rev. Henry Schneider
B	1861	**C-15758**
M	1855*	**C-15758**
D	1855*, 1860	**C-15758**

includes: Berlin (later, Kitchener), as well as other places in the Townships of Waterloo, Wilmot, and Woolwich, Waterloo Co.; and in South Easthope Township, Perth Co.

* In German

Evangelical Association
BD	1860	**C-15758**

includes: Berlin (later, Kitchener), and other places in the Township of Waterloo, as well as Heidelberg, in the Townships of Wellesley, and Woolwich

[St. James' Evangelical Lutheran Church, Elmira]
B	1853-1860	**C-15758**
D	1860	**C-15758**

Evangelical Lutheran Church, Mannheim, New Dundee, and New Hamburg
B	1858, 1860	**C-15758**
D	1860	**C-15758**

includes: places in Wilmot Township, Waterloo Co.; in Brant, and Carrick Townships, Bruce Co.; in Hay, Stanley, and Tuckersmith Townships, Huron Co.; and Blenheim Township, Oxford Co.; as well as Hanover, Grey Co.; and Williamsburgh [Township], Dundas Co.

(cont.)

German Evangelical Lutheran Congregations,
Phillipsburg, Wellesley Village, and New Baden
B   1836-1855, 1858, 1860   **C-15758**
D   1858, 1860   **C-15758**
includes: places in the Townships of Waterloo, Wellesley, and Wilmot, Waterloo Co.; Ellice, Mornington, and North Easthope Townships, Perth Co.; Normanby Township, Grey Co.

German Evangelical Lutheran Church, Preston (later, Cambridge)
B   1853-1855, 1860   **C-15758**
M   1855   **C-15758**
D   1855, 1860   **C-15758**
includes: places in the Townships of North Dumfries, Waterloo, Wilmot, and Woolwich, Waterloo Co.; in the Townships of Brantford, Burford, and South Dumfries, Brant Co.; as well as Blenheim Township, Oxford Co.; Puslinch Township, Wellington Co.; and Beverley Township, Wentworth Co.

[Unorthodox Evangelical Lutheran] Congregation of the Rev. Frederick W. Bindemann, Waterloo Township
M   1855   **C-15758**
includes: Berlin (later, Kitchener), and places in the Townships of North Dumfries, Waterloo, Wellesley, Wilmot, and Woolwich, Waterloo Co.; Carrick Township, Bruce Co.; Normanby Township, Grey Co.; the Townships of Blandford, and Blenheim, Oxford Co.; Hay Township, Huron Co.; the Townships of North Easthope, South Easthope, and Wallace, Perth Co.; the Townships of Peel, Guelph, Nichol, and Puslinch, Wellington Co.; and Hamilton, Wentworth Co.

German Evangelical Lutheran Church, Waterloo Township
B   1860-1861   **C-15758**
D   1860   **C-15758**

Lutheran Congregation of the Rev. Frederick W. Wunderlich
B   1850-1855   **C-15758**
M   1855   **C-15758**

[Amish Mennonite Congregation of Bishop] Peter Litwiller, [Wilmot Township]
BD   1860   **C-15758**
M   1855*   **C-15758**
includes: places in the Townships of Wellesley, and Wilmot, Waterloo Co.; and Mornington Township, Perth Co.

*In German

Mennonite Church, Wilmot Township
BD   1860   **C-15758**

Mennonite Congregation of the Rev. Moses S. Bowman, Latshaws, Wilmot Township
BD   1860   **C-15758**

(cont.)

Mennonite Congregation of [Bishop] Joseph Hagey, [Hagey or Breslau]
BD   1860   **C-15758**

[Mennonite Congregation of the Rev. Abraham Kepler]
BD   [1858]   **C-15758**

[Mennonite] Congregation in New Germany [near Guelph, Wellington Co.]
BMD   1855   **C-15758**

[Mennonite] Congregations
B   1858   **C-15758**
D   1858, 1860   **C-15758**

Primitive Methodist Church, Peel Township, Wellington Co.; and Wellesley Station, Waterloo Co.
B   1845-1858   **C-15758**
D   1858   **C-15758**

Wesleyan Methodist Congregation, Galt (later, Cambridge)
B   1860   **C-15758**
M   1854-1855   **C-15758**
includes: places in the Township of Waterloo, Waterloo Co.; Paris, and the Township of Brantford, Brant Co.; Esquesing Township, Halton Co., and Chinguacousy Township, Peel Co.

Wesleyan Methodist Church, Berlin (later, Kitchener)
B   1860   **C-15758**
includes: places in the Townships of Waterloo, and Wellesley

New Jerusalem (Swedenborgian) Church, Berlin (later, Kitchener)
B   1855-1860   **C-15758**
D   1860   **C-15758**
includes: Waterloo Township, and various places in the Townships of Wilmot and Wellesley

St. Andrew's Presbyterian (Church of Scotland) Church, Galt (later, Cambridge)
B   1837, 1839, 1852-1855, 1860   **C-15758**

Associate Presbyterian Church of the Rev. James Strang, Galt (later, Cambridge)
BD   1855   **C-15758**

Presbyterian Church of Canada, Ayr
M   1855   **C-15758**

Roman Catholic Mission, Berlin (later, Kitchener)
BD   1860   **C-15758**
includes: places in the Townships of Waterloo, and Wilmot

Roman Catholic Mission, Preston (later, Cambridge)
B   1860   **C-15758**
includes: places in the Townships of North Dumfries, and Waterloo

(cont.)

Roman Catholic Mission, New Germany [near Guelph, Wellington Co.]
BD   1860   C-15758
includes: places in the Townships of Waterloo, and
         Woolwich, Waterloo Co.; and the Townships of
         Guelph, and Pilkington, Wellington Co.

St. Agatha's Roman Catholic Church, Wilmot Township
BD   1860   C-15758
includes: places in the Townships of Waterloo, Wellesley,
         Wilmot, and Woolwich, Waterloo Co.; and
         Mornington, and South Easthope Townships,
         Perth Co.

Congregation of the Rev. David Fisher, New Hamburg
B   1852-1860   C-15758
D   1860   C-15758

Congregation of the Rev. Mr. Smith
B   1853-1860   C-15758

Waterloo Township, Waterloo Co.

Civil registers of Waterloo County
B   1836-1861   C-15758
M   1854-1855   C-15758
D   1854-1855, 1858, 1860   C-15758
includes:

   German Baptist Church of the Rev. Henry Schneider
   B   1861   C-15758
   M   1855*   C-15758
   D   1855*, 1860   C-15758
   includes: Berlin (later, Kitchener), as well as other places
            in the Townships of Waterloo, Wilmot, and
            Woolwich, Waterloo Co.; and in South
            Easthope Township, Perth Co.

   * In German

   Evangelical Association
   BD   1860   C-15758
   includes: Berlin (later, Kitchener), and other places in the
            Township of Waterloo, as well as Heidelberg, in
            the Townships of Wellesley, and Woolwich

   German Evangelical Lutheran Congregations,
   Phillipsburg, Wellesley Village, and New Baden
   B   1836-1855, 1858, 1860   C-15758
   D   1858, 1860   C-15758
   includes: places in the Townships of Waterloo, Wellesley,
            and Wilmot, Waterloo Co.; Ellice, Mornington,
            and North Easthope Townships, Perth Co.; and
            Normanby Township, Grey Co.

   German Evangelical Lutheran Church, Preston (later, Cambridge)
   B   1853-1855, 1860   C-15758
   M   1855   C-15758
   D   1855, 1860   C-15758
   includes: places in the Townships of North Dumfries,

(cont.)

   Waterloo, Wilmot, and Woolwich, Waterloo Co.;
   in the Townships of Brantford, Burford, and
   South Dumfries, Brant Co.; as well as Blenheim
   Township, Oxford Co.; Puslinch Township,
   Wellington Co.; and Beverley Township,
   Wentworth Co.

   German Evangelical Lutheran Church, Waterloo Township
   B   1860-1861   C-15758
   D   1860   C-15758

   [Unorthodox Evangelical Lutheran] Congregation of the
   Rev. Frederick W. Bindemann, Waterloo Township
   M   1855   C-15758
   includes: Berlin (later, Kitchener), and places in the
            Townships of North Dumfries, Waterloo,
            Wellesley, Wilmot, and Woolwich, Waterloo Co.;
            Carrick Township, Bruce Co.; Normanby
            Township, Grey Co.; the Townships of
            Blandford, and Blenheim, Oxford Co.; Hay
            Township, Huron Co.; the Townships of North
            Easthope, South Easthope, and Wallace, Perth
            Co.; the Townships of Peel, Guelph, Nichol, and
            Puslinch, Wellington Co.; and Hamilton,
            Wentworth Co.

   Wesleyan Methodist Congregation, Galt (later, Cambridge)
   B   1860   C-15758
   D   1854-1855   C-15758
   includes: places in the Township of Waterloo, Waterloo
            Co.; Paris, and the Township of Brantford, Brant
            Co.; Esquesing Township, Halton Co.; and
            Chinguacousy Township, Peel Co.

   Wesleyan Methodist Church, Berlin (later, Kitchener)
   B   1860   C-15758
   includes: places in the Townships of Waterloo, and
            Wellesley

   New Jerusalem (Swedenborgian) Church, Berlin (later, Kitchener)
   B   1855-1860   C-15758
   D   1860   C-15758
   includes: Waterloo Township, and various places in the
            Townships of Wilmot and Wellesley

   Roman Catholic Mission, Berlin (later, Kitchener)
   BD   1860   C-15758
   includes: places in the Townships of Waterloo, and
            Wilmot

   Roman Catholic Mission, Preston (later, Cambridge)
   B   1860   C-15758
   includes: places in the Townships of North Dumfries,
            and Waterloo

   Roman Catholic Mission, New Germany [near Guelph, Wellington Co.]
   BD   1860   C-15758
   includes: places in the Townships of Waterloo, and

(cont.)

Woolwich, Waterloo Co.; and the Townships of
Guelph, and Pilkington, Wellington Co.

St. Agatha's Roman Catholic Church, Wilmot Township
BD   1860   **C-15758**
includes: places in the Townships of Waterloo, Wellesley,
    Wilmot, and Woolwich, Waterloo Co.; and
    Mornington, and South Easthope Townships,
    Perth Co.

Congregation of the Rev. David Fisher, New Hamburg
B   1852-1860   **C-15758**
D   1860   **C-15758**

Watsons Corners, Lanark Co.

Clayton United Church, Clayton
BMD   1805-1965   **M-3687** and
                                       M-3688
          1876-1965   **M-3243**
includes:

Watson's Corners Presbyterian Church
M   1896-1926   **M-3243**
includes: Flower Station, Poland, Lavant, and Dalhousie
    Township

Dalhousie-Playfair Presbyterian Charge (including the
Presbyterian Churches of: St. James', Dalhousie; and
Zion, Watsons Corners; as well as the Poland
Presbyterian Congregation, Poland; and the Playfair
Presbyterian Congregation, Playfair) (later, the Dalhousie-
Playfair United Church of Canada Church)
communion rolls 1907-1964   **M-3688**

Wellesley, Waterloo Co.

Civil registers of Waterloo County
B   1836-1861   **C-15758**
M   1854-1855   **C-15758**
D   1854-1855, 1858, 1860   **C-15758**
includes:

German Evangelical Lutheran Congregations,
Phillipsburg, Wellesley Village, and New Baden
B   1836-1855, 1858, 1860   **C-15758**
D   1858, 1860   **C-15758**
includes: places in the Townships of Waterloo, Wellesley,
    and Wilmot, Waterloo Co.; Ellice, Mornington,
    and North Easthope Townships, Perth Co.; and
    Normanby Township, Grey Co.

Primitive Methodist Church, Peel Township, Wellington
Co.; and Wellesley Station, Waterloo Co.
B   1845-1858   **C-15758**
D   1858   **C-15758**

Wellesley Township, Waterloo Co.

Civil registers of Waterloo County
B   1836-1861   **C-15758**
M   1854-1855   **C-15758**
D   1854-1855, 1858, 1860   **C-15758**
includes:

Evangelical Association
BD   1860   **C-15758**
includes: Berlin (later, Kitchener), and other places in the
    Township of Waterloo, as well as Heidelberg, in
    the Townships of Wellesley, and Woolwich

German Evangelical Lutheran Congregations,
Phillipsburg, Wellesley Village, and New Baden
B   1836-1855, 1858, 1860   **C-15758**
D   1858, 1860   **C-15758**
includes: places in the Townships of Waterloo, Wellesley,
    and Wilmot, Waterloo Co.; Ellice, Mornington,
    and North Easthope Townships, Perth Co.; and
    Normanby Township, Grey Co.

[Unorthodox Evangelical Lutheran] Congregation of the
Rev. Frederick W. Bindemann, Waterloo Township
M   1855   **C-15758**
includes: Berlin (later, Kitchener), and places in the
    Townships of North Dumfries, Waterloo,
    Wellesley, Wilmot, and Woolwich, Waterloo Co.;
    Carrick Township, Bruce Co.; Normanby
    Township, Grey Co.; the Townships of
    Blandford, and Blenheim, Oxford Co.; Hay
    Township, Huron Co.; the Townships of North
    Easthope, South Easthope, and Wallace, Perth
    Co.; the Townships of Peel, Guelph, Nichol, and
    Puslinch, Wellington Co.; and Hamilton,
    Wentworth Co.

[Amish Mennonite Congregation of Bishop] Peter
Litwiller, [Wilmot Township]
BD   1860   **C-15758**
M   1855*   **C-15758**
includes: places in the Townships of Wellesley, and
    Wilmot, Waterloo Co.; and Mornington
    Township, Perth Co.

*In German

Wesleyan Methodist Church, Berlin (later, Kitchener)
B   1860   **C-15758**
includes: places in the Townships of Waterloo, and
    Wellesley

New Jerusalem (Swedenborgian) Church, Berlin (later,
Kitchener)
B   1855-1860   **C-15758**
D   1860   **C-15758**
includes: Waterloo Township, and various places in the
    Townships of Wilmot, and Wellesley

St. Agatha's Roman Catholic Church, Wilmot Township
BD   1860   **C-15758**
includes: places in the Townships of Waterloo, Wellesley,

(cont.)

Wilmot, and Woolwich, Waterloo Co.; and Mornington, and South Easthope Townships, Perth Co.

Wellington County

Returns of coroners' inquests for Grey, Wellington, Bruce, [and Dufferin] Counties

D	1873	**C-15758**

includes: Durham, Owen Sound, and the Townships of Artemesia, Egremont, Euphrasia, Keppel, Normanby, Osprey, Proton, St. Vincent, and Sydenham, Grey Co.; and Melancthon Township, Dufferin Co.

Wentworth County

Returns of coroners' inquests for Wentworth County

D	1873	**C-15758**

includes: Hamilton

West Flamborough Township, Wentworth Co.

Dundas and Ancaster Presbyterian Church, Dundas

M	1848-1852	**C-3028**

includes:

Ancaster and West Flamboro
M	1848-1852	**C-3028**

West Hawkesbury Township, Prescott Co.

Civil registers of the Surrogate Court for the Eastern and Johnstown Districts

B	1831, 1859, 1862-1865	**C-3030**
M	1831-1857, 1863, 1865	**C-3030** (index)

includes:

Baptist Congregation, Breadalbane, Glengarry Co.
M	1834-1850	**C-3030** (index)

includes: places in the Townships of Kenyon, and Lochiel, Glengarry Co.; as well as in the Townships of Caledonia, East Hawkesbury, West Hawkesbury, and North Plantagenet, Prescott Co.

Congregational Church, 9th Concession, Lochiel Township, Glengarry Co.
M	1833-1835, 1838-1840, 1843-1844	**C-3030** (index)

includes: places in the Townships of Kenyon (including the Indian Lands) and Lochiel, Glengarry Co.; and in the Townships of Caledonia, East Hawkesbury, and West Hawkesbury, Prescott Co.

(cont.)

Methodist Episcopal Church in Canada, Circuits in the Eastern District
B	1831, 1862-1865	**C-3030**
M	1831-1833, 1839-1841, 1843-1844, 1846-1857, 1863	**C-3030** (index)

includes: Townships of Matilda, Mountain, Williamsburgh, and Winchester, Dundas Co.; Lochiel Township, Glengarry Co.; the Townships of Cornwall, Finch, and Osnabruck, Stormont Co.; and West Hawkesbury Township, Prescott Co.

L'Orignal and Plantagenet Presbyterian Church
M	1854-1856	**C-3028**
	1852-1856	**H-1807**

includes:

Hawkesbury
M	1853	**H-1807**

West Hawkesbury Township
M	1853	**H-1807**

Baptist Congregation of Breadalbane, Glengarry Co.
M	1858-1886	**H-1807**

includes: places in the Township of Lochiel, Glengarry Co.; as well as in the Townships of East Hawkesbury, and West Hawkesbury, Prescott Co.

West Lake, Prince Edward Co.

West Lake Monthly Meeting of Friends (Hicksite Quakers)
BD	1829-1866	**M-3841**
M	1829-1907	**M-3841**
removals	1830-1892	**M-3841**

(Records of the Religious Society of Friends, Volumes C-3-77, C-3-78 and C-3-78)

West Lake Monthly Meeting of Friends (Orthodox Quakers)
BD	1769-1886	**M-3819**
M	1846-1880	**M-3820**

(Records of the Religious Society of Friends, Volumes B-2-62 and B-2-68)

Westmeath Township, Renfrew Co.

Shawville United Church, Shawville, Pontiac Co., Que.
BMD	1851-1918	**M-2243**
	1877-1939	**M-2374**

includes:

Presbyterian Church (Church of Scotland), Litchfield Township, Pontiac Co., Que.
BMD	1853-1870, 1874-1904, 1918	**M-2243**

includes: Townships of Bristol, Bryson, Calumet-Island,

(cont.)

Clarendon, Leslie, and Thorne, Pontiac Co., Que.; as well as Ross, and Westmeath Townships, Renfrew Co., Ont., in the early years.

Mississippi Circuit of the Methodist Episcopal (later, the Wesleyan Methodist) Church
B   1829-1843   **H-1809**
includes: places in the Townships of Beckwith, Lanark, Pakenham, and Ramsay, Lanark Co.; in the Townships of Horton, McNab, Pembroke, and Westmeath, Renfrew Co.; and Fitzroy Township, Carleton Co.

Pembroke Circuit of the Wesleyan Methodist Church
B   1841-1843   **H-1809**
includes: Townships of Pembroke, and Westmeath, Renfrew Co., Ont.; as well as Allumette Island, Pontiac Co., Que.

Williamsburg, Dundas Co.

Zion Lutheran Church
BM   1790-1814   **M-1496** (index)
D   1790-1814   **M-1496**
communicants and confirmations, 1808-1814   **M-1496**
includes: Morrisburg, and the Townships of Matilda, and Williamsburgh, Dundas Co.; and the Township of Osnabruck, Stormont Co.

with:

United Anglican Mission of Williamsburgh, Matilda, and Edwardsburgh
BM   1814-1886   **M-1496** (partial index)
D   1814-1886   **M-1496**
communicants and confirmations, 1814-1819, 1829, 1846-1886   **M-1496**
includes: Morrisburg, Williamsburg, and the Townships of Matilda, and Williamsburgh, Dundas Co.; the Township of Osnabruck, Stormont Co.; and the Township of Edwardsburgh, Grenville Co.
(The early registers are in Latin.)

St. Lawrence Lutheran Church, Morrisburg
BMD   1826-1972   **M-2981**
includes:

St. George's (later, St. John's) Evangelical Lutheran Congregation, Williamsburg
BMD   1826-1840   **M-2981**
confirmations 1827-1840   **M-2981**

St. John's, Riverside, and St. Paul's, Morrisburg, Evangelical Lutheran Church
BMD   1840-1895   **M-2981**
confirmations   1841-1863   **M-2981**
communicants, n.d.   **M-2981**

St. John's, Riverside, and St. Peter's, North Williamsburg, Evangelical Lutheran Church
M   1858-1914   **M-2981**

St. John's Evangelical Lutheran Church, Williamsburg, and St. Paul's Lutheran Church, Morrisburg
B   1872-1972   **M-2981**
M   1873-1936   **M-2981**
D   1873-1972   **M-2981**
communicants n.d., 1876-1901   **M-2981**

Williamsburgh Township, Dundas Co.

Zion Lutheran Church, Williamsburg
BM   1790-1814   **M-1496** (index)
D   1790-1814   **M-1496**
communicants and confirmations, 1808-1814   **M-1496**
includes: Morrisburg, and the Townships of Matilda, and Williamsburgh, Dundas Co.; and the Township of Osnabruck, Stormont Co.

with:

United Anglican Mission of Williamsburgh, Matilda, and Edwardsburgh
BM   1814-1886   **M-1496** (partial index)
D   1814-1886   **M-1496**
communicants and confirmations, 1814-1819, 1829, 1846-1886   **M-1496**
includes: Morrisburg, Williamsburg, and the Townships of Matilda, and Williamsburgh, Dundas Co.; the Township of Osnabruck, Stormont Co.; and the Township of Edwardsburgh, Grenville Co.
(The early registers are in Latin.)

Civil registers of the Surrogate Court for the Eastern and Johnstown Districts
B   1831, 1859, 1862-1865   **C-3030**
M   1831-1857, 1863, 1865   **C-3030** (index)
includes:

[Anglican] Parish, Williamsburgh Township
M   1855   **C-3030** (index)

Lutheran Congregation, Williamsburgh Township
M   1832-1843, 1847-1848   **C-3030** (index)
includes: Townships of Matilda, Williamsburgh, and Winchester, Dundas Co.; the Townships of Cornwall, and Osnabruck, Stormont Co.; and Charlottenburg Township, Glengarry Co.

Evangelical Lutheran Congregations, Williamsburg Township
M   1842-1844, 1846-1857   **C-3030** (index)
includes: Townships of Matilda, Williamsburgh, and

Winchester, Dundas Co.; the Townships of Cornwall, and Osnabruck, Stormont Co.; and Charlottenburg Township, Glengarry Co.

Methodist Episcopal Church in Canada, Circuits in the Eastern District
B	1831, 1862-1865	**C-3030**
M	1831-1833, 1839-1841, 1843-1844, 1846-1857, 1863	**C-3030** (index)

includes: Townships of Matilda, Mountain, Williamsburgh, and Winchester, Dundas Co.; Lochiel Township, Glengarry Co.; the Townships of Cornwall, Finch, and Osnabruck, Stormont Co.; and West Hawkesbury Township, Prescott Co.

Wesleyan Methodist Church in Canada, Circuits in the Eastern District
B	1859	**C-3030**
M	1833-1857	**C-3030** (index)

includes: Townships of Matilda, Mountain, Williamsburgh, and Winchester, Dundas Co.; the Townships of Edwardsburgh, and Oxford, Grenville Co.; Sheek Island, and the Townships of Cornwall, Finch, Osnabruck, and Roxborough, Stormont Co.; as well as the Brockville district, Leeds Co.; and other places in the Counties of Dundas, Stormont, and Glengarry

Presbyterian Church of the Rev. John Dickey, Williamsburgh, Matilda, and Winchester Townships
M	1836-1849	**C-3030** (index)

includes: Mountain Township, Dundas Co.; and Osnabruck Township, Stormont Co.

Presbyterian (Church of Scotland) Church of the Rev. T. Scott, Williamsburgh, Matilda, and Winchester Townships
M	1853-1857	**C-3030** (index)

includes: Mountain Township, Dundas Co.; and Osnabruck Township, Stormont Co.

Presbyterian (Free Church) Congregation of the Rev. Robert Lyle
M	1831-1837	**C-3030** (index)

includes: Townships of Matilda, and Williamsburgh, Dundas Co.; and the Townships of Cornwall, and Osnabruck, Stormont Co.

Presbyterian Church of the Rev. Isaac Purkis, Osnabruck Township, Stormont Co.
M	1840, 1842-1849	**C-3030** (index)

Congregation of the Rev. John W. Sills
M	1850-1851	**C-3030** (index)

includes: Williamsburgh Township, Dundas Co.; and the Townships of Cornwall, and Osnabruck, Stormont Co.

(cont.)

Civil registers of Waterloo County
B	1836-1861	**C-15758**
M	1854-1855	**C-15758**
D	1854-1855, 1858, 1860	**C-15758**

includes:

Evangelical Lutheran Church, Mannheim, New Dundee, and New Hamburg, Waterloo County
B	1858, 1860	**C-15758**
D	1860	**C-15758**

includes: places in Wilmot Township, Waterloo Co.; in Brant, and Carrick Townships, Bruce Co.; in Hay, Stanley, and Tuckersmith Townships, Huron Co.; and Blenheim Township, Oxford Co.; as well as Hanover, Grey Co.; and Williamsburgh [Township], Dundas Co.

Osnabruck and Lunenburg Presbyterian Congregations, Stormont Co.
B	1848-1909	**C-3030**
M	1860-1900	**C-3030**
D	1907-1909	**C-3030**

includes:

Canada Presbyterian Church of Lunenburg and Osnabruck, Stormont Co.
M	1860-1900	**C-3030**

includes: Cornwall Township, Finch, Newington, Osnabruck, and Roxborough Township, Stormont Co.; the Indian Lands, Glengarry Co.; and the Townships of Williamsburgh, and Winchester, Dundas Co.

Williamstown, Glengarry Co.

St. Andrew's Presbyterian Church
BM	1779-1810	**C-3030** (index)
BMD	1811-1817	**C-3030** (index)

includes: Stormont Co., Ont.; and Montreal, Que., etc.

Civil registers of the Surrogate Court for the Eastern and Johnstown Districts
B	1831, 1859, 1862-1865	**C-3030**
M	1831-1857, 1863, 1865	**C-3030** (index)

includes:

[Presbyterian] Congregation of the Rev. Peter Watson, Williamstown
M	1865	**C-3030** (index)

includes: Martintown, and Williamstown, and other places in Charlottenburg Township, as well as the Townships of Lancaster, and Lochiel, Glengarry Co.; Cornwall Township, Stormont Co.; and the Townships of North Plantagenet, and South Plantagenet, Prescott Co.

(cont.)

Civil registers for the Eastern District
M   1858-1869   **M-3205**
includes:

St. Andrew's Presbyterian Church (Church of Scotland), Williamstown
M   1858-1860, 1862-1869   **M-3205**

Presbyterian (Free Church) Congregation, Williamstown
M   1867-1869   **M-3205**

St. Mary's Roman Catholic Church, Williamstown
M   1858-1861, 1863-1864   **M-3205**

Wilmot Township, Waterloo Co.

Civil registers of Waterloo County
B   1836-1861   **C-15758**
M   1854-1855   **C-15758**
D   1854-1855, 1858, 1860   **C-15758**
includes:

Wilmot Anglican Mission, Wilmot Township
B   1842-1855   **C-15758**
MD   1854-1855   **C-15758**

St. James' Anglican Church, Wilmot Township
BD   1860   **C-15758**
includes: other places in Wilmot Township; as well as St. George, Brant Co.; and the Townships of Blandford, and East Zorra, Oxford Co.

German Baptist Church of the Rev. Henry Schneider
B   1861   **C-15758**
M   1855*   **C-15758**
D   1855*, 1860   **C-15758**
includes: Berlin (later, Kitchener), as well as other places in the Townships of Waterloo, Wilmot, and Woolwich, Waterloo Co.; and in South Easthope Township, Perth Co.

* In German

German Evangelical Lutheran Congregations, Phillipsburg, Wellesley Village, and New Baden
B   1836-1855, 1858, 1860   **C-15758**
D   1858, 1860   **C-15758**
includes: places in the Townships of Waterloo, Wellesley, and Wilmot, Waterloo Co.; Ellice, Mornington, and North Easthope Townships, Perth Co.; and Normanby Township, Grey Co.

Evangelical Lutheran Church, Mannheim, New Dundee, and New Hamburg
B   1858, 1860   **C-15758**
D   1860   **C-15758**
includes: places in Wilmot Township, Waterloo Co.; in Brant, and Carrick Townships, Bruce Co.; in Hay, Stanley, and Tuckersmith Townships, Huron Co.; and Blenheim Township, Oxford Co.; as well as Hanover, Grey Co.; and Williamsburgh [Township], Dundas Co.

(cont.)

German Evangelical Lutheran Church, Preston (later, Cambridge)
B   1853-1855, 1860   **C-15758**
M   1855   **C-15758**
D   1855, 1860   **C-15758**
includes: places in the Townships of North Dumfries, Waterloo, Wilmot, and Woolwich, Waterloo Co.; in the Townships of Brantford, Burford, and South Dumfries, Brant Co.; as well as Blenheim Township, Oxford Co.; Puslinch Township, Wellington Co.; and Beverley Township, Wentworth Co.

[Unorthodox Evangelical Lutheran] Congregation of the Rev. Frederick W. Bindemann, Waterloo Township
M   1855   **C-15758**
includes: Berlin (later, Kitchener), and places in the Townships of North Dumfries, Waterloo, Wellesley, Wilmot, and Woolwich, Waterloo Co.; Carrick Township, Bruce Co.; Normanby Township, Grey Co.; the Townships of Blandford, and Blenheim, Oxford Co.; Hay Township, Huron Co.; the Townships of North Easthope, South Easthope, and Wallace, Perth Co.; the Townships of Peel, Guelph, Nichol, and Puslinch, Wellington Co.; and Hamilton, Wentworth Co.

[Amish Mennonite Congregation of Bishop] Peter Litwiller, [Wilmot Township]
BD   1860   **C-15758**
M   1855*   **C-15758**
includes: places in the Townships of Wellesley, and Wilmot, Waterloo Co.; and Mornington Township, Perth Co.

*In German

Mennonite Church, Wilmot Township
BD   1860   **C-15758**

Mennonite Congregation of the Rev. Moses S. Bowman, Latshaws, Wilmot Township
BD   1860   **C-15758**

New Jerusalem (Swedenborgian) Church, Berlin (later, Kitchener)
B   1855-1860   **C-15758**
D   1860   **C-15758**
includes: Waterloo Township, and various places in the Townships of Wilmot, and Wellesley

Roman Catholic Mission, Berlin (later, Kitchener)
BD   1860   **C-15758**
includes: places in the Townships of Waterloo, and Wilmot

St. Agatha's Roman Catholic Church, Wilmot Township
BD   1860   **C-15758**
includes: places in the Townships of Waterloo, Wellesley, Wilmot, and Woolwich, Waterloo Co.; and Mornington, and South Easthope Townships, Perth Co.

Wilno, Renfrew Co.

Our Lady of Czestochowa, Queen of Poland (Roman Catholic) Church (formerly, St. Stanislaus Kostka Roman Catholic Church, Hagarty Township)

BMD	1880-1884	**H-1456** (partial index)
B	1877-1880	**H-1456**
	1888-1940	**H-1456** (partial index)
M	1885-1937	**H-1456** (partial index)
	1928-1960	**H-1457**
D	1885-1928	**H-1456** (partial index)
	1928-1943, 1945	**H-1457**
	1961-1975	**H-1457**
ordinations, 1910, 1923-1924		**H-1456**
confirmations, 1912-1913		**H-1456**
	1947-1948, 1950, 1953, 1956, 1959	**H-1457**
first communions, 1946-1947, 1951, 1958-1959		**H-1457**

includes: Townships of Brudenell, Burns, Hagarty, Radcliffe, and Sherwood

(The registers are in French, Latin, and English. Miscellaneous related items are in Polish.)

Winchester Township, Dundas Co.

Civil registers of the Surrogate Court for the Eastern and Johnstown Districts
B	1831, 1859, 1862-1865	**C-3030**
M	1831-1857, 1863, 1865	**C-3030** (index)

includes:

Lutheran Congregation, Williamsburgh Township
M	1832-1843, 1847-1848	**C-3030** (index)

includes: Townships of Matilda, Williamsburgh, and Winchester, Dundas Co.; the Townships of Cornwall, and Osnabruck, Stormont Co.; and Charlottenburg Township, Glengarry Co.

Evangelical Lutheran Congregations, Williamsburgh Township
M	1842-1844, 1846-1857	**C-3030** (index)

includes: Townships of Matilda, Williamsburgh, and Winchester, Dundas Co.; the Townships of Cornwall, and Osnabruck, Stormont Co.; and Charlottenburg Township, Glengarry Co.

Methodist Episcopal Church in Canada, Circuits in the Eastern District
B	1831, 1862-1865	**C-3030**
M	1831-1833, 1839-1841, 1843-1844, 1846-1857, 1863	**C-3030** (index)

includes: Townships of Matilda, Mountain, Williamsburgh, and Winchester, Dundas Co.; Lochiel Township, Glengarry Co.; the Townships of Cornwall, Finch, and Osnabruck, Stormont Co.; and West Hawkesbury Township, Prescott Co.

Wesleyan Methodist Church in Canada, Circuits in the Eastern District
B	1859	**C-3030**
M	1833-1857	**C-3030** (index)

includes: Townships of Matilda, Mountain, Williamsburgh, and Winchester, Dundas Co.; the Townships of Edwardsburgh, and Oxford, Grenville Co.; Sheek Island, and the Townships of Cornwall, Finch, Osnabruck, and Roxborough, Stormont Co.; as well as the Brockville district, Leeds Co.; and other places in the Counties of Dundas, Stormont, and Glengarry

Presbyterian Church of the Rev. John Dickey, Williamsburgh, Matilda, and Winchester Townships
M	1836-1849	**C-3030** (index)

includes: Mountain Township, Dundas Co.; and Osnabruck Township, Stormont Co.

Presbyterian (Church of Scotland) Church of the Rev. T. Scott, Williamsburgh, Matilda, and Winchester Townships
M	1853-1857	**C-3030** (index)

includes: Mountain Township, Dundas Co.; and Osnabruck Township, Stormont Co.

Osnabruck and Lunenburg Presbyterian Congregations, Stormont Co.
B	1848-1909	**C-3030**
M	1860-1900	**C-3030**
D	1907-1909	**C-3030**

includes:

Canada Presbyterian Church of Lunenburg and Osnabruck, Stormont Co.
M	1860-1900	**C-3030**

includes: Cornwall Township, Finch, Newington, Osnabruck, and Roxborough Township, Stormont Co.; the Indian Lands, Glengarry Co.; and the Townships of Williamsburgh, and Winchester, Dundas Co.

Windham Township, Norfolk Co.

Norfolk County Historical Society Collections
B	1783-1863	**M-283**
M	1807-1835	**M-274, M-275** and **M-277**
	1858-1897	**M-283**
D	1840-1899	**M-283**

includes:

(cont.)

Hartford and Fredericksburg (Delhi) Regular Baptist Congregations
B   1783-1863   **M-283**
M   1858-1897   **M-283**
D   1840-1899   **M-283**
includes: Townships of Middleton, South Walsingham, Townsend, and Windham, Norfolk Co.; and Walpole Township, Haldimand Co.
(Pages 12941-12987)

Windsor, Essex Co.

Central Methodist Church
M   1908   **M-7584**

Wolford Township, Grenville Co.

St. Andrew's Presbyterian (Church of Scotland) Church, Toledo (formerly, Presbyterian Congregation of Kitley Township)
B   1846-1852, 1863-1913   **H-1810**
M   1863-1864, 1880-1881,
         1890-1893, 1903, 1907   **H-1810**
D   1894, 1897-1902, 1911   **H-1810**
members, 1847, 1850, 1854,
         1863-1913   **H-1810**
includes: Townships of Bastard, Elizabethtown, Front of Yonge, and Kitley, Leeds Co.; as well as Montague Township, Lanark Co.; and Wolford Township, Grenville Co.

Returns of coroners' inquests for the Counties of Leeds, and Grenville
D   1873   **C-15758**
includes: Brockville, Gananoque, and Elizabethtown Township, Leeds Co.; as well as the Townships of Augusta, and Wolford, Grenville Co.

Woodhouse Township, Norfolk Co.

Norfolk County Historical Society Collections
B   1783-1863   **M-283**
M   1807-1835   **M-274, M-275** and
                                  M-277
         1858-1897   **M-283**
D   1840-1899   **M-283**
includes:

   Civil registers of Norfolk County
   M   1807-1813   **M-274**
         1807-1815   **M-274**
         1826-1828   **M-275**
         1831-1835   **M-277**
   includes: Townships of Charlotteville, and Woodhouse in the London District
   (Pages 829-837, 1040-1041, 2121-2123, 3940-3991)

Woodlawn, Carleton Co.

United Presbyterian Congregation, Fitzroy Harbour
M   1852-1922   **M-1955**
includes: members who later joined congregations in Kilmaurs, Kinburn, Torbolton Township, Woodlawn, etc.

Woodstock, Oxford Co.

Returns of coroners' inquests for Oxford County
D   1873   **C-15758**
includes: Woodstock, and the Townships of Blandford, and Blenheim

Woolwich Township, Waterloo Co.

Civil registers of Waterloo County
B   1836-1861   **C-15758**
M   1854-1855   **C-15758**
D   1854-1855, 1858, 1860   **C-15758**
includes:

   German Baptist Church of the Rev. Henry Schneider
   B   1861   **C-15758**
   M   1855*   **C-15758**
   D   1855*, 1860   **C-15758**
   includes: Berlin (later, Kitchener), as well as other places in the Townships of Waterloo, Wilmot, and Woolwich, Waterloo Co.; and in South Easthope Township, Perth Co.

   * In German

   Evangelical Association
   BD   1860   **C-15758**
   includes: Berlin (later, Kitchener), and other places in the Township of Waterloo, as well as Heidelberg, in the Townships of Wellesley, and Woolwich

   German Evangelical Lutheran Church, Preston (later, Cambridge)
   B   1853-1855, 1860   **C-15758**
   M   1855   **C-15758**
   D   1855, 1860   **C-15758**
   includes: places in the Townships of North Dumfries, Waterloo, Wilmot, and Woolwich, Waterloo Co.; in the Townships of Brantford, Burford, and South Dumfries, Brant Co.; as well as Blenheim Township, Oxford Co.; Puslinch Township, Wellington Co.; and Beverley Township, Wentworth Co.

(cont.)

[Unorthodox Evangelical Lutheran] Congregation of the Rev. Frederick W. Bindemann, Waterloo Township
M   1855   **C-15758**
includes: Berlin (later, Kitchener), and other places in the Townships of North Dumfries, Waterloo, Wellesley, Wilmot, and Woolwich, Waterloo Co.; Carrick Township, Bruce Co.; Normanby Township, Grey Co.; the Townships of Blandford, and Blenheim, Oxford Co.; Hay Township, Huron Co.; the Townships of North Easthope, South Easthope, and Wallace, Perth Co.; the Townships of Peel, Guelph, Nichol, and Puslinch, Wellington Co.; and Hamilton, Wentworth Co.

Roman Catholic Mission, New Germany [near Guelph, Wellington Co.]
BD   1860   **C-15758**
includes: places in the Townships of Waterloo, and Woolwich, Waterloo Co.; and the Townships of Guelph, and Pilkington, Wellington Co.

St. Agatha's Roman Catholic Church, Wilmot Township
BD   1860   **C-15758**
includes: places in the Townships of Waterloo, Wellesley, Wilmot, and Woolwich, Waterloo Co.; and Mornington, and South Easthope Townships, Perth Co.

Yarmouth Township, Elgin Co.

South Yarmouth Monthly Meeting of Friends (Hicksite Quakers)
BD etc.   1743 [or 1797]-1974   **M-3843**
M   1903-1974   **M-3843**

(Records of the Religious Society of Friends, Volumes C-3-93 and C-3-95)

Yonge Street, York Co.

Yonge Street Monthly Meeting of Friends (Hicksite Quakers)
BD   1752-1873   **M-3844**
M   1804-1840   **M-3844**
Sunday School 1861-1871   **M-3845**
includes: Toronto

(Records of the Religious Society of Friends, Volumes C-3-103, C-3-104 and C-3-114)

Toronto Monthly Meeting of Friends (Hicksite Quakers)
M   1941-1942   **M-3839**
includes: Yonge Street

(Records of the Religious Society of Friends, Volume C-3-67)

Yonge Street Monthly Meeting of Friends (Orthodox Quakers)
B   1803-1866   **M-3824**
M   1829-1885   **M-3824**
     1859-1897   **M-3824**
D   1811-1873   **M-3824**
removals   1806-1879   **M-3824**
includes: Toronto

(Records of the Religious Society of Friends, Volumes B-2-92, B-2-93, B-2-87, B-2-92, and B-2-86)

York County

Civil registers of York County
D   1854   **C-15758**
consists of:

     Return of St. Paul's Roman Catholic Graveyard, Toronto
     D   1854   **C-15758**

(cont.)

PRINCE EDWARD ISLAND / ÎLE-DU-PRINCE-ÉDOUARD

Belfast, Queens Co.

St. John's Presbyterian Church
B   1823-1849   **C-3028**
includes: Charlottetown, Pinette, and Rustico, Queens Co., and Murray Harbour, Kings Co., with their environs, P.E.I.; as well as many places in all the counties of Cape Breton Island, and a few in the counties of Pictou, and Antigonish, N.S.

Cascumpèque, comté de Prince

St-Antoine-de-Cascumpèque (Église catholique)
BMD   1839-1868   **M-291**

Charlottetown, Queens Co.

St. John's Presbyterian Church, Belfast
B   1823-1849   **C-3028**
includes: Charlottetown, Pinette, and Rustico, Queens Co., and Murray Harbour, Kings Co., with their environs, P.E.I.; as well as many places in all the counties of Cape Breton Island, and a few in the counties of Pictou, and Antigonish, N.S.

Malpèque, comté de Prince

St-Jean-Baptiste-de-Malpèque (Église catholique)
BMD   1817-1835   **M-16**

Murray Harbour, Kings Co.

St. John's Presbyterian Church, Belfast, Queens Co.
B   1823-1849   **C-3028**
includes: Charlottetown, Pinette, and Rustico, Queens Co., and Murray Harbour, Kings Co., with their environs, P.E.I.; as well as many places in all the counties of Cape Breton Island, and a few in the counties of Pictou, and Antigonish, N.S.

Pinette, Queens Co.

St. John's Presbyterian Church, Belfast
B   1823-1849   **C-3028**
includes: Charlottetown, Pinette, and Rustico, Queens Co., and Murray Harbour, Kings Co., with their environs, P.E.I.; as well as many places in all the counties of Cape Breton Island, and a few in the counties of Pictou, and Antigonish, N.S.

Port Lajoie, comté de [Kings]

Registres d'état civil (Église catholique)
BMD   1721-1744, 1749-1751   **F-595**   (originaux)
           1721-1744, 1749-1751   **C-1472**   (copies)
           1715-1758 Index*   **F-596**   (originaux)
comprend : St-Pierre du Nord

avec :

Port Lajoie (Église catholique)
BMD   1752-1758   **F-595**   (originaux)
           1752-1758   **C-1472**   (copies)
           1715-1758 Index*   **F-596**   (originaux)

*Cet index donne le lieu de résidence mais non les dates des BMD. Il est très difficile de se servir de cet index pour trouver les entrées dans les registres, dont plusieurs sont perdus.

Rustico, comté de Queens

St-Augustin-de-Rustico (Église catholique)
BMD   1812-1817   **C-3027**   (copies, index)
         1817-1819   **C-3027**   (originaux, index)
         1819-1824   **C-3028**   (originaux, index sur **C-3027**)

St. John's Presbyterian Church, Belfast
B   1823-1849   **C-3028**
includes: Charlottetown, Pinette, and Rustico, Queens Co., and Murray Harbour, Kings Co., with their environs, P.E.I.; as well as many places in all the counties of Cape Breton Island, and a few in the counties of Pictou, and Antigonish, N.S.

Saint-Pierre du Nord, comté de [Kings]

Registres d'état civil (Église catholique)
BMD   1721-1744, 1749-1751   **F-595**   (originaux)
           1721-1744, 1749-1751   **C-1472**   (copies)
           1715-1758 Index*   **F-596**   (originaux)
comprend : Port Lajoie

avec :

Port Lajoie (Église catholique)
BMD   1752-1758   **F-595**   (originaux)
           1752-1758   **C-1472**   (copies)
           1715-1758 Index*   **F-596**   (originaux)

*Cet index donne le lieu de résidence mais non les dates des BMD. Il est très difficile de se servir de cet index pour trouver les entrées dans les registres, dont plusieurs sont perdus.

(cont.)

St-Pierre-du-Nord (Église catholique)

BMD	1724-1758	**C-2970** (copies)
	1725-1758	**F-817** (originaux)

Tignish, Prince Co.

Civil registers (Roman Catholic)

M	1844-1869	**M-291**

QUÉBEC

Allen's Corner (later, East Farnham), Brome County

Farnham Monthly Meeting of Friends (Orthodox Quakers), East Farnham (formerly, Allen's Corner)
BMD	1839-1885	MG 17, G3, fiche 22
	1861-1881	24
	1882-1911	25
removals and members	1839-1885	22
members	1885-1911	23

Allumettes, îles des, comté de Pontiac/Pontiac Co.

Missions du comté de Wright (Église catholique)
BMD	1841-1852	**C-2978**
M	1841-1852 Index	**C-2978**

comprend :

    St-Alphonse-de-Liguori-des-Allumettes (Église catholique)
BMD	1841-1848	**C-2978**
M	1841-1852 Index	**C-2978**

Pembroke Circuit of the Wesleyan Methodist Church
B	1841-1843	**H-1809**

includes: Townships of Pembroke, and Westmeath, Renfrew Co., Ont.; as well as Allumette Island, Pontiac Co., Que.

Allumette Island Wesleyan Methodist Circuit
BM	1858-1887	**M-2823**

includes: adjacent parts of Pontiac and Ottawa Counties

Aylmer, comté de Gatineau/Gatineau Co.

Missions du comté de Wright (Église catholique)
BMD	1841-1852	**C-2978**
M	1841-1852 Index	**C-2978**

comprend :

    St-Paul-d'Aylmer (Église catholique)
BMD	1841-1848	**C-2978**
M	1841-1852 Index	**C-2978**

    St-Paul-d'Aylmer (Église catholique)
BMD	1848-1852	**C-2978**
M	1841-1852 Index	**C-2978**

Anglican Missions of Ottawa County, which became:
    St. James' Anglican Church, Hull
    St. George's Anglican Church, Gatineau
    St. Mary Magdalen Anglican Church, Chelsea
BMD	1831-1853	**M-299**
	1854-1940	**M-3689**

includes:

    Christ Church, Aylmer, and St. James', Hull
BMD	1854-1886	**M-3689**

includes: Townships of Eardley, and Hull, Gatineau Co., and Onslow Township, Pontiac Co., Que.; as well as Ottawa, Carleton Co., Ont.

(cont.)

Christ Church Anglican Church, Aylmer
BMD	1864-1920	**M-3695** (index)
	1920-1971	**M-3696** (index)

includes: in the early years, the Townships of Denholm, Hull, and Wakefield, Gatineau Co.; the Townships of Buckingham, and Portland, Papineau Co.; and Templeton Township, Hull Co.

Bassin-de-Châteauguay, Châteauguay Co.

Châteauguay Congregational Church
BMD	1845-1848	**H-1807**

includes: Bassin-de-Châteauguay

Batiscan, comté de Champlain

Ste-Anne-de-Batiscan (Église catholique)
BMD	1680-1762 extraits	**M-866** (index)

Beauharnois, comté de Beauharnois

St-Clément-de-Beauharnois (Église catholique)
BMD	1819-1842	**C-2889**
	1842-1850	**C-2890**

Beaupré, Côte de, comté de Montmorency N° 1

Notre-Dame-de-la-Visitation-du-Château-Richer (Côte de Beaupré) (Église catholique)
B	1661-1702	**M-1624**
M	1661-1701	**M-1624**
D	1661-1702	**M-1624**

L'Ange-Gardien (Côte de Beaupré) (Église catholique)
D	1670-1677	**M-1624**

Beaupré, Sainte-Anne-de-, comté de Montmorency N° 1

Église catholique de Ste-Anne-de-Beaupré
BMD	1657-1702, 1708-1719	**M-1625**

Berthier[ville], comté de Berthier/Berthier Co.

Église catholique de Berthier
BMD	1727-1733, 1751-1761, 1769, 1780-1785 extraits	**M-866** (index)

Christ Church Anglican Church, William Henry (formerly, and later, Sorel), Richelieu Co.
BMD	1784-1896	**H-1807**

includes:

    Berthier[ville]
BM	1796	**H-1807**

Bouchard, îles, comté de L'Assomption

St-Antoine-de-Lavaltrie (Église catholique)
B/MD   1717, 1749-1764,
            1786-1815 extraits   **M-866** (index)
comprend : Saint-Sulpice, et les îles Bouchard

Boucherville, comté de Chambly

Ste-Famille-de-Boucherville (Église catholique)
B/MD   1668-1762 extraits   **M-866** (index)
comprend: Longueuil, comté de Chambly; Fort St-Louis;
        et Varennes, comté de Verchères

Ste-Famille-de-Boucherville (Église catholique)
B/MD   1669-1735   **M-2369**
           1735-1768   **M-2370**
           1768-1790   **M-2371**

[St-Antoine-de-]Longueuil (Église catholique)
B/MD   1679-1684,
           1713-1789 extraits   **M-865** (index)
comprend: Boucherville, comté de Chambly; et Varennes,
        comté de Verchères

Église catholique
B/MD   1696-1697, 1717-1726,
           1760-1800 extraits   **M-866** (index)

Bout-de-l'Île, comté de l'Île-de-Montréal

Ste-Anne-du-Bout-de-l'Île (ou Ste-Anne-de-Bellevue)
(Église catholique)
B/MD   1703-1784 extraits   **M-865** (index)

Bristol, Pontiac Co.

Quyon United Church, Quyon
B/MD   1859-1923   **M-2212**
includes:

    Quyon Methodist Church, Quyon
    B/MD   1903-1923   **M-2212**
    includes: Bristol, North Onslow, and Wyman, etc., as
        well as the Townships of Bristol, Clarendon,
        and Onslow, Pontiac Co.; and Eardley
        Township, Gatineau Co.

Bristol Township, Pontiac Co.

Clarendon Anglican Mission (later, St. Paul's Anglican
Church, Shawville, etc.)
BM   1823-1842 extracts   **M-1303**
B/MD   1842-1898   **M-1303** and
                                  M-1304 (partial
                                          index)
          1864-1873   **M-2819** (index)
          1875-1916   **M-3114** (partial
                                          index)
includes: Townships of Bristol, Clarendon, Leslie,
    Litchfield, Onslow, and Thorne, in:

    St. James' Anglican Church, Hull, Gatineau Co.
    BM   1823-1842 extracts relating
                        to Clarendon   **M-1303**

    St. Paul's Anglican Church, Shawville
    B/MD   1842-1888   **M-1303** (partial
                                         index)
              1888-1898   **M-1304** (index)
    includes also: Calumet-Island, and Mansfield Township,
        Pontiac Co., and Eardley Township,
        Gatineau Co., Que.; as well as Horton
        Township, Renfrew Co., Ont.

Anglican Mission of North Clarendon (later, Charteris),
and district
B/MD   1864-1873   **M-2819** (index)

Anglican Mission of North Clarendon (later, Charteris),
and Thorne Township
B/MD   1875-1891   **M-3114** (partial
                                       index)

Anglican Mission of Thorne Township, and district
B/MD   1891-1913   **M-3114** (partial
                                       index)

Anglican Mission of Thorne and Leslie Townships, and
North Clarendon (later, Charteris)
B/MD   1892-1916   **M-3114** (partial
                                       index)

Anglican Missions of Ottawa County, which became:
    St. James' Anglican Church, Hull
    St. George's Anglican Church, Gatineau
    St. Mary Magdalen Anglican Church, Chelsea
B/MD   1831-1853   **M-299**
           1854-1940   **M-3689**
includes:

    St. James' Anglican Church, Hull, Gatineau Co.
    B/MD   1831-1853   **M-299**
        includes: Townships of Bristol, and Clarendon, Pontiac
            Co.; and the Townships of Eardley, and Hull,
            Gatineau Co.

(cont.)

QUÉBEC

St. John the Evangelist Anglican Church, Quyon
BMD   1857-1909   **M-2226** (index)
       1889-1946   **M-3132** (index)
comprises:

  Onslow Mission, which became:
    St. John the Evangelist Church, Quyon
    St. Mark's Church, Bristol
    St. Luke's Church, Eardley
    St. Matthew's Church, North Onslow
  includes:

  St. John the Evangelist Church, Quyon
  BMD   1857-1889   **M-2226** (index)
        1890-1940   **M-3132** (index)
  includes: Bristol, and North Clarendon

  St. Luke's Church, Eardley, Gatineau Co.
  BMD   1873-1909   **M-2226** (index)

  Bristol Mission (later, St. Thomas' Church, Bristol)
  BMD   1889-1946   **M-3132** (index)

Shawville United Church, Shawville
BMD   1851-1918   **M-2243**
       1877-1939   **M-2374**
includes: Calumet-Island, and the Townships of Bristol,
    Bryson, Clarendon, Leslie, Litchfield, and
    Thorne, in:

  Presbyterian Church (Church of Scotland), Litchfield
  Township
  BMD   1853-1870, 1874-1904,
        1918   **M-2243**
  includes also: Townships of Ross, and Westmeath,
      Renfrew Co., Ont., in the early years

  Clarendon Wesleyan Methodist Circuit, Clarendon
  BMD   1851-1898   **M-2243**
  includes also: Portage-du-Fort Mission, 1860-1879

  Clarendon Regular Baptist Churches, Clarendon
  BMD   1877-1939   **M-2374**
  includes also: North Clarendon, Starks Corners, and
    Wyman

Quyon United Church, Quyon
BMD   1859-1923   **M-2212**
includes: Townships of Bristol, Clarendon, Eardley, and
    Onslow in:

  Onslow Wesleyan Methodist Church, Onslow Township
  BMD   1859-1883   **M-2212**

  Eardley Methodist Church, Eardley Township,
  Gatineau Co.
  BMD   1884-1902   **M-2212**

  Quyon Methodist Church, Quyon
  BMD   1903-1923   **M-2212**
  includes also: Bristol, North Onslow, Wyman, etc.

Bryson Township, Pontiac Co.

Shawville United Church, Shawville
BMD   1851-1918   **M-2243**
       1877-1939   **M-2374**
includes: Calumet-Island, and the Townships of Bristol,
    Bryson, Clarendon, Leslie, Litchfield, and
    Thorne, in:

  Presbyterian Church (Church of Scotland), Litchfield
  Township
  BMD   1853-1870, 1874-1904,
        1918   **M-2243**
  includes also: Townships of Ross, and Westmeath,
      Renfrew Co., Ont., in the early years

  Clarendon Wesleyan Methodist Circuit, Clarendon
  BMD   1851-1898   **M-2243**
  includes also: Portage-du-Fort Mission, 1860-1879

  Clarendon Regular Baptist Churches, Clarendon
  BMD   1877-1939   **M-2374**
  includes also: North Clarendon, Starks Corners, and
    Wyman

St. George's Anglican Church, Campbell's Bay
BMD   1857-1920   **M-2520** (index)
includes:

  Portage-du-Fort Mission, Portage-du-Fort
  BMD   1857-1874   **M-2520** (index)
        1874-1900*   **M-2520** (index)
        1900-1920   **M-2520** (index)
  *Includes: Bryson, and Calumet

Buckingham, Papineau Co.

St. Stephen's Anglican Church
BMD   1845-1877   **M-3856**
       1868-1895   **M-3856** (index)
       1895-1906   **M-3856**
       1906-1922   **M-3856** (index)
       1922-1931   **M-3856** (index on
                                    M-3857)
       1931-1948   **M-3857** (index)
confirmations 1865, 1876-1877   **M-3856**
communicants 1865   **M-3856**

Buckingham Township/Canton de Buckingham, Papineau Co./comté de Papineau

Notre-Dame-de-Bon-Secours-de-la-Petite-Nation
(Église catholique), Montebello
BMD   1830-1849   **C-3023**

avec :

(cont.)

Mission des cantons de Grenville, comté d'Argenteuil, et Buckingham, comté de Papineau (Église catholique)
BMD   1836-1838, 1840-1850   **C-3023**

et :

Mission de Buckingham (Église catholique)
BMD	1839-1845	**C-3023**
	1845-1850	**C-3024**

Christ Church Anglican Church, Aylmer, Gatineau Co.
BMD	1864-1920	**M-3695** (index)
	1920-1971	**M-3696** (index)

includes: in the early years, the Townships of Denholm, Hull, and Wakefield, Gatineau Co.; the Townships of Buckingham, and Portland, Papineau Co.; and Templeton Township, Hull Co.

Calumet-Island/Île du Grand Calumet, Pontiac Co./comté de Pontiac

Clarendon Anglican Mission (later, St. Paul's Anglican Church, Shawville, etc.)
BM	1823-1842 extracts	**M-1303**
BMD	1842-1898	**M-1303** and **M-1304** (partial index)
	1864-1873	**M-2819** (index)
	1875-1916	**M-3114** (partial index)

includes:

St. Paul's Anglican Church, Shawville
BMD	1842-1888	**M-1303** (partial index)
	1888-1898	**M-1304** (index)

includes: Calumet-Island, and the Townships of Bristol, Clarendon, Leslie, Litchfield, Mansfield, Onslow, and Thorne, Pontiac Co., and Eardley Township, Gatineau Co., Que.; as well as Horton Township, Renfrew Co., Ont.

St. George's Anglican Church, Campbell's Bay
BMD   1857-1920   **M-2520** (index)
includes:

Portage-du-Fort Mission, Portage-du-Fort
BMD	1857-1874	**M-2520** (index)
	1874-1900*	**M-2520** (index)
	1900-1920	**M-2520** (index)

*Includes: Bryson, and Calumet

Shawville United Church, Shawville
BMD	1851-1918	**M-2243**
	1877-1939	**M-2374**

includes: Calumet-Island, and the Townships of Bristol, Bryson, Clarendon, Leslie, Litchfield, and Thorne, in:

(cont.)

Presbyterian Church (Church of Scotland), Litchfield Township
BMD   1853-1870, 1874-1904, 1918   **M-2243**
includes also: Townships of Ross, and Westmeath, Renfrew Co., Ont., in the early years

Clarendon Wesleyan Methodist Circuit, Clarendon
BMD   1851-1898   **M-2243**
includes also: Portage-du-Fort Mission, 1860-1879

Clarendon Regular Baptist Churches, Clarendon
BMD   1877-1939   **M-2374**
includes also: North Clarendon, Starks Corners, and Wyman

Missions du comté de Wright (Église catholique)
BMD	1841-1852	**C-2978**
M	1841-1852 Index	**C-2978**

comprend :

Ste-Anne-du-Grand-Calumet (Église catholique)
BMD	1841-1848	**C-2978**
M	1841-1852 Index	**C-2978**

Campbell's Bay, Pontiac Co.

St. George's Anglican Church, Campbell's Bay
BMD   1857-1920   **M-2520** (index)
comprises:

Portage-du-Fort Mission, Portage-du-Fort
BMD	1857-1874	**M-2520** (index)
	1874-1900*	**M-2520** (index)
	1900-1920	**M-2520** (index)

*Includes: Bryson, and Calumet

Mission of Litchfield (Campbell's Bay) and Mansfield (Fort-Coulonge)
BMD   1902-1920   **M-2520** (index)

Cap-de-la-Madeleine, comté de Champlain

Église catholique
BMD   1687, 1737-1741 extraits   **M-867** (index sur **M-866**)

Cap-Saint-Ignace, comté de Montmagny

Église catholique
BMD   1692-1775 extraits   **M-865** (index)

QUÉBEC

Chambly, comté de Chambly

Église catholique
BMD   1746-1789 extraits   **M-865** (index)

Chambly, Fort-, comté de Chambly/Chambly Co.

Église catholique du Fort St-Frédéric ou Fort Beauharnois-à-la-Pointe-à-la-Chevelure (Crown Point), New York, États-Unis
BMD   1732-1760   **C-3023**
           1732-1760 extraits   **M-866** (index)
comprend :

    Fort Chambly (Église catholique)
    B   1759-1760   **C-3023**
    D   1759   **C-3023**

Christ Church Anglican Church, William Henry (formerly, and later, Sorel), Richelieu Co.
BMD   1784-1796   **H-1807**
includes:

    Fort-Chambly
    B   1784-1785   **H-1807**
    BMD   1796   **H-1807**

Champlain, comté de Champlain

Église catholique
BMD   1679-1695 extraits   **M-866** (index)
           1695-1727,
           1733-1763 extraits   **M-867** (index sur **M-866**)
           1764-1780,
           1790-1808 extraits   **M-867** (index sur **M-866**)

Charteris (formerly, North Clarendon), Pontiac Co.

Clarendon Anglican Mission (later, St. Paul's Anglican Church, Shawville, etc.)
BM   1823-1842 extracts   **M-1303**
BMD   1842-1898   **M-1303** and **M-1304** (partial index)
           1864-1873   **M-2819** (index)
           1875-1916   **M-3114** (partial index)
includes: Townships of Bristol, Clarendon, Leslie, Litchfield, Onslow, and Thorne, in:

    St. James' Anglican Church, Hull, Gatineau Co.
    BM   1823-1842 extracts relating to Clarendon   **M-1303**

    St. Paul's Anglican Church, Shawville
    BMD   1842-1888   **M-1303** (partial index)
           1888-1898   **M-1304** (index)
    includes also: Calumet-Island, and Mansfield Township, Pontiac Co., and Eardley Township, Gatineau Co., Que.; as well as Horton Township, Renfrew Co., Ont.

Anglican Mission of North Clarendon (later, Charteris), and district
BMD   1864-1873   **M-2819** (index)

Anglican Mission of North Clarendon (later, Charteris), and Thorne Township
BMD   1875-1891   **M-3114** (partial index)

Anglican Mission of Thorne Township, and district
BMD   1891-1913   **M-3114** (partial index)

Anglican Mission of Thorne and Leslie Townships, and North Clarendon (later, Charteris)
BMD   1892-1916   **M-3114** (partial index)

Shawville United Church, Shawville
BMD   1851-1918   **M-2243**
           1877-1939   **M-2374**
includes: Calumet-Island, and the Townships of Bristol, Bryson, Clarendon, Leslie, Litchfield, and Thorne, in:

Presbyterian Church (Church of Scotland), Litchfield Township
BMD   1853-1870, 1874-1904, 1918   **M-2243**
includes also: Townships of Ross, and Westmeath, Renfrew Co., Ont., in the early years

Clarendon Wesleyan Methodist Circuit, Clarendon
BMD   1851-1898   **M-2243**
includes also: Portage-du-Fort Mission, 1860-1879

Clarendon Regular Baptist Churches, Clarendon
BMD   1877-1939   **M-2374**
includes also: North Clarendon, Starks Corners, and Wyman

(cont.)

Châteauguay, comté de Châteauguay/Châteauguay Co.

Église catholique et mission du Sault-Saint-Louis
(aujourd'hui, St-Joachim-de-Châteauguay)
B/M/D	1727-1728, 1735-1773	**C-2890**
	1774-1817	**C-2891**
	1817-1836	**C-2892**
	1836-1849	**C-2893**

Registres d'état civil (Église catholique)
B/M/D	1751-1762	**C-3023**
	1752-1754, 1758, 1761, 1779-1783 extraits	**M-866** (index)

Châteauguay Congregational Church
B/M/D	1845-1848	**H-1807**

includes: Bassin-de-Châteauguay

Château-Richer, comté de Montmorency Nº 1

Notre-Dame-de-la-Visitation-du-Château-Richer (Côte de Beaupré) (Église catholique)
B	1661-1702	**M-1624**
M	1661-1701	**M-1624**
D	1661-1702	**M-1624**

Chelsea, comté de Gatineau/Gatineau Co.

Anglican Missions of Ottawa County, which became:
St. James' Anglican Church, Hull
St. George's Anglican Church, Gatineau
St. Mary Magdalen Anglican Church, Chelsea
B/M/D	1831-1853	**M-299**
	1854-1940	**M-3689**

includes:

Anglican Mission of Chelsea and Gatineau (later, St. George's Church, Gatineau, and St. Mary Magdalen Church, Chelsea)
B/M/D	1899-1938	**M-3689**
	1934-1940	**M-3689**
confirmations	1888-1912	**M-3689**
communicants	1888-1913	**M-3689**
members	1925-1932	**M-3689**

includes: census of the parish of Chelsea, etc., c. 1818-1933, as well as entries for Hull, Que.; and Ottawa, Ont.

Missions du comté de Wright (Église catholique)
B/M/D	1841-1852	**C-2978**
M	1841-1852 Index	**C-2978**

comprend :

St-Étienne-de-Chelsea
B/M/D	1841-1848	**C-2978**
M	1841-1852 Index	**C-2978**

Clarendon Township, Pontiac Co.

Clarendon Anglican Mission (later, St. Paul's Anglican Church, Shawville, etc.)
B/M	1823-1842 extracts	**M-1303**
B/M/D	1842-1898	**M-1303** and **M-1304** (partial index)
	1864-1873	**M-2819** (index)
	1875-1916	**M-3114** (partial index)

includes: Townships of Bristol, Clarendon, Leslie, Litchfield, Onslow, and Thorne, in:

St. James' Anglican Church, Hull, Gatineau Co.
B/M	1823-1842 extracts relating to Clarendon	**M-1303**

St. Paul's Anglican Church, Shawville
B/M/D	1842-1888	**M-1303** (partial index)
	1888-1898	**M-1304** (index)

includes also: Calumet-Island, and Mansfield Township, Pontiac Co., and Eardley Township, Gatineau Co., Que.; as well as Horton Township, Renfrew Co., Ont.

Anglican Mission of North Clarendon (later, Charteris), and district
B/M/D	1864-1873	**M-2819** (index)

Anglican Mission of North Clarendon (later, Charteris), and Thorne Township
B/M/D	1875-1891	**M-3114** (partial index)

Anglican Mission of Thorne Township, and district
B/M/D	1891-1913	**M-3114** (partial index)

Anglican Mission of Thorne and Leslie Townships, and North Clarendon (later, Charteris)
B/M/D	1892-1916	**M-3114** (partial index)

Anglican Missions of Ottawa County, which became:
St. James' Anglican Church, Hull
St. George's Anglican Church, Gatineau
St. Mary Magdalen Anglican Church, Chelsea
B/M/D	1831-1853	**M-299**
	1854-1940	**M-3689**

includes:

St. James' Anglican Church, Hull, Gatineau Co.
B/M/D	1831-1853	**M-299**

includes: Townships of Bristol, and Clarendon, Pontiac Co.; and the Townships of Eardley, and Hull, Gatineau Co.

(cont.)

St. John the Evangelist Anglican Church, Quyon
BMD   1857-1909   **M-2226** (index)
        1889-1946   **M-3132** (index)
includes:

Onslow Mission, which became:
    St. John the Evangelist Church, Quyon
    St. Mark's Church, Bristol
    St. Luke's Church, Eardley
    St. Matthew's Church, North Onslow
includes:

St. John the Evangelist Church, Quyon
BMD   1857-1889   **M-2226** (index)
      1890-1940   **M-3132** (index)
    includes: Bristol, and North Clarendon

Shawville United Church, Shawville
BMD   1851-1918   **M-2243**
        1877-1939   **M-2374**
includes: Calumet-Island, and the Townships of Bristol, Bryson, Clarendon, Leslie, Litchfield, and Thorne, in:

Presbyterian Church (Church of Scotland), Litchfield Township
BMD   1853-1870, 1874-1904,
        1918   **M-2243**
    includes also: Townships of Ross, and Westmeath, Renfrew Co., Ont., in the early years

Clarendon Wesleyan Methodist Circuit
BMD   1851-1898   **M-2243**
    includes also: Portage-du-Fort Mission, 1860-1879

Clarendon Regular Baptist Churches
BMD   1877-1939   **M-2374**
    includes also: North Clarendon, Starks Corners, and Wyman

Quyon United Church, Quyon
BMD   1859-1923   **M-2212**
includes: Townships of Bristol, Clarendon, Eardley, and Onslow in:

Onslow Wesleyan Methodist Church, Onslow Township
BMD   1859-1883   **M-2212**

Eardley Methodist Church, Eardley Township, Gatineau Co.
BMD   1884-1902   **M-2212**

Quyon Methodist Church, Quyon
BMD   1903-1923   **M-2212**
    includes also: Bristol, North Onslow,, Wyman, etc.

Contrecœur, comté de Verchères

Église catholique de Saint-Ours, comté de Richelieu
BMD   1681-1684,
        1783-1801 extraits   **M-866** (index)

(cont.)

comprend: Contrecœur, Verchères, et Fort Saint-Louis, comté de Verchères

Côte de Beaupré, comté de Montmorency N° 1

Notre-Dame-de-la-Visitation-du-Château-Richer (Côte de Beaupré) (Église catholique)
B   1661-1702   **M-1624**
M   1661-1701   **M-1624**
D   1661-1702   **M-1624**

L'Ange-Gardien (Côte de Beaupré) (Église catholique)
D   1670-1677   **M-1624**

Côte-Saint-Georges, Soulanges Co.

Presbyterian Church of Côte St. George and Dalhousie Mills (Glengarry Co., Ont.)
B   1843-1867, 1870-1874,
        1883   **M-3187**
M   1843-1850, 1862-1873   **M-3187**
BMD   1862-1875, 1882   **M-2228**
communion rolls 1862-1867, n.d.,
        1888-1889   **M-2228**

Coteau-du-Lac, Soulanges Co.

Civil registers of the Surrogate Court for the Eastern and Johnstown Districts, Ont.
B   1831, 1859, 1862-1865   **C-3030**
M   1831-1857, 1863, 1865   **C-3030** (index)
includes:

Presbyterian (Church of Scotland) Church, Lancaster Township, Glengarry Co., Ont.
M   1834-1836   **C-3030** (index)
    includes: Coteau-du-Lac, and Rivière-Beaudette, Soulanges Co., Que.

Denholm Township, Gatineau Co.

Christ Church Anglican Church, Aylmer
BMD   1864-1920   **M-3695** (index)
        1920-1971   **M-3696** (index)
includes: in the early years, the Townships of Denholm, Hull, and Wakefield, Gatineau Co.; the Townships of Buckingham, and Portland, Papineau Co.; and Templeton Township, Hull Co.

Deschambault, comté de Portneuf

Église catholique
BMD   1705-1712 extraits   **M-867** (index)
comprend : La Chevrotière

QUÉBEC

Deux Montagnes, lac des, comté de Deux-Montagnes

Mission du lac des Deux Montagnes (L'Annonciation-de-la-Bienheureuse-Vierge-Marie, Oka) (Église catholique)
BMD	1721-1787 extraits	**C-2895**
	1786-1821	**C-2895**
	1821-1850	**C-2896**

Dunham Township, Missisquoi Co.

Dunham (later, Saint-Armand) Wesleyan Methodist Circuit
B	1806-1825	**H-1807**
D	1807, 1811, 1813	**H-1807**

Dupas, île (ou Île du Pads), comté de Berthier

Église catholique de l'Isle-du-Pads (Île Dupas)
BMD	1709-1726,	
	1750-1756 extraits	**M-866** (index)
	1712-1726, 1750-1774,	
	1762-1790 extraits*	**M-866** (index)

* comprend: Saurel (Sorel), comté de Richelieu

Eardley Township/Canton de Eardley, Gatineau Co./comté de Gatineau

Clarendon Anglican Mission (later, St. Paul's Anglican Church, Shawville, etc.)
BM	1823-1842 extracts	**M-1303**
BMD	1842-1898	**M-1303** and **M-1304** (partial index)
	1864-1873	**M-2819** (index)
	1875-1916	**M-3114** (partial index)

includes:

St. Paul's Anglican Church, Shawville, Pontiac Co.
BMD	1842-1888	**M-1303** (partial index)
	1888-1898	**M-1304** (index)

includes: Calumet-Island, and the Townships of Bristol, Clarendon, Leslie, Litchfield, Mansfield, Onslow, and Thorne, Pontiac Co., and Eardley Township, Gatineau Co., Que.; as well as Horton Township, Renfrew Co., Ont.

(cont.)

Anglican Missions of Ottawa County, which became:
St. James' Anglican Church, Hull
St. George's Anglican Church, Gatineau
St. Mary Magdalen Anglican Church, Chelsea
BMD	1831-1853	**M-299**
	1854-1940	**M-3689**

includes:

St. James' Anglican Church, Hull
BMD	1831-1853	**M-299**

includes: Townships of Bristol, and Clarendon, Pontiac Co.; and the Townships of Eardley, and Hull, Gatineau Co.

St. James' Anglican Church, Hull, and Christ Church Anglican Church, Aylmer
BMD	1854-1886	**M-3689**

includes: Townships of Eardley, and Hull, Gatineau Co., and Onslow Township, Pontiac Co., Que.; as well as Ottawa, Carleton Co., Ont.

St. John the Evangelist Anglican Church, Quyon, Pontiac Co.
BMD	1857-1909	**M-2226** (index)
	1889-1946	**M-3132** (index)

includes:

Onslow Mission, which became:
St. John the Evangelist Church, Quyon
St. Mark's Church, Bristol
St. Luke's Church, Eardley
St. Matthew's Church, North Onslow
includes:

St. Luke's Anglican Church, Eardley
BMD	1873-1909	**M-2226** (index)

Missions du comté de Wright (Église catholique)
BMD	1841-1852	**C-2978**
M	1841-1852 Index	**C-2978**

comprend :

Eardley
BMD	1841-1848	**C-2978**
M	1841-1852 Index	**C-2978**

Quyon United Church, Quyon, Pontiac Co.
BMD	1859-1923	**M-2212**

includes: Townships of Bristol, Clarendon, Eardley, and Onslow, in:

Onslow Wesleyan Methodist Church, Onslow Township, Pontiac Co.
BMD	1859-1883	**M-2212**

Eardley Methodist Church, Eardley Township
BMD	1884-1902	**M-2212**

Quyon Methodist Church, Quyon, Pontiac Co.
BMD	1903-1923	**M-2212**

Includes also: Bristol, North Onslow, Wyman, etc., Pontiac Co.

QUÉBEC

East Farnham, Brome County

Farnham Monthly Meeting of Friends (Orthodox Quakers), East Farnham (formerly, Allen's Corner)
BMD	1839-1885	MG 17, G 3, fiche	22
	1861-1881		24
	1882-1911		25
removals and members	1839-1885		22
members	1885-1911		23

Farnham Township, Brome County

Farnham Monthly Meeting of Friends (Orthodox Quakers), East Farnham (formerly, Allen's Corner)
BMD	1839-1885	MG 17, G 3, fiche	22
	1861-1881		24
	1882-1911		25
removals and members	1839-1885		22
members	1885-1911		23

Fort-Chambly, comté de Chambly/Chambly Co.

Église catholique du Fort St-Frédéric ou Fort Beauharnois-à-la-Pointe-à-la-Chevelure (Crown Point), New York, États-Unis
BMD	1732-1760	**C-3023**
	1732-1760 extraits	**M-866** (index)

comprend :

Fort Chambly (Église catholique)
B	1759-1760	**C-3023**
D	1759	**C-3023**

Christ Church Anglican Church, William Henry (formerly, and later, Sorel), Richelieu Co.
BMD	1784-1796	**H-1807**

includes:

Fort-Chambly
B	1784-1785	**H-1807**
BMD	1796	**H-1807**

Fort-Coulonge, Pontiac Co.

St. George's Anglican Church, Campbell's Bay
BMD	1857-1920	**M-2520** (index)

includes:

Mission of Litchfield (Campbell's Bay) and Mansfield (Fort-Coulonge)
BMD	1902-1920	**M-2520** (index)

Fort Saint-Jean, comté de Saint-Jean/Saint-Jean Co.

St-Jean-[Baptiste-du-Fort-St-Jean-sur-Richelieu] (Église catholique)
BMD	1757-1760	**C-3023**
	1757-1760 extraits	**M-866** (index)

(cont.)

Christ Church Anglican Church, William Henry (formerly, and later, Sorel), Richelieu Co.
BMD	1784-1796	**H-1807**

includes:

Fort Saint-Jean (Dorchester)
B	1784, 1793-1795	**H-1807**
BMD	1796	**H-1807**

Fort Saint-Louis, comté de [Verchères ou Chambly]

Ste-Famille-de-Boucherville (Église catholique), comté de Chambly
BMD	1668-1762 extraits	**M-866** (index)

comprend : Longueuil, comté de Chambly; Fort St-Louis; et Varennes, comté de Verchères

Église catholique de St-Ours, comté de Richelieu
BMD	1681-1684,	
	1783-1801 extraits	**M-866** (index)

comprend : Contrecœur, Verchères, et Fort St-Louis

Fort William Henry, Richelieu Co.

Christ Church Anglican Church, William Henry (formerly, and later, Sorel)
BMD	1784-1796	**H-1807**

includes:

Fort William Henry
B	1784-1794, 1796	**H-1807**
BMD	1796	**H-1807**

Gatineau, Hull Co./comté de Hull

Anglican Missions of Ottawa County, which became:
St. James' Anglican Church, Hull
St. George's Anglican Church, Gatineau
St. Mary Magdalen Anglican Church, Chelsea
BMD	1831-1853	**M-299**
	1854-1940	**M-3689**

includes:

Anglican Mission of Chelsea and Gatineau (later, St. George's Church, Gatineau, and St. Mary Magdalen Church, Chelsea)
BMD	1899-1938	**M-3689**
	1934-1940	**M-3689**
confirmations	1888-1912	**M-3689**
communicants	1888-1913	**M-3689**
members	1925-1932	**M-3689**

includes: census of the parish of Chelsea, etc., c. 1818-1933, as well as entries for Hull, Que.; and Ottawa, Ont.

(cont.)

Missions du comté de Wright (Église catholique)
BMD　　1841-1852　　　　　**C-2978**
M　　　1841-1852 Index　　**C-2978**
comprend :

    St-François-de-Sales-et-la-Visitation-de-la-Gatineau
    BMD　　1841-1848　　　　　**C-2978**
    M　　　1841-1852 Index　　**C-2978**

Grand Calumet Island/Île du Grand Calumet, Pontiac Co./ comté de Pontiac

Clarendon Anglican Mission (later, St. Paul's Anglican Church, Shawville, etc.)
BM　　1823-1842　extracts　　**M-1303**
BMD　 1842-1898　　　　　　**M-1303** and
　　　　　　　　　　　　　　M-1304 (partial index)
　　　　1864-1873　　　　　**M-2819** (index)
　　　　1875-1916　　　　　**M-3114** (partial index)
includes:

    St. Paul's Anglican Church, Shawville
    BMD　　1842-1888　　　　　**M-1303** (partial index)
    　　　　1888-1898　　　　　**M-1304** (index)
    includes: Calumet-Island, and the Townships of Bristol, Clarendon, Leslie, Litchfield, Mansfield, Onslow, and Thorne, Pontiac Co., and Eardley Township, Gatineau Co., Que.; as well as Horton Township, Renfrew Co., Ont.

St. George's Anglican Church, Campbell's Bay
BMD　　1857-1920　　　　　**M-2520** (index)
includes:

    Portage-du-Fort Mission, Portage-du-Fort
    BMD　　1857-1874　　　　　**M-2520** (index)
    　　　　1874-1900*　　　　　**M-2520** (index)
    　　　　1900-1920　　　　　**M-2520** (index)
    *Includes: Bryson, and Calumet

Missions du comté de Wright (Église catholique)
BMD　　1841-1852　　　　　**C-2978**
M　　　1841-1852 Index　　**C-2978**
comprend :

    Ste-Anne-du-Grand-Calumet (Église catholique)
    BMD　　1841-1848　　　　　**C-2978**
    M　　　1841-1852 Index　　**C-2978**

(cont.)

Shawville United Church, Shawville
BMD　　1851-1918　　　　　**M-2243**
　　　　1877-1939　　　　　**M-2374**
includes: Calumet-Island, and the Townships of Bristol, Bryson, Clarendon, Leslie, Litchfield, and Thorne, in:

    Presbyterian Church (Church of Scotland), Litchfield Township
    BMD　　1853-1870, 1874-1904,
    　　　　1918　　　　　　　　**M-2243**
    includes also: Townships of Ross, and Westmeath, Renfrew Co., Ont., in the early years

    Clarendon Wesleyan Methodist Circuit, Clarendon
    BMD　　1851-1898　　　　　**M-2243**
    includes also: Portage-du-Fort Mission, 1860-1879

    Clarendon Regular Baptist Churches, Clarendon
    BMD　　1877-1939　　　　　**M-2374**
    includes also: North Clarendon, Starks Corners, and Wyman

Grenville, canton de, comté d'Argenteuil

Notre-Dame-de-Bon-Secours-de-la-Petite-Nation (Eglise catholique), Montebello, comté de Papineau
BMD　　1830-1850　　　　　**C-3023**
　　　　1845-1850　　　　　**C-3024**
comprend :

    Mission des cantons de Grenville, comté d'Argenteuil, et Buckingham, comté de Papineau (Église catholique)
    BMD　　1836-1838, 1840-1850　**C-3023**

Hull, comté de Gatineau/Gatineau Co.

Civil registers of Ontario
M　　　1816-1869　　　　　**M-5497**
　　　　1858-1869　　　　　**M-7092**
includes:

    Ottawa District (later, Prescott and Russell Counties)
    M　　　1816-1853　　　　　**M-5497**
    includes: Hull, Gatineau Co., Que.; as well as extracts of B 1822-1836 for the districts of Montreal, and Quebec, Que.

Clarendon Anglican Mission (later, St. Paul's Anglican Church, Shawville, etc.)
BM　　1823-1842　extracts　　**M-1303**
BMD　 1842-1898　　　　　　**M-1303** and
　　　　　　　　　　　　　　M-1304 (partial index)
　　　　1864-1873　　　　　**M-2819** (index)
　　　　1875-1916　　　　　**M-3114** (partial index)
includes:

(cont.)

St. James' Anglican Church, Hull
BM   1823-1842 extracts relating
                       to Clarendon   **M-1303**

Anglican Missions of Ottawa County, which became:
   St. James' Anglican Church, Hull
   St. George's Anglican Church, Gatineau
   St. Mary Magdalen Anglican Church, Chelsea
BMD   1831-1853   **M-299**
           1854-1940   **M-3689**
includes:

   St. James' Anglican Church, Hull
   BMD   1831-1853   **M-299**
   includes: Townships of Bristol, and Clarendon, Pontiac
           Co.; and the Townships of Eardley, and Hull,
           Gatineau Co.

   St. James' Anglican Church, Hull, and Christ Church
   Anglican Church, Aylmer
   BMD   1854-1886   **M-3689**
   includes: Townships of Eardley, and Hull, Gatineau Co.,
           and the Township of Onslow, Pontiac Co.,
           Que.; as well as Ottawa, Carleton Co., Ont.

   St. James' Anglican Church, Hull
   BMD   1886-1919   **M-3689**
   includes: Ottawa, Carleton Co., Ont.

Anglican Mission of Chelsea and Gatineau (later, St.
George's Church, Gatineau, and St. Mary Magdalen
Church, Chelsea)
BMD   1899-1938   **M-3689**
           1934-1940   **M-3689**
confirmations 1888-1912   **M-3689**
communicants 1888-1913   **M-3689**
members   1925-1932   **M-3689**
includes: census of the parish of Chelsea, etc.,
       c. 1818-1933, as well as entries for Hull, Que.; and
       Ottawa, Ont.

St-Joseph-de-Wrightville (Église catholique)
M   1913-1929 Index   **H-1807**

Hull Township/Canton de Hull, Gatineau Co./comté
de Gatineau

Anglican Missions of Ottawa County, which became:
   St. James' Anglican Church, Hull
   St. George's Anglican Church, Gatineau
   St. Mary Magdalen Anglican Church, Chelsea
BMD   1831-1853   **M-299**
           1854-1940   **M-3689**
comprises:

   St. James' Anglican Church, Hull
   BMD   1831-1853   **M-299**
   includes: Townships of Bristol, and Clarendon, Pontiac
           Co.; and the Townships of Eardley, and Hull,
           Gatineau Co.

(cont.)

St. James' Anglican Church, Hull, and Christ Church
Anglican Church, Aylmer
BMD   1854-1886   **M-3689**
includes: Townships of Eardley, and Hull, Gatineau Co.,
       and Onslow Township, Pontiac Co., Que.; as
       well as Ottawa, Carleton Co., Ont.

St. James' Anglican Church, Hull
BMD   1886-1919   **M-3689**
includes: Ottawa, Carleton Co., Ont.

Anglican Mission of Chelsea and Gatineau (later,
St. George's Church, Gatineau, and St. Mary Magdalen
Church, Chelsea)
BMD   1899-1938   **M-3689**
           1934-1940   **M-3689**
confirmations 1888-1912   **M-3689**
communicants 1888-1913   **M-3689**
members   1925-1932   **M-3689**
includes: census of the parish of Chelsea, etc.,
       c. 1818-1933, as well as entries for Hull, Que.;
       and Ottawa, Ont.

Christ Church Anglican Church, Aylmer
BMD   1864-1920   **M-3695** (index)
           1920-1971   **M-3696** (index)
includes: in the early years, the Townships of Denholm,
       Hull, and Wakefield, Gatineau Co.; the Townships
       of Buckingham, and Portland, Papineau Co.; and
       Templeton Township, Hull Co.

Missions du comté de Wright (Église catholique)
BMD   1841-1852   **C-2978**
M   1841-1852 Index   **C-2978**
comprend :

   Hull
   BMD   1841-1848   **C-2978**
   M   1841-1852 Index   **C-2978**

Île du Grand Calumet/Grand Calumet Island, comté de
Pontiac/Pontiac Co.

Clarendon Anglican Mission (later, St. Paul's Anglican
Church, Shawville, etc.)
BM   1823-1842 extracts   **M-1303**
BMD   1842-1898   **M-1303** and
                                  M-1304 (partial
                                         index)
           1864-1873   **M-2819** (index)
           1875-1916   **M-3114** (partial
                                       index)
includes:

   St. Paul's Anglican Church, Shawville
   BMD   1842-1888   **M-1303** (partial
                                  index)
           1888-1898   **M-1304** (index)
   includes: Calumet-Island, and the Townships of Bristol,
           Clarendon, Leslie, Litchfield, Mansfield, Onslow,

(cont.)

and Thorne, Pontiac Co., and Eardley Township, Gatineau Co., Que.; as well as Horton Township, Renfrew Co., Ont.

St. George's Anglican Church, Campbell's Bay
BMD   1857-1920   **M-2520** (index)
includes:

Portage-du-Fort Mission, Portage-du-Fort
BMD   1857-1874   **M-2520** (index)
           1874-1900*   **M-2520** (index)
           1900-1920   **M-2520** (index)
*Includes: Bryson, and Calumet

Missions du comté de Wright (Église catholique)
BMD   1841-1852   **C-2978**
M   1841-1852 Index   **C-2978**
comprend:

Ste-Anne-du-Grand-Calumet (Église catholique)
BMD   1841-1848   **C-2978**
M   1841-1852 Index   **C-2978**

Shawville United Church, Shawville
BMD   1851-1918   **M-2243**
           1877-1939   **M-2374**
includes: Calumet-Island, and the Townships of Bristol, Bryson, Clarendon, Leslie, Litchfield, and Thorne, in:

Presbyterian Church (Church of Scotland), Litchfield Township
BMD   1853-1870, 1874-1904,
         1918   **M-2243**
includes also: Townships of Ross, and Westmeath, Renfrew Co., Ont., in the early years

Clarendon Wesleyan Methodist Circuit, Clarendon
BMD   1851-1898   **M-2243**
includes also: Portage-du-Fort Mission, 1860-1879

Clarendon Regular Baptist Churches, Clarendon
BMD   1877-1939   **M-2374**
includes also: North Clarendon, Starks Corners, and Wyman

Île Dupas (ou Île du Pads), comté de Berthier

Église catholique
BMD   1709-1726,
           1750-1756 extraits   **M-866** (index)
           1712-1726, 1750-1774,
           1762-1790 extraits*   **M-866** (index)
*comprend: Saurel (Sorel), comté de Richelieu

Île-Jésus, comté de l'

St-François-de-Sales-de-l'Île-Jésus (Église catholique)
BMD   1727-1761,
           1779-1805 extraits   **M-865** (index)

(cont.)

Église catholique de Lachenaie, comté de L'Assomption
BMD   1683-1744 extraits   **M-866** (index)
comprend: Repentigny, et Saint-Sulpice, comté de L'Assomption; et l'Île-Jésus

Îles Bouchard, comté de L'Assomption

Saint-Antoine-de-Lavaltrie (Église catholique)
BMD   1717, 1749-1764,
           1786-1815 extraits   **M-866** (index)
comprend: Saint-Sulpice, et les Îles Bouchard

Kamouraska, comté de

Église catholique
BMD   1762-1798 extraits   **C-3109**
comprend: Saint-André-de-Kamouraska et Saint-Louis-de-Kamouraska

Lacaille, Pointe-à- (ou Saint-Thomas), comté de Montmagny

Église catholique
BMD   1690, 1738-1739,
           1758-1763 extraits   **M-865** (index)

Lac des Deux Montagnes, comté de Deux-Montagnes

Mission du lac des Deux Montagnes (L'Annonciation-de-la-Bienheureuse-Vierge-Marie, Oka) (Église catholique)
BMD   1721-1787 extraits   **C-2895**
           1786-1821   **C-2895**
           1821-1850   **C-2896**

Lachenaie, comté de L'Assomption

Église catholique de Repentigny
BMD   1681-1727,
           1770-1807 extraits   **M-866** (index)
comprend: Lachenaie

Église catholique
BMD   1683-1744 extraits   **M-866** (index)
comprend: Repentigny, et Saint-Sulpice, comté de L'Assomption; et l'Île-Jésus

Lachevrotière, comté de [Portneuf]

Église catholique de Deschambault
BMD   1705-1712 extraits   **M-867** (index)
comprend: La Chevrotière

QUÉBEC

Lachine, comté de l'Île-de-Montréal

Église catholique
BMD 1676-1711,
1717-1801 extraits **M-865** (index)

Lac-Sainte-Marie, comté de Gatineau

Missions du comté de Wright (Église catholique)
BMD 1841-1852 **C-2978**
M 1841-1852 Index **C-2978**
comprend :

Lac-Sainte-Marie (Église catholique)
BMD 1841-1848 **C-2978**
M 1841-1852 Index **C-2978**

L'Ange-Gardien, comté de Montmorency N° 1

L'Ange-Gardien (Côte de Beaupré) (Église catholique)
D 1670-1677 **M-1624**

L'Annonciation, comté de Deux-Montagnes

Mission du lac des Deux Montagnes (L'Annonciation-de-la-Bienheureuse-Vierge-Marie, Oka) (Église catholique)
BMD 1721-1787 extraits **C-2895**
1786-1821 **C-2895**
1821-1850 **C-2896**

Lanoraie, comté de [Berthier]

Église catholique
BMD 1735, 1738, 1753-1762,
1786-1821 extraits **M-866** (index)

Lapêche, comté de Gatineau

Missions du comté de Wright (Église catholique)
BMD 1841-1852 **C-2978**
M 1841-1852 Index **C-2978**
comprend :

Ste-Cécile-de-la-rivière-à-la-Pêche (Église catholique)
BMD 1841-1848 **C-2978**
M 1841-1852 Index **C-2978**

La Pointe Olivier, [région de Montréal, comté de l'Île-de-Montréal]

Église catholique
BMD 1739, 1746-1747, 1751,
1778-1794,
1801-1803 extraits **M-865** (index)

La Prairie, comté de Laprairie

Église catholique
BMD 1680-1687, 1708-1713,
1727-1729,
1755-1761 extraits **M-866** (index)

L'Assomption, comté de L'Assomption

Église catholique
BMD 1749-1782 extraits **M-865** (index)

Laval, comté de l'Île-Jésus

Ste-Rose-de-Laval (Église catholique)
BMD 1796-1805 **C-2915**
1805-1831 **C-2916**
1831-1850 **C-2917**

Lavaltrie, comté de Berthier

St-Antoine-de-Lavaltrie (Église catholique)
BMD 1717, 1749-1764,
1786-1815 extraits **M-866** (index)
comprend : Saint-Sulpice, et les Îles Bouchard

L'Enfant-Jésus-de-Sorel [Tracy], comté de Richelieu

Archives paroissiales du comté de Richelieu
BMD 1784-1973 **C-7029** à **C-7031**
comprend :

L'Enfant-Jésus-de-Sorel, Tracy (Église catholique)
BMD 1950-1973 **C-7029**

Leslie Township, Pontiac Co.

Clarendon Anglican Mission (later, St. Paul's Anglican Church, Shawville, etc.)
BM 1823-1842 extracts **M-1303**
BMD 1842-1898 **M-1303** and
M-1304 (partial index)
1864-1873 **M-2819** (index)
1875-1916 **M-3114** (partial index)
includes: Townships of Bristol, Clarendon, Leslie, Litchfield, Onslow, and Thorne, in:

St. James' Anglican Church, Hull, Gatineau Co.
BM 1823-1842 extracts relating
to Clarendon **M-1303**

St. Paul's Anglican Church, Shawville
BMD 1842-1888 **M-1303** (partial index)
1888-1898 **M-1304** (index)
(cont.)

includes also: Calumet-Island, and Mansfield Township, Pontiac Co., and Eardley Township, Gatineau Co., Que.; as well as Horton Township, Renfrew Co., Ont.

Anglican Mission of North Clarendon (later, Charteris), and district
BMD   1864-1873   **M-2819** (index)

Anglican Mission of North Clarendon (later, Charteris), and Thorne Township
BMD   1875-1891   **M-3114** (partial index)

Anglican Mission of Thorne Township, and district
BMD   1891-1913   **M-3114** (partial index)

Anglican Mission of Thorne and Leslie Townships, and North Clarendon (later, Charteris)
BMD   1892-1916   **M-3114** (partial index)

Shawville United Church, Shawville
BMD   1851-1918   **M-2243**
            1877-1939   **M-2374**
includes: Calumet-Island, and the Townships of Clarendon, Leslie, Litchfield, and Thorne, in:

Presbyterian Church (Church of Scotland), Litchfield Township
BMD   1853-1870, 1874-1904, 1918   **M-2243**
includes also: Townships of Ross, and Westmeath, Renfrew Co., Ont., in the early years

Clarendon Wesleyan Methodist Circuit, Clarendon
BMD   1851-1898   **M-2243**
includes also: Portage-du-Fort Mission, 1860-1879

Clarendon Regular Baptist Churches, Clarendon
BMD   1877-1939   **M-2374**
includes also: North Clarendon, Starks Corners, and Wyman

Lévis, Lévis Co.

Register of the Royal Canadian Artillery (Army Book 91) — non-commissioned officers and men
B   1871-1911   **C-11775** (index)
M   1870-1915   **C-11775** (index)
D   1895-1905   **C-11775** (index)
includes: Kingston, Ont.; as well as a few entries for Lévis, and Québec, Que.; and for Aldershot, and Barntfield, [England]; and Benares, and Cawnpore [India]

Litchfield Township, Pontiac Co.

Clarendon Anglican Mission (later, St. Paul's Anglican Church, Shawville, etc.)
BM   1823-1842 extracts   **M-1303**
BMD   1842-1898   **M-1303** and
                             M-1304 (partial index)
           1864-1873   **M-2819** (index)
           1875-1916   **M-3114** (partial index)
includes: Townships of Bristol, Clarendon, Leslie, Litchfield, Onslow, and Thorne, in:

St. James' Anglican Church, Hull, Gatineau Co.
BM   1823-1842 extracts relating to Clarendon   **M-1303**

St. Paul's Anglican Church, Shawville
BMD   1842-1888   **M-1303** (partial index)
           1888-1898   **M-1304** (index)
includes also: Calumet-Island, and Mansfield Township, Pontiac Co., and Eardley Township, Gatineau Co., Que.; as well as Horton Township, Renfrew Co., Ont.

Anglican Mission of North Clarendon (later, Charteris), and district
BMD   1864-1873   **M-2819** (index)

Anglican Mission of North Clarendon (later, Charteris), and Thorne Township
BMD   1875-1891   **M-3114** (partial index)

Anglican Mission of Thorne Township, and district
BMD   1891-1913   **M-3114** (partial index)

Anglican Mission of Thorne and Leslie Townships, and North Clarendon (later, Charteris)
BMD   1892-1916   **M-3114** (partial index)

St. George's Anglican Church, Campbell's Bay
BMD   1857-1920   **M-2520** (index)
includes:

Mission of Litchfield (Campbell's Bay) and Mansfield (Fort-Coulonge)
BMD   1902-1920   **M-2520** (index)

Shawville United Church, Shawville
BMD   1851-1918   **M-2243**
           1877-1939   **M-2374**
includes: Calumet-Island, and the Townships of Bristol, Bryson, Clarendon, Leslie, Litchfield, and Thorne, in:

(cont.)

Presbyterian Church (Church of Scotland), Litchfield Township
BMD   1853-1870, 1874-1904,
            1918   **M-2243**
includes also: Townships of Ross, and Westmeath, Renfrew Co., Ont., in the early years

Clarendon Wesleyan Methodist Circuit, Clarendon
BMD   1851-1898   **M-2243**
includes also: Portage-du-Fort Mission, 1860-1879

Clarendon Regular Baptist Churches, Clarendon
BMD   1877-1939   **M-2374**
includes also: North Clarendon, Starks Corners, and Wyman

Longue Pointe, comté de l'Île-de-Montréal

Église catholique
BMD	1724-1792 extraits	**M-865** (index)
	1726, 1749,	
	1755-[1800] extraits	**M-866** (index)

Longueuil, comté de Chambly

Ste-Famille-de-Boucherville (Église catholique)
BMD   1668-1762 extraits   **M-866** (index)
comprend : Longueuil, comté de Chambly; Fort St-Louis; et Varennes, comté de Verchères

[St-Antoine-de-]Longueuil (Église catholique)
BMD   1679-1684,
            1713-1789 extraits   **M-865** (index)
comprend: Boucherville, comté de Chambly; et Varennes, comté de Verchères

Église catholique
BMD   1699-1769,
            1773-1795 extraits   **M-866** (index)

Louiseville (auparavant, Rivière-du-Loup), comté de Maskinongé

Église catholique de St-François-du-Lac, comté de Yamaska
BMD	1687-1719	**C-3024** (index)
	1720-1763	**C-3024**
	1808-1836 extraits	**C-3024**
comprend : des endroits environnants (dont Rivière-du-Loup, ou Louiseville, 1688-1693)

Mansfield Township, Pontiac Co.

Clarendon Anglican Mission (later, St. Paul's Anglican Church, Shawville, etc.)
BM	1823-1842 extracts	**M-1303**
BMD	1842-1898	**M-1303** and
		M-1304 (partial index)
	1864-1873	**M-2819** (index)
	1875-1916	**M-3114** (partial index)

includes:

St. Paul's Anglican Church, Shawville
| BMD | 1842-1888 | **M-1303** (partial index) |
| | 1888-1898 | **M-1304** (index) |
includes: Calumet-Island, and the Townships of Bristol, Clarendon, Leslie, Litchfield, Mansfield, Onslow, and Thorne, Pontiac Co., and Eardley Township, Gatineau Co., Que.; as well as Horton Township, Renfrew Co., Ont.

St. George's Anglican Church, Campbell's Bay
BMD   1857-1920   **M-2520** (index)
includes:

Mission of Litchfield (Campbell's Bay) and Mansfield (Fort-Coulonge)
BMD   1902-1920   **M-2520** (index)

Masham, canton de, comté de Gatineau

Missions du comté de Wright (Église catholique)
| BMD | 1841-1852 | **C-2978** |
| M | 1841-1852 Index | **C-2978** |
comprend :

Ste-Cécile-de-la-rivière-à-la-Pêche (ou Ste-Cécile-de-Masham) (Église catholique)
| BMD | 1841-1848 | **C-2978** |
| M | 1841-1852 Index | **C-2978** |

Montebello, comté de Papineau

Notre-Dame-de-Bon-Secours-de-la-Petite-Nation (Église catholique), Montebello
BMD   1830-1849   **C-3023**

avec :

Missions des cantons de Grenville, comté d'Argenteuil, et Buckingham, comté de Papineau (Église catholique)
BMD   1836-1838, 1840-1850   **C-3023**

et :

Mission de Buckingham (Église catholique)
| BMD | 1839-1845 | **C-3023** |
| | 1845-1850 | **C-3024** |

QUÉBEC

Montréal, comté de l'Île-de-Montréal/Île-de-Montréal Co.

Civil registers of Ontario
M	1816-1869	**M-5497**
	1858-1869	**M-7092**

includes:

Ottawa District (later, Prescott and Russell Counties)
M	1816-1853	**M-5497**

includes: Hull, Gatineau Co., Que.; as well as extracts of B 1822-1836 for the districts of Montreal, and Quebec, Que.

[Christ Church] Anglican Parish of Montreal
BMD	1766-1787	**C-3023**

Christ-Church-de-Montréal (Église anglicane)
B	1767-1768 extraits	**M-868**	(index)
M	1766-1794 extraits	**M-868**	(index)

Christ Church Anglican Church, William Henry (formerly, and later, Sorel), Richelieu Co.
BMD	1784-1796	**H-1807**

includes:

Montreal
B	1785	**H-1807**

Invitations à des funérailles à Montréal
D	1790-1856	**H-1807** (index)

St. John's Evangelical Lutheran Church
BMD	1855-1883	**M-4626**
B	1884-1895	**M-4626** (index)
M	1884-1904	**M-4626** (index)
D	1884-1902	**M-4626** (index)
BMD	1902-1908	**M-4626** (index)
	1909-1923	**M-4626**
B	1895-1925	**M-4626** (index on **M-4627**)
	1926-1939	**M-4627** (index)
M	1904-1939	**M-4627** (index)
D	1902-1939	**M-4627** (index)

(The registers before 1902 were kept in German.)

First Hungarian Lutheran Church of Montreal
BMD	1932-1950	**M-4627**

St. Andrew's Presbyterian Church, Williamstown, Glengarry Co., Ont.
BM	1779-1810	**C-3030** (index)
BMD	1811-1817	**C-3030** (index)

includes: Stormont County, Ont.; Montreal, Que.; etc.

Church of Scotland Garrison Chaplaincy, Montreal
BMD	1862-1869	**C-3023**

Église catholique de Ville-Marie en l'Île-de-Montréal
BMD	1680-1681 extraits	**M-867**	(index)
	1680-1681, 1684-1693	**C-2904**	

Notre-Dame-de-Montréal (Église catholique)
BMD	1642-1680	**C-2900**
	1651-1698	**C-2901**
	1698-1708	**C-2902**
	1709-1722, 1727	**C-2903**
	1727-1728	**C-2904**
	[1648-1763] Index :	
	Abel–Delzenne	**C-15736**
	Demair–Larchevesque	**C-15737**
	Larchevesque–Roby	**C-15738**
	Rocand–Zillion	**C-15739**

[Notre-Dame-de-Montréal] (Église catholique)
B	1642-1680 extraits	**M-867**	(index)
M	1647-1680 extraits	**M-867**	(index)
D	1655-1680 extraits	**M-867**	(index)
BMD	1681-1694 extraits	**M-867**	(index)
	1681-1728 extraits	**M-867**	(index)
	1695-1730 extraits	**M-867**	(index)
	1731-1755 extraits	**M-867**	(index)
	1756-1822 extraits	**M-868**	(index)

North Clarendon, Pontiac Co.

Clarendon Anglican Mission (later, St. Paul's Anglican Church, Shawville, etc.)
BM	1823-1842 extracts	**M-1303**
BMD	1842-1898	**M-1303** and **M-1304** (partial index)
	1864-1873	**M-2819** (index)
	1875-1916	**M-3114** (partial index)

includes: Townships of Bristol, Clarendon, Leslie, Litchfield, Onslow, and Thorne, in:

St. James' Anglican Church, Hull, Gatineau Co.
BM	1823-1842 extracts relating to Clarendon	**M-1303**

St. Paul's Anglican Church, Shawville
BMD	1842-1888	**M-1303** (partial index)
	1888-1898	**M-1304** (index)

includes also: Calumet-Island, and Mansfield Township, Pontiac Co., and Eardley Township, Gatineau Co., Que.; as well as Horton Township, Renfrew Co., Ont.

Anglican Mission of North Clarendon (later, Charteris), and district
BMD	1864-1873	**M-2819** (index)

Anglican Mission of North Clarendon (later, Charteris), and Thorne Township
BMD	1875-1891	**M-3114** (partial index)

Anglican Mission of Thorne Township, and district
BMD	1891-1913	**M-3114** (partial index)

(cont.)

QUÉBEC

Anglican Mission of Thorne and Leslie Townships, and North Clarendon (later, Charteris)
BMD   1892-1916   **M-3114** (partial index)

St. John the Evangelist Anglican Church, Quyon
BMD   1857-1909   **M-2226** (index)
       1889-1946   **M-3132** (index)
includes:

   Onslow Mission, which became:
      St. John the Evangelist Church, Quyon
      St. Mark's Church, Bristol
      St. Luke's Church, Eardley
      St. Matthew's Church, North Onslow
   includes:

      St. John the Evangelist Church, Quyon
      BMD   1857-1889   **M-2226** index
            1890-1940   **M-3132** (index)
      includes: Bristol, and North Clarendon

Shawville United Church, Shawville
BMD   1851-1918   **M-2243**
       1877-1939   **M-2374**
includes:

   Clarendon Regular Baptist Churches
   BMD   1877-1939   **M-2374**
   includes: North Clarendon, Starks Corners, and Wyman

North Onslow, Pontiac Co.

St. John the Evangelist Anglican Church, Quyon
BMD   1857-1909   **M-2226** (index)
       1889-1946   **M-3132** (index)
includes:

   Onslow Mission, which became:
      St. John the Evangelist Church, Quyon
      St. Mark's Church, Bristol
      St. Luke's Church, Eardley
      St. Matthew's Church, North Onslow
   includes:

      St. John the Evangelist Church, Quyon
      BMD   1857-1889   **M-2226** (index)
            1890-1940   **M-3132** (index)
      includes: Bristol, and North Clarendon

      St. Luke's Church, Eardley, Gatineau Co.
      BMD   1873-1909   **M-2226** (index)

Quyon United Church, Quyon
BMD   1859-1923   **M-2212**
includes: Townships of Bristol, Clarendon, and Onslow, Pontiac Co.; and Eardley Township, Gatineau Co., in:

   Onslow Wesleyan Methodist Church, Onslow Township
   BMD   1859-1883   **M-2212**
                                         (cont.)

Eardley Methodist Church, Eardley Township, Gatineau Co.
BMD   1884-1902   **M-2212**

Quyon Methodist Church, Quyon
BMD   1903-1923   **M-2212**
includes also: Bristol, North Onslow, Wyman, etc.

Notre-Dame-de-Bon-Secours, comté de Papineau

Notre-Dame-de-Bon-Secours-de-la-Petite-Nation (Église catholique), Montebello
BMD   1830-1849   **C-3023**

                  avec:

Missions des cantons de Grenville, comté d'Argenteuil, et Buckingham, comté de Papineau (Église catholique)
BMD   1836-1838, 1840-1850   **C-3023**

                  et:

Mission de Buckingham (Église catholique)
BMD   1839-1845   **C-3023**
       1845-1850   **C-3024**

Oka, (lac des Deux Montagnes) comté de Deux-Montagnes

Mission du lac des Deux Montagnes (L'Annonciation-de-la-Bienheureuse-Vierge-Marie) (Église catholique)
BMD   1721-1787 extraits   **C-2895**
       1786-1821   **C-2895**
       1821-1850   **C-2896**

Olivier, la Pointe [région de Montréal, comté de l'Île-de-Montréal]

Église catholique
BMD   1739, 1746-1747, 1751,
       1778-1794,
       1801-1803 extraits   **M-865** (index)

Onslow Township, Pontiac Co.

Clarendon Anglican Mission (later, St. Paul's Anglican Church, Shawville, etc.)
BM   1823-1842 extracts   **M-1303**
BMD   1842-1898   **M-1303** and
                              M-1304 (partial index)
       1864-1873   **M-2819** (index)
       1875-1916   **M-3114** (partial index)
includes: Townships of Bristol, Clarendon, Leslie, Litchfield, Onslow, and Thorne, in:

                                         (cont.)

QUÉBEC

St. James' Anglican Church, Hull, Gatineau Co.
BM   1823-1842 extracts relating
                to Clarendon   **M-1303**

St. Paul's Anglican Church, Shawville
BMD   1842-1888   **M-1303** (partial index)
          1888-1898   **M-1304** (index)
includes also: Calumet-Island, and Mansfield Township, Pontiac Co., and Eardley Township, Gatineau Co., Que.; as well as Horton Township, Renfrew Co., Ont.

Anglican Mission of North Clarendon (later, Charteris), and district
BMD   1864-1873   **M-2819** (index)

Anglican Mission of North Clarendon (later, Charteris), and Thorne Township
BMD   1875-1891   **M-3114** (partial index)

Anglican Mission of Thorne Township, and district
BMD   1891-1913   **M-3114** (partial index)

Anglican Mission of Thorne and Leslie Townships, and North Clarendon (later, Charteris)
BMD   1892-1916   **M-3114** (partial index)

Anglican Missions of Ottawa County, which became:
    St. James' Anglican Church, Hull
    St. George's Anglican Church, Gatineau
    St. Mary Magdalen Anglican Church, Chelsea
BMD   1831-1853   **M-299**
          1854-1940   **M-3689**
includes:

Christ Church, Aylmer, and St. James', Hull, Gatineau Co.
BMD   1854-1886   **M-3689**
includes: Townships of Eardley, and Hull, Gatineau Co., and Onslow Township, Pontiac Co., Que.; as well as Ottawa, Carleton Co., Ont.

St. John the Evangelist Anglican Church, Quyon
BMD   1857-1909   **M-2226** (index)
          1889-1946   **M-3132** (index)
includes:

Onslow Mission, which became:
    St. John the Evangelist Church, Quyon
    St. Mark's Church, Bristol
    St. Luke's Church, Eardley
    St. Matthew's Church, North Onslow
includes:

St. John the Evangelist Church, Quyon
BMD   1857-1889   **M-2226** (index)
          1890-1940   **M-3132** (index)
includes: Bristol, and North Clarendon

St. Luke's Church, Eardley, Gatineau Co.
BMD   1873-1909   **M-2226** (index)

Quyon United Church, Quyon
BMD   1859-1923   **M-2212**
includes: Townships of Bristol, Clarendon, Eardley, and Onslow, in:

Onslow Wesleyan Methodist Church, Onslow Township
BMD   1859-1883   **M-2212**

Eardley Methodist Church, Eardley Township, Gatineau Co.
BMD   1884-1902   **M-2212**

Quyon Methodist Church, Quyon
BMD   1903-1923   **M-2212**
includes also: Bristol, North Onslow, Wyman, etc.

Ottawa County (later, Hull County, and parts of the Counties of Gatineau, Papineau, and Pontiac)

Anglican Missions of Ottawa County, which became:
    St. James' Anglican Church, Hull
    St. George's Anglican Church, Gatineau
    St. Mary Magdalen Anglican Church, Chelsea
BMD   1831-1853   **M-299**
          1854-1940   **M-3689**
comprises:

St. James' Anglican Church, Hull, Gatineau Co.
BMD   1831-1853   **M-299**
includes: Townships of Bristol, and Clarendon, Pontiac Co.; and the Townships of Eardley, and Hull, Gatineau Co.

St. James' Anglican Church, Hull, and Christ Church Anglican Church, Aylmer, Gatineau Co.
BMD   1854-1886   **M-3689**
includes: Townships of Eardley, and Hull, Gatineau Co., and Onslow Township, Pontiac Co., Que.; as well as Ottawa, Carleton Co., Ont.

St. James' Anglican Church, Hull, Gatineau Co.
BMD   1886-1919   **M3689**
includes: Ottawa, Carleton Co., Ont.

Anglican Mission of Chelsea and Gatineau, Gatineau Co., (later, St. George's Church, Gatineau, and St. Mary Magdalen Church, Chelsea)
BMD   1899-1938   **M-3689**
          1934-1940   **M-3689**
confirmations   1888-1912   **M-3689**
communicants   1888-1913   **M-3689**
members   1925-1932   **M-3689**
includes: census of the parish of Chelsea, etc., c. 1818-1933, as well as entries for Hull, Que.; and Ottawa, Ont.

Allumette Island Wesleyan Methodist Circuit, Pontiac Co.
BM   1858-1887   **M-2823**
includes: adjacent parts of Pontiac and Ottawa Counties

QUÉBEC

Pabos, comté de Gaspé-Est

Registres d'état civil d'Acadie et Gaspésie, N.-É.
BM	1679-1686	**C-3021**
BMD	1751-1757	**C-3021**

comprend :

    Ste-Famille-de-Pabos (Église catholique)
BMD	1751-1757	**C-3021**

Petite-Nation, seigneurie de la, comté de Papineau

Notre-Dame-de-Bon-Secours-de-la-Petite-Nation (Église catholique), Montebello
BMD	1830-1849	**C-3023**

    avec :

    Mission des cantons de Grenville, comté d'Argenteuil, et Buckingham, comté de Papineau (Église catholique)
BMD	1836-1838, 1840-1850	**C-3023**

    et :

    Mission de Buckingham (Église catholique)
BMD	1839-1845	**C-3023**
	1845-1850	**C-3024**

Pointe-à-Lacaille (ou Saint-Thomas), comté de Montmagny

Église catholique
BMD	1690, 1738-1739, 1758-1763 extraits	**M-865**	(index)

Pointe-aux-Trembles, comté de l'Île-de-Montréal

Église catholique
BMD	1675-1724,		
	1749-1770 extraits	**M-865**	(index)
	1678-1714 extraits	**M-865**	(index)

Pointe-Claire, comté de l'Île-de-Montréal

Église catholique
BMD	1719-1727,		
	1747-1761 extraits	**M-866**	(index)

Pointe Olivier, La, [région de Montréal, comté de l'Île-de-Montréal]

Église catholique
BMD	1739, 1746-1747, 1751, 1778-1794,		
	1801-1803 extraits	**M-865**	(index)

Pontiac County

Allumette Island Wesleyan Methodist Circuit
BM	1858-1887	**M-2823**

includes: adjacent parts of the Counties of Ottawa, and Pontiac

Portage-du-Fort, Pontiac Co.

St. George's Anglican Church, Campbell's Bay
BMD	1857-1920	**M-2520**	(index)

includes:

    Portage-du-Fort Mission, Portage-du-Fort
BMD	1857-1874	**M-2520**	(index)
	1874-1900*	**M-2520**	(index)
	1900-1920	**M-2520**	(index)

    *Includes: Bryson, and Calumet

Shawville United Church, Shawville
BMD	1851-1918	**M-2243**
	1877-1939	**M-2374**

includes:

    Clarendon Wesleyan Methodist Circuit, Clarendon
BMD	1851-1898	**M-2243**

    includes: Portage-du-Fort Mission, 1860-1879, as well as Calumet-Island, and the Townships of Bristol, Bryson, Clarendon, Leslie, Litchfield, and Thorne

Portland Township, Papineau Co.

Christ Church Anglican Church, Aylmer, Gatineau Co.
BMD	1864-1920	**M-3695**	(index)
	1920-1971	**M-3696**	(index)

includes: in the early years, the Townships of Denholm, Hull, and Wakefield, Gatineau Co.; the Townships of Buckingham, and Portland, Papineau Co.; and Templeton Township, Hull Co.

Potton Township, Brome Co.

Potton Methodist Circuit
BMD	1837-1848	**M-137**	(partial index)

Québec, comté de Québec/Quebec Co.

Civil registers of Ontario
M	1816-1869	**M-5497**
	1858-1869	**M-7092**

includes:

    Ottawa District (later, Prescott and Russell Counties)
M	1816-1853	**M-5497**

    includes: Hull, Gatineau Co., Que.; as well as extracts of

(cont.)

B 1822-1836 for the districts of Montreal, and Quebec, Que.

Holy Trinity Anglican Cathedral

BD	1768-1795	**C-2897** (index)
M	1768-1786	**C-2897** (index)
	1786-1795	**C-2898** (index)
	1789-1795	**C-2898** (index)
B	1789-1795	**C-2898** (index)
D	1789-1795	**C-2898** (index)
BMD	1796-1800	**C-2897** (index)
	1796-1800	**C-2898** (index)

St. Andrew's Presbyterian Church

BMD   1770-1829   **C-2898**

Quebec Garrison Protestant Chaplaincy

BMD	1797-1800, 1817-1825	**C-2898** (index*)
	1825-1826	**C-2899** (index)

*The index for 1824 is on **C-2899**.

Notre-Dame-de-l'Immaculée-Conception-de-Québec (Église catholique)

BM	1621-1667	**M-6802** (originaux, index)
B	1626-1679	**C-2896** (copies)
M	1621-1678	**C-2896** (copies)
D	1640-1671	**C-2896** (copies)
	1640-1679	**M-6802** (originaux, index)
BMD	1651-1668, 1679-1728	**C-2896** (copies)
	1728-1738	**C-2897** (copies)
	1739-1752 extraits	**M-865** (copies, index)

Notre-Dame-des-Anges (Hôpital-général) (Église catholique)

BMD   1728-1783   **C-1472** (index)

Register of the Royal Canadian Artillery (Army Book 91) — non-commissioned officers and men

B	1871-1911	**C-11775** (index)
M	1870-1915	**C-11775** (index)
D	1895-1905	**C-11775** (index)

includes: Kingston, Ont.; as well as a few entries for Lévis, and Quebec, Que.; and for Aldershot, and Barntfield [England]; and Benares, and Cawnpore [India]

Quyon, Pontiac Co.

St. John the Evangelist Anglican Church

BMD	1857-1909	**M-2226** (index)
	1889-1946	**M-3132** (index)

comprises:

  Onslow Mission, which became:
    St. John the Evangelist Church, Quyon
    St. Mark's Church, Bristol
    St. Luke's Church, Eardley
    St. Matthew's Church, North Onslow

(cont.)

includes:

  St. John the Evangelist Church, Quyon

BMD	1857-1889	**M-2226** (index)
	1890-1940	**M-3132** (index)

  includes: Bristol, and North Clarendon

  St. Luke's Church, Eardley, Gatineau Co.

BMD   1873-1909   **M-2226** (index)

  Bristol Mission (later, St. Thomas' Church, Bristol)

BMD   1889-1946   **M-3132** (index)

Quyon United Church

BMD   1859-1923   **M-2212**

includes: Townships of Bristol, Clarendon, and Onslow, Pontiac Co.; and Eardley Township, Gatineau Co., in:

  Onslow Wesleyan Methodist Church, Onslow Township

BMD   1859-1883   **M2212**

  Eardley Methodist Church, Eardley Township, Gatineau Co.

BMD   1884-1902   **M-2212**

  Quyon Methodist Church, Quyon

BMD   1903-1923   **M-2212**

  includes also: Bristol, North Onslow, Wyman, etc.

Repentigny, comté de L'Assomption

Église catholique

BMD	1681-1727,	
	1770-1807 extraits	**M-866** (index)

comprend : Lachenaie

Église catholique de Lachenaie

BMD   1683-1744 extraits   **M-866** (index)

comprend : Repentigny, et Saint-Sulpice, comté de L'Assomption; et l'Île-Jésus

Richelieu County/Comté de Richelieu

Archives paroissiales du comté de Richelieu

BMD	1675-1973	**C-7203** à **C-7206**
	1784-1973	**C-7029** à **C-7031**

comprend :

  Christ Church Anglican Church, Sorel

BMD   1784-1972   **C-7031**

  Saint-Pierre-de-Sorel (Église catholique)

BMD	1675-1847	**C-7203**
	1847-1880	**C-7204**
	1880-1914	**C-7205**
	1914-1973	**C-7206**

  Sainte-Anne-de-Sorel (Église catholique)

BMD   1879-1973   **C-7031**

(cont.)

QUÉBEC

Saint-Joseph-de-Sorel (Église catholique)
BMD 1881-1941 **C-7029**
      1942-1973 **C-7030**

Notre-Dame-de-Sorel (Église catholique)
BMD 1911-1973 **C-7029**

Saint-Maxime, Sorel (Église catholique)
BMD 1946-1973 **C-7030**

Sainte-Victoire (Église catholique)
BMD 1843-1973 **C-7031**

Saint-Robert-sur-Richelieu (Église catholique)
BMD 1855-1972 **C-7030**

Saint-Roch-sur-Richelieu (Église catholique)
BMD 1859-1973 **C-7031**

Marie-Auxiliatrice, Tracy (Église catholique)
BMD 1946-1972 **C-7029**

L'Enfant-Jésus-de-Tracy (Église catholique)
BMD 1950-1973 **C-7029**

Saint-Jean-Bosco, Tracy (Église catholique)
BMD 1954-1973 **C-7029**

Saint-Gabriel-Lalemant (Église catholique)
BMD 1950-1973 **C-7029**

Rigaud, comté de Vaudreuil

Ste-Madeleine-de-Rigaud (Église catholique)
BMD 1802-1825 **C-2885**
     1825-1836 **C-2886**
     1836-1847 **C-2887**
     1847-1850 **C-2888**

Ristigouche, comté de Bonaventure

Ste-Anne-de-Ristigouche (Église catholique)
BMD 1759-1795 **C-3024** (originaux)
     1759-1795 **C-1449** (copies, index)
comprend : autres missions environnantes, dont certaines de l'Acadie

Rivière-à-Lapêche, comté de Gatineau

Missions du comté de Wright (Église catholique)
BMD 1841-1852 **C-2978**
M   1841-1852 Index **C-2978**
comprend :

    Ste-Cécile-de-la-rivière-à-la-Pêche (Église catholique)
    BMD 1841-1848 **C-2978**
    M   1841-1852 Index **C-2978**

Rivière-Beaudette, Soulanges Co.

Civil registers of the Surrogate Court for the Eastern and Johnstown Districts, Ont.
B 1831, 1859, 1862-1865 **C-3030**
M 1831-1857, 1863, 1865 **C-3030** (index)
includes:

    Presbyterian (Church of Scotland) Church, Lancaster Township, Glengarry Co., Ont.
    M 1834-1836 **C-3030** (index)
    includes: Coteau-du-Lac, and Rivière-Beaudette, Soulanges Co., Que.

Rivière-des-Prairies, comté de l'Île-de-Montréal

St-Joseph-de-la-Rivière-des-Prairies (Église catholique)
BMD 1687, 1702-1709 extraits **M-865** (index)
     1711-1792 extraits **M-866** (index)
     1704-1761, 1786-1788,
     1798-1801 extraits **M-866** (index)

Rivière-du-Loup (aujourd'hui, Louiseville), comté de Maskinongé

Église catholique de St-François-du-Lac
BMD 1687-1719 **C-3024** (index)
     1720-1763 **C-3024**
     1808-1836 extraits **C-3024**
comprend : des endroits environnants (dont Rivière-du-Loup ou Louiseville, 1688-1693)

Saint-André-d'Argenteuil, comté d'Argenteuil

St-André-d'Argenteuil (Église catholique)
BMD 1833-1850 **C-2904**

Saint-André-de-Kamouraska, comté de Kamouraska

Église catholique de Kamouraska
BMD 1762-1798 extraits **C-3109**
comprend : Saint-André-de-Kamouraska et Saint-Louis-de-Kamouraska

Saint-André-Est, Argenteuil Co.

St. Andrew's East Anglican Church
BMD 1812   **C-2904**
     1812-1849 **C-2905**

St. Andrew's East Presbyterian Church
BMD 1818-1850 **C-2905**

Sainte-Anne-de-Beaupré, comté de Montmorency N° 1

Église catholique de Ste-Anne-de-Beaupré
BMD   1657-1702, 1708-1719   **M-1625**

Sainte-Anne-de-Bellevue, comté de l'Île-de-Montréal

Ste-Anne-du-Bout-de-l'Île (ou Ste-Anne-de-Bellevue) (Église catholique)
BMD   1703-1784 extraits   **M-865** (index)

Sainte-Anne-de-Sorel, comté de Richelieu

Archives paroissiales du comté de Richelieu
BMD   1784-1973   **C-7029 à C-7031**
comprend :

   Ste-Anne-de-Sorel (Église catholique)
   BMD   1879-1973   **C-7031**

Sainte-Anne-des-Plaines, comté de Terrebonne

Église catholique de Ste-Anne-des-Plaines
BMD   1788-1820   **C-2913**
      1820-1839   **C-2914**
      1840-1850   **C-2915**

Sainte-Anne-du-Bout-de-l'Île, comté de l'Île-de-Montréal

Église catholique de Ste-Anne-du-Bout-de-l'Île (ou Ste-Anne-de-Bellevue)
BMD   1703-1784 extraits   **M-865** (index)

Saint-Antoine-de-Lavaltrie, comté de Berthier

St-Antoine-de-Lavaltrie (Église catholique)
BMD   1717, 1749-1764,
      1786-1815 extraits   **M-866** (index)
comprend : Saint-Sulpice et les Îles Bouchard

Saint-Armand-Ouest, Missisquoi Co.

Dunham (later, Saint-Armand) Wesleyan Methodist Circuit
B   1806-1825   **H-1807**
D   1807, 1811, 1813   **H-1807**

Saint-Benoît, comté de Deux-Montagnes

Église catholique de St-Benoît
BMD   1799-1810   **C-2905**
      1810-1823   **C-2906**
      1823-1834   **C-2907**
      1834-1850   **C-2908**

Sainte-Cécile-de-Masham, comté de Gatineau

Missions du comté de Wright (Église catholique)
BMD   1841-1852   **C-2978**
M   1841-1852 Index   **C-2978**
comprend :

   Ste-Cécile-de-la-rivière-à-la-Pêche (ou Ste-Cécile-de-Masham) (Église catholique)
   BMD   1841-1848   **C-2978**
   M   1841-1852 Index   **C-2978**

Saint-Eustache, comté de Deux-Montagnes

Église catholique de St-Eustache-de-la-Rivière-du-Chêne
BMD   1771-1802 extraits   **M-865**
      1769-1777   **C-2908**
      1777-1801   **C-2909**
      1801-1815   **C-2910**
      1815-1829   **C-2911**
      1829-1848   **C-2912**
      1848-1850   **C-2913**

Saint-François-du-Lac, comté de Yamaska

Église catholique de St-François-du-Lac
BMD   1687-1719   **C-3024** (index)
      1720-1763   **C-3024**
      1808-1836 extraits   **C-3024**
comprend : des endroits environnants (dont Rivière-du-Loup, ou Louiseville, 1688-1693)

Saint-Gabriel-Lalemant, comté de Richelieu

Archives paroissiales du comté de Richelieu
BMD   1784-1973   **C-7029 à C-7031**
comprend :

   Saint-Gabriel-Lalemant (Église catholique)
   BMD   1950-1973   **C-7029**

Saint-Georges, Côte-, Soulanges Co.

Presbyterian Church of Côte St. George and Dalhousie Mills, [Glengarry Co., Ont.]
B   1843-1867, 1870-1874,
      1883   **M-3187**
M   1843-1850, 1862-1873   **M-3187**
BMD   1862-1875, 1882   **M-2228**
communion rolls 1862-1867, n.d.,
      1888-1889   **M-2228**

QUÉBEC

Saint-Hermas, comté de Deux-Montagnes

Église catholique de St-Hermas
BMD	1837-1843	**C-3024**
	1843-1850	**C-3025**

Saint-Jean, Fort, comté de Saint-Jean/Saint-Jean Co.

St-Jean-[Baptiste-du-Fort-St-Jean-sur-Richelieu] (Église catholique)
BMD	1757-1760	**C-3023**	
	1757-1760 extraits	**M-866**	(index)

Christ Church Anglican Church, William Henry (formerly, and later, Sorel), Richelieu Co.
BMD	1784-1796	**H-1807**

includes:

Fort Saint-Jean (Dorchester)
B	1784, 1793-1795	**H-1807**
BMD	1796	**H-1807**

Saint-Joachim-de-Châteauguay (antérieurement, Sault-Saint-Louis), comté de Châteauguay

Église catholique et mission du Sault-Saint-Louis (aujourd'hui, St-Joachim-de-Châteauguay)
BMD	1727-1728, 1735-1773	**C-2890**
	1774-1817	**C-2891**
	1817-1836	**C-2892**
	1836-1849	**C-2893**

Registres d'état civil (Église catholique)
BMD	1751-1762	**C-3023**	
	1752-1754, 1758, 1761, 1779-1783 extraits	**M-866**	(index)

Saint-Joseph-de-Sorel, comté de Richelieu

Archives paroissiales du comté de Richelieu
BMD	1784-1973	**C-7029** à **C-7031**

comprend :

St-Joseph-de-Sorel (Église catholique)
BMD	1881-1941	**C-7029**
	1942-1973	**C-7030**

Saint-Laurent, comté de l'Île-de-Montréal

Église catholique
BMD	1721, 1748-1799 extraits	**M-866**	(index)

Saint-Louis, Fort, comté de [Verchères ou Chambly]

Ste-Famille-de-Boucherville (Église catholique)
BMD	1668-1762 extraits	**M-866**	(index)

comprend : Longueuil, comté de Chambly; Fort St-Louis; et Varennes, comté de Verchères

Église catholique de St-Ours, comté de Richelieu
BMD	1681-1684,		
	1783-1801 extraits	**M-866**	(index)

comprend : Contrecœur, Verchères, et Fort St-Louis, comté de Verchères

Saint-Louis-de-Kamouraska, comté de Kamouraska

Église catholique de Kamouraska
BMD	1762-1798 extraits	**C-3109**

comprend : Saint-André-de-Kamouraska et Saint-Louis-de-Kamouraska

Saint-Louis-de-Terrebonne, comté de Terrebonne

St-Louis-de-Terrebonne (Église catholique)
BMD	1725-1732	**C-3025**	(index)

Sainte-Madeleine-de-Rigaud, comté de Vaudreuil

Ste-Madeleine-de-Rigaud (Église catholique)
BMD	1802-1825	**C-2885**
	1825-1836	**C-2886**
	1836-1847	**C-2887**
	1847-1850	**C-2888**

Saint-Michel-de-Vaudreuil, comté de Vaudreuil

St-Michel-de-Vaudreuil (Église catholique)
BMD	1783-1809	**C-2923**
	1809-1835	**C-2924**

Saint-Ours, comté de Richelieu

Église catholique
BMD	1681-1684,		
	1783-1801 extraits	**M-866**	(index)

comprend : Contrecœur, Verchères, et Fort St-Louis, comté de Verchères

Église catholique
BMD	1718-1726, 1751-1752, 1757-1758 extraits	**M-866**	(index)

QUÉBEC

Saint-Pierre-de-Sorel, comté de Richelieu

St-Pierre-de-Sorel (Église catholique)
BMD	1675-1847	**C-7203**
	1847-1880	**C-7204**
	1880-1914	**C-7205**
	1914-1973	**C-7206**

Saint-Régis, comté de Huntingdon

Mission iroquoise (catholique) de St-Jean-François-de-St-Régis
BMD	1764-1830	**C-3025**

Saint-Robert, comté de Richelieu

Archives paroissiales du comté de Richelieu
BMD   1784-1973   **C-7029** à **C-7031**
comprend :

St-Robert-sur-Richelieu (Église catholique)
BMD	1855-1972	**C-7030**

Saint-Roch-de-Richelieu, comté de Richelieu

Archives paroissiales du comté de Richelieu
BMD   1784-1973   **C-7029** à **C-7031**
comprend :

St-Roch-sur-Richelieu (Église catholique)
BMD	1859-1973	**C-7031**

Saint-Roch-des-Aulnaies, comté de L'Islet

St-Roch-des-Aulnaies (Église catholique)
BMD	1734-1764, 1777-1781	**C-3025** (index)

Sainte-Rose, comté de l'Île-Jésus

Ste-Rose-de-Laval (Église catholique)
BMD	1796-1805	**C-2915**
	1805-1831	**C-2916**
	1831-1850	**C-2917**

Sainte-Scholastique, comté de Deux-Montagnes

Ste-Scholastique (Église catholique)
BMD	1825-1828	**C-2917**
	1828-1843	**C-2918**
	1843-1850	**C-2919**

Saint-Sulpice, comté de L'Assomption

Église catholique de Lachenaie
BMD   1683-1744 extraits   **M-866** (index)
comprend : Repentigny, et Saint-Sulpice, comté de L'Assomption; et l'Île-Jésus

St-Antoine-de-Lavaltrie, comté de Berthier (Église catholique)
BMD   1717, 1749-1764,
       1786-1815 extraits   **M-866** (index)
comprend : Saint-Sulpice et les Îles Bouchard

Saint-Thomas, Pointe- (ou Pointe-à-Lacaille), comté de Montmagny

Église catholique
BMD   1690, 1738-1739,
       1758-1763 extraits   **M-865** (index)

Sainte-Victoire, comté de Richelieu

Archives paroissiales du comté de Richelieu
BMD   1784-1973   **C-7029** à **C-7031**
comprend :

Ste-Victoire (Église catholique)
BMD	1843-1973	**C-7031**

Sault-au-Récollet, comté de l'Île-de-Montréal

Église catholique
BMD	1736-1777 extraits	**M-865** (index)
	1750-1805 extraits	**M-865** (index)

La-Visitation-du-Sault-au-Récollet (Église catholique)
BMD	1736-1760	**C-2919**
	1760-1823	**C-2920**
	1823-1850	**C-2921**

Sault-Saint-Louis, comté de Châteauguay

Église catholique et mission du Sault-Saint-Louis (aujourd'hui, St-Joachim-de-Châteauguay)
BMD	1727-1728, 1735-1773	**C-2890**
	1774-1817	**C-2891**
	1817-1836	**C-2892**
	1836-1849	**C-2893**

Registres d'état civil (Église catholique)
BMD   1751-1762   **C-3023**
       1752-1754, 1758, 1761,
       1779-1783 extraits   **M-866** (index)

Shawville, Pontiac Co.

Clarendon Anglican Mission (later, St. Paul's Anglican Church, Shawville, etc.)
BM	1823-1842 extracts	**M-1303**
BMD	1842-1898	**M-1303** and **M-1304** (partial index)
	1864-1873	**M-2819** (index)
	1875-1916	**M-3114** (partial index)

includes: Townships of Bristol, Clarendon, Leslie, Litchfield, Onslow, and Thorne, in:

St. James' Anglican Church, Hull, Gatineau Co.
BM   1823-1842 extracts relating to Clarendon   **M-1303**

St. Paul's Anglican Church, Shawville
BMD	1842-1888	**M-1303** (partial index)
	1888-1898	**M-1304** (index)

includes also: Calumet-Island, and Mansfield Township, Pontiac Co., and Eardley Township, Gatineau Co., Que.; as well as Horton Township, Renfrew Co., Ont.

Anglican Mission of North Clarendon (later, Charteris), and district
BMD   1864-1873   **M-2819** (index)

Anglican Mission of North Clarendon (later, Charteris), and Thorne Township
BMD   1875-1891   **M-3114** (partial index)

Anglican Mission of Thorne Township, and district
BMD   1891-1913   **M-3114** (partial index)

Anglican Mission of Thorne and Leslie Townships, and North Clarendon (later, Charteris)
BMD   1892-1916   **M-3114** (partial index)

Shawville United Church, Shawville
BMD	1851-1918	**M-2243**
	1877-1939	**M-2374**

includes: Calumet-Island, and the Townships of Bristol, Bryson, Clarendon, Leslie, Litchfield, and Thorne, in:

Presbyterian Church (Church of Scotland), Litchfield Township
BMD   1853-1870, 1874-1904, 1918   **M-2243**
includes also: Townships of Ross, and Westmeath, Renfrew Co., Ont., in the early years

Clarendon Wesleyan Methodist Circuit
BMD   1851-1898   **M-2243**
includes also: Portage-du-Fort Mission, 1860-1879

(cont.)

Clarendon Regular Baptist Churches
BMD   1877-1939   **M-2374**
includes also: North Clarendon, Starks Corners, and Wyman

Sorel, comté de Richelieu/Richelieu Co.

Christ Church Anglican Church, William Henry (formerly, and later, Sorel)
BMD   1784-1796   **H-1807**
comprises:

Fort William Henry, Richelieu Co.
B	1784-1794, 1796	**H-1807**
BMD	1796	**H-1807**

Fort Saint-Jean (Dorchester), Saint-Jean Co.
B	1784, 1793-1795	**H-1807**
BMD	1796	**H-1807**

Fort-Chambly, Chambly Co.
B	1784-1785	**H-1807**
BMD	1796	**H-1807**

Montreal, Île-de-Montréal Co.
B   1785   **H-1807**

Berthier[ville], Berthier Co.
BM   1796   **H-1807**

Albany, New York State, U.S.A.
B   1785   **H-1807**

Schenectady, New York State, U.S.A.
B   1785   **H-1807**

Archives paroissiales du comté de Richelieu
BMD	1675-1973	**C-7203 à C-7206**
	1784-1973	**C-7029 à C-7031**

comprend :

Christ Church Anglican Church
BMD   1784-1972   **C-7031**

St-Pierre-de-Sorel (Église catholique)
BMD	1675-1847	**C-7203**
	1847-1880	**C-7204**
	1880-1914	**C-7205**
	1914-1973	**C-7206**

Ste-Anne-de-Sorel (Église catholique)
BMD   1879-1973   **C-7031**

St-Joseph-de-Sorel (Église catholique)
BMD	1881-1941	**C-7029**
	1942-1973	**C-7030**

Notre-Dame-de-Sorel (Église catholique)
BMD   1911-1973   **C-7029**

(cont.)

St-Maxime, Sorel (Église catholique)
BMD   1946-1973   **C-7030**

L'Enfant-Jésus-de-Sorel, Tracy (Église catholique)
BMD   1950-1973   **C-7029**

Église catholique de Saurel [Sorel]
BMD   1679-1682,
       1726-1730 extraits   **M-866** (index)
       1681-1682,
       1725-1726 extraits   **M-866** (index)

Église catholique de l'Isle-du-Pads [Île Dupas], comté de Berthier
BMD   1712-1726, 1750-1774,
       1762-1790 extraits   **M-866** (index)
comprend : Saurel (Sorel)

Sorel, seigneurie de, comté de Richelieu

St-Pierre-de-Sorel (Église catholique),
Christ Church (Église anglicane), etc.
B   1672-1881 extraits   **C-14034**
M   1734-1886 extraits   **C-14034**
D   1803-1882 extraits   **C-14034**

Starks Corners, Pontiac Co.

Shawville United Church, Shawville
BMD   1851-1918   **M-2243**
       1877-1939   **M-2374**
includes:

   Clarendon Regular Baptist Churches
   BMD   1877-1939   **M-2374**
   includes: North Clarendon, Starks Corners, and Wyman, as well as other places in the Townships of Bristol, Clarendon, Leslie, Litchfield, Onslow, and Thorne

Templeton, comté de Hull

Missions du comté de Wright (Église catholique)
BMD   1841-1852   **C-2978**
M   1841-1852 Index   **C-2978**
comprend :

   St-François-de-Templeton
   BMD   1841-1848   **C-2978**
   M   1841-1852 Index **C-2978**

Templeton Township, Hull Co.

Christ Church Anglican Church, Aylmer, Gatineau Co.
BMD   1864-1920   **M-3695** (index)
       1920-1971   **M-3696** (index)
includes: in the early years, the Townships of Denholm,
(cont.)

Hull, and Wakefield, Gatineau Co.; the Townships of Buckingham, and Portland, Papineau Co.; and Templeton Township, Hull Co.

Terrebonne, comté de Terrebonne

St-Louis-de-Terrebonne (Église catholique)
BMD   1725-1732   **C-3025** (index)

Église catholique
BMD   1727-1797 extraits   **M-866** (index)

Thorne Township, Pontiac Co.

Clarendon Anglican Mission (later, St. Paul's Anglican Church, Shawville, etc.)
BM   1823-1842 extracts   **M-1303**
BMD   1842-1898   **M-1303** and
                            M-1304 (partial index)
       1864-1873   **M-2819** (index)
       1875-1916   **M-3114** (partial index)
includes: Townships of Bristol, Clarendon, Leslie, Litchfield, Onslow, and Thorne, in:

   St. James' Anglican Church, Hull, Gatineau Co.
   BM   1823-1842 extracts relating
                             to Clarendon   **M-1303**

   St. Paul's Anglican Church, Shawville
   BMD   1842-1888   **M-1303** (partial index)
          1888-1898   **M-1304** (index)
   includes also: Calumet-Island, and Mansfield Township, Pontiac Co., and Eardley Township, Gatineau Co., Que.; as well as Horton Township, Renfrew Co., Ont.

   Anglican Mission of North Clarendon (later, Charteris), and district
   BMD   1864-1873   **M-2819** (index)

   Anglican Mission of North Clarendon (later, Charteris), and Thorne Township
   BMD   1875-1891   **M-3114** (partial index)

   Anglican Mission of Thorne Township, and district
   BMD   1891-1913   **M-3114** (partial index)

   Anglican Mission of Thorne and Leslie Townships, and North Clarendon (later, Charteris)
   BMD   1892-1916   **M-3114** (partial index)

   Shawville United Church
   BMD   1851-1918   **M-2243**
          1877-1939   **M-2374**
   includes: Calumet-Island, and the Townships of Bristol,
(cont.)

QUÉBEC

Bryson, Clarendon, Leslie, Litchfield, and Thorne, in:

Presbyterian Church (Church of Scotland), Litchfield Township
BMD   1853-1870, 1874-1904, 1918   **M-2243**
includes also: Townships of Ross, and Westmeath, Renfrew Co., Ont., in the early years

Clarendon Wesleyan Methodist Circuit
BMD   1851-1898   **M-2243**
includes also: Portage-du-Fort Mission, 1860-1879

Clarendon Regular Baptist Churches
BMD   1877-1939   **M-2374**
includes also: North Clarendon, Starks Corners, and Wyman

Tracy, comté de Richelieu

Archives paroissiales du comté de Richelieu
BMD   1784-1973   **C-7029** à **C-7031**
comprend :

    Marie-Auxiliatrice-de-Tracy (Église catholique)
    BMD   1946-1972   **C-7029**

    L'Enfant-Jésus-de-Tracy (Église catholique)
    BMD   1950-1973   **C-7029**

    St-Jean-Bosco-de-Tracy (Église catholique)
    BMD   1954-1973   **C-7029**

Trois-Rivières, comté de Saint-Maurice

Église protestante et garnison de Trois-Rivières
BMD   1768-1786, 1790-1792   **C-2923** (index)

Immaculée-Conception-de-Trois-Rivières (Église catholique)

B	1635-1671	**C-2921** (index sur **C-2922**)
	1671-1751	**C-2922** (index)
	1751-1763	**C-2922** (index sur **C-2923**)
M	1654-1677, 1699-1751	**C-2922** (index)
	1751-1763	**C-2923** (index)
D	1634-1699	**C-2921** (index)
	1699-1751	**C-2922** (index)
	1751-1755	**C-2922** (index sur **C-2923**)
	1755-1763	**C-2923** (index)
confirmations 1688-1698		**C-2922**

(Les index ne mentionnent pas les noms des Indiens)

(cont.)

[Immaculée-Conception-de-Trois-Rivières] (Église catholique)

B	1648-1679 extraits	**M-867**	(index)
D	1634-1677 extraits	**M-867**	(index)
BMD	1679-1699 extraits	**M-867**	(index)
confirmations 1688-1698		**M-867**	(index)

Église catholique de Trois-Rivières

BMD	1650-1699 extraits	**M-866**	(index)
	1654-1675 extraits	**M-867**	(index)

Registres d'état civil
Chapelle-de-la-Sainte-Vierge (Église catholique)
M   1654-1677 extraits   **M-867** (index)

Registres d'état civil
Chapelle-de-la-Conception (Église catholique)

D	1636-1679 extraits	**M-867**	(index)
BMD	1639-1699 extraits	**M-867**	(index)

Varennes, comté de Verchères

Ste-Famille-de-Boucherville (Église catholique), comté de Chambly
BMD   1668-1762 extraits   **M-866** (index)
comprend : Longueuil, comté de Chambly; Fort St-Louis; et Varennes, comté de Verchères

[St-Antoine-de-]Longueuil (Église catholique), comté de Chambly
BMD   1679-1684, 1713-1789 extraits   **M-865** (index)
comprend : Boucherville, comté de Chambly; et Varennes, comté de Verchères

Église catholique de Varennes
BMD   1693-1800 extraits   **M-866** (index)
    1697-1722, 1728, 1749-1761, 1773-1803 extraits   **M-866** (index)

Vaudreuil, comté de Vaudreuil

St-Michel-de-Vaudreuil (Église catholique)
BMD   1783-1809   **C-2923**
    1809-1835   **C-2924**

Verchères, comté de Verchères

Église catholique de Saint-Ours, comté de Richelieu
BMD   1681-1684, 1783-1801 extraits   **M-866** (index)
comprend : Contrecœur, Verchères, et Fort St-Louis, comté de Verchères

Église catholique de Verchères
BMD   1724-1727, 1751-1788 extraits   **M-866** (index)

Ville-Marie, comté de l'Île-de-Montréal

Église catholique de Ville-Marie en l'Île-de-Montréal
BMD	1680-1681 extraits	**M-867**	(index)
	1680-1681, 1684-1693	**C-2904**	
annulation	1660-1663 extraits	**M-867**	(index)

Voir aussi : Montréal

Wakefield, comté de Gatineau

Missions du comté de Wright (Église catholique)
BMD	1841-1852	**C-2978**
M	1841-1852 Index	**C-2978**

comprend :

   St-Joseph-de-Wakefield (Église catholique)
BMD	1841-1848	**C-2978**
M	1841-1852 Index	**C-2978**

Wakefield Township, Gatineau Co.

Christ Church Anglican Church, Aylmer
BMD	1864-1920	**M-3695**	(index)
	1920-1971	**M-3696**	(index)

includes: in the early years, the Townships of Denholm, Hull, and Wakefield, Gatineau Co.; the Townships of Buckingham, and Portland, Papineau Co.; and Templeton Township, Hull Co.

William Henry, Richelieu Co.

Christ Church Anglican Church, William Henry (formerly, and later, Sorel)
BMD	1784-1796	**H-1807**

comprises:

   Fort William Henry
B	1784-1794, 1796	**H-1807**
BMD	1796	**H-1807**

   Fort Saint-Jean (Dorchester), Saint-Jean Co.
B	1784, 1793-1795	**H-1807**
BMD	1796	**H-1807**

   Fort-Chambly, Chambly Co.
B	1784-1785	**H-1807**
BMD	1796	**H-1807**

   Montreal, Île-de-Montréal Co.
B	1785	**H-1807**

   Berthier[ville], Berthier Co.
BM	1796	**H-1807**

   Albany, New York State, U.S.A.
B	1785	**H-1807**

   Schenectady, New York State, U.S.A.
B	1785	**H-1807**

William Henry, Fort, Richelieu Co.

Christ Church Anglican Church, William Henry (formerly, and later, Sorel)
BMD	1784-1796	**H-1807**

includes: Fort William Henry

Wright, comté de (aujourd'hui, comtés de Hull, Gatineau, et des parties des comtés de Papineau et Pontiac)

Missions du comté de Wright (Église catholique)
BMD	1841-1848	**C-2978**
M	1841-1852 Index	**C-2978**

comprend :

   St-Paul-d'Aylmer, comté de Gatineau
   St-François-de-Sales-et-la-Visitation-de-la-Gatineau, comté de Hull

et :

autres missions sur l'Outaouais :

   St-Étienne-de-Chelsea, comté de Gatineau
   St-Alphonse-de-Liguori-des-Allumettes, comté de Pontiac
   Ste-Anne-du-Grand-Calumet, comté de Pontiac
   St-François-de-Templeton, comté de Hull
   Lac-Sainte-Marie, comté de Gatineau
   St-Joseph-de-Wakefield, comté de Gatineau
   St-Jacques-de-Bytown (ou St-Jacques-d'Embrun), comté de Russell, Ont.
   Ste-Cécile-de-la-rivière-à-la-Pêche (ou Ste-Cécile-de-Masham), comté de Gatineau
   Hull, comté de Gatineau
   Eardley, comté de Gatineau

avec :

   St-Paul-d'Aylmer (Église catholique)
BMD	1848-1852	**C-2978**
M	1841-1852 Index	**C-2978**

Wyman, Pontiac Co.

Shawville United Church, Shawville
BMD	1851-1918	**M-2243**
	1877-1939	**M-2374**

includes:

   Clarendon Regular Baptist Churches
BMD	1877-1939	**M-2374**

   includes: North Clarendon, Starks Corners, and Wyman, as well as other places in the Townships of Bristol, Bryson, Clarendon, Leslie, Litchfield, and Thorne

Quyon United Church, Quyon
BMD	1859-1923	**M-2212**

includes:

(cont.)

QUÉBEC

Quyon Methodist Church, Quyon
BMD   1903-1923   **M-2212**
includes: Bristol, North Onslow, Wyman, and other places in the Townships of Bristol, Clarendon, and Onslow, Pontiac Co.; and Eardley Township, Gatineau Co.

SASKATCHEWAN

Balgonie, Rural Municipality No. 158

St. Joseph's Roman Catholic Church
B	1827-1932	**H-1812**
M	1872-1915	**H-1812**
D	1899-1916	**H-1812**
first communions, 1863-1913		**H-1812**

(Mainly births)

Carlton House (Fort Pelly), Rural Municipality No. 301

Registers of the Rev. William Cockran, Assistant Chaplain (Anglican) to the Hudson's Bay Company and Missionary of the Church Missionary Society

BMD   1828-1829   **A-86**

includes: Oxford House, the Red River Settlement (later, St. John's Cathedral, Winnipeg), the Rapids of the Red River (later, St. Andrew's-on-the-Red, Lockport), and York Factory, Man.; as well as Carlton House (Fort Pelly), and Cumberland House, Sask.

See also: Hudson's Bay Company returns (page 3)

Cumberland House

Registers of the Rev. William Cockran, Assistant Chaplain (Anglican) to the Hudson's Bay Company and Missionary of the Church Missionary Society

BMD   1828-1829   **A-86**

includes: Oxford House, the Red River Settlement (later, St. John's Cathedral, Winnipeg), the Rapids of the Red River (later, St. Andrew's-on-the-Red, Lockport), and York Factory, Man.; as well as Carlton House (Fort Pelly), and Cumberland House, Sask.

Rupert's Land Anglican Missions, Red River Settlement, Man.
B	1838 extracts	**H-1812**
M	1821, 1823 extracts	**H-1812**
D	1821-1822, 1864 extracts	**H-1812**

includes:

St. John's Anglican Cathedral, Winnipeg, Man.
B	1838 extracts	**H-1812**
M	1821, 1823 extracts	**H-1812**
D	1821-1822 extracts	**H-1812**

includes: Cumberland House, Sask.; as well as Norway House, Pembina, Red River Settlement, Indian Settlement, and York Factory, Man.

See also: Hudson's Bay Company returns (page 3)

Fort Île-à-la-Crosse
See: Hudson's Bay Company returns (page 3)

Fort Pelly (Carlton House), Rural Municipality No. 301

Registers of the Rev. William Cockran, Assistant Chaplain (Anglican) to the Hudson's Bay Company and Missionary of the Church Missionary Society

BMD   1828-1829   **A-86**

includes: Oxford House, the Red River Settlement (later, St. John's Cathedral, Winnipeg), the Rapids of the Red River (later, St. Andrew's-on-the-Red, Lockport), and York Factory, Man.; as well as Carlton House (Fort Pelly), and Cumberland House, Sask.

See also: Hudson's Bay Company returns (page 3)

Neudorf, Rural Municipality No. 185

Christ Evangelical Lutheran Church

BMD   1894-1961   **M-854**   (partial index)

comprises:

Zion Evangelical Lutheran Church
B	1894-1955	**M-854**	(index)
M	1898-1960	**M-854**	
D	1898-1961	**M-854**	
confirmations	1898-1960	**M-854**	(index)
membership lists 1898-1961		**M-854**	

Zion Reformed Church
B	1913, 1918, 1922-1957	**M-854**
M	1927-1956	**M-854**
D	1923-1955	**M-854**
confirmations 1924-1941, 1950, 1953		**M-854**
membership lists 1922-1957		**M-854**

(These registers were kept in German.)

Swarthmore, Rural Municipality No. 409

Swarthmore Monthly Meeting of Friends (Orthodox Quakers)

BMD   1836-1929   **M-3825**

(Records of the Religious Society of Friends, Volume B-3-9)

Dawson

St. Mary's Roman Catholic Church
BMD   1898-1956   **M-906**

Outside Canada

Hors du Canada

CZECHOSLOVAKIA / TCHÉCOSLOVAQUIE

Holy Ghost Roman Catholic Church, Winnipeg, Manitoba, Canada
B   1850-1920   **H-1812**
M   c. 1901   **H-1812**
includes:

Czechoslovakia
B   1873-1918   **H-1812**
(In Latin, Czechoslovakian, and German.)

Great Britain: War Office 42/52-63

Files on pension applications of widows and children of military officers deceased while serving or on half pay

BMD   1775-1908   **B-4682 to B-4694**
comprises:

King's German Legion — Officers

Acton	— Buhre	B-4682
Carey	— Duvel	B-4683
Ebel	— Heinemann	B-4684
Heinemann	— von Lesperg	B-4685
von Lesperg	— Naterman	B-4686
Naterman	— Ruman	B-4687
Ruman	— von Uslar	B-4688
von Uslar	— Zimmerman	B-4689

(In German, English, etc.)

British American Regiments — Officers

Adhemar	— Barclay	B-4689
Barclay	— Chartier de Lotbinière	B-4690
Chartier de Lotbinière	— Hatch	B-4691
Hatfield	— McDonell	B-4692
McDonell	— Robinson	B-4693
Robinson	— Wyley	B-4694

(In English, French, etc.)

Register of the **Royal Canadian Artillery** Army Book 91) — non-commissioned officers and men

B	1871-1911	**C-11775** (index)
M	1870-1915	**C-11775** (index)
D	1895-1905	**C-11775** (index)

includes: Kingston, Ont., as well as a few entries for Lévis, and Québec, Que., Canada; and for **Aldershot**, and **Barntfield**, [England]; and Benares, and Cawnpore, [India]

Cayenne

Registres d'état civil de la Guyane
BMD   1763-1792 extraits*   **C-3119**
comprend :

    St-Sauveur-de-Cayenne (Église catholique)
    BMD   1764-1792 extraits   **C-3119**

Kourou

Registres d'état civil de la Guyane
BMD   1763-1792 extraits*   **C-3119**
comprend :

    Kourou
    B   1764 extraits   **C-3119**
    D   1763-1764, 1768,
            1770 extraits   **C-3119**

Sinnamary

Registres d'état civil de la Guyane
BMD   1763-1792 extraits*   **C-3119**
comprend :

    St-Joseph-de-Sinnamary (Église catholique)
    BMD   1764-1767, 1771-1782,
            1784-1792 extraits   **C-3119**

---

*Ces extraits concernent les habitants de l'Acadie, de l'Île Royale et de l'Île Saint-Jean réfugiés en Guyane et établis à Kourou, Sinnamari et dans la paroisse Saint-Sauveur-de-Cayenne.

Holy Ghost Roman Catholic Church, Winnipeg, Manitoba, Canada
B   1850-1920   **H-1812**
M   c. 1901   **H-1812**
includes:

Hungary
B   1877   **H-1812**
(In Hungarian.)

INDIA / INDE

Register of the Royal Canadian Artillery (Army Book 91) — non-commissioned officers and men

B	1871-1911	**C-11775** (index)
M	1870-1915	**C-11775** (index)
D	1895-1905	**C-11775** (index)

includes: Kingston, Ont., as well as a few entries for Lévis, and Québec, Que., Canada; and for Aldershot, and Barntfield, [England]; and **Benares**, and **Cawnpore**, [India]

Holy Ghost Roman Catholic Church, Winnipeg, Manitoba, Canada
B 1850-1920 **H-1812**
M c. 1901   **H-1812**
includes:

Poland
B 1850-1920 **H-1812**
(In Latin and Polish.)

Île Miquelon

Registres d'état-civil de l'Île Miquelon
BMD	1763-1776	**C-3119**
	1763-1791, 1816-1830	**F-598** à **F-599**

comprend :

Notre-Dame-des-Ardilliers-de-la-Ville-de-Miquelon
(Église catholique)
BMD	1763-1774, 1776	**C-3119**	(copies)
M	1767, 1770, 1772, 1774	**C-3119**	(copies)
BMD	1763-1771, 1773-1775, 1777-1778, 1783-1789	**F-598**	(originaux, index)
	1790-1791	**F-599**	(originaux, index sur **F-598**)
	1816-1825	**F-599**	(originaux)
	1826-1830	**F-599**	(originaux, index)

Île Saint-Pierre

Registres d'état-civil de l'Île Miquelon et de l'Île Saint-Pierre
BMD	1763-1776	**C-3119**
	1763-1830	**F-598** à **F-601**

comprend :

St-Pierre (Église catholique)
BMD	1763-1787	**F-600**	(originaux, index sur **F-598**)
	1788-1791	**F-601**	(originaux, index sur **F-598**)
	1792-1822	**F-601**	(originaux)
	1775-1776	**C-3119**	(copies)

UNION OF SOVIET SOCIALIST REPUBLICS / UNION DES RÉPUBLIQUES SOCIALISTES SOVIÉTIQUES

Holy Ghost Roman Catholic Church, Winnipeg, Manitoba, Canada
B   1850-1920   **H-1812**
M   c. 1901   **H-1812**
includes:

Galicia (Austrian Empire, later the U.S.S.R.)
B   1861-1898   **H-1812**
M   c. 1901   **H-1812**
(In Latin, Polish, Russian, Ukrainian, and German)

Russia
B   1869, 1884   **H-1812**
(In Russian)

Albany, New York

Christ Church Anglican Church, William Henry (formerly, and later, Sorel), Richelieu Co., Quebec, Canada
B/MD	1784-1796	**H-1807**

includes:

Albany
B	1785	**H-1807**

Annette Island, Alaska

William Duncan's Metlakahtla Christian Mission, Annette Island
B	1861-1918	**M-2331**
M	1881-1899	**M-2331**
D	1881-1918	**M-2331**

comprises:

C.M.S. Anglican Mission of Fort Simpson and Metlakatla, British Columbia, Canada
B	1861-1863, 1874-1884	**M-2331**
D	1862	**M-2331**

William Duncan's Metlakahtla Christian Mission, Metlakatla, British Columbia, Canada
B	1882-1887	**M-2331**
M	1881-1886	**M-2331**
D	1881-1887	**M-2331**

William Duncan's Metlakahtla Christian Mission, Metlakatla, Annette Island
B	1890-1918	**M-2331**
M	1891-1899	**M-2331**
D	1887-1918	**M-2331**

Arkansas, Poste des, Arkansas

Mission du Poste des Arkansas (Église catholique)
B	1744	**C-2899**

At(t)akapas, Poste des (Nouvelle-Acadie; aujourd'hui, Saint-Martinville), Louisiane

St-Martin-des-Atakapas (Église catholique)
BD	1756, 1765-1766	**C-2237** ou **C-2900**
BMD	1771-1773	**C-2237** ou **C-2900**
B	1773-1779, 1791-1794	**C-2237** ou **C-2900**
BM	1778-1779	**C-2237** ou **C-2900**

comprend : des actes concernant les habitants de l'Acadie réfugiés en Louisiane, ainsi que des mentions concernant les missions suivantes: Pointe-Coupée, Opelousas, L'Ascension-de-La-Fourche-des-Chétimachas, St-Bernard-des-Atakapas, St-Joseph-des-Atakapas, St-Martin-des-Atakapas, St-François-des-Nakitoches (Natchitoches)

Beauharnois-à-la-Pointe-à-la-Chevelure, Fort (Fort Saint-Frédéric ou Fort Crown Point), New York

Église catholique du Fort Beauharnois ou Fort Saint-Frédéric
B/MD	1732-1760	**C-3023**
	1732-1760 extraits	**M-866** (index)

comprend :

Fort Chambly (Église catholique), Québec, Canada
B	1759-1760	**C-3023**
D	1759	**C-3023**

Biloxi, Fort du, Louisiane

Église catholique du Fort du Biloxy
D	1720-1723	**F-597**

Chambly, Fort-, comté de Chambly, Québec, Canada

Église catholique du Fort St-Frédéric ou Fort Beauharnois-à-la-Pointe-à-la-Chevelure (Crown Point), New York, États-Unis
B/MD	1732-1760	**C-3023**
	1732-1760 extraits	**M-866** (index)

comprend :

Fort Chambly (Église catholique)
B	1759-1760	**C-3023**
D	1759	**C-3023**

Chartres, Fort de (par après, Fort Cavendish), Illinois

Chapelle de l'aumônerie du Fort de Chartres (Église catholique)
B/MD	1723-1724	**F-597**

Ste-Anne-du-Fort-de-Chartres (Église catholique)
BMD	1721-1755	**C-2899**
MD	1757-1765	**C-2899**

(cont.)

Condé-de-la-Mobile, Fort (antérieurement, Fort Louis-de-la-Louisiane; par après, Fort Charlotte), Alabama

Notre-Dame-de-l'Immaculée-Conception-de-la-Mobile
(Église catholique)
BM   1704-1764 extraits   **C-2224**
comprend :

    Fort Louis ou Fort Condé-de-la-Mobile
    (Église catholique)
    B   1704, 1707, 1717,
          1727-1728, 1731-1735,
          1737, 1741-1746,
          1748-1751, 1756,
          1764 extraits   **C-2224**
    M   1726, 1738-1739, 1741,
          1747, 1760, 1762,
          1764 extraits   **C-2224**

Crown Point, Fort (Fort Beauharnois-à-la-Pointe-à-la-Chevelure, ou Fort Saint-Frédéric), New York

Église catholique du Fort Beauharnois ou Fort Saint-Frédéric
BMD   1732-1760   **C-3023**
          1732-1760 extraits   **M-866** (index)
comprend :

    Fort Chambly (Église catholique), Québec, Canada
    B   1759-1760   **C-3023**
    D   1759   **C-3023**

Detroit, Michigan

Ste-Anne-du-Détroit (Église catholique)
BMD   1704-1800   **C-2893** à **C-2895**
comprend :

    Fort Pontchartrain-du-Détroit (Église catholique)
    B   1704-1718   **C-2893**
    M   1710-1718   **C-2893**
    D   1707-1718   **C-2893**
    BMD   1709-1765   **C-2893**
          [1760]-1800   **C-2894**

    Mission des Hurons de la Pointe-de-Montréal-du-Détroit
    (Église catholique)
    B   1761-1767   **C-2894**

    L'Assomption-de-la-Pointe-de-Montréal-du-Détroit
    (Église catholique)
    B   1767-1771   **C-2894**
    M   1764-1765, 1768-1771   **C-2894**
    D   1768-1772   **C-2894**
    BMD   1772-1777   **C-2894**
          1777-1783   **C-2895**

    L'Assomption-de-Sandwich-du-Détroit
    (Église catholique)
    BMD   1781-1799   **C-2895**

Duquesne-à-la-Belle-Rivière, Fort (Pittsburgh), Pennsylvanie

L'Assomption-de-la-Très-Sainte-Vierge-à-la-Belle-Rivière
(Église catholique)
D   1753-1754*   **C-3023**
BD   1754-1756   **C-3023**
*comprend : Fort de la Presqu'Île et Fort de la Rivière-aux-Bœufs, ainsi que Fort Duquesne-à-la-Belle-Rivière

Fort Beauharnois-à-la-Pointe-à-la-Chevelure (Fort Crown Point ou Fort Saint-Frédéric), New York

Église catholique du Fort Beauharnois ou Fort Saint-Frédéric
BMD   1732-1760   **C-3023**
          1732-1760 extraits   **M-866** (index)
comprend :

    Fort Chambly (Église catholique), Québec, Canada
    B   1759-1760   **C-3023**
    D   1759   **C-3023**

Fort du Biloxi, Louisiane

Église catholique du Fort du Biloxy
D   1720-1723   **F-597**

Fort Cavendish (antérieurement, Fort de Chartres), Illinois
Voir : Fort de Chartres

Fort Chambly, comté de Chambly, Québec, Canada

Église catholique du Fort Saint-Frédéric ou Fort Beauharnois-à-la-Pointe-à-la-Chevelure, New York
BMD   1732-1760   **C-3023**
          1732-1760 extraits   **M-866** (index)
comprend :

    Fort Chambly (Église catholique), Québec, Canada
    B   1759-1760   **C-3023**
    D   1759   **C-3023**

Fort Charlotte, Alabama
Voir : Fort Condé-de-la-Mobile

Fort de Chartres (par après, Fort Cavendish), Illinois

Chapelle de l'aumônerie du Fort de Chartres
(Église catholique)
BMD   1723-1724   **F-597**

(cont.)

Ste-Anne-du-Fort-de-Chartres (Église catholique)
BMD   1721-1755   **C-2899**
MD   1757-1765   **C-2899**

Fort Condé-de-la-Mobile (antérieurement, Fort Louis-de-la-Louisiane; par après, Fort Charlotte), Alabama

Notre-Dame-de-l'Immaculée-Conception-de-la-Mobile (Église catholique)
BM   1704-1764 extraits   **C-2224**
comprend :

    Fort Louis ou Fort Condé-de-la-Mobile (Église catholique)
    B   1704, 1707, 1717,
         1727-1728, 1731-1735,
         1737, 1741-1746,
         1748-1751, 1756,
         1764 extraits   **C-2224**
    M   1726, 1738-1739, 1741,
         1747, 1760, 1762,
         1764 extraits   **C-2224**

Fort Crown Point (Fort Beauharnois-à-la-Pointe-à-la-Chevelure ou Fort Saint-Frédéric), New York

Église catholique du Fort Beauharnois ou Fort Saint-Frédéric
BMD   1732-1760   **C-3023**
        1732-1760 extraits   **M-866** (index)
comprend :

    Fort Chambly (Église catholique), Québec, Canada
    B   1759-1760   **C-3023**
    D   1759   **C-3023**

Fort Duquesne-à-la-Belle-Rivière (Pittsburgh), Pennsylvanie

L'Assomption-de-la-Très-Sainte-Vierge-à-la-Belle-Rivière (Église catholique)
D   1753-1754*   **C-3023**
BD   1754-1756   **C-3023**
*comprend : Fort de la Presqu'Île et Fort de la Rivière-aux-Bœufs, ainsi que Fort Duquesne-à-la-Belle-Rivière

Fort Louis-de-la-Louisiane (par après, Fort Condé-de-la-Mobile, puis, Fort Charlotte), Alabama

Notre-Dame-de-l'Immaculée-Conception-de-la-Mobile (Église catholique)
BM   1704-1764 extraits   **C-2224**
comprend :

(cont.)

Fort Louis ou Fort Condé-de-la-Mobile (Église catholique)
B   1704, 1707, 1717,
    1727-1728, 1731-1735,
    1737, 1741-1746,
    1748-1751, 1756,
    1764 extraits   **C-2224**
M   1726, 1738-1739, 1741,
    1747, 1760, 1762,
    1764 extraits   **C-2224**

Fort Pontchartrain-du-Détroit, Michigan

Ste-Anne-du-Détroit (Église catholique)
BMD   1704-1800   **C-2893** à **C-2895**
comprend :

    Fort Pontchartrain-du-Détroit (Église catholique)
    B   1704-1718   **C-2893**
    M   1710-1718   **C-2893**
    D   1707-1718   **C-2893**
    BMD   1709-1765   **C-2893**
        [1760]-1800   **C-2894**

Fort de la Presqu'Île, Pennsylvanie

L'Assomption-de-la-Très-Sainte-Vierge-à-la-Belle-Rivière (Église catholique)
D   1753-1754*   **C-3023**
BD   1754-1756   **C-3023**
*comprend : Fort de la Presqu'Île et Fort de la Rivière-aux-Bœufs, ainsi que Fort Duquesne-à-la-Belle-Rivière (Pittsburgh)

Fort de la Rivière-aux-Bœufs, Pennsylvanie

L'Assomption-de-la-Très-Sainte-Vierge-à-la-Belle-Rivière (Église catholique)
D   1753-1754*   **C-3023**
BD   1754-1756   **C-3023**
*comprend : Fort de la Presqu'Île et Fort de la Rivière-aux-Bœufs, ainsi que Fort Duquesne-à-la-Belle-Rivière (Pittsburgh)

Fort Saint-Frédéric (Fort Beauharnois-à-la-Pointe-à-la-Chevelure (ou Fort Crown Point), New York

Église catholique du Fort Beauharnois ou Fort Saint-Frédéric
BMD   1732-1760   **C-3023**
        1732-1760 extraits   **M-866** (index)
comprend :

    Fort Chambly (Église catholique), Québec, Canada
    B   1759-1760   **C-3023**
    D   1759   **C-3023**

Fort Saint-Philippe, Louisiane

La-Visitation-du-Village-de-Saint-Philippe
(Église catholique)
BMD   1761-1765   **C-2899**

Iberville, Louisiane

St-Gabriel-d'Iberville (Église catholique)
B	1773-1774	**C-2224** ou
		C-2899
M	1773-1859	**C-2224** ou
	1773-1816	**C-2899**
	1816-1859	**C-2900**

Kaskaskia, Illinois

Notre-Dame-de-l'Immaculée-Conception-des-Kaskaskias
(Église catholique)
B	1695-1735, 1759-1799	**C-2899**
	1722-1724	**F-597**
M	1723-1724	**F-597**
	1724-1729, 1741-1798	**C-2899**
D	1720-1727, 1764-1834	**C-2899**
	1723-1724	**F-597**

La Fourche, Louisiane

St-Martin-des-Atikapas, Saint-Martinville
(Église catholique)
BD	1756,1765-1766	**C-2237** ou
		C-2900
BMD	1771-1773	**C-2237** ou
		C-2900
B	1773-1779, 1791-1794	**C-2237** ou
		C-2900
BM	1778-1779	**C-2237** ou
		C-2900

comprend: des actes concernant les habitants de l'Acadie réfugié en Louisiane, ainsi que des mentions concernant les missions suivantes: Pointe-Coupée, Opelousas, L'Ascension-de-La-Fourche-des-Chétimachas, St-Bernard-des-Atakapas, St-Joseph-des-Atakapas, St-Martin-des-Atakapas, St-François-des-Nakitoches (Natchitoches)

L'Assomption-de-la-Pointe-de-Montréal-du-Détroit (par après, Sandwich) comté d'Essex, Ontario, Canada
Voir: Sandwich

Louis-de-la-Louisiane, Fort (par après, Fort Condé-de-la-Mobile, et puis, Fort Charlotte), Alabama

Notre-Dame-de-l'Immaculée-Conception-de-la-Mobile
(Église catholique)
BM   1704-1764 extraits   **C-2224**
comprend :

Fort Louis ou Fort Condé-de-la-Mobile
(Église catholique)
B	1704, 1707, 1717,	
	1727-1728, 1731-1735,	
	1737, 1741-1746,	
	1748-1751, 1756,	
	1764 extraits	**C-2224**
M	1726, 1738-1739, 1741,	
	1747, 1760, 1762,	
	1764 extraits	**C-2224**

Metlakatla, Annette Island, Alaska

William Duncan's Metlakahtla Christian Mission, Annette Island
B	1861-1918	**M-2331**
M	1881-1899	**M-2331**
D	1881-1918	**M-2331**

comprises:

C.M.S. Anglican Mission of Fort Simpson and Metlakatla, British Columbia, Canada
B	1861-1863, 1874-1884	**M-2331**
D	1862	**M-2331**

William Duncan's Metlakahtla Christian Mission, Metlakatla, British Columbia, Canada
B	1882-1887	**M-2331**
M	1881-1886	**M-2331**
D	1881-1887	**M-2331**

William Duncan's Metlakahtla Christian Mission, Metlakatla, Annette Island, Alaska
B	1890-1918	**M-2331**
M	1891-1899	**M-2331**
D	1887-1918	**M-2331**

Michilimackinac, Michigan

Ste-Anne-de-Mackinac, (Église catholique)
BMD   1695-1799   **C-2900**
comprend :

Mission de St-Ignace (Église catholique)
B	1695, 1712-1781,	
	1786-1799	**C-2900**
M	1744-1799	**C-2900**
D	1754-1799	**C-2900**

Mobile, Alabama

Notre-Dame-de-l'Immaculée-Conception-de-la-Mobile
(Église catholique)
BM 1704-1764 extraits **C-2224**
comprend :

    Fort Louis-de-la-Louisiane ou Fort Condé-de-la-Mobile
    (Église catholique)
    B   1704, 1707, 1717,
           1727-1728, 1731-1735,
           1737, 1741-1746,
           1748-1751, 1756,
           1764 extraits   **C-2224**
    M   1726, 1738-1739, 1741,
          1747, 1760, 1762,
          1764 extraits   **C-2224**

Natchitoches (Nakitoches), Poste des, Louisiane

Notre-Dame-de-l'Immaculée-Conception-de-Natchitoches
(Église catholique)
BMD   1729-1796   **M-702**
comprend :

    St-François-du-Poste-des-Natchitoches
    (Église catholique)
    B   1729-1730, 1734-1796   **M-702**
    M   1734-1761, 1764-1792   **M-702**
    D   1734-1788   **M-702**
    (Des parties de ces registres sont en latin ou en
    espagnol.)

St-Martin-des-Atakapas, Saint-Martinville
(Église catholique)
BD   1756, 1765-1766   **C-2237** ou
                                C-2900
BMD   1771-1773   **C-2237** ou
                                C-2900
B   1773-1779, 1791-1794   **C-2237** ou
                                C-2900
BM   1778-1779   **C-2237** ou
                                C-2900
comprend : des actes concernant les habitants de l'Acadie
         réfugiés en Louisiane, ainsi que des mentions
         concernant les missions suivantes : Pointe-
         Coupée, Opelousas, L'Ascension-de-La-
         Fourche-des-Chétimachas, St-Bernard-des-
         Atakapas, St-Joseph-des-Atakapas, St-Martin-
         des-Atakapas, St-François-des-Nakitoches
         (Natchitoches)

Nouvelle-Acadie (Poste des At(t)akapas) (aujourd'hui,
Saint-Martinville), Louisiane

St-Martin des Atakapas, Saint-Martinville
(Église catholique)
BD   1756, 1765-1766   **C-2237** ou
                                C-2900

(cont.)

BMD   1771-1773   **C-2237** ou
                                C-2900
B   1773-1779, 1791-1794   **C-2237** ou
                                C-2900
BM   1778-1779   **C-2237** ou
                                C-2900
comprend : des actes concernant les habitants de l'Acadie
         réfugiés en Louisiane, ainsi que des mentions
         concernant les missions suivantes : Pointe-
         Coupée, Opelousas, L'Ascension-de-La-
         Fourche-des-Chétimachas, St-Bernard-des-
         Atakapas, St-Joseph-des-Atakapas, St-Martin-
         des-Atakapas, St-François-des-Nakitoches
         (Natchitoches)

Nouvelle-Orléans, Louisiane

Paroisses catholiques de la Nouvelle-Orléans
B   1728-1730   **F-597**
D   1721-1730, 1734   **F-597**

Opelousas, Poste des, Louisiane

St-Martin-des-Atakapas, Saint Martinville
(Église catholique)
BD   1756, 1765-1766   **C-2237** ou
                                C-2900
BMD   1771-1773   **C-2237** ou
                                C-2900
B   1773-1779, 1791-1794   **C-2237** ou
                                C-2900
BM   1778-1779   **C-2237** ou
                                C-2900
comprend : des actes concernant les habitants de l'Acadie
         réfugiés en Louisiane, ainsi que des mentions
         concernant les missions suivantes : Pointe-
         Coupée, Opelousas, L'Ascension-de-La-
         Fourche-des-Chétimachas, St-Bernard-des-
         Atakapas, St-Joseph-des-Atakapas, St-Martin-
         des-Atakapas, St-François-des-Nakitoches
         (Natchitoches)

St-Landry-des-Opelousas (Église catholique)
B   1776-1785   **M-703**
M   1784-1795   **M-703**
D   1779-1806   **M-703**
(Ces registres sont en espagnol.)

Oswego, New York

St. John's Anglican Church, Bath, Ontario, Canada
B   1787-1813   **H-1810**
M   1787-1816   **H-1810**
D   1787-1813   **H-1810**
comprises:

(cont.)

St. Thomas' Anglican Church, Ernestown Township, Lennox and Addington Co., Ontario
B	1788-1813	**H-1810**
M	1787-1813, 1814, 1816	**H-1810**
D	1788-1813	**H-1810**

includes: Amherst Island, and the Townships of Adolphustown, Camden, and Fredericksburg, Lennox and Addington Co.; the Townships of Ameliasburg, Marysburgh, and Sophiasburgh, Prince Edward Co.; the Townships of Sidney, and Thurlow, Hastings Co.; and Kingston, Frontenac Co., Ont., Canada; as well as Oswego, N.Y., U.S.A.

St. Paul's Anglican Church, Fredericksburg Township
B	1787-1813	**H-1810**
M	1788-1812	**H-1810**
D	1787-1813	**H-1810**

includes: Amherst Island, and the Townships of Adolphustown, Camden, Ernestown, and Richmond, Lennox and Addington Co.; the Townships of Ameliasburg, Hallowell, Marysburgh, and Sophiasburgh, Prince Edward Co.; the Townships of Sidney, and Thurlow, Hastings Co.; and the Townships of Cramahé, and Percy, Northumberland Co., Ont., Canada; as well as Oswego, N.Y., U.S.A.

Ouabache (Wabash) (dit Poste de Vincennes), Indiana

St-François-Xavier-sur-Ouabache (Église catholique)
BM	1749-1786	**C-2896** (index)
D	1750-1758, 1767, 1770-1771, 1777-1778, 1781, 1784-1786	**C-2896** (index)

Petersham, Massachusetts

Civil registers
M	1767-1773	**M-138**

Pittsburgh, Pennsylvanie

L'Assomption-de-la-Très-Sainte-Vierge-à-la-Belle-Rivière (Église catholique)
D	1753-1754*	**C-3023**
BD	1754-1756	**C-3023**

*comprend: Fort de la Presqu'Île et Fort de la Rivière-aux-Bœufs, ainsi que Fort Duquesne-à-la-Belle-Rivière (Pittsburgh)

Pointe-à-la-Chevelure, New York

Voir: Crown Point, Fort

Pointe-Coupée, Louisiane

St-Martin-des-Atakapas, Saint-Martinville (Église catholique)
BD	1756, 1765-1766	**C-2237** ou **C-2900**
BMD	1771-1773	**C-2237** ou **C-2900**
B	1773-1779, 1791-1794	**C-2237** ou **C-2900**
BM	1778-1779	**C-2237** ou **C-2900**

comprend: des actes concernant les habitants de l'Acadie réfugiés en Louisiane, ainsi que des mentions concernant les missions suivantes: Pointe-Coupée, Opelousas, L'Ascension-de-La-Fourche-des-Chétimachas, St-Bernard-des-Atakapas, St-Joseph-des-Atakapas, St-Martin-des-Atakapas, St-François-des-Nakitoches (Natchitoches)

Pointe-de-Montréal-du-Détroit (par après, Sandwich), comté d'Essex, Ontario, Canada

Ste-Anne-du-Détroit (Église catholique), Detroit, Michigan
BMD	1704-1800	**C-2893** à **C-2895**

comprend:

Mission des Hurons de la Pointe-de-Montréal-du-Détroit (Église catholique)
B	1761-1767	**C-2894**

L'Assomption-de-la-Pointe-de-Montréal-du-Détroit (Église catholique)
B	1767-1771	**C-2894**
M	1764-1765, 1768-1771	**C-2894**
D	1768-1772	**C-2894**
BMD	1772-1777	**C-2894**
	1777-1783	**C-2895**

L'Assomption-de-Sandwich-du-Détroit (Église catholique)
BMD	1781-1799	**C-2895**

Pontchartrain-du-Détroit, Fort, Michigan

Ste-Anne-du-Détroit (Église catholique)
BMD	1704-1800	**C-2893** à **C-2895**

comprend:

Fort Pontchartrain-du-Détroit (Église catholique)
B	1704-1718	**C-2893**
M	1710-1718	**C-2893**
D	1707-1718	**C-2893**
BMD	1709-1765	**C-2893**
	[1760]-1800	**C-2894**

UNITED STATES OF AMERICA / ÉTATS-UNIS

Prairie-du-Rocher, Illinois

St-Joseph-de-la-Prairie-du-Rocher (Église catholique)
BMD   1761-1799   **C-2899**

Presqu'Île, Fort de la, Pennsylvanie

L'Assomption-de-la-Très-Sainte-Vierge-à-la-Belle-Rivière (Église catholique)
D	1753-1754*	**C-3023**
BD	1754-1756	**C-3023**

*comprend : Fort de la Presqu'Île et Fort de la Rivière-aux-Bœufs, ainsi que Fort Duquesne-à-la-Belle-Rivière (Pittsburgh)

Rivière-aux-Bœufs, Fort de la, Pennsylvanie

L'Assomption-de-la-Très-Sainte-Vierge-à-la-Belle-Rivière (Église catholique)
D	1753-1754*	**C-3023**
BD	1754-1756	**C-3023**

*comprend : Fort de la Presqu'Île et Fort de la Rivière-aux-Bœufs, ainsi que Fort Duquesne-à-la-Belle-Rivière (Pittsburgh)

Saint-Frédéric, Fort (Fort Beauharnois-à-la-Pointe-à-la-Chevelure ou Fort Crown Point), New York

Église catholique du Fort Saint-Frédéric ou Fort Beauharnois
BMD	1732-1760	**C-3023**
	1732-1760 extraits	**M-866** (index)

comprend :

    Fort Chambly (Église catholique), Québec, Canada
B	1759-1760	**C-3023**
D	1759	**C-3023**

Saint-Martinville (antérieurement, Poste des At(t)akapas ou Nouvelle-Acadie), Louisiane

St-Martin-des-Atakapas, Saint-Martinville (Église catholique)
BD	1756, 1765-1766	**C-2237** ou **C-2900**
BMD	1771-1773	**C-2237** ou **C-2900**
B	1773-1779, 1791-1794	**C-2237** ou **C-2900**
BM	1778-1779	**C-2237** ou **C-2900**

comprend : des actes concernant les habitants de l'Acadie réfugiés en Louisiane, ainsi que des mentions (cont.)

concernant les missions suivantes : Pointe-Coupée, Opelousas, L'Ascension-de-La-Fourche-des-Chétimachas, St-Bernard-des-Atakapas, St-Joseph-des-Atakapas, St-Martin-des-Atakapas, St-François-des-Nakitoches (Natchitoches)

Saint-Philippe, Fort, Louisiane

La-Visitation-du-Village-de-Saint-Philippe (Église catholique)
BMD   1761-1765   **C-2899**

Sandwich (antérieurement, Pointe-de-Montréal-du-Détroit), comté d'Essex/Essex Co., Ontario, Canada

Ste-Anne-du-Détroit (Église catholique), Detroit, Michigan
BMD   1704-1800   **C-2893** à **C-2895**
comprend :

    Mission des Hurons de la Pointe-de-Montréal-du-Détroit (Église catholique)
    B   1761-1767   **C-2894**

    L'Assomption-de-la-Pointe-de-Montréal-du-Détroit (Église catholique)
B	1767-1771	**C-2894**
M	1764-1765, 1768-1771	**C-2894**
D	1768-1772	**C-2894**
BMD	1772-1777	**C-2894**
	1777-1783	**C-2895**

    L'Assomption-de-Sandwich-du-Détroit (Église catholique)
    BMD   1781-1799   **C-2895**

St. John's Anglican Church
BMD   1802-1827   **C-3030** (index)

Schenectady, New York

Christ Church Anglican Church, William Henry (formerly, and later, Sorel), Richelieu Co., Quebec, Canada
BMD   1784-1796   **H-1807**
includes:

    Schenectady
    B   1785   **H-1807**

Vincennes, Poste de, Indiana

St-François-Xavier-sur-Ouabache (Wabash) (Église catholique)
BM	1749-1786	**C-2896** (index)
D	1750-1758, 1767, 1770-1771, 1777-1778, 1781, 1784-1786	**C-2896** (index)

Wabash (Ouabache) (dit Poste de Vincennes), Indiana

St-François-Xavier-sur-Ouabache (Wabash)
(Église catholique)

BM	1749-1786	**C-2896** (index)
D	1750-1758, 1767, 1770-1771, 1777-1778, 1781, 1784-1786	**C-2896** (index)

Woodbury, Connecticut

S.P.G. Anglican Mission of Gagetown, Queens Co., New Brunswick, Canada

BM   1786-1792   **H-1806**

includes: Carleton Parish, Kent Co.; Kingston, and Sussex, Kings Co.; Hampstead, Long Island, Waterborough, and Wickham, Queens Co.; Lancaster, and St. John, St. John Co.; Maugerville, Sunbury Co.; Fredericton, York Co., N.B., Canada; and Woodbury, Conn., U.S.A.

Geographic Index

Index géographique

GEOGRAPHIC INDEX / INDEX GÉOGRAPHIQUE

Page

ARCHIVES OF THE HUDSON'S BAY COMPANY / ARCHIVES DE LA COMPAGNIE DE LA BAIE D'HUDSON

RUPERT'S LAND / TERRE DE RUPERT

British Columbia

Fort Kamloops (Thompson's River Post)	3
Fort New Caledonia (Fort St. James)	3
Fort St. James (Fort New Caledonia)	3
Thompson's River Post (Fort Kamloops)	3

Manitoba

Albany House	3
Beaver Creek	3
Berens River	3
Brandon House	3
Dynevor	3
Fort Alexander	3
Fort Douglas	3
Fort Garry	3
Fort Gibraltar	3
Lockport	3
Nelson River District	3
Norway House	3
Oxford House	3
Pembina	3
Pigeon River	3
Red River Settlement	3
Rivière-du-Pat [Rivière-du-Pas]	3
Rock River Depot	3
St. Peter's Indian Reserve, Sugar Point	3
Swan River	3
The Pas	3
White Horse Plains House	3
Winnipeg	3
York Factory	3

North West Territories

Fort McPherson	3
Fort Simpson	3
Peel's River Fort	3

Ontario

Fort Rainy Lake (Fort Frances)	3

Saskatchewan

Cumberland House	3
Fort Île-à-la-Crosse	3
Fort Pelly	3

CANADA

BRITISH COLUMBIA / COLOMBIE-BRITANNIQUE

Cariboo District

Fort New Caledonia	7
Fort St. James	7
New Caledonia, Fort	7
St. James, Fort	7

West Coast Area

Fort Simpson	7
Metlakatla	7
Port Simpson	7

Yale District

Fort Kamloops	7
Kamloops, Fort	7
Thompson's River Post	7

MANITOBA

Consol District

Rivière-du-Pat	11
The Pas	12

Cornwallis Municipality

Brandon House	9

Ellice District

Beaver Creek	9

Interlake District

Lockport	10
Lower Mapleton	10
Mapleton	10

North Central District

Arden	9
Beautiful Plains	9
Gladstone	9
Palestine	11
Westbourne	12
White Mud River	12

North District

Albany House	9
Berens River House	9
Fort Alexander	9
Nelson River District	10
Norway House	10
Oxford House	10
Pigeon River	11
Rock River Depot	11
York Factory	13

Parklands District

Swan River House	12

MANITOBA (cont.)

Portage-La-Prairie Municipality
Dynevor 9
St. Peter's Indian Reserve 12
Sugar Point 12

South Central District
Pembina 11

Southwest District
Hamilton 9
Hamiota 9
Little Saskatchewan 10
Minnedosa 10

Winnipeg Municipality
Fort Douglas 9
Fort Garry 9
Fort Gibraltar 9
Red River Settlement 11
St. Boniface 11
White Horse Plains House 12
Winnipeg 12

NEW BRUNSWICK / NOUVEAU-BRUNSWICK

Albert, comté d'
Chipoudy (Chipoudie) 16
Hillsborough 18
Hopewell 18
Shepody 23

Carleton County
Northampton Parish 20
Woodstock Parish 24

Gloucester, comté de
Caraquet 15

Kent County/Comté de Kent
Bouctouche/Buctouche 15
Carleton Parish 15
Coates Mills 16
Cocagne 16
Dundas Parish 16
Grande-Digue 17
L'Ardoine 19
Pointe-Sapin 20
Richibucto/Richibouctou 21
Richibucto Harbour 21
Richibucto Parish 21
Richibucto River 21
Saint-Charles-de-Kent 22
Saint-Louis[-de-Kent] 22
Wellington Parish 24

Kings County
Apohaqui 15
Hampton 17
Kings County 18
Kingston 18
Lester Brook 19
Milligan Brook 19
Milliken 19

Penobsquis 20
Smiths Creek 23
Sussex 24
Wards Creek 24

Madawaska, comté de
Saint-Basile 22

Northumberland, comté de
Baie-des-Vents 15
Baie-Sainte-Anne 15
Néguac 20

Nouveau-Brunswick, Missions du 20

Queens County/Comté de Queens
Gagetown Parish 17
Hampstead 17
Jemseg (Jemsek) 18
Long Island 19
Rivière Saint-Jean 21
Waterborough 24
Wickham 24

Saint John County
Lancaster 19
St. John 22

Sunbury County
Burton Parish 15
Maugerville 19
Sheffield 23

Westmorland County/Comté de Westmorland
Barachois 15
Botsford 15
Cap-Tourmentin 15
Chimogoui (Chimougoui) 16
Didiche [Tidnish Bridge] 16
Haute-Aboujagane 17
Memramcook 19
Naboiyagan (Naboujagan) 19
Petitcodiac/Petitcoudiac 20
Petitcodiac River 20
Sackville 21
Saint-Anselme 22
Saint-Henri-de-Barachois 22
Salisbury 22
Scoudouc 22
Shediac 22
Shediac Cape 22
Shediac Parish 23
Shediac River 23
Shemogue 23
Westmorland County 24

York County/Comté d'York
Dumfries Parish 16
Ekoupag (Ekouipahag) 17
Fredericton 17
Kingsclear 18
Kingsclear Parish 18
Prince William Parish 20
Queensbury Parish 21
Rivière Saint-Jean 21
Southampton Parish 24

(cont.)

GEOGRAPHIC INDEX / INDEX GÉOGRAPHIQUE

NEWFOUNDLAND AND LABRADOR / TERRE-NEUVE ET LABRADOR

Labrador
Hebron	25
Nain	25
Okak	25
Ramah	25
Zoar	25

Newfoundland
St. John's	25
St. John's District	25
Trinity	25

NORTHWEST TERRITORIES / TERRITOIRES DU NORD-OUEST

District of Mackenzie
Fort McPherson	27
Fort Simpson	27
Peel's River Fort	27

NOVA SCOTIA / NOUVELLE-ÉCOSSE

Acadie et Gaspésie ... 29

Annapolis County/Comté d'Annapolis
Annapolis	29
Bridgetown	30
Clements	31
Cornwallis	31
Cornwallis Township	31
Dalhousie	31
Granville	32
Graywood (Greywood)	32
Lake La Rose	34
Perotte	36
Port-Royal	37
Wilmot	38
Wilmot Township	38

Antigonish County ... 29

Cape Breton County/Comté du Cap-Breton
Baleine, Havre de la	29
Havre de la Baleine	32
Havre du Petit-Laurent-le-Bec	33
Lorembec	35
Lorraine Head	35
Louisbourg	35
Petit-Laurent-le-Bec, Havre du	37
Sydney	38

Cape Breton Island/Île du Cap-Breton ... 30

Colchester County
Londonderry	35
Onslow	36
Truro	38

Cumberland County/Comté de Cumberland
Beaubassin	30
Cumberland	31
Cumberland County	31

(cont.)

Elysian Fields	31
Fort Lawrence	31
Franklin Manor	32
Maccan	36
Mines, Rivière-des-	36
Minudie Marsh	36
Nappan	36
Rivière-des-Mines	38

Digby County/Comté de Digby
Baie Sainte-Marie	29
Church Point	31
Cornwallis	31
Cornwallis Township	31
Digby	31
Sainte-Marie, Baie	38

Hants County
[Douglas]	31
Douglas Township	31
Falmouth	31
Newport	36
Rawdon	37

Île du Cap-Breton/Cape Breton Island ... 33

Île Royale (Île du Cap-Breton) ... 34

Kings County/Comté de Kings
Aylesford	29
Grand-Pré	32
Horton	33
Horton Township	33
Mines, Les	36

Lunenburg County
Chester	30
Lunenburg	35
Mahone Bay	36

Pictou County ... 37

Queens County
Liverpool	34
Liverpool Township	34
Milton	36
Rosette	38

Richmond, comté de
Fourchu (Fourché)	32
Havre du Saint-Esprit	33
Petit-Nord	37
Port-au-Basque	37
Port-Fourchu (Fourché)	37
Saint-Esprit, Havre du	38

Shelburne County
Shelburne	38

ONTARIO

Bathurst District ... 44

Bay of Quinté Region ... 44

GEOGRAPHIC INDEX / INDEX GÉOGRAPHIQUE

ONTARIO (cont.)

Brant County
Brantford Township	48
Burford Township	50
Paris	100
St. George	110
South Dumfries Township	114

Bruce County
Brant Township	48
Bruce County	49
Carrick Township	52

Carleton County/Comté de Carleton
Antrim	42
Ashton	42
Bathurst District	44
Bells Corners	46
Bytown (see/voir Ottawa)	50
Carleton County	51
Carp	52
Dwyer Hill	60
Fallowfield	66
Fitzroy Harbour	67
Fitzroy Township	67
Goulbourn Township	71
Hazeldean	74
Huntley	76
Huntley Township	76
Johnstown District	77
Kilmaurs	79
Kinburn	79
Lowry	84
March Township	85
Marchhurst	85
Ottawa	98
Ottawa District	99
Richmond	108
Stittsville	115
Torbolton Township	117
Woodlawn	128

Dufferin County
Dufferin County	59
Melancthon Township	89

Dundas County
Dundas County	60
Eastern District	61
Inkerman	77
Matilda Township	86
Morrisburg	91
Mountain Township	92
Pleasant Valley	103
Riverside	108
Williamsburg	124
Williamsburgh Township	124
Winchester Township	127

Durham County
Cavan Township	53

Eastern District
Eastern District	61

Elgin County
Aylmer	43
Bayham	45
Corinth	55
Dexter	58

(cont.)

Fairview	66
North Bayham	94
Port Stanley	104
Richmond Village	108
St. Thomas	111
Sparta	115
Summers Corners	116
Yarmouth Township	129

Essex County/Comté d'Essex
Amherstburg	41
Colchester	55
Essex County	66
L'Assomption-de-la-Pointe-de-Montréal-du-Détroit	82
Maidstone	85
Pointe-de-Montréal-du-Détroit	103
Sandwich	111
Sandwich Township	111
Windsor	128

Frontenac County
Bay of Quinté Region	44
Elphin	64
Kingston	79
Loughborough Township	84
Mecklenburg District	87
Midland District	89
Pittsburgh Township	102
Portland Township	104
Quinté Region, Bay of	105
Snow Road	113

Georgian Bay Region
Georgian Bay Region	70
Indian Lands	76

Glengarry County
Alexandria	40
Breadalbane	48
Charlottenburg Township	53
Dalhousie Mills	57
Dalkeith	58
Dunvegan	60
Eastern District	61
Glengarry County	70
Indian Lands	76
Kenyon Township	78
Kirkhill	80
Laggan	81
Lancaster	81
Lancaster Township	82
Lochiel	82
Lochiel Township	82
McCrimmon	84
Martintown	86
Maxville	87
Notfield	96
St. Raphael West	110
Williamstown	125

Grenville County/Comté de Grenville
Augusta Township	43
Edwardsburgh Township	63
Grenville County	71
Johnstown District	77
Kemptville	78
Oxford Township	99
Rideau District	108
Wolford Township	128

ONTARIO (cont.)

Grey County
- Artemesia Township 42
- Durham 60
- Egremont Township 63
- Euphrasia Township 66
- Grey County 72
- Hanover 73
- Keppel Township 79
- Normanby Township 94
- Osprey Township 98
- Owen Sound 99
- Proton Township 105
- St. Vincent Township 111
- Sydenham Township 116

Haldimand County
- Hartford 74
- Walpole Township 119

Halton County
- Esquesing Township 65

Hastings County
- Bay of Quinté Region 44
- Mecklenburg District 87
- Midland District 89
- Quinté Region, Bay of 105
- Rawdon Township 107
- Sidney Township 112
- Thurlow 117
- Thurlow Township 117
- Tyendinaga Township 119

Huron County
- Dungannon 60
- Hay Township 74
- Kirkton 80
- London District 83
- Stanley Township 115
- Tuckersmith Township 118
- Usborne Township 119

Indian Lands, Western Ontario 76

Johnstown District 77

Kenora District
- Fort Hope, [Albany River, north of Lake Nepigon] 68
- Patricia District 100

Kent County
- Chatham 54
- Orford Township 97

Lambton County
- Sarnia 111

Lanark County
- Almonte 40
- Appleton 42
- Ashbury 42
- Ashton 42
- Bathurst District 44
- Bathurst Township 44
- Beckwith Township 45
- Blakeney 47
- Carleton Place 52

(cont.)

- Cedar Hill 53
- Clayton 54
- Clyde Forks 55
- Dalhousie Township 57
- Darling Township 58
- Drummond Township 59
- Flower Station 68
- Franktown 68
- Harper 73
- Hopetown 75
- Lanark 81
- Lanark County 81
- Lanark Township 81
- Lavant Township 82
- McDonalds Corners 85
- Middleville 89
- Mississippi Lake 90
- Montague Township 91
- North Sherbrooke Township 96
- Pakenham 99
- Pakenham Township 100
- Perth 101
- Playfair 103
- Poland 104
- Prestonvale 105
- Ramsay Township 107
- Rideau District 108
- Rosetta 109
- Sherbrooke (North) Township 112
- Smith's Falls 113
- Tatlock 116
- Watson's Corners 122

Leeds County
- Bastard Township 43
- Bellamy Pond 46
- Brockville 49
- Elizabethtown Township 63
- Front of Yonge Township 70
- Gananoque 70
- Johnstown District 77
- Kitley Township 80
- Leeds County 82
- Smith's Falls 113
- Toledo 117

Lennox and Addington County
- Adolphustown Township 39
- Amherst Island Township 41
- Bath 44
- Bay of Quinté Region 44
- Camden Township 51
- Centreville 53
- Ernestown Township 64
- Fredericksburgh Township 68
- Mecklenburg District 87
- Midland District 89
- North Fredericksburgh Township 95
- Quinté Region, Bay of 105
- Richmond Township 108
- Sheffield Township 112
- South Fredericksburgh Township 114

Lincoln County
- Queenston 105
- St. Catharines 110

London District 83

ONTARIO (cont.)

Manitoulin District
- Manitoulin Island ... 85

Mecklenburg District ... 87

Middlesex County
- Biddulph Township ... 47
- Granton ... 71
- London District ... 83
- London Township ... 83
- Middlesex County ... 89
- Muncey ... 92
- Saintsbury ... 111
- Strathroy ... 116

Midland District ... 89

Muskoka District
- Aspdin ... 43
- Beausoleil Island ... 45
- Stephenson Township ... 115
- Stisted Township ... 115

Norfolk County
- Charlotteville Township ... 54
- Delhi ... 58
- Fredericksburg ... 68
- Hartford ... 74
- London District ... 83
- Middleton Township ... 89
- Norfolk County ... 93
- South Walsingham Township ... 114
- Townsend Township ... 118
- Windham Township ... 127
- Woodhouse Township ... 128

Northumberland County
- Alderville ... 40
- Alnwick Township ... 40
- Bay of Quinté Region ... 44
- Cramahé Township ... 57
- Haldimand Township ... 72
- Hamilton Township ... 73
- Murray Township ... 92
- Percy Township ... 101
- Quinté Region, Bay of ... 105
- South Monaghan Township ... 114

Ontario County
- Ontario County ... 96
- Pickering ... 102

Ontario Province ... 96

Ottawa District ... 99

Oxford County
- Blandford Township ... 47
- Blenheim Township ... 47
- East Zorra Township ... 61
- London District ... 83
- Norwich ... 96
- Oxford County ... 99
- Woodstock ... 128

Parry Sound District
- French River ... 70
- Henvey Inlet ... 75
- McMurrich Township ... 85
- Parry Island ... 100
- Parry Sound District ... 100
- Shawanaga Township ... 112

Patricia District
- Fort Hope, [Albany River, north of Lake Nepigon] ... 68
- Patricia District ... 100

Peel County
- Chinguacousy Township ... 54

Perth County
- Blanshard Township ... 47
- Ellice Township ... 63
- Kirkton ... 80
- Mornington Township ... 91
- North Easthope Township ... 95
- Prospect Hill ... 105
- South Easthope Township ... 114
- Wallace Township ... 119

Peterborough County
- Asphodel Township ... 43
- Douro Township ... 59
- Dummer Township ... 59
- Elmhill ... 64
- Ennismore Township ... 64
- Harvey Township ... 74
- Lakefield ... 81
- North Douro ... 94
- North Monaghan Township ... 95
- Otonabee Township ... 98
- Peterborough ... 102
- Peterborough County ... 102
- Smith Township ... 113

Prescott County
- Caledonia Township ... 50
- East Hawkesbury Township ... 60
- Eastern District ... 61
- Hawkesbury ... 74
- L'Orignal ... 84
- North Plantagenet Township ... 95
- Ottawa District ... 99
- Plantagenet ... 103
- Prescott County ... 104
- Riceville ... 108
- South Plantagenet Township ... 114
- West Hawkesbury Township ... 123

Prince Edward County
- Ameliasburgh Township ... 41
- Bay of Quinté Region ... 44
- Hallowell Township ... 72
- Hillier Township ... 75
- Marysburgh Township ... 86
- Mecklenburg District ... 87
- Midland District ... 89
- Quinté Region, Bay of ... 105
- Sophiasburgh Township ... 113
- West Lake ... 123

Quinté Region, Bay of ... 105

Rainy River District
- Fort Frances ... 68
- Fort Lac-La-Pluie ... 68
- Fort Rainy Lake ... 68
- Lac-La-Pluie ... 80
- Lac-La-Pluie, Fort ... 81

(cont.)

ONTARIO (cont.)

Renfrew County
Boyd	48
Brudenell Township	49
Burns Township	50
Castleford	53
Dewar's Settlement	58
Hagarty Township	72
Horton Township	75
Loch Winnoch	82
McNab Township	85
Pembroke Township	101
Radcliffe Township	107
Renfrew County	107
Ross Township	109
Sherwood Township	112
Stewartville	115
Westmeath Township	123
Wilno	127

Rideau District ... 108

Russell County/Comté de Russell
Cambridge Township	51
Eastern District	61
Embrun	64
Ottawa District	99
Russell County	110

Simcoe County
Christian Island, Georgian Bay	54

Stormont County
Cornwall	56
Cornwall Township	56
Eastern District	61
Finch Township	66
Lunenburg	84
Newington	93
North Lunenburg	95
Osnabruck Township	97
Roxborough Township	109
St. Andrews	110
Sheek Island	112
Stormont County	115

Thunder Bay District
Fort William	68
Port Arthur	104
Thunder Bay	116

Victoria County
Emily Township	64
Lindsay	82
Ops Township	96

Waterloo County
Ayr	43
Baden	43
Berlin	46
Breslau	49
Cambridge	50
Elmira	64
Galt	70
Hagey	72
Heidelberg	75
Kitchener	80
Latshaws	82
Mannheim	85
[New] Baden	92
New Dundee	92
New Hamburg	93
North Dumfries Township	94
Phillipsburg	102
Preston	104
St. Agatha	110
Waterloo County	119
Waterloo Township	121
Wellesley	122
Wellesley Township	122
Wilmot Township	126
Woolwich Township	128

Welland County
Pelham Township	101
Thorold	116

Wellington County
Guelph Township	72
New Germany	93
Nichol Township	93
Peel Township	100
Pilkington Township	102
Puslinch Township	105
Wellington County	123

Wentworth County
Ancaster Township	41
Beverly Township	46
Dundas	59
Flamborough (West) Township	67
Hamilton	73
Wentworth County	123
West Flamborough Township	123

York County
Toronto	118
Yonge Street	129
York County	129

PRINCE EDWARD ISLAND / ÎLE-DU-PRINCE-ÉDOUARD

King's County/Comté de King's
Murray Harbour	131
Port Lajoie	131
St-Pierre du Nord	131

Prince County/Comté de Prince
Cascumpèque	131
Malpèque	131
Tignish	132

Queen's County/Comté de Queen's
Belfast	131
Charlottetown	131
Pinette	131
Rustico	131

(cont.)

QUÉBEC

Argenteuil County/Comté d'Argenteuil
- Grenville, canton de 142
- Saint-André-d'Argenteuil 153
- Saint-André-Est 153

Beauharnois, comté de
- Beauharnois 133

Berthier, comté de/Berthier County
- Berthier[ville] 133
- Dupas (du Pads), île 140
- Île Dupas (Isle du Pads) 144
- Lanoraie 145
- Lavaltrie 145
- Saint-Antoine-de-Lavaltrie 154

Bonaventure, comté de
- Ristigouche 153

Brome County
- Allen's Corner 133
- East Farnham 141
- Farnham Township 141
- Potton Township 151

Chambly County/Comté de Chambly
- Boucherville 134
- Chambly 137
- Chambly, Fort- 137
- Fort-Chambly 141
- [Fort Saint-Louis] 141
- Longueuil 147
- [Saint-Louis, Fort] 155

Champlain, comté de
- Batiscan 133
- Cap-de-la-Madeleine 136
- Champlain 137

Châteauguay County/Comté de Châteauguay
- Bassin-de-Châteauguay 133
- Châteauguay 138
- Saint-Joachim-de-Châteauguay 155
- Sault-Saint-Louis 156

Deux-Montagnes, comté de
- Deux Montagnes, lac des 140
- Lac des Deux Montagnes 144
- L'Annonciation 145
- Oka 149
- Saint-Benoît 154
- Saint-Eustache 154
- Saint-Hermas 155
- Sainte-Scholastique 156

Gaspé-Est, comté de
- Pabos 151

Gatineau County/Comté de Gatineau
- Aylmer 133
- Chelsea 138
- Denholm Township 139

(cont.)

- Eardley Township 140
- Hull 142
- Hull Township/Canton de Hull 143
- Lac-Sainte-Marie 145
- Lapêche 145
- Masham, canton de 147
- Ottawa County 150
- Rivière-à-Lapêche 153
- Sainte-Cécile-de-Masham 154
- Wakefield 160
- Wakefield Township 160
- Wright, comté de 160

Hull County/Comté de Hull
- Gatineau 141
- Ottawa County 150
- Templeton 158
- Templeton Township 158
- Wright, comté de 160

Huntingdon, comté de
- Saint-Régis 156

Île-de-Montréal County/Comté de l'Île-de-Montréal
- Bout-de-l'Île 134
- Lachine 145
- La Pointe Olivier 145
- Longue Pointe 147
- Montréal 148
- Olivier, la Pointe 149
- Pointe-aux-Trembles 151
- Pointe-Claire 151
- Pointe Olivier, La 151
- Rivière-des-Prairies 153
- Sainte-Anne-de-Bellevue 154
- Saine-Anne-du-Bout-de-l'Île 154
- Saint-Laurent 155
- Sault-au-Récollet 156
- Ville-Marie 160

Île-Jésus, comté de l'
- Île-Jésus, comté de l' 144
- Laval 145
- Sainte-Rose 156

Kamouraska, comté de
- Kamouraska, comté de 144
- Saint-André-de-Kamouraska 153
- Saint-Louis-de-Kamouraska 155

Laprairie, comté de
- La Prairie 145

L'Assomption, comté de
- Bouchard, îles 134
- Îles Bouchard 144
- Lachenaie 144
- L'Assomption 145
- Repentigny 152
- Saint-Sulpice 156

Laval, [comté de]
- Sainte-Rose-de-Laval 156

QUÉBEC (cont.)

Lévis, [comté de]
Lévis 146

L'Islet, comté de
Saint-Roch-des-Aulnaies 156

Maskinongé, comté de
Louiseville 147
Rivière-du-Loup 153

Missisquoi County
Dunham Township 140
Saint-Armand-Ouest 154

Montmagny, comté de
Cap-Saint-Ignace 136
Lacaille [Saint-Thomas], Pointe-à- 144
Pointe-à-Lacaille [Saint-Thomas] 151
Saint-Thomas [Pointe-à-Lacaille] 156

Montmorency N° 1, comté de
Beaupré, Côte de 133
Beaupré, Sainte-Anne-de- 133
Château-Richer 138
Côte de Beaupré 139
L'Ange-Gardien 145
Sainte-Anne-de-Beaupré 154

Ottawa County 150

Papineau County/Comté de Papineau
Buckingham 135
Buckingham Township 135
Montebello 147
Notre-Dame-de-Bon-Secours 149
Ottawa County 150
Petite-Nation, seigneurie de la 151
Portland Township 151
Wright, comté de 160

Pontiac County/Comté de Pontiac
Allumettes, îles des 133
Bristol 134
Bristol Township 134
Bryson Township 135
Calumet-Island 136
Campbell's Bay 136
Charteris 137
Clarendon Township 138
Fort-Coulonge 141
Grand Calumet Island 142
Île du Grand Calumet 143
Leslie Township 145
Litchfield Township 146
Mansfield Township 147
North Clarendon 148
North Onslow 149
Onslow Township 149
Ottawa County 150
Pontiac County 151
Portage-du-Fort 151
Quyon 152
Shawville 157
Starks Corners 158
(cont.)

Thorne Township 158
Wright, comté de 160
Wyman 160

Portneuf, comté de
Deschambault 139
Lachevrotière 144

Quebec County/Comté de Québec
Québec 151

Richelieu County/Comté de Richelieu
Fort William Henry 141
L'Enfant-Jésus-de-Sorel 145
Richelieu County/Comté de Richelieu ... 152
Sainte-Anne-de-Sorel 154
Saint-Gabriel-Lalemant 154
Saint-Joseph-de-Sorel 155
Saint-Ours 155
Saint-Pierre-de-Sorel 156
Saint-Robert 156
Saint-Roch-de-Richelieu 156
Sainte-Victoire 156
Sorel 157
Sorel, seigneurie de 158
Tracy 159
William Henry 160
William Henry, Fort 160

Saint-Jean, comté de/Saint-Jean County
Fort Saint-Jean 141
Saint-Jean, Fort 155

Saint-Maurice, comté de
Trois-Rivières 159

Soulanges County
Côte-Saint-Georges 139
Côteau-du-Lac 139
Rivière-Beaudette 153
Saint-Georges, Côte- 154

Terrebonne, comté de
Sainte-Anne-des-Plaines 154
Saint-Louis-de-Terrebonne 155
Terrebonne 158

Vaudreuil, comté de
Rigaud 153
Sainte-Madeleine-de-Rigaud 155
Saint-Michel-de-Vaudreuil 155
Vaudreuil 159

Verchères, comté de
Contrecœur 139
[Fort Saint-Louis] 141
[Saint-Louis, Fort] 155
Varennes 159
Verchères 159

Wright, comté de 160

Yamaska, comté de
Saint-François-du-Lac 154

SASKATCHEWAN

Cumberland House 163

Fort Île-à-la-Crosse 163

Rural Municipality 158
Balgonie 163

Rural Municipality 185
Neudorf 163

Rural Municipality 301
Carlton House 163
Fort Pelly 163

Rural Municipality 409
Swarthmore 163

YUKON TERRITORY / TERRITOIRE DU YUKON

Dawson 165

OUTSIDE CANADA / HORS CANADA

CZECHOSLOVAKIA/TCHÉCOSLOVAQUIE

Czechoslovakia 169

GREAT BRITAIN/GRANDE-BRETAGNE

Aldershot 171
Barntfield 171
Great Britain: War Office 171

GUYANE FRANÇAISE/FRENCH GUIANA

Cayenne 173
Kourou 173
Sinnamary 173

HUNGARY/HONGRIE

Hungary 175

INDIA/INDE

Benares 177
Cawnpore 177

POLAND/POLOGNE

Poland 179

SAINT-PIERRE-ET-MIQUELON

Île Miquelon 181
Île Saint-Pierre 181

UNION OF SOVIET SOCIALIST REPUBLICS/ UNION DES RÉPUBLIQUES SOCIALISTES SOVIÉTIQUES

Galicia 183

Russia 183

UNITED STATES OF AMERICA/ÉTATS-UNIS

Alabama
Condé-de-la-Mobile, Fort 186
Fort Charlotte 186
Fort Condé-de-la-Mobile 187
Fort Louis-de-la-Louisiane 187
Louis-de-la-Louisiane, Fort 188
Mobile 189

Alaska
Annette Island 185
Metlakatla 188

Arkansas
Arkansas, Poste des 185

Connecticut
Woodbury 192

GEOGRAPHIC INDEX / INDEX GÉOGRAPHIQUE

UNITED STATES / ÉTATS-UNIS (cont.)

Illinois
Chartres, Fort de	185
Fort Cavendish	186
Fort de Chartres	186
Kaskaskia	188
Prairie-du-Rocher	191

Indiana
Ouabache (Wabash)	190
Vincennes, Poste de	191
Wabash (Ouabache)	192

Louisiane
At[t]akapas, Poste des	185
Biloxi, Fort du	185
Fort du Biloxi	186
Fort Saint-Philippe	188
Iberville	188
La Fourche	188
Natchitoches (Nakitoches), Poste des	189
Nouvelle-Acadie	189
Nouvelle-Orléans	189
Opelousas, Poste des	189
Pointe-Coupée	190
Saint-Martinville	191
Saint-Philippe, Fort	191

Massachusetts
Petersham	190

Michigan
Détroit	186
Fort Pontchartrain-du-Détroit	187
Michilimakinak	188
Pontchartrain-du-Détroit, Fort	190

New York
Albany	185
Beauharnois-à-la-Pointe-à-la-Chevelure, Fort	185
Crown Point, Fort	186
Fort Beauharnois-à-la-Pointe-à-la-Chevelure	186
Fort Crown Point	187
Fort Saint-Frédéric	187
Oswego	189
Pointe-à-la-Chevelure	190
Saint-Frédéric, Fort	191
Schenectady	191

Ontario, Canada
L'Assomption-de-la-Point-de-Montréal-du-Détroit	188
Pointe-de-Montréal-du-Détroit	190
Sandwich	191

Pennsylvanie
Duquesne-à-la-Belle-Rivière, Fort	186
Fort Duquesne-à-la-Belle-Rivière	187
Fort de la Presqu'Île	187
Fort de la Rivière-aux-Bœufs	187
Pittsburgh	190
Presqu'Île, Fort de la	191
Rivière-aux-Bœufs, Fort de la	191

Quebec, Canada
Chambly, Fort-	185
Fort-Chambly	186